ISBN 978-1-5279-3167-1
PIBN 10926198

1 MONTH OF
FREE
READING

at
www.ForgottenBooks.com

By purchasing this book you are eligible for one month membership to ForgottenBooks.com, giving you unlimited access to our entire collection of over 1,000,000 titles via our web site and mobile apps.

To claim your free month visit:
www.forgottenbooks.com/free926198

English
Français
Deutsche
Italiano
Español
Português

www.forgottenbooks.com

Mythology Photography **Fiction**
Fishing Christianity **Art** Cooking
Essays Buddhism Freemasonry
Medicine **Biology** Music **Ancient
Egypt** Evolution Carpentry Physics
Dance Geology **Mathematics** Fitness
Shakespeare **Folklore** Yoga Marketing
Confidence Immortality Biographies
Poetry **Psychology** Witchcraft
Electronics Chemistry History **Law**
Accounting **Philosophy** Anthropology
Alchemy Drama Quantum Mechanics
Atheism Sexual Health **Ancient History**
Entrepreneurship Languages Sport
Paleontology Needlework Islam
Metaphysics Investment Archaeology
Parenting Statistics Criminology
Motivational

DISTRICT OF COLUMBIA APPROPRIATION BILL

STATEMENTS

BEFORE THE

SUBCOMMITTEE OF THE COMMITTEE ON APPROPRIATIONS UNITED STATES SENATE

SIXTY-THIRD CONGRESS
SECOND SESSION

ON

H. R. 10523

AN ACT MAKING APPROPRIATIONS TO PROVIDE FOR THE
EXPENSES OF THE GOVERNMENT OF THE DISTRICT
OF COLUMBIA FOR THE FISCAL YEAR ENDING
JUNE 30, 1915, AND FOR OTHER PURPOSES

JANUARY 30, 1914

Printed for the use of the Committee on Appropriations

WASHINGTON
GOVERNMENT PRINTING OFFICE
1914

SUBCOMMITTEE ON DISTRICT OF COLUMBIA APPROPRIATION BILL.

JOHN WALTER SMITH, Maryland, *Chairman.*

JOHN F. SHAFROTH, Colorado.   JACOB H. GALLINGER, New Hampshire.
LUKE LEA, Tennessee.   WILLIAM P. DILLINGHAM, Vermont.

KENNEDY F. REA, *Clerk.*

2

DISTRICT OF COLUMBIA APPROPRIATION BILL.

FRIDAY, JANUARY 23, 1914.

COMMITTEE ON APPROPRIATIONS,
UNITED STATES SENATE,
Washington, D. C.

The subcommittee met at 10.30 a. m.

Present: Senators Smith of Maryland (chairman), Lea, and Gallinger.

Senator Martin, the chairman of the committee, sat with the subcommittee. Messrs. Oliver P. Newman, Frederick L. Siddons, and Lieut. Col. Chester Harding, Commissioners of the District of Columbia, appeared.

STATEMENT OF THE DISTRICT COMMISSIONERS.

The ACTING CHAIRMAN (Mr. Smith of Maryland). The subcommittee is ready to hear the commissioners.

Commissioner NEWMAN. Mr. Chairman, and gentlemen of the committee, we have a few things that we would like to bring to the attention of the committee. We do not anticipate that we will consume a great deal of time. Our original estimates of course were transmitted in the usual way. Upon them, as you know, we had a very exhaustive hearing before the subcommittee of the House Committee on Appropriations.

In compliance with a request of the subcommittee of the House Appropriations Committee we did not ask for the inclusion in the District of Columbia appropriation bill of projects which are distinctly legislative. However, we presented in our estimates the amounts which some of the projects which we hoped to see established would require. The subcommittee eliminated most matters of new legislation, though the bill as it was reported to the House and as it passed the House carried some new legislation.

In view of the very direct request made by the House subcommittee, which we understand was the request of the entire committee and not merely of the subcommittee, we refrained from asking to have new legislation put in the pending District of Columbia appropriation bill, and we do not care to ask this subcommittee now to put in matters which are distinctly in a large way legislative. So, in presenting our case, we will limit ourselves almost entirely to matters strictly of appropriation.

Some few little inconsistencies occurred either in the preparation of the bill or in its handling on the floor of the House, which we

3

would like to get straightened out. We would be very glad to have the subcommittee as it passes along consider those items.

Senator SMITH of Maryland. State the items to which you allude.

Commissioner NEWMAN. Do you care to take up the bill paragraph by paragraph?

Senator SMITH of Maryland. We would like to hear you on the matters you wish to discuss, and we will go through with the bill in that way.

DISPOSAL OF CITY REFUSE.

Commissioner NEWMAN. One thing which we think it is essential should be given attention at this time is the matter of garbage and waste disposal, which is in the engineer commissioner's department.

Senator SMITH of Maryland. Where is the item for garbage and waste disposal?

Commissioner NEWMAN. It is in the margin on page 27. Col. Harding will explain it to the committee.

Col. HARDING. The disposal of city waste generally—garbage, ashes, and general house waste—at the present time is handled under contracts, which from their nature must be long-term contracts, and in the particular cases in question they have run for a period of five years. These contracts expire on the 30th of June, 1915. If provision is not made, as we recommend, for the matter being handled directly as a municipal operation by the District with its own plant in this appropriation bill it will be necessary to enter into other long-term contracts, effective from the 1st of July, 1915, which postpones the change which we feel is very desirable. We therefore deem it very important to have this matter, which is new legislation, carried in this appropriation bill.

Senator GALLINGER. I see that you ask $7,500 for the investigation. What is the purpose? To inquire into the methods adopted in other municipalities?

Col. HARDING. Yes, sir; the purpose of that appropriation is to enable us to make investigations in other cities and to employ expert assistants in the preparation of plans and specifications for entering into a contract for the construction of a plant so as to have the plant available, and that we may submit an estimate the coming year for expending the funds now expended under contract.

Senator SMITH of Maryland. I understand that you have a contract for the disposal of garbage up to July, 1915, and the object of this appropriation of $7,500 is to investigate the best manner in which to dispose of it yourselves. Is that the idea?

Col. HARDING. Yes; not only to investigate, but actually to prepare the plans and specifications for the construction of the plant, so that we will be ready, after having expended this appropriation, actually to construct the plant when an appropriation for it is made and have it ready by the date that is mentioned.

Senator SMITH of Maryland. Do you know what is the amount you now pay?

Senator GALLINGER. The amount is $179,945 for all these items. It will be found on page 27, line 5.

Senator SMITH of Maryland. That is the yearly cost?

Senator GALLINGER. Undoubtedly. That is the appropriation for the one year.

Commissioner NEWMAN. The point, Senator, is that unless we are in shape the 1st of July, 1915, to do this ourselves we shall have to make another contract, which, because of the character of the work, must be a long-term contract. In order to get an advantageous contract it must be for a long term.

Senator SMITH of Maryland. Have you compared the cost of the disposal of garbage here with the cost in other cities so as to ascertain what it costs other cities to dispose of their garbage?

Col. HARDING. Yes, sir; certain investigations have been made.

Senator SMITH of Maryland. Does the cost here seem to be high comparatively?

Col. HARDING. It seems to be high comparatively, and it may be reasoned out to be high as compared with the cost under municipal operation on account of the fact that we will then obtain revenue from the disposal of by-products from these wastes by treating them and selling them after treatment. In other words, it is estimated by the man in charge of the work that in all probability this service will become eventually self-maintaining as a municipal function.

Senator GALLINGER. Of course, that is a mere theory, Colonel, is it not? The parties who are doing this work now are doubtless utilizing by-products to a reasonable extent, are they not?

Col. HARDING. They are, of course.

Senator GALLINGER. Have you investigated this matter or inquired into it sufficiently to satisfy yourselves that they are getting an inordinate profit?

Col. HARDING. I can not say that they are getting an inordinate profit. The situation, however, is this: In order properly to dispose of these materials and to reduce them so as to obtain revenue from the by-products, it is necessary for the contractor to have quite an elaborate and expensive plant. It is estimated that, in round numbers, an adequate plant would cost perhaps half a million dollars, all told. A contractor entering into a contract for a period of five years has to provide for the cost of the construction of the plant. If for any reason he does not get the contract another time, the District must pay in its contract price to the next contractor a sufficient amount to justify him to construct his plant.

Senator GALLINGER. The same would be true of the District government, would it not?

Col. HARDING. No, sir; the District government would extend its investment in the plant through a long period of years, not for every period of five years.

Senator GALLINGER. Where is the plant now situated?

Col. HARDING. The reduction plant is outside of the District, at Cherry Hill, Va., about 40 miles away.

Senator GALLINGER. I think the Virginia Senators have on one or two occasions entered a protest against the District government using their territory for purposes of this kind. I will ask the Senator from Virginia, the chairman of the Committee on Appropriations, if some objection has not been made to it.

Senator MARTIN. Yes; there was objection to some proposed location of the reduction plant. I do not recall the exact facts, but there was a proposition to locate it near Occoquan, and there was great objection to it.

Senator GALLINGER. There was very great objection to it.

Senator MARTIN. The location of such a plant anywhere is an objection under the present uses. I know that on the Richmond Fredericksburg & Potomac road when the train passes one spot it is very obnoxious for a considerable distance now to passengers on the cars. When there was a proposition to have the Government erect a plant of its own and locate it near Occoquan the suggestion was made that there are new methods which would remove the obnoxious features which now prevail.

Senator SMITH of Maryland. I think we have had some experience in Baltimore City lately in regard to the processs of reducing and utilizing garbage.

Senator MARTIN. It seems to me that the appropriation of $179,945 is necessary now to meet existing obligations. I suppose that to be the case.

Senator SMITH of Maryland. We expect that to remain as it is.

Senator MARTIN. But the inquiry was as to whether a reasonable amount is being expended now and how the cost here compares with the cost in other cities. That was the inquiry to which the engineer commissioner was addressing himself.

Commissioner SIDDONS. May I add, Senator, that it is necessary, of course, to fulfill our contract obligation.

Senator MARTIN. That is my understanding. That, of course, is not in question, but inquiry was made in regard to it in considering the wisdom and necessity of making an appropriation of $7,500 for an investigation of the subject. It seems to me that that will be well worth the cost of the investigation.

Senator GALLINGER. On that point I will venture to ask the commissioners if it might not be well for a somewhat smaller appropriation to be made and not to include the preparation of plans and specifications; in other words, to ascertain whether or not it is wise to construct the plant. After the commissioners have inquired into the expenditures in other cities, if we are getting the work done at a reasonable and fair rate, there would not seem to be any wisdom in the Government constructing a plant and doing the work under the direction of the municipal authorities.

Senator MARTIN. The language proposed by the commissioners meets your suggestion. It reads:

For the purpose of investigating and reporting upon the collection and disposal of garbage and other city waste originating in the District of Columbia.

That meets what you suggest?

Senator GALLINGER. Precisely.

Senator SMITH of Maryland. It goes still further and says—

including the preparation of plans and specifications for the construction of disposal plants, the necessary accessories, and the employment of personal services and such other incidental expenses as may be necessary to carry out the purposes of this appropriation.

In order to determine whether it would be desirable to have the plant or not, they would want to know what it would cost.

Senator MARTIN. I think so. It would tend to make the bidders come down to the lowest point when they knew the Government was prepared to put up a plant if their price was exorbitant. It seems to me the investigation is well worth $7,500.

Senator SMITH of Maryland. Is not $7,500 a pretty large appropriation?

Senator MARTIN. It struck me as being exceedingly small for the purposes covered.

Col. HARDING. I should like to say that this estimate of $7,500 is a reduction of $2,500 in the estimate made to us by the superintendent of street cleaning for this purpose. After we had decided to put this amount in our estimates that official came to me and asked me if it would not be possible to increase it to the original estimate. I asked him to justify it in detail to me if he could. He did it to the extent of corresponding with those in charge of such plants elsewhere and having a rough estimate made of the probable cost of the plant, and, in view of the time involved in the preparation of plans and an appropriate salary to the man who was doing it, he made a pretty clear showing that $7,500 would hardly cover what he proposed to have covered, which involved not only the question of investigation as to whether this would be a good thing to do or not, in general, but the preparation of plans and specifications in detail so that we could give you a definite estimate of the cost of the proposition when we came to ask for authority to build the plant.

Senator GALLINGER. Can you state approximately, from the investigations that have already been made, the amount which was suggested for the construction of a plant?

Senator SMITH of Maryland. He said it would be about half a million dollars.

Col. HARDING. My recollection of it is that it is between $400,000 and $500,000. I have that in a report at my office from the superintendent of street cleaning, but I did not bring the report with me. However, my recollection is that it is between $400,000 and $500,000. This estimate refers to the garbage collection and disposal plant only.

Senator GALLINGER. Would the preparation of these plans properly come under the direction of the municipal architect, or would you have to employ outside architects?

Col. HARDING. He would direct all such matters as to the building, but the machinery and the special plant would come under the direction of the expert whom we would employ.

Senator GALLINGER. What process have you in mind, incineration, or some other method of destroying the waste?

Col. HARDING. Incineration as to certain classes of waste, and reduction, as they call it, as to other classes; so that we will make grease from garbage instead of absolutely destroying it.

Senator GALLINGER. There is a very marked difference, as I recall it, in the cost of the two kinds of plant.

Col. HARDING. Yes, sir; there would be no revenue from by-products from incineration to speak of, but from reduction there would be a considerable revenue. As I understand the matter, modern plants are so arranged as to be practically free from nuisance to the localities in which they are situated.

Senator GALLINGER. But those are the expensive kind of plants.

Col. HARDING. Yes.

Senator SMITH of Maryland. It is the more expensive plant that does away with the nuisance.

Col. HARDING. It is, and that is the type of plant we have in contemplation. In view of the urgent request of the superintendent of street cleaning that we should increase this estimate from $7,500 to $10,000, the commissioners have decided to ask you, gentlemen, to make the increase if you grant the item at all, it being considered that we will not spend any more than is necessary to accomplish the purpose.

Senator MARTIN. In your estimate you fix the amount at $7,500.

Col. HARDING. Yes, sir; and now we would like to change it to $10,000 on a further showing by the superintendent of street cleaning.

Senator MARTIN. I think he ought to have made his showing at the proper time.

Commissioner NEWMAN. If there was any error, it was ours, Senator.

Senator SMITH of Maryland. I do not believe we would be able to increase the amount after the estimate has been submitted. As far as my judgment goes $10,000 is a good deal of money to investigate a matter of that kind. Of course, it takes experts and all that kind of thing, but the estimate has been submitted for $7,500, and I am rather inclined to think that the subcommittee, from what the members say, feel kindly toward it.

Senator GALLINGER. Col. Harding, I will ask you if Col. Judson did not go over the same ground and make an investigation?

Col. HARDING. He made an investigation so far as ascertaining the desirability of the plant was concerned, but not as to plans and specifications.

Senator GALLINGER. I think he visited other cities and examined plants.

Col. HARDING. Yes; he did.

Senator GALLINGER. I suppose there is some report from him on file.

Col. HARDING. There is a report. This is not the first time that this item has been urged by the commissioners.

Senator GALLINGER. Oh, no; that is true. I remember that we discussed it at considerable length with the commissioners on two or three former occasions. Personally, I will venture to suggest, Mr. Chairman, that the matter appeals to me very strongly as an advisable thing to do; but, of course, we can determine later on when we take up the bill in detail.

Senator SMITH of Maryland. I think it would be well if the subcommittee should determine if the examination can be made for $7,500, or whether it will probably be necessary to appropriate $10,000 for the purpose.

Col. HARDING. I believe that the further showing of the superintendent of streets will make clear the difficulty of accomplishing the purpose of this particular clause for the amount of $7,500. I think it would be very much better to raise the amount to $10,000.

Senator SMITH of Maryland. Is there anything further you wish to say on this point?

Col. HARDING. Perhaps, Mr. Chairman, it might be well for me to send to you, or bring to you when I come again, the details of the report of the superintendent of street cleaning in which he justifies the estimate of $10,000.

Senator SMITH of Maryland. We would be very glad to have it.

Senator GALLINGER. I will venture to suggest that Col. Harding insert it in the hearing at this point.

Senator Lea. I also suggest that he bring the preliminary report of the investigation made by Col. Judson, so that we may see all that has been accomplished on this line.

Senator Smith of Maryland. Very well.

The matter referred to is as follows:

STATEMENT IN DETAIL REGARDING ESTIMATE OF $10,000 FOR INVESTIGATING THE COLLECTION AND DISPOSAL OF GARBAGE AND CITY WASTE BY THE COMMISSIONERS OF THE DISTRICT OF COLUMBIA, INCLUDING PREPARATION OF PLANS AND SPECIFICATIONS FOR PLANT.

NOVEMBER 11, 1913.

The ENGINEER COMMISSIONER
(Through Capt. Brooke) :

In connection with the request to Congress for an appropriation of $7,500, appearing in the estimates for the fiscal year 1915, to investigate the methods of collection and disposal of city waste most suited to this city, to prepare plans and specifications for the necessary disposal plants, buildings, wharves, etc., and to prepare an accurate estimate of the cost of construction, to be submitted to Congress for an appropriation, I have written a letter to Mr. Irwin S. Osborn, sanitary engineer, and to the municipal architect, requesting their opinions as to what the amount of this appropriation should be, and forward herewith the replies to these letters.

The municipal architect's estimate of the cost of the work, which will be done in this office, is $11,500, and Mr. Osborn's estimate for the additional cost for the services of an expert in such matters is from $1,500 to $2,000. Selecting the smaller estimate of Mr. Osborn, in combination with that of the municipal architect, brings the estimate to $13,000.

My original estimate was $11,087, but to be on the safe side, I recommended that a request be made to Congress for an appropriation of $15,000. Col. Judson reduced this to $10,000, which was the amount requested in the estimates for 1913 and 1914. For 1915 the amount was again cut to $7,500.

J. W. PAXTON,
Superintendent of Street Cleaning.

OCTOBER 28, 1913.

Mr. IRWIN S. OSBORN,
Department of Public Service, Columbus, Ohio.

MY DEAR MR. OSBORN : The question of an investigation as to the best methods and initial cost for municipal ownership and operation of city waste disposal plants is again under consideration. My original estimate of $15,000 was cut to $10,000 before it was submitted to Congress, and this year it has again been cut to $7,500, and I am trying to get more expert opinion on the subject than I am able to furnish.

Referring to the copy of a letter to the municipal architect, inclosed herewith, which is self-explanatory, I would appreciate it very much if you would write me your opinion of the length of time the services of an expert would have to be employed, and what would be the cost of draftsmen and other expenses as outlined in this letter to the municipal architect, under the heading "Work to be designed, specified, and estimated by the disposal expert, personal services, and other requirements to be provided by the office of the municipal architect."

Thanking you in advance for any attention which you give to this matter, I remain

Very truly, yours.

J. W. PAXTON,
Superintendent of Street Cleaning.

OCTOBER 28, 1913.

Mr. SNOWDEN ASHFORD,
Municipal Architect, District of Columbia.

DEAR SIR : I have submitted an approximate estimate to the engineer commissioner of the initial cost to the District of Columbia of the collection and disposal equipment for the handling of all city wastes, except night soil, amounting to $803,572.

The question has arisen as to the cost of making a complete investigation of this matter to decide on the best method of disposal, to plan out a system of collection, to design, prepare plans, and draw up specifications for the disposal plant, buildings, wharves, etc., and to prepare an accurate estimate of the cost to be submitted to Congress in requesting appropriations for this purpose.

Te engineer commissioner's idea is to employ an expert to take charge of this investigation, to decide on the method of disposal, and design the plants, with the exception of such buildings, wharves, etc., which you can look after in cooperation with the disposal expert; but all personal services and other expenses, except the salary and traveling expenses of the expert, are to be paid by your office and charged to the appropriation for the purpose. I would appreciate it very much if you will give me an estimate of the amount of such expenses.

I submit herewith items selected for the total estimate which will require engineering expenses:

Work to be designed, specified, and estimated by the disposal expert, personal services and other requirements to be provided by the office of the municipal architect.

Garbage:

Garbage conveyor equipment	$20,000
4 digestor units, including roller presses	40,000
Drying equipment	20,000
Evaporators	20,000
Grease equipment	10,000
Tar plant and piping	40,000
Percolator and equipment	20,000
Coal conveyors	5,000

Refuse:

Incinerator	15,000
Boilers	4,500
Conveyors	5,000
4 presses	2,000
Tar equipment	2,000
	203,500

Work to be designed, specified, and estimated by the office of the municipal architect.

Garbage:

1 stable	$50,000
2 main buildings and several outbuildings	100,000

Combined garbage and refuse:

1 loading wharf	30,000
1 unloading wharf	30,000
5 barges	15,000
Three-fourths cost of tugboat	22,500

Refuse:

1 stable	20,000
1 sorting building	30,000
1 building for incinerator	20,000
Ashes: 1 stable	50,000
Total	367,500

Very respectfully,

J. W. PAXTON,
Superintendent of Street Cleaning.

315 MANNING CHAMBERS,
Toronto, Canada.

Mr. J. W. PAXTON,
Superintendent of Street Cleaning, Washington, D. C.

MY DEAR MR. PAXTON: Your letter of October 28 was forwarded to me at Toronto, where I have been retained to design and install complete work in connection with collection and disposal of all municipal waste.

I have gone over the copy of the letter to the municipal architect that you inclosed and note the manner in which you propose to handle the work in connection with plans for waste disposal.

It is my opinion that in designing a plant for disposal, the laying out of the buildings, as well as the machinery and equipment, should be under the direction of one person, and if the design of buildings are to be worked up by the municipal architect, that he also lay out plans for installation of equipment. The building work must of necessity agree with the type of equipment installed, especially as pertains to conveyers, foundations, structural steel of building, and its use for supporting equipment. The layout of the buildings must be such that it will meet the conditions that arise in making the installations of equipment. It would be difficult to determine where one class of work stopped and the other started.

Under the circumstances, wouldn't you find it desirable to have the complete proposition laid out by your architect. and only have such work as done by the expert be in an advisory capacity? The expert to furnish such information as necessary to have the whole work developed properly; the expert to furnish specifications, sketches, and check up the work done by the architect from the engineering standpoint. If this was the case, the larger cost would be taken care of by the architect's office.

I do not know as to what detail you would want the drawings worked up. but with the amount available you could not get out detail working drawings for work of such magnitude. but would have to confine the work to complete general drawings, from which a detail estimate could be made. If Congress then made an appropriation for construction the details could be developed.

Under this plant I should think that you should allow $1.500 to $2,000 for expert fees and expense. the amount depending on such work as you desired to have him handle or the amount necessary to permit the whole to be done by the architect acting in a consulting capacity.

If, after the plans were completed and appropriation was made by Congress, you could employ an experienced man to see that the details were worked up and works properly constructed.

I had hoped to be in Washington last summer. but changed my plans rather hurriedly to go to Europe to study methods of refuse collection and disposal. as well as street cleaning. I plan to make a trip through the eastern cities in the future. and I trust I can arrange to spend a day with you.

I noticed somewhere since my return that you had an article in one of the engineering papers on your work in Washington. I have failed to find time to find it, and if you have a reprint I would be very glad to receive one.

I was very glad to have you write me, and if at any time I can assist you in any way would be glad to hear from you.

Very truly, yours,

IRWIN S. OSBORN.

NOVEMBER 10, 1913.

Mr. J. W. PAXTON,
Superintendent of Street Cleaning, District of Columbia.

DEAR SIR: In reply to your letter of October 28. requesting an estimate of the cost of making an investigation, preparing plans and specifications. and making estimates, etc., for a disposal system, I have the honor to submit the following:

On the work to be designed, specified. and estimated by a disposal expert, the personal services required in this office will amount to about 2 per cent of the cost of the work, on the assumption that there will be considerable detail drawing connected with such work.

The plans, specifications, and estimates for the buildings. wharves. and other structures connected with the work will cost about 2 per cent of the cost of the building, etc., or a total cost of $11,500.

This figure does not include the cost of inspection, which is usually paid from the appropriation for the building, and cost about 1½ per cent, making the total cost of the plans. specifications, and superintendence 3½ per cent of the cost of the work.

Very respectfully,

SNOWDEN ASHFORD.
Municipal Architect, District of Columbia.

REPORT OF IVESTIGATION MADE BY LIEUT. COL. WILLIAM V. JUDSON, AND J. W. PAXTON, SUPERINTENDENT OF STREET CLEANING, AS TO THE COST OF CONSTRUCTING AND OPERATING MUNICIPALLY OWED PLANTS FOR THE COLLECTION AND DISPOSAL OF CITY WASTES.

NOVEMBER 1, 1911.

Maj. W. V. JUDSON,
    Engineer Commissioner, District of Columbia.

SIR: As the result of a trip recently made by yourself and the writer to Cleveland, Toledo, and Columbus, Ohio, for the purpose of investigating the garbage-reduction plants at these points, I have, at your request, collected considerable information and prepared the following estimates in regard to the cost of construction and operation of municipally owned plants and equipment for the collection and disposal of city wastes, as compared with the present cost of doing this work by contract, to be used in preparing a request to Congress to make an appropriation for a more thorough investigation of this matter.

This kind of work is almost invariably done under contract, and the contractors being unwilling to furnish information, I have been obliged to rely largely upon the reports of the municipally owned plants at Cleveland and Columbus, and I am also very much indebted to Mr. Irwin S. Osborne, the designer, builder, and operator of the Columbus reduction plant, for the most valuable of the information obtained.

Respectfully submitted.

J. W. PAXTON,
Superintendent of Street Cleaning.

Approximate estimate of the cost of the collection and reduction of garbage and dead animals under the direct control of the Commissioners of the District of Columbia on the basis of transportation by water from Washington to Occoquan, where the reduction plant will be located and prison labor used where possible.

TABLE SHOWING THE NUMBER OF HORSES REQUIRED FOR THE COMBINED COLLECTION OF ASHES AND GARBAGE.

Months.	Average number of horses per month for garbage.	Average number of horses per month for ashes.	Average number of horses per month for both services.
1910.			
July	98	36	134
August	111	36	147
September	105	39	144
October	86	49	135
November	80	103	183
December	94	118	212
1911.			
January	85	122	207
February	85	123	208
March	85	121	206
April	85	100	185
May	89	71	160
June	90	58	148
Average for the year	1,093 / 91	976 / 81	2,069 / 172

Maximum number for ashes, 123 horses.
Maximum number for garbage, 111 horses.

Combination ashes and garbage.

           Horses.
Maximum _____ 212
Minimum _____ 134

Difference _____ 78

The number of horses for garbage is proportioned as follows: 91, average number for the year (garbage): 172 average number for the year (garbage and ashes) = × maximum number required for garbage: 212 maximum number for garbage and ashes, and a similar proportion for the number required for ashes.

Record of garbage service for fiscal year ending June 30, 1911.

(Furnished by the contractor.)

Months.	Vehicles.			Men.			Horses.			Tons.			Loads.		
	Average number week days.	Average number Sundays.	Maximum for 1 day.	Average number week days.	Average number Sundays.	Maximum for 1 day.	Average number week days.	Average number Sundays.	Maximum for 1 day.	Total number week days.	Total number Sundays.	Maximum for 1 day.	Total number week days.	Total number Sundays.	Maximum for 1 day.
July	74	14	88	93	21	107	98	18	107	4,286	121	248	3,762	103	207
August	88	12	94	104	23	120	111	16	116	5,532	103	333	4,787	83	280
September	81	12	90	101	20	120	106	16	112	5,150	104	329	4,355	83	255
October	65	13	71	85	21	91	86	16	92	4,001	127	237	3,346	104	188
November	54	12	61	71	21	81	80	16	84	3,491	91	160	2,707	72	128
December	59	29	84	60	30	84	94	46	123	3,292	163	149	2,754	140	117
January	53	11	59	70	13	79	85	20	101	3,500	126	162	2,668	90	117
February	53	12	59	70	18	72	85	19	96	3,064	106	159	2,396	75	118
March	53	11	55	90	14	72	85	20	90	3,371	97	158	2,633	70	115
April	53	11	58	70	18	75	88	21	86	3,497	161	166	2,686	114	117
May	80	12	67	81	14	85	90	20	95	3,961	110	211	3,147	84	161
June	64	12	68	81	15	88	90	19	95	3,667	104	212	3,040	78	161
Entire year	63	13	71	79	18	90	91	20	99	46,882	1,412	210	38,281	1,096	163

Garbage.

CAPACITY OF REDUCTION PLANT.

Tons of garbage collected during the fiscal year ended June 30, 1911	48,214
Tons collected during the month of August, 1910, maximum for the year	5,638
Tons average for the month of August, 1910, assuming 26 working days	213
Tons maximum collected for one day	333
Occurring in August, 1911 (see note A):	
Tons average monthly collection	4,018
Tons average daily collection for 26 working days per month	154

Assume plant with maximum capacity of 320 tons per day working 24 hours, operated on an average of 12 hours per day, or one-half of three 8-hour shifts.

INITIAL COST.

Collection:

112 horses (maximum), at $240 (see note B)	$26,880
112 sets single harness (maximum), at $30	3,360
94 wagons (maximum), at $210	19,740
94 extra wagon boxes (maximum), at $60	5,640
1 stable	50,000
1 stable site	20 000
1 loading wharf	15,000
3 barges, at $3.000	9,000
Tug boat, one-half charged to garbage	15,000
	164,620
Incidentals, 10 per cent	16,462
	181,082

Disposal:

Conveyor equipment	20,000
4 digestor units, each unit consisting of 4 digestors and 1 roller press	40,000
Drying equipment	20.000
Evaporators	20,000
Grease equipment	10.000
Power plant and piping	40,000
Percolator equipment	20,000
Buildings	100,000
1 unloading wharf for garbage and coal	20,000
Coal handling, conveyors, etc	5,000
	295,000
Incidentals, 10 per cent	29,500
	324,500

OPERATION.

Collection:

Assistant superintendent	$2,000	
5 inspectors, at $1,000	5,000	
Average 79 drivers, at $1.75 per day, for 313 days	43.272	
Average 18 drivers, at $1.75 per day, for 52 days	1,638	
6 laborers, unloading wharf, at $1.50 per day, for 365 days	3,285	
Stable labor, average 91 plus extra 9 equals 100 horses, at 20 cents per day per horse, for 365 days	7,300	
Supervision and labor		62,495
100 horses (forage, 45.5 cents; shoeing, 6 cents; medicine, one-half cent, equals 52 cents), at 52 cents per day per horse, for 365 days	18,980	
Forage and shoeing		18,980

Collection—Continued.

Repairs 112 sets single harness (maximum), at 4 cents per day per set, for 365 days	$1, 635
Repairs to 94 wagons (minimum), at 10 cents per day per wagon, for 365 days	3, 431
Renewals, 94 boxes, at $60	5, 640
Repairs to stable and wharves	4, 000
Repairs and renewals	$14, 706
Repairs to floating equipment	4, 000
6 laborers, floating equipment, $1.50 per day, for 365 days	3, 285
One-half coal and crew tugboat, $10 per day, for 365 days	3, 650
Transportation of garbage	10, 935
3 per cent interest, 5 per cent depreciation, or 8 per cent of initial cost of $18,082	14, 487
Total cost of operation (collection)	121, 603

Disposal:

Skilled labor required for three 8-hour shifts—

1 superintendent, at $7 per day	7. 00
1 assistant superintendent, at $5 per day	5. 00
3 general foremen, at $3 per day	9. 00
3 foremen, at $2 per day	6. 00
1 master mechanic, at $4 per day	4. 00
2 assistant master mechanics, at $3 per day	6. 00
4 machinists, at $3 per day	12. 00
3 engineers, at $3.50 per day	10. 50
2 unloading foremen, at $2.50 per day	5. 00
3 pressmen, at $2.50 per day	7. 50
3 digestor men, at $2.50 per day	7. 50
3 dryer men, at $2.50 per day	7. 50
3 grease men, at $2.50 per day	7. 50
3 evaporator men, at $2.50 per day	7. 50

Prison laborers required for three 8-hour shifts—

15 unloading, 6 pressroom, 12 digestor room, 6 firemen, 2 grounds, 9 extra, total 50, at 75 cents	37. 50
Total per day	.139. 50
One-half of three 8-hour shifts	. 69. 75
One-half of three 8-hour shifts for 365 days	25, 458. 75
Superintendence and labor	25, 459
Coal and power	50, 000
Repairs and renewals	10, 000
Fixed charges: 3 per cent interest plus 5 per cent depreciation or 8 per cent of initial cost of $324,500	25, 960
Total cost of operation (disposal)	111, 419

Income:

Cost of operation (collection)	121, 603	
Cost of operation (disposal)	111, 419	
Total cost of operation		233, 022
Solids, 15 per cent of 48,214 tons, 7,232 tons, at $8	57, 856	
Grease, 3¾ per cent of 48,214 tons, 1,808 tons, at $80	144, 640	
Income		202, 496
Net cost garbage collection and disposal		30, 526
Present cost of garbage collection and disposal by contract		68, 400. 00
Estimated cost District ownership and operation		30, 526. 00
Estimated amount yearly advantage of municipal ownership		37, 874. 00

Disposal:

Pay roll, 52 weeks, at $400	$20,800.00
Repairs, 12 months, at $100	1,200.00
Rent land, 12 months, at $25	300.00
Fixed charges	10,500.00
	32,800.00

Collection	32,207.50
Disposal	32,800.00
Cost of operation	65,007.50

Income:

7,825 tons crumbled news, at $4	31,300.00
313 tons mixed rags, at $12	3,756.00
Registered bottles	1,200.00
Mixed bottles	2,400.00
Tin cans and scrap iron	2,400.00
Junk	1,200.00
	42,256.00
Yearly payment from District of Columbia	17,000.00
Income	59,256.00
Yearly loss	5,751.50

Note.—The yearly collections from the District of Columbia are about the same as Buffalo, N. Y., where they have a refuse incinerator owned by the municipality, and their latest figures show operating expenses $38,530.60 and income $39,175.97; but it is not known whether these figures include fixed charges. M. R. Ready says that in figuring on this contract he neglected to consider fixed charges. Prices on salable refuse are very low at present, and it would be possible, with the highest prices, to increase the present income on salable products by about 50 per cent. The former contractor was a competitor for the present contract. He had had three years' previous experience, a plant which, it is assumed, was paid for by his former contract, and a large business of this kind in New York, which should have enabled him to obtain higher prices on salable products. The above figures indicate that the present contractor is operating at a loss. The former contractor's bid on this contract was $34,500. It is estimated that the present contractor's bid should have been:

Cost of operation	$65,007.50
Plus 20 per cent profit	13,001.50
Total	78,009.00
Less income from salable products	42,256.00
Bid	35,753.00

Assume bid for the next five-year period, say, $35,000, which does not make allowance for future growth of the District.

ESTIMATED COST OF THE COLLECTION AND DISPOSAL OF REFUSE UNDER THE DIRECT CONTROL OF THE COMMISSIONERS ON THE BASIS OF THE INCINERATOR PLANT BEING LOCATED AT OCCOQUAN, USING PRISON LABOR FOR PICKING, ETC., AND THE STEAM DEVELOPED, IN THE REDUCTION PLANT, THE REFUSE BEING TRANSPORTED BY WATER FROM WASHINGTON TO OCCOQUAN.

Record of refuse service during fiscal year ending June 30, 1911.

(Furnished by the contractor.)

Months.	Average number per day.			Total cubic yards per month.	Loads, total number per month.
	Vehicles.	Men.	Horses.		
July....................	25	27	27	10,628	1,561
August..................	23	25	25	10,436	1,328
September...............	22	24	24	8,151	1,037
October.................	23	24	24	8,675	1,106
November................	22	23	23	8,252	1,031
December................	22	24	24	7,308	901
January.................	23	24	24	8,367	1,042
February................	23	24	24	7,218	891
March...................	24	25	25	8,696	1,076
April...................	24	25	25	8,875	1,097
May.....................	27	28	28	11,432	1,427
June....................	27	28	28	10,748	1,328
Entire year.............	23	25	25	108,789	13,825

108,789 cubic yards of refuse collected during the fiscal year ending June 30, 1911, at 171 pounds to the cubic yard, equals 9,301 tons.

Population, Buffalo, 425,000, where 15,000 tons of rubbish per year is collected.

Refuse.

INITIAL COST.

Collection :

40 horses, at $240_____	$9,600
30 wagons, at $100_____	3,000
40 sets single harness, at $30_____	1,200
2 sets double harness, at $75_____	150
Stable and site_____	30,000
1 loading wharf_____	15,000
2 barges, at $3,000_____	6,000
One-fourth tugboat_____	7,500
Incidentals, 10 per cent_____	7,245
	79,695

Disposal :

Incinerator_____	15,000
Boilers_____	4,500
Building for incinerator_____	20,000
Sorting building_____	30,000
Conveyors_____	5,000
4 presses_____	2,000
Power equipment_____	2,000
Unloading wharf_____	10,000
Incidentals, 10 per cent_____	8,850
	97,350

OPERATION.

Collection :

1 assistant superintendent_____	$2,000
2 inspectors, at $1,000_____	2,000
30 drivers, at $1.75 per day for 313 days_____	16,432
2 dumpmen, at $1.50 per day for 313 days_____	939
Stable labor, 40 horses, at 20 cents per day per horse for 365 days.	2,920

Collection—Continued.

40 horses (forage, 45.5 cents; shoeing 6 cents; medicine, one-half cent), 52 cents per day per horse for 365 days_____ $7,592
Repairs to 30 wagons, at 10 cents per day for 313 days_____ 939
Repairs to stable_____ 1,000
Repairs to 30 sets harness, at 4 cents per day per set for 313 days__ 376
3 per cent interest plus 5 per cent depreciation, or 8 per cent of $79,695_____ 6,376

40,574

Transportation on, say, 10,000 tons refuse Washington to Occoquan, using unit price estimated for garbage, $0.23_____ 2,300

42,874

Disposal:

1 assistant superintendent, at $4_____ $4.00
1 mason, at $3.50_____ 3.50
3 assistant engineers, at $2.50_____ 7.50
60 prison laborers, at $0.75_____ 45.00

60.00

Labor and supervision, at $60 per day for 313 days_____ 18,780
Repairs and renewals_____ 4,000
3 per cent interest plus 5 per cent depreciation, or 8 per cent of initial cost of $97,350_____ 7,788

30,568

Income:

About one-third of refuse collected is burned, the balance being salable. Refuse has about one-seventh fuel power of coal, or it will evaporate 1 pound of water per pound of refuse.
One-third of 10,000 tons equals 6,666,000 pounds of steam, at 2 cents per 100_____ $1,333
Revenue from Buffalo collecting 15,000 tons is $39,176. Washington contractor's present estimated revenue $42,256, assumed for this estimate_____ 42,256

43,589

SUMMARY.

Estimated cost of future contract_____ 35,000
Total cost of collection_____ $42,874
Total cost of disposal_____ 30,568

Total cost of collection and disposal_____ 73,442
Income _____ 43,589

Total net cost_____ 29,853

Estimated yearly saving by municipal ownership_____ 5,147

Comparing an incinerator with utilization at Occoquan with incinerator in Washington.

Saving by using prison labor, 60 laborers, at 75 cents per man per day, for 313 days _____ $14,085
Credit for steam developed, $1,333, less interest and depreciation on boilers, 8 per cent of $4,500, or $360_____ 973

15,058

Transportation by water from Washington to Occoquan, 10,000 tons, at 23 cents_____ 2,300

Total yearly advantage of plant at Occoquan_____ 12,758

APPROXIMATE ESTIMATE OF THE COLLECTION AND DISPOSAL OF ASHES UNDER THE DIRECT CONTROL OF THE COMMISSIONERS.

Record of ash service for the fiscal year ending June 30, 1911.

(Furnished by the contractor.)

Month.	Vehicles.		Men.		Horses.		Total weight for month.	Cubic yards.		Total number loads per month.
	Average number per day.	Maximum for 1 day.	Average number per day.	Maximum for 1 day.	Average number per day.	Maximum for 1 day.		Total cubic yards for month.	Maximum cubic yards for 1 day.	
July	18	18	33	34	36	36	912,360	7,608	319	1,388
August	18	18	34	34	36	36	704,240	5,627	286	1,115
September	19	22	35	38	39	44	7,225,600	5,973	280	1,392
October	24	45	42	90	49	90	10,804,400	8,972	600	2,273
November	51	55	108	108	103	108	23,984,800	20,005	886	4,991
December	58	64	118	132	118	132	28,358,400	23,632	920	5,008
January	60	64	122	132	122	128	26,312,000	21,820	868	5,455
February	61	70	123	140	123	140	23,635,200	19,696	912	4,914
March	60	64	121	128	121	128	25,224,000	21,020	900	5,255
April	50	64	100	128	100	128	18,705,600	15,588	788	3,897
May	35	37	71	74	71	74	14,428,800	12,024	464	3,006
June	29	30	58	60	58	60	11,275,200	9,396	392	2,349
Entire year	40	45	80	91	81	92	191,570,600	171,361	623	41,938

Cleveland and Columbus are both manufacturing towns, and a larger portion of their population consists of a poorer class of people than is found in Washington. Washington has a much larger floating population. It is thought for this reason that Washington not only produces more garbage per capita, but that the garbage is of a higher commercial value. It is also thought that the collection service in Washington is better and that a larger proportion of the garbage produced is collected. The estimated cost of collection per ton of garbage for Washington compares very closely with Cleveland and Columbus. In these two cities the area covered in collecting a ton of garbage is about twice as great as in Washington, but Washington makes this up by giving collections about twice as often.

NOTES.

A. Three hundred and thirty-three tons is shown as the maximum for one day, occurring on Monday, but the average for this day and the next two succeeding days is 242, showing that a plant one-quarter smaller than the one assumed for this estimate would have handled the garbage for the year ending June 30, 1911, and therefore the 320 tons per day plant assumed would probably take care of the growth of the District for a number of years to come.

B. The advantage of combining the collection of garbage and ashes is that when garbage collections are heavy ash collections are light, and vice versa; but referring to page 2, the table indicates that even with the combined service there is required 58 per cent more horses in the maximum month than in the minimum month. For an economical operation arrangements should be made either to purchase the minimum and hire the extra horses when needed or purchase the maximum and use the surplus in some other branch of the service when not needed, but the equipment, such as wagons, etc., being of a special kind, the maximum will have to be purchased.

C. The inital cost of the Cleveland plant is low, because it was bought from the former contractor secondhand. In Columbus a large portion of the garbage is collected by private parties, which practice the city hopes to eliminate, but the plant was built with ample capacity to take all the garbage produced, and consequently the initial cost and interest and depreciation are high in proportion to the garbage collected by the city at present.

D. The cost of operation per ton of garbage for labor and supervision at the Columbus plant will decrease considerably as the plant is operated toward its full capacity. At both Columbus and Cleveland the cost of labor is much higher than here, and the estimate for Washington is based on using prison labor at one-half cost of outside labor.

E. The price of fuel is more than twice as much in Washington as in either Columbus or Cleveland.

F. Irwin Blair, secretary of the Kutztown Foundry & Machine Works, manufacturers and designers of reduction equipment, who has been in this business more than 20 years, states that he usually figures the cost of operation of reduction plants, not including interest and depreciation, at $1.75, and income at from $4 to $5 per ton of garbage collected.

G. Mr. Blair says that the reason the percentage of tankage is low at the Cleveland plant is because they do not evaporate their stick water and mix the product with the tankage, which is done at the Columbus plant.

DEAD ANIMALS.

At Cleveland and Columbus the collection and disposal of dead animals is included with the garbage, which would be done in Washington under a municipally owned and operated system.

As the collection and disposal of dead animals would cost about the same as garbage, and as they yield a slightly larger income, the use of the unit prices estimated for garbage in the following estimate for dead animals is conservative:

Table showing number and estimated weight of dead animals collected fiscal year ended June 30, 1911.

Number and kinds.	Weight of each.	Total.
	Pounds.	*Pounds.*
6,150 dogs	30	184,500
8,970 cats	10	89,700
547 rats	1	547
638 horses	1,000	638,000
176 chickens	4	704
239 miscellaneous	10	2,390
		915,841

Income:

458 tons dead animals, at $4.20	$1,923.60	
638 horsehides, at $4	2,552.00	
		$4,475.60

Collection:

458 tons dead animals, at $2.52	1,154.16	

Reduction:

458 tons dead animals, at $2.31	1,057.98	
		2,212.14

Income	2,263.46
Amount at present paid for this service	2,855.00
Estimated amount saving by municipal ownership	5,118.46

Financial statement of present refuse collection and disposal in Washington, D. C., based on approximate information furnished by the contractor, M. R. Ready.

INITIAL COST AND FIXED CHARGES.

Collection:

30 wagons, at $75	$2,250.00
40 horses, at $150	6,000.00
40 sets single harness, at $22.50	900.00
2 sets double harness, at $40	80.00
	9,230.00
5 per cent interest and depreciation, 20 per cent	2,307.50

Disposal:

Plant	42,000.00
5 per cent interest and 20 per cent depreciation	10,500.00

NOTE: The depreciation is based on 100 per cent in five years, this being the contract period. The former contractor received practically nothing for his plant on the termination of his contract.

OPERATION.

Collection:

Pay roll, 52 weeks, at $400	20,800.00
Forage and material for horseshoeing, for 40 horses, $0.50 per day per horse, 365 days	7,300.00
Repairs to wagons and harness per year	1,200.00
Rent stables, 12 months, at $50	600.00
Fixed charges	2,307.50
	32,207.50

Disposal:
```
    Pay roll, 52 weeks, at $400_____$20, 800. 00
    Repairs, 12 months, at $100_____ 1, 200. 00
    Rent land, 12 months, at $25_____   300. 00
    Fixed charges_____ 10, 500. 00
                                                              _____
                                                               32. 800. 00
                                                              ============
Collection _____ 32, 207. 50
Disposal _____ 32, 800. 00
                                                              _____
    Cost of operation_____ 65, 007. 50
                                                              ============
```

Income:
```
    7,825 tons crumbled news, at $4_____ 31, 300. 00
    313 tons mixed rags, at $12_____ 3, 756. 00
    Registered bottles _____ 1, 200. 00
    Mixed bottles _____ 2, 400. 00
    Tin cans and scrap iron_____ 2, 400. 00
    Junk_____ 1, 200. 00
                                                              _____
                                                               42, 256. 00
Yearly payment from District of Columbia_____ 17, 000. 00
                                                              _____
    Income_____ 59, 256. 00
Yearly loss_____ 5, 751. 50
```

NOTE.—The yearly collections from the District of Columbia are about the same as Buffalo, N. Y., where they have a refuse incinerator owned by the municipality, and their latest figures show operating expenses $38,530.60 and income $39,175.97; but it is not known whether these figures include fixed charges. M. R. Ready says that in figuring on this contract he neglected to consider fixed charges. Prices on salable refuse are very low at present, and it would be possible, with the highest prices, to increase the present income on salable products by about 50 per cent. The former contractor was a competitor for the present contract. He had had three years' previous experience, a plant which, it is assumed, was paid for by his former contract, and a large business of this kind in New York, which should have enabled him to obtain higher prices on salable products. The above figures indicate that the present contractor is operating at a loss. The former contractor's bid on this contract was $34,500. It is estimated that the present contractor's bid should have been:
```
    Cost of operation_____ $65, 007. 50
    Plus 20 per cent profit_____ 13, 001. 50
                                                          _____
        Total_____ 78, 009. 00
    Less income from salable products_____ 42, 256. 00
                                                          _____
    Bid _____ 35, 753. 00
```

Assume bid for the next five-year period, say, $35,000, which does not make allowance for future growth of the District.

ESTIMATED COST OF THE COLLECTION AND DISPOSAL OF REFUSE UNDER THE DIRECT CONTROL OF THE COMMISSIONERS ON THE BASIS OF THE INCINERATOR PLANT BEING LOCATED AT OCCOQUAN, USING PRISON LABOR FOR PICKING, ETC., AND THE STEAM DEVELOPED, IN THE REDUCTION PLANT, THE REFUSE BEING TRANSPORTED BY WATER FROM WASHINGTON TO OCCOQUAN.

Record of refuse service during fiscal year ending June 30, 1911.

(Furnished by the contractor.)

Months.	Average number per day.			Total cubic yards per month.	Loads, total number per month.
	Vehicles.	Men.	Horses.		
July....................	25	27	27	10,628	1,561
August..................	23	25	25	10,436	1,328
September...............	22	24	24	8,151	1,037
October.................	23	24	24	8,675	1,106
November................	22	23	23	8,252	1,031
December................	22	24	24	7,308	901
January.................	23	24	24	8,367	1,042
February................	23	24	24	7,218	891
March...................	24	25	25	8,696	1,076
April...................	24	25	25	8,875	1,097
May.....................	27	28	28	11,432	1,427
June....................	27	28	28	10,748	1,328
Entire year.............	23	25	25	108,789	13,825

108,789 cubic yards of refuse collected during the fiscal year ending June 30, 1911, at 171 pounds to the cubic yard, equals 9,301 tons.
Population, Buffalo, 425,000, where 15,000 tons of rubbish per year is collected.

Refuse.

INITIAL COST.

Collection:

40 horses, at $240	$9,600
30 wagons, at $100	3,000
40 sets single harness, at $30	1,200
2 sets double harness, at $75	150
Stable and site	30,000
1 loading wharf	15,000
2 barges, at $3,000	6,000
One-fourth tugboat	7,500
Incidentals, 10 per cent	7,245
	79,695

Disposal:

Incinerator	15,000
Boilers	4,500
Building for incinerator	20,000
Sorting building	30,000
Conveyors	5,000
4 presses	2,000
Power equipment	2,000
Unloading wharf	10,000
Incidentals, 10 per cent	8,850
	97,350

OPERATION.

Collection:

1 assistant superintendent	$2,000
2 inspectors, at $1,000	2,000
30 drivers, at $1.75 per day for 313 days	16,432
2 dumpmen, at $1.50 per day for 313 days	939
Stable labor, 40 horses, at 20 cents per day per horse for 365 days	2,920

Collection—Continued.

40 horses (forage, 45.5 cents; shoeing 6 cents; medicine, one-half cent), 52 cents per day per horse for 365 days_____ $7,592

Repairs to 30 wagons, at 10 cents per day for 313 days_____ 939

Repairs to stable_____ 1,000

Repairs to 30 sets harness, at 4 cents per day per set for 313 days__ 376

3 per cent interest plus 5 per cent depreciation, or 8 per cent of $79,695-- 6,376

‾‾‾‾‾‾‾‾
40,574

Transportation on, say, 10,000 tons refuse Washington to Occoquan, using unit price estimated for garbage, $0.23_____ 2,300

‾‾‾‾‾‾‾‾
42,874

Disposal:

1 assistant superintendent, at $4_____ $4.00

1 mason, at $3.50_____ 3.50

3 assistant engineers, at $2.50_____ 7.50

60 prison laborers, at $0.75_____ 45.00

‾‾‾‾‾‾
60.00

Labor and supervision, at $60 per day for 313 days_____ 18,780

Repairs and renewals_____ 4,000

3 per cent interest plus 5 per cent depreciation, or 8 per cent of initial cost of $97,350--- 7,788

‾‾‾‾‾‾‾‾
30,568

Income:

About one-third of refuse collected is burned, the balance being salable. Refuse has about one-seventh fuel power of coal, or it will evaporate 1 pound of water per pound of refuse.

One-third of 10,000 tons equals 6,666,000 pounds of steam, at 2 cents per 100_____ $1,333

Revenue from Buffalo collecting 15,000 tons is $39,176. Washington contractor's present estimated revenue $42,256, assumed for this estimate-- 42,256

‾‾‾‾‾‾‾‾
43,589

SUMMARY.

Estimated cost of future contract_____ 35,000

Total cost of collection_____ $42,874

Total cost of disposal_____ 30,568

Total cost of collection and disposal_____ 73,442

Income _____ 43,589

Total net cost_____ 29,853

Estimated yearly saving by municipal ownership_____ 5,147

Comparing an incinerator with utilization at Occoquan with incinerator in Washington.

Saving by using prison labor, 60 laborers, at 75 cents per man per day, for 313 days _____ $14,085

Credit for steam developed, $1,333, less interest and depreciation on boilers, 8 per cent of $4,500, or $360_____ 973

‾‾‾‾‾‾‾
15,058

Transportation by water from Washington to Occoquan, 10,000 tons, at 23 cents_____ 2,300

Total yearly advantage of plant at Occoquan_____ 12,758

APPROXIMATE ESTIMATE OF THE COLLECTION AND DISPOSAL OF ASHES UNDER THE DIRECT CONTROL OF THE COMMISSIONERS.

Record of ash service for the fiscal year ending June 30, 1911.

(Furnished by the contractor.)

Month.	Vehicles.		Men.		Horses.		Total weight for month.	Cubic yards.		Total number loads per month.
	Average number per day.	Maximum for 1 day.	Average number per day.	Maximum for 1 day.	Average number per day.	Maximum for 1 day.		Total cubic yards for month.	Maximum cubic yds for 1 day.	
July	18	18	33	34	36	36	912,360	7,606	319	1,383
August	18	18	34	34	36	36	704,240	5,027	296	1,116
September	19	22	36	38	39	44	7,225,600	5,973	280	1,302
October	24	45	42	90	49	90	10,804,400	8,972	900	2,273
November	51	55	108	106	103	108	23,984,800	20,005	856	4,991
December	58	64	118	132	118	132	28,358,400	23,632	920	5,908
January	60	64	122	128	122	128	26,312,000	21,820	868	5,485
February	61	70	123	140	123	140	22,635,200	19,696	912	4,914
March	60	64	121	128	121	128	25,224,000	21,020	900	5,255
April	50	64	100	128	100	128	18,705,600	15,588	788	3,997
May	35	37	71	74	71	74	14,498,800	12,024	464	3,006
June	29	30	58	60	58	60	11,275,200	9,396	392	2,349
Entire year	40	45	80	91	81	92	191,570,600	171,361	623	41,038

Cleveland and Columbus are both manufacturing towns, and a larger portion of their population consists of a poorer class of people than is found in Washington. Washington has a much larger floating population. It is thought for this reason that Washington not only produces more garbage per capita, but that the garbage is of a higher commercial value. It is also thought that the collection service in Washington is better and that a larger proportion of the garbage produced is collected. The estimated cost of collection per ton of garbage for Washington compares very closely with Cleveland and Columbus. In these two cities the area covered in collecting a ton of garbage is about twice as great as in Washington, but Washington makes this up by giving collections about twice as often.

NOTES.

A. Three hundred and thirty-three tons is shown as the maximum for one day, occurring on Monday, but the average for this day and the next two succeeding days is 242, showing that a plant one-quarter smaller than the one assumed for this estimate would have handled the garbage for the year ending June 30, 1911, and therefore the 320 tons per day plant assumed would probably take care of the growth of the District for a number of years to come.

B. The advantage of combining the collection of garbage and ashes is that when garbage collections are heavy ash collections are light, and vice versa; but referring to page 2, the table indicates that even with the combined service there is required 58 per cent more horses in the maximum month than in the minimum month. For an economical operation arrangements should be made either to purchase the minimum and hire the extra horses when needed or purchase the maximum and use the surplus in some other branch of the service when not needed, but the equipment, such as wagons, etc., being of a special kind, the maximum will have to be purchased.

C. The inital cost of the Cleveland plant is low, because it was bought from the former contractor secondhand. In Columbus a large portion of the garbage is collected by private parties, which practice the city hopes to eliminate, but the plant was built with ample capacity to take all the garbage produced, and consequently the initial cost and interest and depreciation are high in proportion to the garbage collected by the city at present.

D. The cost of operation per ton of garbage for labor and supervision at the Columbus plant will decrease considerably as the plant is operated toward its full capacity. At both Columbus and Cleveland the cost of labor is much higher than here, and the estimate for Washington is based on using prison labor at one-half cost of outside labor.

E. The price of fuel is more than twice as much in Washington as in either Columbus or Cleveland.

F. Irwin Blair, secretary of the Kutztown Foundry & Machine Works, manufacturers and designers of reduction equipment, who has been in this business more than 20 years, states that he usually figures the cost of operation of reduction plants, not including interest and depreciation, at $1.75, and income at from $4 to $5 per ton of garbage collected.

G. Mr. Blair says that the reason the percentage of tankage is low at the Cleveland plant is because they do not evaporate their stick water and mix the product with the tankage, which is done at the Columbus plant.

DEAD ANIMALS.

At Cleveland and Columbus the collection and disposal of dead animals is included with the garbage, which would be done in Washington under a municipally owned and operated system.

As the collection and disposal of dead animals would cost about the same as garbage, and as they yield a slightly larger income, the use of the unit prices estimated for garbage in the following estimate for dead animals is conservative:

Table showing number and estimated weight of dead animals collected fiscal year ended June 30, 1911.

Number and kinds.	Weight of each.	Total.
	Pounds.	*Pounds.*
6,150 dogs	30	184,500
8,970 cats	10	89,700
547 rats	1	547
638 horses	1,000	638,000
176 chickens	4	704
239 miscellaneous	10	2,390
		915,841

Income:
    458 tons dead animals, at $4.20 _____ $1,923.60
    638 horsehides, at $4 _____ 2,552.00
                                                                  $4,475.60
Collection:
    458 tons dead animals, at $2.52 _____ 1,154.16
Reduction:
    458 tons dead animals, at $2.31 _____ 1,057.98
                                                                  2,212.14

    Income _____ 2,263.46
Amount at present paid for this service _____ 2,855.00

    Estimated amount saving by municipal ownership_____ 5,118.46

Financial statement of present refuse collection and disposal in Washington, D. C., based on approximate information furnished by the contractor, M. R. Ready.

INITIAL COST AND FIXED CHARGES.
Collection:
    30 wagons, at $75 _____ $2,250.00
    40 horses, at $150 _____ 6,000.00
    40 sets single harness, at $22.50 _____ 900.00
    2 sets double harness, at $40 _____ 80.00
                                                                  9,230.00
    5 per cent interest and depreciation, 20 per cent_____ 2,307.50
Disposal:
    Plant _____ 42,000.00
    5 per cent interest and 20 per cent depreciation_____ 10,500.00

NOTE: The depreciation is based on 100 per cent in five years, this being the contract period. The former contractor received practically nothing for his plant on the termination of his contract.

OPERATION.
Collection:
    Pay roll, 52 weeks, at $400 _____ 20,800.00
    Forage and material for horseshoeing, for 40 horses, $0.50 per day per horse, 365 days _____ 7,300.00
    Repairs to wagons and harness per year_____ 1,200.00
    Rent stables, 12 months, at $50 _____ 600.00
    Fixed charges _____ 2,307.50
                                                                          32,207.50

Disposal:

Pay roll, 52 weeks, at $400	$20,800.00
Repairs, 12 months, at $100	1,200.00
Rent land, 12 months, at $25	300.00
Fixed charges	10,500.00
	32,800.00

Collection	32,207.50
Disposal	32,800.00
Cost of operation	65,007.50

Income:

7,825 tons crumbled news, at $4	31,300.00
313 tons mixed rags, at $12	3,756.00
Registered bottles	1,200.00
Mixed bottles	2,400.00
Tin cans and scrap iron	2,400.00
Junk	1,200.00
	42,256.00
Yearly payment from District of Columbia	17,000.00
Income	59,256.00
Yearly loss	5,751.50

NOTE.—The yearly collections from the District of Columbia are about the same as Buffalo, N. Y., where they have a refuse incinerator owned by the municipality, and their latest figures show operating expenses $38,530.60 and income $39,175.97; but it is not known whether these figures include fixed charges. M. R. Ready says that in figuring on this contract he neglected to consider fixed charges. Prices on salable refuse are very low at present, and it would be possible, with the highest prices, to increase the present income on salable products by about 50 per cent. The former contractor was a competitor for the present contract. He had had three years' previous experience, a plant which, it is assumed, was paid for by his former contract, and a large business of this kind in New York, which should have enabled him to obtain higher prices on salable products. The above figures indicate that the present contractor is operating at a loss. The former contractor's bid on this contract was $34,500. It is estimated that the present contractor's bid should have been:

Cost of operation	$65,007.50
Plus 20 per cent profit	13,001.50
Total	78,009.00
Less income from salable products	42,256.00
Bid	35,753.00

Assume bid for the next five-year period, say, $35,000, which does not make allowance for future growth of the District.

ESTIMATED COST OF THE COLLECTION AND DISPOSAL OF REFUSE UNDER THE DIRECT CONTROL OF THE COMMISSIONERS ON THE BASIS OF THE INCINERATOR PLANT BEING LOCATED AT OCCOQUAN, USING PRISON LABOR FOR PICKING, ETC., AND THE STEAM DEVELOPED, IN THE REDUCTION PLANT, THE REFUSE BEING TRANSPORTED BY WATER FROM WASHINGTON TO OCCOQUAN.

Record of refuse service during fiscal year ending June 30, 1911.

(Furnished by the contractor.)

Months.	Average number per day.			Total cubic yards per month.	Loads, total number per month.
	Vehicles.	Men.	Horses.		
July...............................	25	27	27	10,628	1,561
August............................	23	25	25	10,436	1,328
September.........................	22	24	24	8,151	1,037
October...........................	23	24	24	8,676	1,106
November..........................	22	23	23	8,252	1,031
December..........................	22	24	24	7,306	901
January...........................	23	24	24	8,367	1,042
February..........................	23	24	24	7,218	891
March.............................	24	25	25	8,696	1,076
April.............................	24	25	25	8,875	1,097
May...............................	27	28	28	11,432	1,427
June..............................	27	28	28	10,748	1,328
Entire year.......................	23	25	25	108,789	13,825

108,789 cubic yards of refuse collected during the fiscal year ending June 30, 1911, at 171 pounds to the cubic yard, equals 9,301 tons.

Population, Buffalo, 425,000, where 15,000 tons of rubbish per year is collected.

Refuse.

INITIAL COST.

Collection:

40 horses, at $240_____	$9,600
30 wagons, at $100_____	3,000
40 sets single harness, at $30_____	1,200
2 sets double harness, at $75_____	150
Stable and site_____	30,000
1 loading wharf_____	15,000
2 barges, at $3,000_____	6,000
One-fourth tugboat_____	7,500
Incidentals, 10 per cent_____	7,245
	79,695

Disposal:

Incinerator_____	15,000
Boilers_____	4,500
Building for incinerator_____	20,000
Sorting building_____	30,000
Conveyors_____	5,000
4 presses_____	2,000
Power equipment_____	2,000
Unloading wharf_____	10,000
Incidentals, 10 per cent_____	8,850
	97,350

OPERATION.

Collection:

1 assistant superintendent_____	$2,000
2 inspectors, at $1,000_____	2,000
30 drivers, at $1.75 per day for 313 days_____	16,432
2 dumpmen, at $1.50 per day for 313 days_____	939
Stable labor, 40 horses, at 20 cents per day per horse for 365 days.	2,920

Collection—Continued.

40 horses (forage, 45.5 cents; shoeing 6 cents; medicine, one-half cent), 52 cents per day per horse for 365 days	$7,592
Repairs to 30 wagons, at 10 cents per day for 313 days	939
Repairs to stable	1,000
Repairs to 30 sets harness, at 4 cents per day per set for 313 days	376
3 per cent interest plus 5 per cent depreciation, or 8 per cent of $79,695	6,376
	40,574
Transportation on, say, 10,000 tons refuse Washington to Occoquan, using unit price estimated for garbage, $0.23	2,300
	42,874

Disposal:

1 assistant superintendent, at $4	$4.00
1 mason, at $3.50	3.50
3 assistant engineers, at $2.50	7.50
60 prison laborers, at $0.75	45.00
	60.00
Labor and supervision, at $60 per day for 313 days	18,780
Repairs and renewals	4,000
3 per cent interest plus 5 per cent depreciation, or 8 per cent of initial cost of $97,350	7,788
	30,568

Income:

About one-third of refuse collected is burned, the balance being salable. Refuse has about one-seventh fuel power of coal, or it will evaporate 1 pound of water per pound of refuse.

One-third of 10,000 tons equals 6,666,000 pounds of steam, at 2 cents per 100	$1,333
Revenue from Buffalo collecting 15,000 tons is $39,176. Washington contractor's present estimated revenue $42,256, assumed for this estimate	42,256
	43,589

SUMMARY.

Estimated cost of future contract		35,000
Total cost of collection	$42,874	
Total cost of disposal	30,568	
Total cost of collection and disposal	73,442	
Income	43,589	
Total net cost		29,853
Estimated yearly saving by municipal ownership		5,147

Comparing an incinerator with utilization at Occoquan with incinerator in Washington.

Saving by using prison labor, 60 laborers, at 75 cents per man per day, for 313 days		$14,085
Credit for steam developed, $1,333, less interest and depreciation on boilers, 8 per cent of $4,500, or $360		973
		15,058
Transportation by water from Washington to Occoquan, 10,000 tons, at 23 cents		2,300
Total yearly advantage of plant at Occoquan		12,758

APPROXIMATE ESTIMATE OF THE COLLECTION AND DISPOSAL OF ASHES UNDER THE DIRECT CONTROL OF THE COMMISSIONERS.

Record of ash service for the fiscal year ending June 30, 1911.

(Furnished by the contractor.)

Month	Vehicles.		Men.		Horses.		Total weight for month.	Cubic yards.		Total number loads per month.
	Average number per day.	Maximum for 1 day.	Average number per day.	Maximum for 1 day.	Average number per day.	Maximum for 1 day.		Total cubic yards for month.	Maximum cubic yards for 1 day.	
July	18	18	33	34	36	36	912,360	7,608	319	1,383
August	18	18	34	34	36	36	704,240	5,627	286	1,115
September	19	22	35	38	39	44	7,225,600	5,973	280	1,392
October	24	46	42	90	49	90	10,804,400	8,972	800	2,273
November	51	55	103	108	103	108	23,984,800	20,005	886	4,991
December	58	64	118	132	118	132	28,358,400	23,632	920	5,908
January	60	64	122	132	122	128	26,312,000	21,820	868	5,465
February	61	64	123	140	123	140	23,635,200	19,696	912	4,914
March	50	64	121	128	121	128	25,224,000	21,020	800	5,255
April	50	64	100	128	100	128	18,705,600	15,588	788	3,897
May	35	37	71	74	71	74	14,428,800	12,024	464	3,006
June	29	30	58	60	58	60	11,275,200	9,396	392	2,349
Entire year	40	45	80	91	81	92	191,570,600	171,361	623	41,938

Cleveland and Columbus are both manufacturing towns, and a larger portion of their population consists of a poorer class of people than is found in Washington. Washington has a much larger floating population. It is thought for this reason that Washington not only produces more garbage per capita, but that the garbage is of a higher commercial value. It is also thought that the collection service in Washington is better and that a larger proportion of the garbage produced is collected. The estimated cost of collection per ton of garbage for Washington compares very closely with Cleveland and Columbus. In these two cities the area covered in collecting a ton of garbage is about twice as great as in Washington, but Washington makes this up by giving collections about twice as often.

NOTES.

A. Three hundred and thirty-three tons is shown as the maximum for one day, occurring on Monday, but the average for this day and the next two succeeding days is 242, showing that a plant one-quarter smaller than the one assumed for this estimate would have handled the garbage for the year ending June 30, 1911, and therefore the 320 tons per day plant assumed would probably take care of the growth of the District for a number of years to come.

B. The advantage of combining the collection of garbage and ashes is that when garbage collections are heavy ash collections are light, and vice versa; but referring to page 2, the table indicates that even with the combined service there is required 58 per cent more horses in the maximum month than in the minimum month. For an economical operation arrangements should be made either to purchase the minimum and hire the extra horses when needed or purchase the maximum and use the surplus in some other branch of the service when not needed, but the equipment, such as wagons, etc., being of a special kind, the maximum will have to be purchased.

C. The inital cost of the Cleveland plant is low, because it was bought from the former contractor secondhand. In Columbus a large portion of the garbage is collected by private parties, which practice the city hopes to eliminate, but the plant was built with ample capacity to take all the garbage produced, and consequently the initial cost and interest and depreciation are high in proportion to the garbage collected by the city at present.

D. The cost of operation per ton of garbage for labor and supervision at the Columbus plant will decrease considerably as the plant is operated toward its full capacity. At both Columbus and Cleveland the cost of labor is much higher than here, and the estimate for Washington is based on using prison labor at one-half cost of outside labor.

E. The price of fuel is more than twice as much in Washington as in either Columbus or Cleveland.

F. Irwin Blair, secretary of the Kutztown Foundry & Machine Works, manufacturers and designers of reduction equipment, who has been in this business more than 20 years, states that he usually figures the cost of operation of reduction plants, not including interest and depreciation, at $1.75, and income at from $4 to $5 per ton of garbage collected.

G. Mr. Blair says that the reason the percentage of tankage is low at the Cleveland plant is because they do not evaporate their stick water and mix the product with the tankage, which is done at the Columbus plant.

DEAD ANIMALS.

At Cleveland and Columbus the collection and disposal of dead animals is included with the garbage, which would be done in Washington under a municipally owned and operated system.

As the collection and disposal of dead animals would cost about the same as garbage, and as they yield a slightly larger income, the use of the unit prices estimated for garbage in the following estimate for dead animals is conservative:

Table showing number and estimated weight of dead animals collected fiscal year ended June 30, 1911.

Number and kinds.	Weight of each.	Total.
	Pounds.	*Pounds.*
6,150 dogs	30	184,500
8,970 cats	10	89,700
547 rats	1	547
638 horses	1,000	638,000
176 chickens	4	704
239 miscellaneous	10	2,390
		915,841

Income:
```
    458 tons dead animals, at $4.20_____ $1,923.60
    638 horsehides, at $4_____  2,552.00
                                                                 $4,475.60
Collection:
    458 tons dead animals, at $2.52_____  1,154.16
Reduction:
    458 tons dead animals, at $2.31_____  1,057.98
                                                                  2,212.14

        Income _____  2,263.46
Amount at present paid for this service_____  2,855.00

        Estimated amount saving by municipal ownership_____  5,118.46
```

Financial statement of present refuse collection and disposal in Washington, D. C., based on approximate information furnished by the contractor, M. R. Ready.

INITIAL COST AND FIXED CHARGES.

Collection:
```
    30 wagons, at $75_____ $2,250.00
    40 horses, at $150_____  6,000.00
    40 sets single harness, at $22.50_____    900.00
    2 sets double harness, at $40_____     80.00

                                                            9,230.00
    5 per cent interest and depreciation, 20 per cent_____  2,307.50
Disposal:
    Plant _____  42,000.00
    5 per cent interest and 20 per cent depreciation_____  10,500.00
```

NOTE: The depreciation is based on 100 per cent in five years, this being the contract period. The former contractor received practically nothing for his plant on the termination of his contract.

OPERATION.

Collection:
```
    Pay roll, 52 weeks, at $400_____ 20,800.00
    Forage and material for horseshoeing, for 40 horses, $0.50 per
        day per horse, 365 days_____  7,300.00
    Repairs to wagons and harness per year_____  1,200.00
    Rent stables, 12 months, at $50_____    600.00
    Fixed charges _____  2,307.50

                                                           32,207.50
```

Disposal:

Pay roll, 52 weeks, at $400	$20,800.00
Repairs, 12 months, at $100	1,200.00
Rent land, 12 months, at $25	300.00
Fixed charges	10,500.00
	32,800.00

Collection	32,207.50
Disposal	32,800.00
Cost of operation	65,007.50

Income:

7,825 tons crumbled news, at $4	31,300.00
313 tons mixed rags, at $12	3,756.00
Registered bottles	1,200.00
Mixed bottles	2,400.00
Tin cans and scrap iron	2,400.00
Junk	1,200.00
	42,256.00
Yearly payment from District of Columbia	17,000.00
Income	59,256.00
Yearly loss	5,751.50

NOTE.—The yearly collections from the District of Columbia are about the same as Buffalo, N. Y., where they have a refuse incinerator owned by the municipality, and their latest figures show operating expenses $38,530.60 and income $39,175.97; but it is not known whether these figures include fixed charges. M. R. Ready says that in figuring on this contract he neglected to consider fixed charges. Prices on salable refuse are very low at present, and it would be possible, with the highest prices, to increase the present income on salable products by about 50 per cent. The former contractor was a competitor for the present contract. He had had three years' previous experience, a plant which, it is assumed, was paid for by his former contract, and a large business of this kind in New York, which should have enabled him to obtain higher prices on salable products. The above figures indicate that the present contractor is operating at a loss. The former contractor's bid on this contract was $34,500. It is estimated that the present contractor's bid should have been:

Cost of operation	$65,007.50
Plus 20 per cent profit	13,001.50
Total	78,009.00
Less income from salable products	42,256.00
Bid	35,753.00

Assume bid for the next five-year period, say, $35,000, which does not make allowance for future growth of the District.

ESTIMATED COST OF THE COLLECTION AND DISPOSAL OF REFUSE UNDER THE DIRECT CONTROL OF THE COMMISSIONERS ON THE BASIS OF THE INCINERATOR PLANT BEING LOCATED AT OCCOQUAN, USING PRISON LABOR FOR PICKING, ETC., AND THE STEAM DEVELOPED, IN THE REDUCTION PLANT, THE REFUSE BEING TRANSPORTED BY WATER FROM WASHINGTON TO OCCOQUAN.

Record of refuse service during fiscal year ending June 30, 1911.

(Furnished by the contractor.)

Months.	Average number per day.			Total cubic yards per month.	Loads, total number per month.
	Vehicles.	Men.	Horses.		
July.....................	25	27	27	10,628	1,561
August..................	23	25	25	10,436	1,328
September.............	22	24	24	8,151	1,037
October................	23	24	24	8,675	1,106
November.............	22	23	23	8,252	1,031
December.............	22	24	24	7,308	901
January................	23	24	24	8,367	1,042
February..............	23	24	24	7,218	891
March.................	24	25	25	8,696	1,076
April..................	24	25	25	8,875	1,097
May...................	27	28	28	11,432	1,427
June...................	27	28	28	10,748	1,328
Entire year..........	23	25	25	108,789	13,825

108,789 cubic yards of refuse collected during the fiscal year ending June 30, 1911, at 171 pounds to the cubic yard, equals 9,301 tons.

Population, Buffalo, 425,000, where 15,000 tons of rubbish per year is collected.

Refuse.

INITIAL COST.

Collection:
- 40 horses, at $240_____ $9,600
- 30 wagons, at $100_____ 3,000
- 40 sets single harness, at $30_____ 1,200
- 2 sets double harness, at $75_____ 150
- Stable and site_____ 30,000
- 1 loading wharf_____ 15,000
- 2 barges, at $3,000_____ 6,000
- One-fourth tugboat_____ 7,500
- Incidentals, 10 per cent_____ 7,245

79,695

Disposal:
- Incinerator_____ 15,000
- Boilers _____ 4,500
- Building for incinerator_____ 20,000
- Sorting building_____ 30,000
- Conveyors_____ 5,000
- 4 presses_____ 2,000
- Power equipment_____ 2,000
- Unloading wharf_____ 10,000
- Incidentals, 10 per cent_____ 8,850

97,350

OPERATION.

Collection:
- 1 assistant superintendent_____ $2,000
- 2 inspectors, at $1,000_____ 2,000
- 30 drivers, at $1.75 per day for 313 days_____ 16,432
- 2 dumpmen, at $1.50 per day for 313 days_____ 939
- Stable labor, 40 horses, at 20 cents per day per horse for 365 days_____ 2,920

Collection—Continued.

40 horses (forage, 45.5 cents; shoeing 6 cents; medicine, one-half
cent), 52 cents per day per horse for 365 days_____ $7, 592
Repairs to 30 wagons, at 10 cents per day for 313 days_____ 939
Repairs to stable_____ 1, 000
Repairs to 30 sets harness, at 4 cents per day per set for 313 days__ 376
3 per cent interest plus 5 per cent depreciation, or 8 per cent
of $79,695_____ 6, 376

    40, 574

Transportation on, say, 10,000 tons refuse Washington to Occoquan,
using unit price estimated for garbage, $0.23_____ 2, 300

    42, 874

Disposal:

1 assistant superintendent, at $4_____ $4. 00
1 mason, at $3.50_____ 3. 50
3 assistant engineers, at $2.50_____ 7. 50
60 prison laborers, at $0.75_____ 45. 00

    60. 00

Labor and supervision, at $60 per day for 313 days_____ 18, 780
Repairs and renewals_____ 4, 000
8 per cent interest plus 5 per cent depreciation, or 8 per cent of
initial cost of $97,350_____ 7, 788

    30, 568

Income:

About one-third of refuse collected is burned, the balance being
salable. Refuse has about one-seventh fuel power of coal, or
it will evaporate 1 pound of water per pound of refuse.
One-third of 10,000 tons equals 6,666,000 pounds of steam, at
2 cents per 100_____ $1, 333
Revenue from Buffalo collecting 15,000 tons is $39,176. Wash-
ington contractor's present estimated revenue $42,256, assumed
for this estimate_____ 42, 256

    43, 589

SUMMARY.

Estimated cost of future contract_____ 35, 000
Total cost of collection_____ $42. 874
Total cost of disposal_____ 30, 568

Total cost of collection and disposal_____ 73, 442
Income _____ 43, 589

Total net cost_____ 29, 853

Estimated yearly saving by municipal ownership_____ 5, 147

*Comparing an incinerator with utilization at Occoquan with incinerator in
Washington.*

Saving by using prison labor, 60 laborers, at 75 cents per man per day,
for 313 days_____ $14, 085
Credit for steam developed, $1,333, less interest and depreciation on
boilers, 8 per cent of $4,500, or $360_____ 973

    15, 058

Transportation by water from Washington to Occoquan, 10,000 tons,
at 23 cents_____ 2, 300

Total yearly advantage of plant at Occoquan_____ 12, 758

APPROXIMATE ESTIMATE OF THE COLLECTION AND DISPOSAL OF ASHES UNDER THE DIRECT CONTROL OF THE COMMISSIONERS.

Record of ash service for the fiscal year ending June 30, 1911.

(Furnished by the contractor.)

Month	Vehicles		Men		Horses		Total weight for month.	Cubic yards.		Total number loads per month.
	Average number per day.	Maximum for 1 day.	Average number per day.	Maximum for 1 day.	Average number per day.	Maximum for 1 day.		Total cubic yards for month.	Maximum cubic yards for 1 day.	
July	18	18	33	34	36	36	912,360	7,606	319	1,383
August	18	18	34	34	36	36	704,240	5,627	296	1,115
September	19	22	35	38	39	44	7,225,600	5,973	280	1,392
October	24	45	42	90	49	90	10,804,400	8,972	600	2,273
November	51	55	108	108	103	108	23,984,800	20,005	856	4,991
December	58	64	118	132	118	132	28,358,400	23,632	920	5,908
January	60	64	122	132	122	128	26,312,000	21,820	868	5,455
February	61	70	123	140	123	140	23,635,200	19,696	912	4,914
March	60	64	121	128	121	128	25,224,000	21,020	900	5,255
April	50	64	100	128	100	128	18,705,600	15,588	788	3,997
May	35	37	71	74	71	74	14,428,800	12,024	464	3,006
June	29	30	58	60	58	60	11,275,200	9,396	392	2,349
Entire year	40	45	80	91	81	92	191,570,600	171,361	623	41,938

and the Bronx, or at the rate of about 57 cents per ton collected, or $1.88 per ton picked out. During 1904 the weekly privileges sold for sums varying from $1,175 to $1,920. About 30 per cent of the rubbish collected was picked out.

Financial statement, one day's work at Delancey Slip plant.

Cost of disposal of rubbish on land fills:
1,050 cubic yards delivered, compressed on scows, after trimming, to 315 cubic yards; 315 cubic yards, at $0.1569_____ $49. 42
Cost, incinerator:
Labor—
Ash removal, 7.6 cubic yards, at $0.1569_____ $1. 20
Supplies and repairs_____ 8. 00
Interest, 3½ per cent on $34,193_____ 3. 28
_____ 12. 48

Saving per day_____ 36. 94
Saving per year (39.4 per cent on cost)_____ 13, 483. 00

Cost, electric-light station:
Cost of buying electricity_____ 80. 00
Labor _____ $20. 00
Supplies, repairs, and sundries_____ 8. 00
Interest, 3½ per cent on $49,391_____ 4. 74
_____ 32. 74

Saving per day_____ 47. 26
Saving per year (35 per cent on cost)_____ 17, 250. 00

The total saving, therefore, on the combined plant is $30,733 per annum, or 36.7 per cent on the cost.

NOTE.—There is included in the above no cost for labor charges in the incinerator plant, because the privilege of picking out the marketable refuse on the belt conveyor is under contract, and the contractor pays to the city a sum which slightly exceeds the expenses of labor in the incinerator building, including the operations of the boilers. Taxes are not included.

FROM "THE COLLECTION AND DISPOSAL OF MUNICIPAL WASTE."

(William F. Morse, in Municipal Journal and Engineer, 1908.)

Col. Waring applied a method he saw at Budapest, consisting of an endless belt, over which the refuse passed and from which those portions having a commercial value were picked out. He applied this method to New York City by having a separate collection made of the refuse and sorting it out.

"This experiment proved that there was a far greater value in city refuse than had been generally known; that the preliminary separation could readily be made at the house; that a separate force of men and carts could be profitably employed for collection; that the refuse could be sorted, baled, and marketed, the worthless portions being destroyed without nuisance in the neighborhood of the works; and that there was revenue for the city in the process."

Year.	Loads.	Collections.	Payments to city by contractor.	Value to city per ton.
1898..................................	15,356	6,710	$4,144	$0.617
1899..................................	12,946	5,660	3,109	.549
1900..................................	7,422	3,330	3,000	[1] 1.10

[1] Seven months.

The quantities and component parts of refuse received in 1899 were as follows:

Paper, books, strawboard, etc_____pounds__ 3, 058, 616
Rags, carpets, clothing, shoes, etc_____do____ 576, 812
Iron, copper, brass, lead, and rubber_____do____ 132, 438
Bottles, proprietary _____do____ 29, 000
Bottles, common _____barrels__ 350

Of the whole annual quantity, by weight, thus treated 37 per cent was sorted and sold, 60 per cent was burned, and 3 per cent to 5 per cent was incombustible an was taken away with the ashes, which formed about 17 per cent of the quantity burned. About 75 horsepower in steam was derived from combustion, of which less than 25 per cent was utilized.

Percentage of salable portions in 100 parts of refuse:

	Per cent.
Paper, 6 different grades	74. 5
Rags, clothing, bagging, twine	12. 2
Carpet, 4 grades	3. 3
Bottles, common and proprietary	2. 5
Metal—iron, brass, lead, and zinc	2. 1
Tin, all sizes and kinds	1. 4
Leather, shoes and scraps	1. 9
Rubber—shoes, hose, and mats	. 2
Barrels, whole	1. 4
Other salable material	. 5
	100

At Boston a boiler of 200 horsepower can be maintained by the heat from the destructor. (Capacity, 500 cubic yards in 24 hours.)

The rubbish (New York) is picked over at the dumps and stations by a trimming contractor, who pays the city for the privilege. The value of this marketable refuse to the city is about $3.20 (city receives about $1,920 per week for 600 tons, the marketable proportion 35 per cent of the daily collections of 300 tons). The commissioner of street cleaning has stated that this figure is too low, probably it should be increased 50 per cent. The total yearly amount of marketable material is 93,600 tons, and the payment made for the privilege of everything salable is $110,000.

Experience with this plant (Delancey Slip) seems to have demonstrated that, in competition with coal-fed plants of equal size, rubbish-incinerating plants can furnish steam power economically.

Approximate cost of the refuse-disposal station and all the machinery, inclusive of the chimney, was $50,000 (Buffalo). The gross returns from recovered articles and steam supply to the sewerage-pumping station for 4 months 10 days, May 20 to September 30, 1907, was $11,957.83. After deducting the cost of operating and adding the allowances formerly made to the sanitary company (contractor previous to municipal operation) for steam, the net returns from the station for the period named was about $5,000, or at the rate of $1,250 per month, or $15,000 per year.

The recovered articles included 2,362,417 pounds of paper, 83,703 pounds of rags, 53,626 bottles, and 4 cart loads of tins.

If garbage, refuse, rubbish, coal, and clinker, and other waste products of the city can be successfully dealt with by the contractors after being delivered to them in a separated condition, and if such work be remunerative to the contractors, why should not the town itself do its own work of waste disposal and recover at least a part of the profit it now allows others to make, applying this profit to the expense of the collection and disposal service.

The value of garbage for commercial products lies chiefly in the amount of grease extracted. This is assumed to be 3 per cent, which equals 60 pounds from an average ton of garbage—larger perhaps than is usually obtained. * * * There is a constant market for the grease at prices which vary from 2½ to 3 cents per pound. The tankage averages about 400 pounds to each ton of garbage.

The following data are taken from the report of W. T. Brooke, city engineer of Norfolk, Va., 1898–1902. The year 1896 when the crematory (Engle garbage crematory) was operated by a contractor was omitted:

Total loads mixed garbage and refuse	58, 793
Expenses of operation and maintenance:	
Labor	$16, 735. 64
Fuel, coal	9, 237. 31
Repairs and sundries	3, 263. 39
Total expenses	29, 236. 34

Fifty-eight thousand seven hundred and ninety-three loads is estimated to equal 60,000 tons. or cost per ton of 50 cents for operating and maintenance.

During this time two steel chimneys have been supplied, furnace relined once, besides usual repairs.

Reports on the Smith Siemens Crematory, Atlantic City, N. J., made by J. P. Fetherson, street cleaning service, New York City, for the period September 1, 1901, to September 1, 1902, shows cost per ton of garbage burned to be $1.52. Cost for 1900 to 1902 shows average cost per ton of $1.485. Average cost of collection, $1.22 per ton. This crematory was operated by producer gas.

Unofficial report for Davis Crematory at Trenton, N. J., gives cost of about 62 cents per ton.

The cost of incineration at Montreal as stated by Dr. Pelletier follows:

From figures furnished by the department in charge * * * 13,659 tons destroyed during 1901 at a cost of 98½ cents per ton. This, however, is not the exact cost due to repairs, etc. It is now well established that the net cost for the incineration of a ton of garbage is 39 cents per ton.

NOTE.—It is understood that this is operating cost only, not including interest charges on capital cost or depreciation.

Test at Brown's Crematory, Boston, Mass., April 25, 1893:

Cost per ton of garbage consumed, $1.22.

Cost of Engle Crematory at Chicago Exposition was 63 cents per ton for labor and fuel.

Report of operation Heenan & Froude Destructor, Vancouver, British Columbia.

Character of refuse estimated by weight:

	Per cent.
Household garbage	82
Trade refuse	12
Decayed fruit and vegetables	3
Manure	1. 5
Meat and fish offal	1
Sawdust	. 5

Collection cost per ton 1.55, not deducting revenue, or $1.15 deducting revenue.

Complete cost of construction, building, extras, chimney, destructor plant, boilers, and accessories, $41,193.

Cost of operation, 46 cents per ton, deducting revenue; 56 cents per ton, not deducting revenue; 91 cents per ton, counting in interest and sinking fund.

Cost of operation and value of by-products of reduction plant, New Bedford, Mass.

Daily average tons treated, 20.

Value of 1 ton of garbage, as delived to plant, prices as of Sept. 1, 1907	$4. 282
Actual cost of reduction	1. 995
Gain per ton	2. 287
Gain, 20 tons, 312 days	14, 270. 88
Depreciation on 25-ton plant	6, 500. 00
	7, 770. 80
Yield of grease, 53 to 60 lbs _____per cent__	3. 34
Yield of tankage, 400 to 460 lbs _____do____	. 15

Coal per ton of garbage reduced, 394 pounds. On 30 tons per day, cost of reduction per ton would not exceed $1.50. At full capacity of the plant (60 tons) cost would not exceed $1. Tankage is valued at from $4 to $12 per ton, depending on the amount of ammonia present.

Concerning the relative value of incineration and reduction methods for the final disposal of this material, much has been said and written. The problem is very complex. What is a merit in one city is a demerit in another.

Generally speaking, in a city whose population is under the 100,000 mark, the returns from a reduction method of disposal are too small to warrant building a plant, unless the contract price paid by the city for the work is high and the terms of the contract long (ten years or more). For such cities cremation is unquestionably the method to adopt.

Again, generally speaking, in a city whose population is over 100,000, reduction should be the method adopted if the cost alone is considered.

It has been demonstrated time and again that a reduction plant can be operated near a thickly populated district without creating any offense whatever. For example, the old plant of the American Product Co., not over 2 miles from the city hall, Philadelphia, and across the river from the suburban district of West Philadelphia. This plant has been in almost continuous operation for the past 12 years, and whoever heard of any complaint as to its being unsanitary or a menace to public health. If care is taken in the design of a reduction plant, there is absolutely no complaint, provided intelligence is used in its operation. A crematory can also be conducted in a highly sanitary manner, but against most existing plants, in this country at least, complaints have been entered, based on the fumes or from the small particles of unburned garbage and dust discharged from the stacks.

Success of both systems, however, from a sanitary standpoint, rests almost entirely with the health officers of the city. As far as sanitation goes, there is very little to choose between cremation and reduction. It must be remembered that the raw material is subject to rapid decay, and it is the hauling of this material from the receptacle to the wagon and from the wagon to the plant that complaints arise rather than from the plant itself, be it a crematory or a reduction plant.

It was said by Co. Waring, in relation to the wastes of New York, that there was annually thrown away in the discarded matter a sum of money sufficient to pay for the collection and disposal of the wastes of the city. In three years Col. Waring demonstrated that this was not entirely a theoretical idea, but one that could be carried out if it were attempted with thorough knowledge of the requirement, a sufficient amount of money to do the word, and the aid of a mayor and council who would support reform.

In the largest cities the disposal of garbage by the crematory has met with very unsatisfactory results. The largest plants now operated are of four different types of construction, but none gives results that correspond with the contracts under which they were built. The incinerators at Atlanta and Los Angeles, built under a stipulation to burn 200 tons per day, are not able to destroy more than half that amount. The 140-ton incinerator at Winnepeg has never yet been able to meet the contract conditions as to quantity and cost, and is not yet accepted by the city. The crematory a Milwaukee has never met the specifications of amounts destroyed or cost of operating. Incinerator at Montreal does not consume the specified quantities and the operating costs are more than double those estimated.

An examination of the work done by American creamatories for a period of over 20 years make it very clear that the actual cost of destroying garbage and refuse when fuel is necessary will approximate a sum of 50 cents a ton, and this may be taken as the lowest price which can reasonably be expected for a successful operation throughout all the yearly period. Statements made that the garbage can be destroyed at 22 cents to 35 cents per ton for operating costs, labor, and fuel, are not borne out by facts.

The operating cost of destructors, according to four installations now at work runs from 50 cents to 70 cents per ton for actual expense of labor. If power is developed, the operating costs will fall from 50 cents to 30 cents or less per ton. It must be borne in mind that these figures do not include the expense of depreciation or construction interest.

Assuming a permanent fireproof building two stories high, 50 by 60 feet, the cost of building and land in the city of New York, equipment would be:

2 gas engines, electric generators, and necessary machinery for lifting, sorting, and handling 50 tons per day	$85,000.00

Cost of operation:

Interest, depreciation, repairs, taxes, insurance, 18 per cent	15,300.00
Labor	13,600.00
Supplies	1,600.00
Total	30,500.00
Electric current sold	53,557.55
Select wastes sold, 855 tons, at $2.50	2,137.50
Total	55,695.05
Cost	30,500.00
Profit	25,195.05

Power, August 1, 1911, "The Combustion of Town Refuse" (3,000 words). Milwaukee Bureau of Economy and Efficiency, Bulletin No. 5, June, 1911, "The Refuse Incinerator," 75 pages. Engineering and Contracting, July 5, 1911, "Economic Disposal of Garbage." Minneapolis Engineer, May, 1911, "The design of an Incinerating Plant." Journal of Ohio Society of Mechanical and Electrical and Steam Engineers, volume 3, No. 2, "Engineering features of the Columbus Garbage Reduction Plant." Enginering News, May 25, 1911, "Data on Street Cleaning Efficiency in Berlin." Canadian Engineer, March 30, 1911, "Garbage Creamatory at Houston, Tex." Municipal Engineer, April, 1911, "Reduction Plant at Columbus, Ohio." Canadian Engineer, February, 2, 1911, "The Installation of an Incinerator." School of Mines, Quarterly, January, 1911, "Disposal of City Wastes." Municipal Engineer, February, 1911, "Garbage and Refuse Collection and Disposal." Scientific American Supplement, January, 14, 1911, "Disposal of Garbage in Various Cities" (foreign). Engineering Record, January 21, 1911, "Plant for Handling and Destroying Destructor Clinker." Municipal Journal and Engineer, December 28, 1910, "Eastern Garbage Incinerator." Electrical Review (London), December 9, 1910, "Combined Destructor and Electrical Plant." Municipal Engineering Journal, January 7, 1910, "Snow Plows"; December 21, 1910, "Snow Removal in New York," Engineering Record, August 13, 1910; September 24, 1910; October 8, 1910; July 16, 1910; November 19, 1910; March 18, 1911; June 3, 1911. Enginering News, March 6, 1911; March 23, 1911.

MOTOR VEHICLES AND HORSE-DRAWN VEHICLES.

Senator SMITH of Maryland. What is the next item to which the commissioners desire to call our attention?

Commissioner NEWMAN. The next item we want to bring to the committee's attention is the matter of transportation on page 13, beginning with the last paragraph on page 12. It is under the general contingent and miscellaneous expense fund of the District. Beginning near the bottom of page 13, it reads:

For maintenance, care, and repair of automobiles, motor cycles, and motor trucks, acquired for the government of the District of Columbia, that are not otherwise herein provided for, including such personal services in connection therewith not otherwise herein authorized, as the commissioners shall in writing specially order, and for the purchase of one additional motor vehicle herein specified; namely:

Automobiles for the offices of the civilian commissioners and the engineer commissioner, including the building inspection and street cleaning divisions; surveyor's office, and electrical department, 12 in all, including one to be purchased hereunder for the service of the civilian commissioners;

The engineer commissioner has an automobile and we made an estimate for one for each of the civilian commissioners. The subcommittee of the House recommended the allowance of two automobiles for the civilian commissioners—one for each commissioner—but the full Appropriations Committee of the House provided one automobile for the joint use of the two civilian commissioners. We want first to bring particularly to the attention of the committee the reason why we ask for automobiles for ourselves at all.

Senator GALLINGER. Before you discuss the item, may I make a suggestion?

Commissioner NEWMAN. Certainly.

Senator GALLINGER. The House, I think wisely, has combined all the appropriations in the former bill which were scattered through the bill and has massed them in one item, as I understand.

Commissioner NEWMAN. Except, of course, the police and fire departments.

Senator GALLINGER. I understand.

Commissioner NEWMAN. I think there are one or two other exceptions.

Senator GALLINGER. It is a very wise plan.

Commissioner NEWMAN. Of course there is no particular reason why the items should be carried separately. The House committee has grouped them together for the purpose of a more comprehensive consideration of the question.

I have found since I have been commissioner that it has been absolutely impossible for me to get over the District of Columbia as we ought and find out what the District government is doing and how it is doing and to observe conditions that need attention. Each civilian commissioner is supplied with a horse and vehicle, but it is impossible to cover the District with a horse and vehicle. It simply can not be done. I happen to have, in the division of departments among the commissioners, the charitable and correctional institutions, and it has been impossible for me to get around to them as I feel I ought to get around so as to know how they are being conducted. Commissioner Siddons happens to have the police and fire departments. It has been impossible for him to get around for the personal observation and examination of those services which he feels he ought to make.

It was in recognition of this actual official need that the House subcommittee made the recommendation for motor cars, and it was a recognition of that need, I think, which prompted the full committee to allow one car for the joint use of the two civilian commissioners. It seems to me it would be a rather difficult and cumbersome arrangement, as the chances are that we would seldom want to go out together at the same time, but almost every day would want to go out separately. We might want to go simultaneously, but it would be to see different things and to do different things.

The House placed a limit of $2,000 on the purchase of all cars that carry more than two people, which is satisfactory to us, and I think proper.

There is one other point in this connection. There is a provision here that no officer or employee of the District for whom a motor vehicle is provided shall have a horse-drawn vehicle. If it went through as it stands, for Mr. Siddons and myself, the two civilian commissioners, horse-drawn vehicles would be eliminated and replaced by one motor-driven vehicle. If you should conclude to allow the one motor vehicle, we would like to suggest that you leave one horse-drawn vehicle. Of course, if you allow the two motors, the horses would be replaced entirely, but it would be increasingly difficult for us to get around if the horses were taken away and only one car provided in their place.

In this connection there is another little inconsistency in regard to the assistants to the engineer commissioner, which Col. Harding can explain better than I can.

Senator GALLINGER. What you would suggest, Mr. Commissioner, to secure the two automobiles for the civilian commissioners, would be on page 14, line 8, to substitute " 13 " for " 12 " and the word " two " for the word " one " in the same line.

Commissioner NEWMAN. I think the first change would be in line 3.

Senator GALLINGER. And "one" would have to be changed to "two" in line 3.

Senator SMITH of Maryland. I understand the House allowed one for the two civilian commissioners.

Commissioner NEWMAN. Yes, sir.

Senator SMITH of Maryland. At what cost?

Commissioner NEWMAN. At not more than $2,000.

Senator GALLINGER. In line 17 the amount $9,150 would have to be changed to $11,150, adding $2,000 to the appropriation in all for motor vehicles.

Commissioner NEWMAN. I think Col. Harding will have something to say about that when we come to the maintenance items.

You will observe further on that the House has taken what I am sure ought to be an effective precaution against the possibility of these machines being used for anything except the official business of the District of Columbia. They provide that they shall be of uniform color and shall have displayed conspicuously in letters six inches high on the cars "City Service," which, I think, ought effectively to prevent their improper use, if there was any tendency to use them improperly.

Senator SMITH of Maryland. Well, Col. Harding, what have you to say about it?

Col. HARDING. With reference to the engineer department, the current law provides for an automobile for the use of the engineer commissioner and his assistants. When the provision for automobiles was asked by the commissioners of the House committee it was the idea of the commissioners that for inspection purposes the automobile is very much better in the long run; that it is more efficient, and that, therefore, it is more economical to use motor-driven vehicles instead of horse-drawn vehicles. It was therefore proposed that where the commissioners saw fit to recommend motor vehicles they should be provided, and that in such cases the horse-driven vehicles should be taken away, so that there would be no question at all about both motor vehicles and horse-drawn vehicles being furnished, that being entirely unnecessary in our judgment.

The House committee did not authorize, as we estimated and suggested, a motor-driven vehicle for each of my two assistants. They, however, included in their appropriation a provision which deprives these assistants of their horse-drawn vehicles. As the matter stands, therefore, there is one automobile available for the use of the engineer commissioner and his two assistants, and no provision at all for horse-drawn vehicles, so that on the occasions when it is necessary for me to use the automobile there is no provision for transportation for my assistants, and when they use the automobile there is no provision for transportation for myself.

The suggestion I should like to make, if it is not deemed proper to grant automobiles for my two assistants, is to restore to them the horse-drawn vehicles which they now have, in connection with the amount of money appropriated for the maintenance of the motor vehicles provided by the bill in its present shape.

Senator SMITH of Maryland. On what page?

Commissioner NEWMAN. On page 14, lines 6, 7, and 8.

Col. HARDING. I will say with regard to the appropriation of $9,150, which provides for the purchase of this one automobile for the civilian commissioners and for the maintenance of that machine and all the other machines which are now authorized. we have gone over that item carefully and find that it is impossible to provide for the maintenance of the number of machines authorized with that amount of money. The estimate that we make, which I have here shown in the form of a table, is $13,034 instead of $9,150. If the additional machine is provided for the civilian commissioners that item would be still further increased by $2,000 for the original purchase of the machine, and by an item of some $600 for the maintenance of that additional machine. So the total amount instead of $9,150 should be $15,634, provided the additional machine is authorized.

Commissioner SIDDONS. Mr. Chairman, may I while on this contingent and miscellaneous items call the attention of the committee to one matter?

Senator SMITH of Maryland. All right, sir.

Commissioner SIDDONS. In the estimate the commissioners transmitted to Congress, on page 16, you will find the item.

Senator SMITH of Maryland. Pardon me, gentlemen; the total amount of $15,634, instead of $9,150, includes the 2,000 machines additional I understand.

Senator LEA. It includes the additional machine.

Commissioner NEWMAN. One additional machine.

Senator SMITH of Maryland. And also for horses?

.Col. HARDING. No, sir; the fund that is available for the maintenance of horses would be sufficient.

Senator SMITH of Maryland. Have you the horses now or would you have to buy them?

Col. HARDING. We have the horses. We are now, of course, operating under the current law.

Commissioner NEWMAN. You see, Senator, this clause says there shall be no horse-drawn vehicles for any officer or employee who has an automobile. They allowed one automobile for the use of the two civilian commissioners, and that cut out both horse-drawn vehicles. The same is true with the present authorization for the engineer commissioner's automobile. It is for the use of the engineer commissioner and his assistants. That is the existing authorization in law. So, if this provision is enacted, it would take from the engineer commissioner and his assistants their horse-drawn vehicles.

Senator SMITH of Maryland. You may proceed, Commissioner Siddons.

STREET-CAR TICKETS.

Commissioner SIDDONS. The item omitted by the House, gentlemen, is that found on the margin on page 16, street-car tickets:

That the Commissioners of the District of Columbia are hereby authorized, in their discretion, to furnish necessary transportation in connection with official business of the government of the District of Columbia by the purchase of car tickets from appropriations contained in this act.

The reason for that item is, briefly, as follows: After the enactment of the public-utilities law the then utilities commission ruled that by virtue of its provisions the practice which had theretofore prevailed of permitting policemen and firemen to ride free on the street cars of the District could no longer be permitted, and an order carried out that view of the law. So the free transportation of these officers was refused. The embarrassment and, I think, distress on the part of the police officers and firemen that followed led to an effort on the part of the commissioners to secure an opinion from the Comptroller of the Treasury whether or not under the existing contingent appropriations car tickets could be provided to police officers and firemen when engaged upon official missions about the District. The opinion of the comptroller was adverse. He said that under the existing law the commissioners could not do that.

Thereupon, we submitted to the House Committee on Appropriations an estimate supplied by the chief of police and by the chief of the fire department as to what this transportation would cost a year, the chief of police estimating that it would cost $5,000 for his department and the chief of the fire department estimating that it would cost $650 per year for his department. That was submitted, and the contingent appropriation here should be increased by those two amounts and this language read into the contingent appropriation item, in order to overcome the objections raised by the opinion of the Comptroller of the Treasury. I wish to renew very earnestly to your committee the estimate and recommendation that we have made in that particular.

I may say that the ruling of the Public Utilities Commission and the opinion of the comptroller have meant to the policemen and firemen, who are sent all about the city on official business, that they now have to pay their own street car fare, and in doing so it puts a monthly burden upon them that ranges from three or four dollars up even as high as $12 per month, and they are not able to afford it. The same is true with regard to the firemen. Of course there are not so many firemen sent about the city on official business, but they are required to go to different parts of the city where crowds are gathered in buildings. They are required to be there on duty. They are very frequently called to their fire houses from their homes on official business. We feel very strongly that if Congress will give this appropriation it will be doing a simple act of justice to these men.

Senator SMITH of Maryland. Then, as I understand, you are asking for transportation for them only when they are on duty?

Commissioner SIDDONS. When they are on official duty; yes, sir.

Senator SMITH of Maryland. I am not expressing an opinion either for or against it. Does this include transportation to and from their homes?

Commissioner SIDDONS. Of course, we have not had to pass upon that question; but, speaking for myself, I should say that it should not include transportation when a policeman is leaving his home in the morning to go to his precinct station house to begin his duty, nor when he leaves it at the close of his day's work.

Senator SMITH of Maryland. Was this estimate made upon the basis of excluding that?

Commissioner SIDDONS. Oh, yes. That was our notion. We do not ask for them any different consideration or any special favors. If they were to be given transportation in going between their homes and their places of official business, every other employee of the District ought to have it, too, in my judgment. We do not ask it for that purpose; but these officers are constantly sent, every day—policemen, of course, in much greater numbers than firemen, but firemen also—to different parts of the District of Columbia, and it has become an exceedingly heavy burden. The chief of police reports to. me that it is being reflected in a somewhat impaired efficiency. The question of time is involved. They have to walk now where they rode before, because they can not afford to and will not expend their own car fare in riding on the street cars. He tells me he is beginning to see the unfortunate effect of all that in the somewhat impaired efficiency of the force.

I wish to add in that connection, Senator, that the commissioners do not favor permitting policemen and firemen to ride free and receive from the transportation companies a favor of that sort. We want to pay the street car companies for that transportation when it is afforded for official business. If we were asked officially our opinion on the subject, we should be opposed to permitting a restoration of the old system of free transportation; but we do wish to provide these men in this manner with transportation when they are sent about the District.

Senator GALLINGER. Mr. Commissioner, is not your proposal broader than you suggest? The language is:

That the Commissioners of the District of Columbia are hereby authorized, in their discretion, to furnish necessary transportation in connection with official business of the government of the District of Columbia by the purchase of car tickets, etc.

Would not that give you authority to purchase tickets for all your employees?

Commissioner SIDDONS. The language as used would do so, Senator.

Senator GALLINGER. Would it not be better for us to deal frankly and make an appropriation for the police and fire departments?

Commissioner SIDDONS. I should have no objection to it, except that I think car tickets have been supplied in the past, for instance, to food inspectors, inspectors of the health department, and possibly to other inspectors. I am not sure about that. The engineer commissioner might be able to tell. Have not the building inspectors been supplied with them?

Col. HARDING. Yes, sir; that is true in certain departments of the engineering branch. The buildings inspector's office and the plumbing inspector's office of the District have been for years purchasing car tickets and supplying them to their employees for their travel about the city on official duty, and those accounts have passed the Treasury Department without question. I understand, however, that the particular difficulty about the police department and the fire department is that, in the opinion of the comptroller, the wording of the law appropriating their contingent fund is such as would make any portion of the fund available for the purchase of car tickets for their transportation.

Senator SMITH of Maryland. If you were to make this provision specifically for the policemen and firemen would not the same usage prevail that now prevails, so that you would have the same right as at present to give tickets to people to whom you are now giving them for official purposes?

Col. HARDING. It would be a question, Senator, whether the comptroller would rule that this special legislation with reference to those departments might not preclude furnishing tickets to other departments.

Senator SMITH of Maryland. Whether it might not preclude what you are doing now?

Col. HARDING. Yes, sir.

Commissioner NEWMAN. The expenditure we are making now for the men in these other departments is from the contingent funds of those departments. If I remember correctly, and I think I do, there is no specific authorization in those contingent paragraphs for the purchase of street car tickets; but the comptroller has passed the accounts, because in interpreting the law he has thought there was a general authorization under its general terms, "necessary expenses," or something of that kind, and that it was permissible to do so. I think the reason this language was made broad was because if transportation is now specifically provided for firemen and policemen the comptroller might say: "Congress did not specifically provide it for these other departments, but has specifically provided it for the police and fire departments, and therefore it evidently did not intend to give it to the other departments."

Senator SMITH of Maryland. Senator Gallinger, has this matter ever been up before the committee before?

Senator GALLINGER. No. The street car companies formerly transported the members of the police and fire departments free of charge.

Senator SMITH of Maryland. It does seem like a good deal of a hardship on these people to have to pay for their own transportation when they are attending to their official business, when possibly it is really to the advantage of the District that they shall go more quickly than they might go on foot.

Commissioner NEWMAN. It is a very serious situation, Senator.

Commissioner SIDDONS. It is, indeed.

Senator SMITH of Maryland. I am of the impression that, as a rule, the policemen in most cities have free transportation. That is my impression now.

Commissioner NEWMAN. We felt, after a very careful investigation and study of the public utilities law, that it does not permit them to ride free.

Senator SMITH of Maryland. Of course, if you granted them transportation to and from their homes, that would be far-reaching.

Commissioner NEWMAN. We would not favor that at all.

Senator GALLINGER. Just one or two questions: I understood the commissioner to say that the necessary appropriation for tickets for the police would be about $5,000. Am I right?

Commissioner SIDDONS. That is the estimate, Senator.

Senator GALLINGER. And how much for the firemen?

Commissioner SIDDONS. $650. That is the estimate of the chief of the fire department.

Senator GALLINGER. What is the amount needed for the employees of the other departments to whom you have been giving tickets?

Col. HARDING. They are covered, Senator, in the current appropriations. They are provided for. There is no question about the availability of those appropriations.

Senator GALLINGER. But if the comptroller should make a technical ruling, which he is liable to do, could you suggest to the committee approximately how much additional that would be?

Col. HARDING. For the engineer department, about $1,000.

Commissioner SIDDONS. I would not venture to tell you what it would amount to for the health department, Senator. I would not undertake to say.

Senator LEA. Could you furnish us with that information?

Commissioner SIDDONS. I think we could procure an estimate based upon the actual expenditure on that account in past years.

Senator LEA. I would suggest that that estimate be furnished and included in the hearings.

Senator SMITH of Maryland. It can be furnished; yes.

Senator GALLINGER. I will raise this question simply for information: The provision here is that these tickets shall be used only for official business. Will you have any check at all on that?

Commissioner NEWMAN. Oh; yes, sir.

Senator GALLINGER. In what way? For instance, heretofore, when they had free transportation, policemen have been in the habit of getting on a car and riding a couple of blocks. I have noticed it over and over and over again. I presume it was all well enough as long as they had free transportation. Now, what check would you have on their using these tickets as between official and nonofficial business?

Commissioner NEWMAN. We would have the check of our subordinate, who is the immediate superior of the policeman, who knows where the policeman is, where he goes, and why he goes.

Senator GALLINGER. Yes; if they would only keep a record of those trips.

Col. HARDING. In the building and plumbing departments the tickets are issued by the head of the office to the employee when he is about to start out on the particular journey, and at the end of the month a return is made by the head of the department of the state of his ticket account.

Senator GALLINGER. That would be an absolute check, if it should be done in that way.

Commissioner SIDDONS. That is in contemplation, I know, with respect to the police and fire departments. For instance, to-day the detective sergeants and detective officers attached to headquarters are permitted, under a ruling of the comptroller, to receive street-car tickets. They are distributed to them as they go out on official business.

Senator GALLINGER. I understand that.

Commissioner NEWMAN. Of course the man at the head of the bureau knows. He sends them out, and when he sends them he gives them the tickets.

Senator SMITH of Maryland. It would appear from the language of the estimate you have given here that this amount of money will be sufficient to purchase tickets for all necessary transportation in connection with official business of the government of the District of Columbia.

Commissioner SIDDONS. The $5,000 and the $650?

Senator SMITH of Maryland. Yes.

Commissioner SIDDONS. No, Senator; I did not mean to give you that impression.

Senator SMITH of Maryland. Would it not be construed in that way?

Commissioner SIDDONS. Let me explain that we propose that there shall be added to the total contingent appropriation two sums, $5,000 and $650, the estimates of the transportation required by these two departments.

Senator SMITH of Maryland. Yes; I understand that you say that is for the police and fire departments. At the same time, the way it reads here it apparently covers all of the transportation.

Commissioner NEWMAN. The rest of it is already carried in the bill, Senator.

Senator LEA. The remainder for the other departments, as I understand, is already carried in the contingent fund.

Commissioner NEWMAN. In the contingent fund of the particular department.

Senator SMITH of Maryland. At the same time you do not think it would be well to state that it is for the policemen and the firemen?

Commissioner SIDDONS. Personally I should not have any objection, provided only it would not be construed as being confined to them, and thus prohibit the issuance of transportation to any of the others.

Senator SMITH of Maryland. I understand that it is confined to them.

Senator MARTIN. If the others are provided for in some other place, it ought to be confined to them.

Commissioner SIDDONS. I think it ought, Senator.

Senator SMITH of Maryland. This is strictly for those two departments?

Senator GALLINGER. I think the commissioner was fearful that there might be an adverse ruling by the comptroller as to the tickets furnished to the other officials, in which event they would want to fall back on this provision.

Commissioner SIDDONS. That was the object.

Senator SMITH of Maryland. I think it would be well for you to submit an estimate stating what this is for, so that it may be known by reference to the estimate what this sum is being asked for; for instance, $5,000 for the police department and $650 for the fire department. Then the committee will have your statement, as a matter of reference, as to what it is being asked for.

Commissioner NEWMAN. You would like an estimate from us of the cost per year of furnishing these tickets to all of the departments?

Senator SMITH of Maryland. That is right.

Commissioner NEWMAN. That we will supply you.

Senator SMITH of Maryland. So that we will know just what we are dealing with.

Senator GALLINGER. I think that is very desirable.

(The estimate referred to was subsequently furnished by the commissioners, and is as follows:)

EXECUTIVE OFFICE,
COMMISSIONERS OF THE DISTRICT OF COLUMBIA,
Washington, January 24, 1914.

Hon. JOHN WALTER SMITH.
*Chairman of the Subcommittee on Appropriations for the
District of Columbia, United States Senate.*

SIR: The Commissioners of the District of Columbia have the honor to invite your attention to the necessity of specifically providing for the use of car tickets within the District of Columbia for official purposes, and to suggest that there be inserted in the bill, H. R. 10523, now pending before your committee, on page 13, after line 21, the following language:

"That the Commissioners of the District of Columbia are hereby authorized, in their discretion, to furnish necessary transportation in connection with official business of the government of the District of Columbia by the purchase of car tickets from appropriations contained in this act."

There are so many appropriations affected that it is deemed desirable that the legislation should be in general terms rather than to attempt the insertion of authority in each of the appropriations affected throughout the bill.

In this connection the commissioners have the honor to transmit herewith a statement prepared by the auditor, District of Columbia, showing the use of car tickets during the fiscal year ended June 30, 1913.

The foregoing suggested amendment will not increase the expenditures under appropriations, but will make specific provision for the use of this character of transportation within the District of Columbia when authorized by the commissioners and will enable the commissioners to continue to furnish this character of transportation within the District of Columbia, which is absolutely necessary in the transaction of the municipal business and the authority for which it has been the custom for many years to grant.

In a decision dated July 29, 1913, on the question of the use of car tickets the Comptroller of the Treasury of the United States said:

" In the act of March 4, 1913 (37 Stat., 758, 776, and 782), specific provisions have been made for purchase of car tickets for the Treasury Department, Departments of the Interior and Justice, thus showing that when Congress intends car tickets to be furnished for local travel it makes specific provision therefor."

The Public Utilities Commission having decided that the street railway companies in the District of Columbia are not authorized to furnsh free transportaton to policemen and firemen, and the Comptroller of the Treasury having decided that the appropriations for contingent expenses of the police department and for contingent expenses of the fire department are not available for the purchase of car tickets without express authorization, and as the appropriations for the contingent expenses of the police department and of the fire department are not adequate for the additional expenditures required for this purpose even though the appropriations contained the specific authorization, the commissioners suggest the insertion of two items, that for the police department to be inserted on page 48, between lines 19 and 20, in the following language and amount: " For the purchase of car tickets for official use, $5.000 "; and, under the head of fire department, on page 51, between lines 6 and 7, the following item: " For the purchase of car tickets for official use, $650."

With these amendments it is believed that the matter of car tickets for the District of Columbia will be satisfactorily adjusted.

Very respectfully,

O. P. NEWMAN,
*President of the Board of Commissioners
of the District of Columbia.*

Statement of expenditures for car tickets from District of Columbia appropriations, fiscal year ended June 30, 1913.

Commissioner Johnston	$15.00
Commissioners Judson and Harding	20.00
Secretary's office	40.00
Auditor's office	30.00
Assessor's office	215.00
Collector's office	20.00
Corporation counsel's office	25.00
Record division, engineer department	5.00
Building-inspection division	245.00
Plumbing-inspection division	70.00
Superintendent of weights, measures, and markets' office	5.00
Surveyor's office	20.00
Insurance department	40.00
Sewer division	30.00
Street-cleaning division	40.00
Board of Charities	200.00
Purchasing officer's office	10.00
Child-labor inspectors	120.00

Municipal court	$5.00
Juvenile court	170.00
Probation system	150.00
Collections by distraint	75.00
Public Utilities Commission	29.50
Electrical department	100.00
Gas and laboratory inspection	90.00
To maintain public order during inaugural ceremonies	107.50
Metropolitan police	20.00
Fire department	1.00
Health department, inspectors	890.00
Sewer division, from operating-account fund	5.00
Surface division, engineer department	205.00
Industrial Home School	20.00
Industrial Home School, colored	40.00
Board of Children's Guardians	325.00
Workhouse	100.00
Tuberculosis Hospital	15.00
Municipal lodging house	5.00
Home for the aged and infirm	40.00
Temporary home for ex-Union soldiers and sailors	10.00
Public schools	360.00
Free public libraries	100.00
Parking commission	5.00
Fish wharf and market	5.00
Water department	375.00
Total	4,398.00

A. TWEEDALE,
Auditor, District of Columbia.

WASHINGTON, D. C., *November 25, 1913.*

Senator LEA. The former Public Utilities Commission, as I understand, stopped the granting of free transportaiton to firemen and policemen?

Commissioner NEWMAN. Yes, sir.

Senator LEA. Was that a voluntary ruling of the commission?

Commissioner NEWMAN. Yes, sir.

Senator LEA. On account of the provisions of the act creating the Utilities Commission?

Commissioner NEWMAN. We thought the public utilities law prohibited that character of transportation.

Senator GALLINGER. Did you not get a ruling from the comptroller to that effect, too?

Commissioner NEWMAN. Not on that point.

Col. HARDING. The comptroller would not pass on a question of that kind.

Senator LEA. In a great many cities the charters of the street railway companies, as part of their franchise tax, provide that certain employees, especially firemen and policemen, shall be carried free.

Commissioner NEWMAN. Yes, sir. That is not the case here.

Senator LEA. I do not see anything harmful in that practice, because it is a tax that they are paying to the city—not a gratuity that they are granting to some employee.

Commissioner NEWMAN. That is all right.

Senator SMITH of Maryland. At the same time, that is not the case here, and it would be asking a favor of these compaines, and the commissioners feel that they do not want to be under obligations to them. I can see that.

I wish you would have a separate paragraph drawn up indicating the different amounts for the different departments, please.

Commissioner NEWMAN. We shall do so.

Replying just a moment to Senator Lea, as far as the policemen and firemen alone are concerned, it is a little objectionable to me personally that an officer or agent of the District government, particularly one whose duty it is to enforce the law—many of the regulations of the public utilities commission which affect the street railway companies are enforced by the policemen—should be accepting a gratuity from these companies. In the mind of the policeman or fireman I think it would be a gratuity. It would not be much of an item, broadly speaking; but the thing that has particularly influenced me in the matter is not only the policemen and firemen, but the other employees of the District. It seems to me there is no more reason why policemen or firemen should be carried free by the street car companies than health inspectors and building inspectors and elevator inspectors and other employees of the District should be carried free. It would be a discrimination against all the other employees of the District.

Senator LEA. In a good many cities the franchise granted by the municipality has a proviso that the firemen and policemen, when in uniform, shall be carried without any cost to the city or to them.

Col. HARDING. There is no such provision in the charters of the local companies; and the idea of the utilities commission was merely to make a strict interpretation of the law, which in terms forbade furnishing free transportation to any person.

BATHING BEACH.

Senator SMITH of Maryland. What is the next item?

Commissioner NEWMAN. On page 27, Mr. Chairman, there is an item with regard to the bathing beach. A total of $4,830 is asked for the maintenance of the existing bathing beach, down below the Monument. That item was stricken out on the floor of the House on a point of order. We should like to have it restored. We wish to recommend it.

Senator SMITH of Maryland. The total is $4,830 for the bathing beach?

Commissioner NEWMAN. Yes, sir; that is for the maintenance of the existing bathing beach.

Senator GALLINGER. The House did the same thing last year and the Senate restored it, and we won out in conference on it.

Commissioner NEWMAN. We should like to recommend it.

Senator GALLINGER. Has there not been some very severe criticism from some source as to the pollution of the water at the bathing beach?

Commissioner NEWMAN. I can not exactly call it a criticism, Senator. It was an initial action of our own. We discovered from our own inquiry last summer that at one time the water was in bad condition; but we remedied that to a very great extent by having a more rapid inflow and outflow, and I think there is now no justification for the abandonment of those grounds.

Senator GALLINGER. The bathing beach was very largely patronized. I chance to know that myself, because I visited it two or three times with a view to ascertaining whether or not people were going there, and they were going there in very large numbers. It seemed to me, in view of the small appropriation, that it was a desirable thing.

Senator SMITH of Maryland. This has been in before?

Senator GALLINGER. For several years; yes.

Senator SMITH of Maryland. It was eliminated on a point of order?

Commissioner NEWMAN. Yes, sir.

PERMANENT IMPROVEMENTS.

Commissioner SIDDONS. May I call your attention to a correction that should be made on page 51? It is very slight, but in the interest of accuracy it should be made. It is on page 51, under the head of "Permanent improvements." The word "Tenley" should be "Tenleytown."

Senator SMITH of Maryland. On what line?

Commissioner NEWMAN. Line 13.

Senator GALLINGER. Yes; it should be "Tenleytown," of course.

Commissioner SIDDONS. It is a small matter, but of course the correction should be made.

Senator SMITH of Maryland. All right.

PROPOSED PROPERTY DIVISION.

Col. HARDING. On page 18, on the margin, under the heading of "Contingent and miscellaneous expenses," as estimated, new, and omitted, the commissioners asked in their estimate for an appropriation and an authorization to create what would really be a property division of the District office, for the purpose of taking care systematically of District property and fixing the responsibility for lost property; also for the purchase of a stock of general supplies from which issues would be made, and for the construction of a central warehouse. The estimate was not allowed by the subcommittee of the House; but on page 83 of the bill the following provision was inserted by the committee:

That all persons in the employment of the government of the District of Columbia having, as a result of such employment, custody of or chargeable with property, other than real estate, belonging to the District of Columbia shall, at such times and in such form as the Commissioners of the District shall require, make returns to said commissioners of all such property remaining in their possession, and the condition thereof, etc.

My suggestion is that it is impracticable to carry out the provisions of section 7, page 83, unless some provision is made in the appropriation for creating a force to take care of the matter. If the Senate does not restore the provision we ask for on page 18, I think the legislation proposed on page 83 should be omitted and the matter left in its present status.

The question was very fully argued before the subcommittee of the House Appropriations Committee, and I would refer you to the hearings there for the reasons that were urged for the establishment of this central warehouse and this new force. I have nothing to add to what is stated there, but I should like to suggest that if the item is omitted the legislation proposed should be omitted also, as being impossible to carry out with our present force.

Senator SMITH of Maryland. We will take that under consideration.

DESIGNATION OF OFFICIAL VEHICLES.

Senator GALLINGER. Let me ask the commissioners about this heading "City service," and how it found its way on page 15? This is all city service. I suppose you have no objection to that going out?

Commissioner SIDDONS. That is another thing I had intended mentioning. I am very glad the Senator called attention to it. I think the words "City service" ought to be changed to "District service."

Senator GALLINGER. There is no objection to striking it out or changing it, is there?

Senator SMITH of Maryland. It is not city service; it is District service.

Commissioner SIDDONS. Yes; it is District service. There is not any such thing as city service.

Senator GALLINGER. It is all District service.

Senator SMITH of Maryland. Of course, that includes Georgetown and the District of Columbia?

Senator GALLINGER. Yes.

Commissioner NEWMAN. I think the purpose of it was to put a sign that everybody would see upon District vehicles which would prevent their use for anything except official purposes.

Senator GALLINGER. It is with reference to that, then, is it?

Commissioner NEWMAN. In view of the fact that we do not want to use the vehicles for any but official purposes, we have no objection to that sign being on them.

Commissioner SIDDONS. My suggestion was that if the Senate should conclude that such a sign should go on these vehicles, it certainly ought to be correct. It should be " District service " and not " City service."

Senator LEA. It is not on any other Government vehicles, is it? It is not on those used by the heads of departments?

Commissioner SIDDONS. No; it is not on those used by the heads of departments. On all vehicles belonging to the District of Columbia the words "District of Columbia " are painted, except upon the vehicles used by the commissioners.

Senator GALLINGER. This subhead really follows the item of the designation of vehicles, and can not have reference to that. It seems to me entirely unnecessary and inconsequential.

Col. HARDING. If that question is going to be taken up at all, I would suggest, as a practical matter, that the height of these letters is unnecessarily great. Six inches is pretty high. It perhaps would be impossible to comply with this requirement in the case of some of our vehicles.

Commissioner SIDDONS. Senator, may I say that I do not understand that these words " city service " are intended as a topical heading? They follow the colon just above. The provision is that these vehicles shall have these words painted upon them in letters 6 inches high.

Commissioner Newman. That was not one of the commissioners' messengers. That increase was on the broad general ground that a human being can not live on $480 a year. We recommended that in several instances.

Col. Harding. One of the messengers to whom Mr. Newman has just referred is mentioned on page 9, line 2, ".Messengers, one, $600." Our estimate there was $720. The individual covered by that item is my messenger, and he is one of the men to whom Mr. Newman referred.

Commissioner Newman. Of the three to whom I referred, two are found on line 10, page 2—Mr. Siddons's messenger and my own.

SECRETARIES TO COMMISSIONERS.

Col. Harding. On page 8 of the bill there is one increase which was recommended by the commissioners and not granted by the House, which I should like especially to urge before this committee. That is my secretary, covered under the item of " Clerks," on line 24, page 8, " three, at $1,500 each." My secretary is one of those three. I will ask the committee to change that item so as to read " One at $1,600 and two at $1,500."

The reason why this increase is urged is because, under the current law, the secretary to the president of the Board of Commissioners receives $1,600 a year, and the commissioners decided that there was not any difference in the amount of work or in the amount of responsibility in the two cases to justify that difference in pay. I should simply like to call the attention of the committee to our original estimate of $1,600.

Senator Gallinger. This increase would make it uniform, then, and would appropriate the same amount for the secretaries to the three commissioners?

Commissioner Siddons. It would.

Col. Harding. It would, with the explanation which Mr. Siddons will make.

Commissioner Siddons. I should like to call the attention of the members of the Senate committee to the appropriation on page 2 for my secretary. His salary is now $1,500. The commissioners estimated, as Col. Harding has just stated, $1,600.

Senator Smith of Maryland. He gets $1,500 now, and you are asking for $1,600?

Commissioner Siddons. Yes.

Senator Gallinger. Those are assistant secretaries, are they not?

Commissioner Newman. They are carried in that way.

Senator Smith of Maryland. Do I understand you to say, Col. Harding, that there are others serving in the same capacity that get $1,600?

Col. Harding. One, the secretary to the president of the board of commissioners, gets $1,600. What we are now asking is that the secretaries for the other two commissioners shall be paid a similar sum.

Commissioner Newman. Their duties are practically the same; there is no difference.

Senator Smith of Maryland. There is no difference in the work?

Commissioner Newman. No, sir; it is just an even rate all around.

MESSENGERS TO COMMISSIONERS.

Senator GALLINGER. Going back to the suggestion about increasing the salaries of your messengers, in the consideration of this bill in prior years we have found that if we made an increase in the compensation of one official, however small it might be, there was immediately a clamor that they should all be increased to the same amount. Would there not be some danger in making the salary of a messenger $720? Personally, I do not think it is too much; but would there not be some danger that the messengers running all through the bill, hundreds in number, would feel that they ought to have the same salary?

Commissioner NEWMAN. The justification for it, in our minds, Senator, is that there is that much difference in their duties and hours of labor.

Col. HARDING. The commissioners had the same problem to solve, naturally, in making the estimates. They decided that the difference in the hours and really in the amount of work in the case of the messengers to the commissioners justified that difference between their pay and the pay of the messengers generally throughout the building.

Senator GALLINGER. Do they have to report at an earlier hour, Colonel?

Col. HARDING. They possibly report at the same hour, but they stay there longer. They stay there until we go, which is sometimes 6 o'clock at night.

Senator SMITH of Maryland. Do you work them over eight hours?

Col. HARDING. Yes, sir; they work over eight hours.

Commissioner NEWMAN. Almost every day.

Senator SMITH of Maryland. I presume thy are not actively at work all the time, though; they just have to wait and stay there. That is the difficulty, Senator Gallinger, that there are so many who get the same pay that they would have some pretext to have this increase apply to them. It is a question of where they are located; but you will find all through here that the messengers get $600.

Commissioner SIDDON. There are a number in the bill who are only getting $480.

Senator SMITH of Maryland. Yes; that is true.

Senator GALLINGER. We have had the same trouble heretofore with janitors of school buildings. Some schools undoubtedly require of the janitor greater service and longer service than others. They have more rooms to look after. We knew, however, that if we increased one they would all pounce on it and insist that we ought to make it uniform. We had that trouble. However, Mr. Chairman, I think the argument the commissioners make in this particular respect is worthy of very serious consideration.

Senator SMITH of Maryland. We will take it under consideration.

GENERAL RECOMMENDATIONS.

Commissioner NEWMAN. There is one general recommendation we would like to make. All the way through the bill there are some items which were in the bill as reported to the House and which have been thrown out on a point of order. In some cases increases of salaries were disallowed on a point of order.

Senator SMITH of Maryland. Not because they were objected to?

Commissioner NEWMAN. Not because they were considered on their merits.

Senator SMITH of Maryland. Of course, they were objected to by somebody.

Commissioner NEWMAN. Yes, sir; but we should like to recommend the restoration of all of those things which went out of the bill on points of order and were not considered on their merits.

Senator GALLINGER. They were approved by the committee?

Commissioner NEWMAN. That is the point; yes, sir. They were approved by the committee after very complete inquiry and consideration. They are all indicated in the bill now before you, and we should like to make a blanket recommendation that they be restored.

PUBLIC LIBRARIAN.

Commissioner NEWMAN. Following my statement that we wanted to make a sort of blanket recommendation for the items which have been approved by the House committee but changed on the floor of the House on points of order, there is one item of which I happen to have personal knowledge to which I should like to call the attention of the committee. That is the salary of the public librarian.

Senator SMITH of Maryland. On what page is that found?

Commissioner NEWMAN. Page 11, line 9. His salary at present is $3,500. He is an exceedingly efficient officer, and under the handicap of inadequate facilities and inadequate force and organization he is doing very excellent work. We recommended in our estimates that his salary be made $4,500, an increase of $1,000. The committee reported $4,000, but the additional $500 was stricken out in the House. I should like particularly to urge that the $500 be restored.

Senator SMITH of Maryland. Then, as I understand, the House committee wanted to put it at $4,000?

Commissioner NEWMAN. $4,000.

Senator SMITH of Maryland. But it was stricken out on a point of order when it went in, and you would like to have the $4,000 maintained? Is that it?

Commissioner NEWMAN. Yes, sir. That is merely one of the general items that I described, but it is one which I think is particularly meritorious.

MAINTENANCE OF HORSES AND VEHICLES.

Col. HARDING. There is an item, on page 26, line 19, to which I should like to direct attention. It is a provision for an allowance to inspectors and foremen for maintenance of horses and vehicles used in the performance of official duties, of not to exceed $20 per month. The current appropriation act, the one under which we are now operating, provides a limit of $30 per month instead of $20 per month for that maintenance. Our estimate was $30, just as heretofore appropriated. The matter did not come up in detail at all in the hearings before the House committee, and I do not know why the reduction was made—whether it was inadvertently done or intentionally done.

Senator SMITH of Maryland. They are now getting $30?

Col. Harding. They are now getting $30.

Senator Smith of Maryland. And it has been reduced, according to this bill, to $20?

Col. Harding. Yes, sir; and a pretty strong representation is made that $20 is not adequate for the purpose.

Senator Smith of Maryland. We will take that up. What is the next item?

RECOMMENDATIONS FROM PERSONS OTHER THAN COMMISSIONERS.

Commissioner Newman. I think those are the only particular items that we desire to call to the attention of the committee.

We should like to suggest to the committee that in case you receive suggestions and recommendations from sources other than the District Commissioners for changes in the appropriations for new projects, and one thing and another, which we anticipate you are quite likely to receive, we should appreciate it very much if we could be given an opportunity to express our opinion of the matter before you act upon it.

Senator Smith of Maryland. We shall take pleasure in calling your attention to it. We have done that all along in matters of legislation, and we shall be very glad to get your views about anything that may come up.

Commissioner Siddons. In that connection I will say that in consultation with Col. Harding this morning, Mr. Newman not being in the building, I gave permission to two police patrol drivers, representing themselves and their fellows, to endeavor to interest the members of the committee in an increase in salary they were asking, and if the Senators cared to entertain it at all. They sought permission from us this morning to do that. I said that if the committee cared to hear from them they would have our consent to making their representation.

I say that in connection with what Mr. Newman has just said to you.

Senator Gallinger. Would they not better submit it in writing? I think they have heretofore done that.

Commissioner Siddons. That is in the hands of this honorable committee, of course.

Senator Smith of Maryland. I think that would be better.

Senator Lea. What heads of departments do the commissioners desire the committee to hear?

Commissioner Newman. I do not think we care to bring heads of departments before you now unless you care to hear from them in order to get a clear understanding of the various items. We shall be very glad to send up or bring up anyone you wish to interrogate.

Senator Lea. But you do not desire to present them, as far as you are concerned, as I understand?

Commissioner Newman. No; I think not, at this time, although we do not wish to close the door to that for good.

Senator Smith of Maryland. We shall go over these items one by one, as you know. We wanted to hear from you gentlemen first, so as to see what you had to say. Then we will go over them, and if there is any further information we want, of course we will let you know.

SUBSCRIPTIONS BY PUPILS.

Senator GALLINGER. There are one or two items that I will venture, with the permission of the chairman, to interrogate the commissioners about, if they choose to express their views One is the blue slip pasted on page 44 of the bill, reading as follows:

No part of any money appropriated by this act shall be paid to any person employed under or in connection with the public schools of the District of Columbia who shall solicit or receive or permit to be solicited or received on any public-school premises any subscription or donation of money or other thing of value from pupils enrolled in such public schools for presentation of testimonials or for any purposes other than for the promotion of school athletics, school gardens, and commencement exercises of high schools.

Commissioner NEWMAN. That was adopted on the floor of the House.

Senator GALLINGER. I see they have exempted subscriptions for the promotion of school athletics, school gardens, and commencement exercises of high schools.

Commissioner NEWMAN. Yes.

Senator GALLINGER. I did not observe that that was changed on the floor. I thought the original proposition was altogether too broad.

Commissioner SIDDONS. I might say that I have heard from a number of teachers who apparently are not even satisfied with the enlargement in the last line of the new legislation. It is felt, in some schools at least, that it is going to cripple some of their undertakings, but unless you or the committee wish to hear from the board of education on the subject I am not prepared to make any further comment about it. I am in sympathy with the prohibition against soliciting subscriptions for presentation of testimonials. I think, myself, it is a very excellent provision. There are some undertakings in the high schools, perhaps, other than those referring to school athletics and commencement exercises of high schools, that may be affected. I am not clear in my own mind that it is at all serious, and, unless the board of education wish to make some representations, I have nothing to add.

Senator GALLINGER. Then, we can interrogate the superintendent if he appears before the committee, as he probably will.

AVENUE OF THE PRESIDENTS.

Senator GALLINGER. I will ask one other question, with the permission of the chairman. Did the commissioners recommend that the name of Sixteenth Street should be restored, and the present designation of "Avenue of the Presidents" dispensed with?

Commissioner NEWMAN. No, sir.

Senator GALLINGER. That was not a recommendation of the commissioners?

Commissioner NEWMAN. No, sir. It was inserted, I think, on the floor of the House.

Commissioner SIDDONS. It was done in Committee of the Whole, as I remember.

Senator GALLINGER. That is all I care to know, whether or not it was on the recommendation of the commissioners.

STREET IMPROVEMENTS.

Commissioner NEWMAN. There is a very large item in the bill pertaining to street improvements, both city and suburban. We submitted our estimates as to those items, and the entire subcommittee of the House, all of its members, personally inspected practically all of the improvements we recommended. They made a very careful examination, and I think they came to a very good conclusion as a result of it. While they are not in entire conformity with our recommendations, we are satisfied to accept their decision. However, if this committee should desire to inquire further into those questions, we shall be very glad to do as we did with the House committee—get machines and take you over the city and have you see the various improvements for which the bill provides.

Senator GALLINGER. You think the House has dealt with reasonable generosity in reference to new streets?

Commissioner NEWMAN. I think it is a very good result; yes, sir.

Senator SMITH of Maryland. Are there any streets here that they have left out about which you have anything especially to say?

Commissioner NEWMAN. There are one or two that we would have liked to have had included, but we do not care to urge them.

Senator GALLINGER. The probabilities are that parties interested in the improvement of some of these streets will come to us and urge them. It would be agreeable to the commissioners if the subcommittee should inquire of the commissioners about the matter afterwards.

Commissioner NEWMAN. We should most earnestly ask, Senator, that you do inquire of us before acting upon requests of that character.

Senator SMITH of Maryland. What do you think about what is known as the "Borland amendment"? As I understand, it is provided by that amendment that the property holders shall bear all of the expense, not only of paving the sidewalk, but also of paving the street.

Commissioner NEWMAN. Yes, sir.

Senator SMITH of Maryland. You have read it, have you?

Commissioner NEWMAN. Yes, sir.

Senator GALLINGER. Is that in the bill?

Senator SMITH of Maryland. Yes; it has been adopted.

Senator GALLINGER. That is a pretty serious change.

Senator SMITH of Maryland. It seems to me a radical change.

Commissioner NEWMAN. I will say in reply to your question, Senator Smith, that the commissioners as a board have never given consideration to the Borland amendment, so that what I say is only my individual opinion and feeling. Purely as an abstract question, I believe most emphatically that adjacent benefited property should bear the cost of public improvements. I do not feel, however, that at this particular time that principle could be with exact justice adopted in the District of Columbia.

Senator SMITH of Maryland. The improvement of these streets is not for the benefit of the property holders alone, but the streets are used by the entire city.

Commissioner NEWMAN. I understand that.

Senator SMITH of Maryland. It seems to me it is unfair—I am speaking now individually only—to have a property holder bear the entire expense of improving the street while the city gets the benefit of it to a certain extent and pays nothing.

Senator GALLINGER. I know of no municipality where that is done.

Commissioner NEWMAN. It is the rule throughout the Middle West.

Senator LEA. Is it not the rule that they pay only a certain proportion?

Commissioner NEWMAN. I think it is the rule that they pay all of it, except the intersections.

Senator GALLINGER. Here the property owner pays one-half of the expense for sidewalks and the Government one-half, and the Government pays the entire cost of the street.

Commissioner NEWMAN. Yes, sir.

Senator GALLINGER. As I understand, this proposition is that the abutting property owner shall pay the entire cost of the sidewalk and to the middle of the street?

Commissioner NEWMAN. Yes, sir; with the exception of intersections.

Senator GALLINGER. That is a pretty serious matter.

Senator SMITH of Maryland. A very serious matter, and it is unjust, in my judgment. I think it is entirely unjust, because the city gets the benefit of it. The property owner may never go on the street himself. He may never use it. He may never put his foot on it.

Commissioner NEWMAN. Of course over a protracted period—if you carry the thing over a period sufficient to obtain street improvements for the whole municipality it makes no difference whether it is paid from a general fund or whether it is paid by the owner of abutting property.

Senator GALLINGER. It makes a difference to the property owner, though.

Senator SMITH of Maryland. Yes; it makes a difference to him.

Commissioner NEWMAN. Only for the time being. Of course it does make a difference here on account of the half-and-half arrangement.

Senator GALLINGER. Yes.

Commissioner NEWMAN. But as an abstract question, in an ordinary municipality the expense to the property holder would be approximately the same whether the entire community were paved with money from a general fund or whether each man paid for that in front of his own property.

The feeling I have about the situation here is that there has been a very large expenditure in the District—properly so, of course, because the streets ought to be well improved—for street improvements and that there are some sections of the city which have not had as much street improvement as other sections; and those sections, generally speaking, have been the ones in which people in poor circumstances live. I feel that it would be an injustice to them to apply this principle at this time. This very bill, in its list of streets to be improved, is drawn on the theory of making the improvement where the block is built up, or nearly built up, and where the improvement of private property has been accomplished, or nearly accomplished. I think in a great majority of cases of the items they are in the communities and along the streets on which the people of less means live. To put upon those people at this time the burden of paying for their entire street improvement, whereas for a great many years past the improvements in other sections, where the more well-to-do live, have been made from a general fund, I think would be unjust.

Senator SMITH of Maryland. Speaking of the poorer class of people, Mr. Commissioner, they would pay for this, although a great many of them have really no use of the streets at all. They have no vehicles, and they do not go over them.

Commissioner NEWMAN. They do not use them, except, of course, that a person who lives on a paved street——

Senator SMITH of Maryland. He has to get to his property. At the same time, these streets are used for other purposes by people from other parts of the city entirely.

Commissioner NEWMAN. Yes; but it is more desirable to live on a street that is improved than on one that is unimproved.

Senator SMITH of Maryland. Undoubtedly. They ought to pay a portion of it.

Commissioner NEWMAN. The feeling I have is that in justice to everyone we ought to go along for two or three years more on the present arrangement until we finish paving the streets upon which private improvement is practically completed, and get a more nearly uniform system.

Senator SMITH of Maryland. Then, for the present, your opinion is that this is a little ahead of time?

Commissioner NEWMAN. Yes, sir. That, you understand, is my individual opinion, because the commissioners as a board have never considered this matter.

Senator SMITH of Maryland. So far as I am concerned, that is my individual opinion.

Senator GALLINGER. If we ever should reach the point where we will ask the adjacent property owner to pay for the entire sidewalk, I hope we will give very serious consideration to the question whether under any circumstances he should be required to pay for the street. The street is a public highway. Everybody uses it; and it seems to me the property owner ought not to be compelled to pay for the paving of half the street in front of his premises.

SURPLUS REVENUES OF DISTRICT OF COLUMBIA.

Senator GALLINGER. Another item which I have observed in the bill, and which has been discussed more or less in the newspapers, is the requirement in the bill as it now stands that the surplus revenues of the District of Columbia shall be covered back into the Treasury of the United States and credited to a certain fund. You have given consideration to that item, have you?

Commissioner NEWMAN. We have given individual thought to it, I think, to a very great extent. We have not as a board, and I think not as individuals, arrived at a conclusion as to whether or not that is equitable, and whether it should or should not obtain. I have not done so personally.

Senator SMITH of Maryland. That is an interference with the half-and-half principle, is it not?

Commissioner NEWMAN. Yes, sir.

Commission SIDDONS. Assuming that it is a blow, if you please, at the so-called half-and-half principle—and that is the way I read the amendment—I am not prepared to say, expressing merely my individual opinion, whether the present financial relation known as the half-and-half principle is unsound or unfair or not. I have had a great deal of difficulty for a number of years past, in thinking about it, in formulating in my own mind what ought to be the true basis of this financial relation, this joint contribution. I have assumed that the action of Congress, continued for many years, had its origin and inception in what at that time, at least, was an equitable arrangement, so regarded and so considered. Whether or not it was an equitable arrangement which should continue for all time is a matter about which I am not at the present moment able to express an opinion satisfactory to myself. Therefore, it could not under any circumstances be satisfactory to you. I want more time.

The elements and factors that fairly belong to a consideration of that subject are quite numerous. They are vital. They begin, as I think, with the constitutional supremacy of the Federal Congress over the National Capital. From that we pass to the question of the land that has been withdrawn from taxation from time to time by the Federal Government for use for Federal purposes, which has grown to a very considerable amount. That, too, becomes, as it seems to me, fairly an element in it. Questions of the extent to which the Federal Government as such benefits by the various activities of the municipal government I think play a part in it.

I can well consider that the Federal Government enjoys the advantage of our police department; it enjoys the advantage of our fire department; it may enjoy the advantages of other municipal activities. There are some others from which, perhaps, it is not so clear that the Federal Government as such gets any benefit. The people at large do not.

So I am not willing and, indeed, not able to express an opinion on the subject at present.

Senator GALLINGER. The converse of that would lead us to the conclusion that the municipality derives great advantage from the Federal activities.

Commission SIDDONS. That is undoubtedly true.

Commission NEWMAN. Yes; that it undoubtedly true.

Commissioner SIDDONS. The fact that this is the National Capital, that here the Federal Government monthly and annually appropriates a very large amount of money to its employees stationed here, must be of very great advantage to the people of the District and of the community as organized society.

Senator SMITH of Maryland. At the same time, as the matter now stands, on the basis of the money that is being appropriated for the use of the District, a larger amount of revenue is being collected than is necessary for the payment by the District of its one-half. That is, the amount of revenue more than equals one-half of the amount necessary to be distributed; and that will have to be taken care of somehow.

Commissioner NEWMAN. That, of course, raises another question.

Senator SMITH of Maryland. The question of reduced taxation or something of that sort?

Commissioner NEWMAN. No; it raises a question of opinion as to the money necessary for the local government. I think we could in a very proper, advantageous, and economical manner expend all of this revenue.

Senator SMITH of Maryland. There is a question in the minds of some people whether, where they raise so much money, it does not lead to extravagance.

Commissioner NEWMAN. Yes, sir; and I think unquestionably it has a tendency to do that very thing. However, at this particular time we feel convinced that all of the money raised by local taxation, plus an equal amount from the Federal Government, could be economically and advantageously expended.

Senator GALLINGER. I was about to make that very observation—that if I had my way there would not be any of this money turned back into the Treasury. I should expend it and let the Government put up an equal amount for the present, at least. I believe it could be advantageously expended.

Commissioner SIDDONS. May I venture a suggestion? According to the newspapers and debates in Congress and a recent opinion by the comptroller, it may be—I do not know, but it may be—that the District of Columbia is indebted in some amount to the Federal Government. If that is so, then if there is any surplus, at least we should be permitted to extinguish or liquidate any liability we are under to the Federal Government. My official information is that by the close of the present fiscal year the District of Columbia will have completely liquidated its floating and unfunded indebtedness, and will have reduced its outstanding bonded indebtedness to an amount slightly over $7,000,000. Each year sees the annual appropriation of $950,000 which is used for the payment, first, of the interest on the outstanding bonds, and the balance to their retirement as the Treasurer of the United States sees an opportunity to retire them by their purchase in the open market at prices which would justify the investment for the purpose of cancellation and retirement.

Therefore I think we here in the District, and Congress to the extent of its interest in the District, may all congratulate ourselves that the District of Columbia is in a very remarkably sound financial condition when contrasted with any municipality of like size anywhere else in this country. We are in a singularly fortunate position.

Now, however, there comes a claim that we still owe the Federal Government money growing out of old issues of bonds. You are probably all familiar with the recent opinion by the comptroller on the subject.

Senator SMITH of Maryland. I think he has decided that it is due; has he not?

Commissioner SIDDONS. He has decided that it is due. If it is due, and Congress thinks now is the time to pay, I venture to suggest that resort should be had to the surplus to the extent of liquidating that indebtedness.

Senator SMITH of Maryland. We could pay it out of the surplus to that extent, but the surplus more than equals that indebtedness.

Commissioner NEWMAN. Yes; I think the surplus would provide for that and still leave something over.

Senator SMITH of Maryland. Some hundreds of thousands of dollars more?

Commissioner SIDDONS. Yes; it would, sir.

Commissioner NEWMAN. The feeling I have had thus far, as a result not only of my experience and consideration of this matter as a commissioner, but of several years' prior consideration, is that, first, the people of the United States want Washington to be a great and beautiful Capital. I do not think there is any question about that. They want a city here on a great and magnificent scale.

Senator SMITH of Maryland. I think that is the general sentiment.

Commissioner NEWMAN. I think that can be accepted as a fact. I think it can be also accepted as a fact that it would be a financial impossibility and an economic injustice to expect the people of the District of Columbia to provide the money to do that. They can not do it.

Senator SMITH of Maryland. It should not be asked.

Commissioner NEWMAN. They could not do it. It would be a financial impossibility and economically unjust.

Senator SMITH of Maryland. The Government wants what any ordinary city would not require.

Commissioner NEWMAN. Yes, sir.

Senator SMITH of Maryland. Therefore it is not fair to require the people of this city to put up money to make a capital such as the people of the United States want this Capital to be.

Commissioner NEWMAN. Yes, sir. It is not only not fair, sir, but they could not do it.

Senator SMITH of Maryland. Not only is it true that they could not do it, but it would be unfair to expect the people to do it when they are handicapped as they are here. There are many things in the way of industrial enterprises that might come to an ordinary city that, as a capital, we do not want here, that would increase the assessable basis of property, and from which the city could derive a revenue, but that we do not want. The people of this country are unwilling for this city to be a city of that kind. Therefore I think the Government ought to be willing to make up a deficiency of that character. The streets here, for instance, are very much wider than usual.

Commissioner NEWMAN. Yes, sir.

Senator SMITH of Maryland. A great many things go to make up sources of expense that ordinarily would not be considered in cities with other advantages and characteristics.

Commissioner NEWMAN. Yes, sir. It is a fact that this country wants that kind of a capital. It is a fact that the people of this community could not establish and maintain such a city. Therefore it also must be a fact that to some extent the Government must assist in establishing and maintaining such a city. The question which is immediately brought to an issue by the amendment referred to by Senator Gallinger is: What should the Government do in dollars and cents, or in a percentage? Specifically, what should the Government do and how should it do it? On that matter I am not ready to express an opinion at this time.

Senator GALLINGER. The late Senator Hoar, of Massachusetts, who was a very wise man, as we all know, once made a suggestion on the floor of the Senate that attracted a good deal of attention. It was that if the half-and-half principle ever should be abandoned, Congress should make appropriations for the District of Columbia precisely as it does for the War Department or the Navy Department; that the citizens of the District of Columbia should be taxed, the tax rate being fixed at a reasonable amount as compared to other cities, and that any deficit that was found to exist after the citizens had paid their taxes on an equitable basis should be appropriated by the Government. That thought is worthy of consideration if we are going to break down the half-and-half principle.

Senator SMITH of Maryland. I think the tax rate at present is about $1.50, is it not?

Commissioner NEWMAN. $1.50 per hundred on the basis of a two-thirds valuation.

Senator SMITH of Maryland. That is not a high tax rate for a city.

Commissioner NEWMAN. No.

Senator SMITH of Maryland. That is a low tax rate.

Senator GALLINGER. It is very low.

Senator SMITH of Maryland. There is no question about that. It is quite a low tax rate, and the people have no right to complain of a tax of that character.

There is one question that I should like to ask. I have asked it several times, and I have been unable to find anyone who knows positively about it. When people who own stocks and bonds come here to live and become citizens of the District of Columbia, are those stocks and bonds taxed?

Commissioner NEWMAN. They are exempt. All intangible personal property is exempt.

Senator SMITH of Maryland. It seems to me that is unfair. Is there any reason why a man should come here to live in order to get exemption from taxation? The property of a great many very rich people consists almost entirely of stocks and bonds. They have to pay a tax on them elsewhere.

Commissioner NEWMAN. Of course, there is a growing feeling in the country that it is difficult to exact accurately a tax of that character.

Senator SMITH of Maryland. I know that, but it is being done. They are being searched out and found and taxed. In my State they are taxed.

Commissioner NEWMAN. Personally, it is repugnant to my theory of taxation.

Senator SMITH of Maryland. That may be so. Nevertheless, we must treat all people alike. If they are taxed in other States and other cities there is no reason why, by virtue of their living in the city of Washington or in the District of Columbia, they should be exempt, because if so they are not paying their proportion of the expense of running the Government.

Commissioner SIDDONS. No; assuming the soundness of the personal-property tax law, certainly it is not fair that rich people coming here to escape taxation should be allowed to escape.

Senator SMITH of Maryland. No. There is a very great temptation for men of large means to come here to live if they can thereby free themselves from taxes.

Commissioner SIDDONS. It may be so, sir. Of course, that assumes the soundness of the personal-property tax. There is, too, the other consideration that in enacting a personal-property tax law all personal property ought to be taxed and not merely a portion of it. We have a personal-property tax law here, but it is a tax only on certain tangible goods.

Senator SMITH of Maryland. As I understand, it is only the tangible property that is taxed.

Commissioner NEWMAN. Practically it is only the visible property.

Senator SMITH of Maryland. Yes; that is correct.

Commissioner SIDDONS. If a personal-property tax law is sound at all—and I share with Mr. Newman the belief——

Senator SMITH of Maryland. I am not discussing the right or wrong of the theory. I am only taking the conditions as they exist in this country to-day, and asking whether, as long as they are taxed in other States, people with large holding of stocks and bonds should be allowed to come here to escape taxation?

Senator GALLINGER. When the personal-property tax law was enacted that matter was very warmly discussed in the committee, at least. I felt then, and feel now, that men holding stocks and bonds and coming here to make their homes ought to be taxed. As it is now a man who owns a little home, however modest it may be, has his real estate tax to pay and he has his personal-property tax, while the man who owns a $100,000 home or a $200,000 home and has most of his property in stocks and bonds escapes taxation except upon his house and furniture.

Commissioner SIDDONS. It may be that some people in coming here have had in mind the avoidance of taxation. On the other hand, I think it is likely that many of the wealthy people who come to Washington and build their mansions and live here three or four or five months of the year and live elsewhere during the rest of the year have their sources of revenue elsewhere, the corporations, the stocks and bonds of which they own, do business elsewhere, and in a great many cases you will find they are taxed on that property elsewhere than in the District of Columbia.

Senator SMITH of Maryland. Of course there is not double taxation.

Senator GALLINGER. In many cases it is true, as Commissioner Siddons says, that they come from States where intangibles are taxed, and they do not escape taxation by coming here.

Senator SMITH of Maryland. It is only in cases where they are not taxed here, that there certainly ought to be some taxation elsewhere, under the present conditions of taxation.

Gentlemen, is there anything further you wish to talk with the committee about?

Commissioner SIDDONS. There has just been sent up to me a memorandum, which I have had no chance at all to look at, prepared by the chief of the fire department, with regard to estimates that were submitted by the commissioners in behalf of that department and which were omitted or modified in the House bill. Not having examined it, I can not express any opinion about the memorandum, but with your permission I should like to leave it with you for your consideration.

Senator LEA. Does that appear in the House hearings?

Commissioner SIDDONS. No, Senator.

Senator GALLINGER. Probably all the items appear there.

Commissioner SIDDONS. I may say, in explanation, that I called on the chief of the fire department to inform me as to whether or not there were any items which we had included in our estimates which had been omitted by the House, or modified, which were considered by the department to be vital, and I told him in case there were such items he should prepare a memorandum and let me have it. I assume that this is the memorandum. It has just been handed to me here, and I have had no opportunity to even look at it.

Senator GALLINGER. This list is headed items included in the department's estimates, and not included in the appropriation bill as it passed the House of Representatives.

Commissioner SIDDONS. I have not examined the list. I could indicate the items that I think vital.

Senator SMITH of Maryland. Would it not be better to ask the commissioners to look over this list and hand it back to us after they have done so?

Commissioner SIDDONS. I submitted it to you now only because it came to me here.

Senator SMITH of Maryland. We would submit it to you, anyway. These matters are to be submitted to you first, before they are acted upon.

Senator GALLINGER. And doubtless the police department will want a great many items included which are not in the bill as it comes to us from the House, and I think the commissioners ought to scan those pretty carefully.

Senator SMITH of Maryland. No doubt we will want you to come before us again.

Commissioner NEWMAN. Any time you say, Mr. Chairman, we will be at your disposal.

Senator SMITH of Maryland. We will let you know if there is anything required of you. So far as I understand, you have nothing to volunteer now, but if anything comes up we will let you know about it.

Commissioner NEWMAN. Very well.

(At 12.55 o'clock p. m. the subcommittee adjourned its hearing until Monday, January 26, 1914, at 10.30 o'clock a. m.)

MONDAY, JANUARY 26, 1914.

COMMITTEE ON APPROPRIATIONS,
UNITED STATES SENATE,
Washington, D. C.

The subcommittee met at 10.30 o'clock a. m.

Present: Senators Smith of Maryland (chairman), Gallinger, and Dillingham.

NATIONAL LIBRARY FOR THE BLIND.

Hon. Ernest W. Roberts, Representative in Congress from the ninth district of Massachusetts, Mrs. Ernest W. Roberts, and Miss

Ella Loraine Dorsey appeared representing the National Library for the Blind.

The CHAIRMAN (Senator Smith of Maryland). Mr. Roberts, the subcommittee will be very glad to hear you.

STATEMENT OF HON. ERNEST W. ROBERTS OF MASSACHUSETTS.

Representative ROBERTS. Mr. Chairman, I appear before the subcommittee this morning in the interest of the National Library for the Blind. The District appropriation bill last year carried an appropriation of $5,000 in aid of that institution. I wish to make a brief statement to the committee in the strong hope that they will see fit to continue that amount annually for this institution.

Senator SMITH of Maryland. I understand that you had this appropriation previously, but it was left out of the pending bill in the House.

Representative ROBERTS. We had it last year, but it was left out of the bill in the House.

I wish to emphasize what I have to say by a very brief statement of the action of the Government in regard to deaf, dumb, and blind. In 1857 or 1858 the Federal Government began assisting in the education of deaf, dumb. and blind. Amos Kendall, at that time a prominent man in official life in Washington, took a deep interest in this subject and gave a certain quantity of land and a building for the education of deaf, dumb. and blind—all three of these unfortunate classes—the express condition being that the property would be maintained by private charity or by the Government.

The Government began by appropriations of $3,000 annually for the education of all three of these classes of unfortunates. That was continued until about 1865, when, for some reason, the blind were excluded from education at the institution which had been founded by Amos Kendall. That institution is known now as the Columbia Institution for the Deaf.

The Federal Government from year to year increased its benefactions for the education of the deaf and dumb until we have appropriated directly and indirectly down to the present time nearly $4,000,000—something like $3,700,000—for the education of the deaf and dumb.

Meanwhile the blind, after they were excluded from the Columbia Institution. were cared for by a provision of law which provided that only the indigent blind should be educated, at some institution in Maryland or elsewhere, and an indefinite appropriation was made for that purpose. That continued down until about five years ago, according to my recollection, when the indefinite appropriation was repealed and a fixed appropriation of at first $6.000, now $7,000, annually was provided for the education of the indigent blind.

There is another point I want to speak of in regard to the indigent blind. The total amount, as near as I can ascertain from the Secretary of the Interior, who was charged with administering the indefinite appropriation—that has been expended for the blind is about $200,000. I can give the exact figures a little later.

The point I wish to make is that while the Government started out treating the deaf, dumb, and blind on an equal footing and making equal provision for them, and while Amos Kendall's gift, accepted and enjoyed by this Government, was for the equal benefit of the deaf, dumb, and blind, for some reason the blind were set to one side in 1865 and very little or nothing has been done for them, either those able to care for themselves or the indigent, in comparison with the total amount of the benefactions of the Government for the deaf and dumb, both those of means and those who were indigent.

I am not as well able to speak of the work of the National Library for the Blind as its secretary, Miss Dorsey, who is here, and with the permission of the chairman I will ask Miss Dorsey to give to the committee the scope of their work, the people who are interested, and what they are hoping to accomplish with the small aid from the Government which they are asking.

Senator SMITH of Maryland. The subcommittee will be glad to hear Miss Dorsey.

STATEMENT OF MISS ELLA LORAINE DORSEY.

Miss DORSEY. Mr. Chairman and gentlemen of the subcommittee, the question of our work applies particularly to the blind who have had their intelligence awakened and their hands trained in the great institutional schools but have no way of earning a livelihood after leaving the same. When they have been specially trained a small number can become self-supporting, but the majority can find nothing to do outside of the trades. Some can bind brooms; some can cane chairs; some tune pianos. Some can teach music, but not all. Our great hope and object in opening the library and our great effort has been to give employment to the educated blind who are otherwise obliged to live a life dependent either on the charity of the public, the State or community, or, in many cases, on the insufficient means of their relatives.

We find that in our country there are five embossed types in use among the blind, which results in a further limitation of the pupils in the various schools, and so in our Library we adopted the type universal in 23 of the old countries—that is, the English Braille. In building up our Library we found that by using this type we could begin at once to exchange with other countries their new books for ours, and thus provide not only a wider literature for the amusement of the blind, who have scant means to amuse themselves, but also immediate employment for the blind in making these new books and the music for exchange.

There have been machines invented for doing it. There are special presses and there are special typewriters and slates by which the blind can transcribe anything into embossed type; and there are typewriters which, by a special guide, enable the blind to write in sighted type from dictation or from the Braille shorthand.

We found that by these means we could give employment in their homes to adult blind or we could bring them from their homes here. We had applications from all over the country from blind, asking for work that they could do in their homes by means of these typewriters, slates, and other appliances. We have from 40 States in the Union appeals from the blind to be employed in this work.

The way we are able to employ them at a distance is by making and sending them the Braille alphabet and a set of our rules for Braille transcribers and the paper. We have to furnish the paper.

Then we send whatever book it is desired to copy in this raised type. Mrs. Roberts has with her some of the work that they do, by which you can see its special features.

Last year Senator Curtis, of Kansas, who took a deep interest in the blind, had inserted in the District of Columbia appropriation bill by the District of Columbia Committee a provision for $5,000 with which to help us buy the necessary appliances and apparatus, to buy the paper, and to bear the expense of the transportation to the blind in their homes of the books and paper. In returning the embossed book the Government gives us postage free.

Mrs. Duncan Upshaw Fletcher, Mrs. Everis Anson Hayes, and Mrs. Albert Burleson were the moving spirits in raising $330 for the purchase of a large Braille press, and this gift we will receive in about 10 days.

Senator Fletcher, in his generous compassion for the blind, had inserted in the tariff bill an amendment by which the Braille press, cubarithms, and other apparatus for the education of the blind can be brought in from France free of tax. I call this a press, but it is a hand-worked machine, the type of which is composed of the Braille unit, and by which tangible printing is done, as you will see here, the blind reading it by the touch. This press, coming to us free of duty, will be a most valuable gift to the blind, and will enable us to furnish employment to many more of them.

In our work we are obliged to have the undivided services of a special teacher of the blind, and we need to pay her a given salary. She is the only salaried officer we have, because the rest of us are able as well as willing and eager and glad to give our services free of charge. She has, however, to support herself and to support an aged mother. So she is the one to whom a salary must be paid. Out of the appropriation given us that salary of $1,200 a year was secured. We have quarters, for which we pay a small rental, where the blind go and spend the day in learning how to do this work and in carrying on the work of the library.

We have the pleasure of announcing that 15 of the District blind are rendered self-supporting and at least partly independent by what they make in this National Library for the Blind and that we have contributed to the literature of the blind 83 new books which have been made by our blind copyists. We have issued an edition of 350 copies of " Rules for transcribing Braille," a pamphlet of 17 pages. We have made and distributed 600 alphabets, and an edition of 100 copies of Our Syrian Guest, with its prefatory psalm; also a calendar, and the blind employees prepared and printed a set of resolutions setting forth their valuation of the national library and what it has meant to the blind here and elsewhere. We have offered to print the schoolbooks for the first year's experiment with the blind children of the District in the public school as our offering.

I should like to say, Mr. Chairman, that no words are too fine to be said in praise of the institutional schools. They are the greatest benefactions that can be imagined, but they can only carry the blind to the close of their education. Of course, when the blind leave them they must return to homes or communities, where, if they have no trade or training, they are dependent, or they must ask the charitable institutions from which they have been taken as children to readmit them as charity inmates.

In one of the great schools where one of the most brilliant of its young women was educated, it occurred to her in the last month of her life there, "What is to become of me when I leave here? I have no home; I have no friends." She went to the head of the institution and said: "What will I do when I leave here?" The only answer he could make her was, "Well, they will receive you back at the poor-house from which you were taken."

Mr. Chairman, our work helps to rescue and relieve that type of man or woman who, educated in good surroundings, living under hygenic conditions, among congenial companions, and with mental resources, yet must return to dependence and poverty, and the terrible solitude of that perpetual darkness unless they have some means of making a living.

We are enabled to aid the blind through the love and care our director gives them. Through her we learn to know what are their needs, and by means of this little library we are establishing branches throughout the country with the same idea of work, the same idea of employment, and we are sending out the means of employment.

Mr. Roberts spoke of the deaf.

These people of ours are overwhelmed with a misfortune which deafness does not even approximate. In the magnificent institution at Kendall Green those men and those women in spite of their infirmity are so well trained, so well taught, that they are returned to their State and country as valuable citizens. They are returned with the power to aid in the development of both, and continue their own. With deafness they are not handicapped. It is not a bar to them. The law is open to them; medicine is open to them; the ministry is open to them. There are a dozen places open to them. But when a man comes out of a school for the blind, unless he can make brooms or tune pianos or teach music, he has no career open to him. There are exceptions, but I speak of the average blind man. A woman is still more handicapped, for although she may be taught to sew she can not sew fast enough to compete with those who have machines and whose eyesight is good. A few only can teach, and the clerical work they can do is limited. The courage and the gallant patience they show in trying to learn must move one to the deepest compassion.

Our director has made a point always of urging them to additional effort, and what we are trying to do is to raise the standard of their work to a point wherein what we teach them they can compete successfully with the sighted.

There are very few things in which the blind may compete successfully with the sighted. The darkness affects them physiologically. We know that if we who are sighted are in a dark room, however familiar, we move cautiously for fear of meeting some unknown obstacle and receiving either a blow or a nervous fright.

There is this veil of darkness between them and the outer world, and it can never be lifted or lightened. They are given in the institutional schools everything except the sort of every-day competition which inspires them with confidence in strange surroundings and opens up the possibility of generally making their way outside. They are specialized, guarded, and provided for so carefully that when they finish their 10 or 12 years' course they return to their families and their communities as strangers and must begin an adjustment of daily life as well as an effort for self-support.

We are trying to open a loophole in the wall of darkness which surrounds these unfortunate citizens. There are 80,000 blind in the country, and of this number we are hoping to reach at least a proportion. As I said, applicants in 40 States have made appeals to us for this form of work. They average from 4 to 12 in each of these 40 States, and in one State 22 applied. We have on file applications for work from 390 people who literally are begging to be given the chance that any citizen with sight now has, viz, the right to have a little corner in the world for himself and to be self-supporting.

Senator GALLINGER. How many persons now take advantage of this library?

Miss DORSEY. We have our report here, to which I can refer.

Senator GALLINGER. Just state the number approximately.

Senator SMITH of Maryland. No matter about the report. Tell us the number. We must be brief in this matter. We want to get all the information we can, but we have not much time. How many are there who have received the benefits of the library?

Miss DORSEY. There are 70 readers and 15 workers. Three work there daily. The other 12 work in their own homes.

Senator GALLINGER. Has the library any relation to the so-called Polytechnic Institute for the Blind?

Miss DORSEY. None at all.

Senator GALLINGER. That is a separate institution?

Miss DORSEY. Absolutely. We are incorporated under the laws of the District of Columbia. Our incorporators live in eight or ten other cities. Mr. John Cadwalader is one of them. Mr. Charles Bell, who is now present, is our treasurer. We have a very interesting representation throughout the country. We find that it aids in a way the proposition to help the blind by having some of our officers scattered through the country, as they are representative men and women.

Senator SMITH of Maryland. Do you receive any outside donations?

Miss DORSEY. We have a membership and the appropriation.

Senator SMITH of Maryland. What does it amount to in the aggregate?

Miss DORSEY. About $300. Our members pay a small fee of $2 annually, and then we have eight or ten life members, and hope to increase the number. They pay $50 apiece.

Senator SMITH of Maryland. What are the total receipts?

Miss DORSEY. From outside sources not more than $300 or $400.

Senator SMITH of Maryland. Then, you say that you have life members who give $50 apiece?

Miss DORSEY. That is their life fee, and the money is invested and the interest on it is paid to the blind transcribers for copying short stories into Braille.

Senator SMITH of Maryland. What is the total amount of money that you receive from all sources for the library?

Miss DORSEY. Exclusive of the one appropriation, not more than about $400.

Senator SMITH of Maryland. How long have you been getting the appropriation of $5,000 from the Government?

Miss DORSEY. We have had only one. Senator Curtis obtained that for us last year, and we were enabled thereby to buy the appliances and the paper. The paper is an expensive item; it has to be of a special texture and costs $90 a ton.

Senator SMITH of Maryland. You were before the House committee?

Miss DORSEY. No; Senator Curtis saw to everything. He and Senator Martin, of Virginia; Senator Gore, of Oklahoma; and Senator Perkins, of California, were the four who especially interested themselves in this benefaction to the blind.

Senator GALLINGER. Let me understand exactly the scope of your work. You say that there are 40 States making an appeal to you. Do not most of those States take care of their own blind?

Miss DORSEY. Indeed they do. They educate their blind children and care for the defective and helpless; two States have employment bureaus; but these applicants are people who have no support after leaving school, and who are anxious to become self-supporting citizens, and to do something toward making at least a shelter for themselves. The schools can not reach this particular class of the blind, and we appeal to you because we are trying to help them to independent citizenship.

Senator GALLINGER. Let me ask just one further practical question, Miss Dorsey. I sympathize with anything that will help the blind. I notice there are four applications from New Hampshire.

Miss DORSEY. Yes.

Senator GALLINGER. Do you propose to admit people from the various States and expend a portion of this money toward supporting these people?

Miss DORSEY. Toward furnishing work and helping them to support themselves after the educational period is over; for, as soon as their education is finished they must return to such homes as they have.

Mrs. ROBERTS. They can have no presses for use in their own homes; but they can have typewriters for the writing of Braille point, and slates, if we can furnish them, as you will notice this book contains this sort of work [exhibiting].

Senator GALLINGER. I know the difficulty in getting the States to take care of the blind, and I should not care how many such machines were purchased for those people.

Miss DORSEY. Do not imagine that the people of the States do not take care of their blind. They educate them with admirable care, but in the period which comes after the education unless they are absolutely helpless, there is no way to support them in their own homes. It is simply with us a question of helping them do this. It has assumed a national scope in response to the widespread appeal. Within every State in the Union there are various generous undertakings to help the blind, and yet there is no provision for them beyond the school period, or before the helpless old-age period when they must go into institutions.

Senator GALLINGER. We have several appropriations—I was somewhat instrumental in getting them—for the so-called polytechnic institute here. They do a different work. They furnish employment for the blind of the city of Washington, at least, that is their claim. It has been intimated sometimes that they are not quite doing what they claim, but I do not know how that may be. We made appropriations to buy printing presses for them and all that sort of thing. You say that your work is entirely independent of that?

Miss DORSEY. Entirely so.

Senator GALLINGER. I think they are located on H Street. I notice that your location is on H Street.

Miss DORSEY. I do not know their location. I thought they were down on one of the streets running north and south. We are on H between Seventeenth and Eighteenth. We have an apartment in the "Milton," where we do our work. They are in no way associated with our library. I think their efforts are made to teach trades— such as typesetting, for instance; but I do not know.

Senator SMITH of Maryland. Their work is more professional.

Senator GALLINGER. They make, or claim to make, post cards.

Miss DORSEY. They have a sighted member who sets type for them and then they can print and fold, but they can not set ordinary type yet. That may come for them some day. I hope it will.

Senator GALLINGER. As I remember, we put in the appropriation of $5,000 last year without any restriction, but I think in conference the House insisted that it should be for one year. You will observe, Mr. Chairman, that it runs for but one year.

Senator SMITH of Maryland. And this year it was cut out?

Senator GALLINGER. It was not put in by the House last year. It was put in by the Senate and retained in conference.

Miss DORSEY. Mr. Chairman, when you asked me about the actual sum of money we receive, I omitted to state there is one benefactor who has arranged for our rent until the end of this year. It is $45 a month, and secures us a place to work. As it is a special benefaction, I do not know whether you would include it in "income."

Senator SMITH of Maryland. I just wanted to get an idea of the donations and the money you receive outside the Government appropriation.

Senator GALLINGER. You say that you are incorporated?

Miss DORSEY. We are incorporated under the laws of the District of Columbia. We felt obliged to do that, because if we receive money contributions we ought to be responsible for them.

Our officers include:

Dr. Thomas Nelson Page, honorary president.
Mrs. Ernest W. Roberts, president.
Miss Helen Keller, chairman of the board of councillors.
Mr. Charles J. Bell, American Security and Trust Co., treasurer.
Mrs. William E. Clark, assistant treasurer.
Miss Etta Jossyln Giffin, director.
Miss Ella Loraine Dorsey, recording secretary.
Vice presidents: Mr. John Cadwalader, Philadelphia (of the great Overbrook School for the Blind); Bishop Whitehead, Pittsburgh; Mrs. Charles Gleed, Kansas; Gen. Dangerfield Parker, United States Army; Dr. William Holland Wilmer, District of Columbia (the famous oculist); Admiral Dewey, United States Navy; Mrs. Colfelt (Rebecca McManes Colfelt), at large; Mr. H. J. Baxter, Minnesota; Senator George C. Perkins, California; Dr. Emile Berliner (a noted scientist and philanthropist), at large.
Chairmen of national committees: Mrs. Champ Clark, membership; Mrs. Murray Galt Motter, house; Mrs. William Hitz, entertainment (daughter-in-law of the philanthropist who taught Helen Keller); Mrs. R. Giffin, rules; Mrs. Horace Mann Towner, circulation of books; Dr. E. Folkmar, bureau of informa-

tion (head of the Woman's Clinic) ; Miss Hilda Erikson, foreign correspondence; Miss Jessie Wilson (now Mrs. Sayre), ticket bureau; Miss Sybil Hayes, clippings; Mrs. Duncan U. Fletcher, press.

ADDITIONAL STATEMENT OF REPRESENTATIVE ERNEST W. ROBERTS.

Representative Roberts. Mr. Chairman, there is one other feature of the work of this institution which Miss Dorsey did not emphasize as I think it should be. In addition to furnishing a certain amount of employment for the blind throughout the country the National Library for the Blind is engaged in furnishing additional literature for the blind, which circulates all over the country, and which is available to the blind who are under instruction in various institutions and blind who are living in their own homes. In other words, they are building up a library of books in this Braille point which are circulated throughout the country. If I am not mistaken an arrangement is made whereby you get exchange with foreign countries.

Miss Dorsey. With foreign countries.

Representative Roberts. So these books are not confined in their use to the District of Columbia, where they originate, but they go all over the country and to foreign lands. One of the objects of the institution is to build up this library, and they have adopted the plan in building it up of at the same time furnishing employment to the blind who have graduated from schools or those, perhaps, who have never attended school. So there is a double object and a double benevolence that is being conferred by the operation of the institution.

Senator Smith of Maryland. It is not limited to the District of Columbia, but applies to all the States of the Union!

Representative Roberts. It applies to all the States of the Union, and it is accompanied as well by the increase of and exchange of literature for the blind.

If I may be pardoned for just a moment, Mr. Chairman, on the subject of the blind there is another matter in which I have taken a personal interest and which I should like to call to the attention of the committee, and that is the wording of the appropriation as it has been carried for fifty-odd years for the education of the blind.

As I said a few moments ago, in the beginning of the Government appropriations they were considered as indigent, and only indigent deaf, dumb, and blind could get any benefit from the appropriations which the Government saw fit to make. That treatment of the deaf, dumb, and blind continued down to 1901, when an act was passed which removed the stigma of pauperism from the deaf and dumb, and since 1901 the money appropriated annually in this bill for the education of the deaf and dumb at the Columbia Institution is available for any deaf and dumb person who is certified by the superintendent of schools for the District as being of teachable age and one who should receive the benefit of that fund. Notwithstanding that the deaf and dumb are taken out from under the stigma of pauperism, the blind have still continued under it right down to the present moment, and in the bill you have before you there is only provision for an appropriation for the education of indigent blind.

It has occurred to me that the blind people are under perhaps the greatest handicap that people can have, and to impose the added humiliation of pauperism, before they can get any benefit from the small appropriation of $7,000 that is provided for their education, is certainly not an enlightened way to treat that unfortunate class of people.

Senator GALLINGER. The two preceding appropriations deal with the deaf and dumb, the white and the colored. There is no restriction.

Representative ROBERTS. There is no restriction.

Senator GALLINGER. Suppose we should strike out the word "indigent," would not the appropriation necessarily have to be increased?

Representative ROBERTS. I hardly think so, because the school authorities, especially when Dr. Davidson was superintendent, were right on the point of opening the public schools here to the blind. I do know how familiar the committee may be on this point, but other cities of the country have done that. Chicago began in 1900 admitting blind children into the public schools, recognizing that the community is just as much under obligations to educate a blind child as it is to educate a sighted child. That plan has been followed by New York, Milwaukee, Racine, Cincinnati, Cleveland, Newark, Jersey City, and others. So there are a number of cities now that are taking the blind children into the public schools and educating them right along with the sighted children with very beneficial results.

Senator SMITH of Maryland. Certainly the funds are not appropriated for indigent school children, and they all get the benefit of it.

Representative ROBERTS. All are getting the benefit.

Senator SMITH of Maryland. There is no reason why the restriction should be imposed upon the blind, whether indigent or not, any more than in the other cases.

Representative ROBERTS. It so occurs to me.

Senator SMITH of Maryland. I think your point is well taken.

Senator GALLINGER. There is no question but that they should be put on all fours.

Representative ROBERTS. That is my point, and I hope the committee will take it into consideration and remove the restriction which is now put upon that class of people.

Senator SMITH of Maryland. Your idea is that if children other than indigent go to the schools, there is no reason why blind children other than indigent should not be taught, too.

Representative ROBERTS. That is just it.

Mrs. ROBERTS. I wish to call attention to this book which they have made [exhibiting]. They have made and bound it. I do not think even sighted men could do a better piece of work. Shall I leave this with the committee?

Senator SMITH of Maryland. Very well, if you would like to leave it.

Mrs. ROBERTS. You might like to look over this table.

Representative ROBERTS. Mr. Chairman, just one further word. If the committee is interested in having the exact figures of the appropriations for the indigent blind down to 1908, I have them here.

Senator SMITH of Maryland. You can leave that with us, too.

Representative ROBERTS. The total is $105,446.90 down to and including 1894.

Senator SMITH of Maryland. Since when?

Representative ROBERTS. Since 1866; that is, since the blind were taken out of the Columbia Institution. From 1894 down to 1908 the total is $96,061.98. A trifle over $200,000 has been appropriated in all for the benefit of the blind.

We are very much obliged to you, Mr. Chairman.

STATEMENT OF CHARLES J. BELL.

Mr. BELL. Mr. Chairman, I would like to state that I have watched the work done by the ladies in charge of the National Library for the Blind for the past two years and have seen the very valuable work they are attempting to do in the interests of that unfortunate class. With the very small amount of money available they have begun the nucleus of what I believe will be a very large institution, and I think they should be encouraged by an appropriation.

Senator SMITH of Maryland. You believe it not only beneficial to the District of Columbia, but——

Mr. BELL. To the country at large.

Senator SMITH of Maryland. To reach out to the entire country?

Mr. BELL. To the entire country.

IMPROVEMENT OF SEVENTH STREET NW., FROM NEW YORK AVENUE TO Q STREET.

A. J. Driscoll, president of the Midcitizens' Association; Charles S. Shreve, John Shugrue, S. R. Waters, A. H. Plugge, W. M. Whyte, and M. G. Ruppert appeared.

Senator SMITH of Maryland. Gentlemen, we want you to give us all the information that is necessary, but we ask you to be as brief as possible and submit what you have to state in the most concise way, because we have a great deal to do and we can not give you very much time. At the same time we do not want to cut you off unnecessarily.

STATEMENT OF CHARLES S. SHREVE.

Mr. SHREVE. Mr. Chairman, I will strive to be brief and to the point. I appear on behalf of the Midcitizens' Association of this city, many of the members of that association being merchants and property owners on Seventh Street from New York Avenue to Q Street NW., are in favor of the appropriation that was asked for by the District Commissioners of $30,000 for repaving Seventh Street NW. with concrete from New York Avenue to Q. We did not in any way appear before the House committee.

Senator SMITH of Maryland. Did you not ask for the appropriation in any way?

Mr. SHREVE. Not before the House committee. We appeared before the District Commissioners and they saw the absolute necessity of the appropriation.

I wish to say that at this time more than at any other time this appropriation for repaving Seventh Street is most imperative. Seventh Street is without doubt one of the oldest, if not the oldest, business street running north and south in the city of Washington. For over have a century it has been the thoroughfare for the farmers and other growers out in Maryland to come down Seventh Street extended, what was then known as Brightwood · Avenue, and bring their produce to the markets.

Seventh Street was paved with wooden blocks in 1872. At that time it was considered a great innovation to pave a street with wooden blocks. That proved a failure, and it was paved with granite blocks about the year 1874, and that granite-block pavement still remains on Seventh Street from New York Avenue to Q Street.

In 1898 Seventh Street between E and F NW. was paved with concrete, and in 1904 the street was concreted from G Street up to New York Avenue, where it stops at present. At that time it was the intention or the hope of the District Commissioners to follow it immediately with a continuation of the paving of concrete on Seventh Street above New York Avenue.

Senator GALLINGER. It seems to me that you are guilty of laches in this case. As I remember it, the Senate put this appropriation in the District of Columbia appropriation bill heretofore and lost it in conference. You should have gone to the House committee, it seems to me.

Mr. SHREVE. Of course, not knowing how we should proceed in those matters, as we had the commissioners to assure us of the necessity and they were aware of the present deplorable condition of the street, I had not thought whatever but that it would go through. The merchants of Seventh Street have been for the last 20 years trying to have the street concreted.

Senator SMITH of Maryland. Do I understand that the item was cut out by the House?

Senator GALLINGER. I feel quite sure it went out in conference.

Senator SMITH of Maryland. That ought to have been some notice to you to go to the House committee first.

Mr. SHREVE. Heretofore we never thought that that was the case.

Senator SMITH of Maryland. Proceed with your statement, Mr. Shreve.

Mr. SHREVE. When in the olden days Seventh Street was surfaced with blocks, as it is at present. All the streets in the city were surfaced with blocks, and when the merchants and farmers came down Seventh Street it was without doubt one of the most busy streets in the city. With the advent of concrete, Eighth Street NW. was concreted, although not a business street, and Sixth Street was concreted, and as the farmers would reach Seventh Street and Florida Avenue they thereupon began to turn off their course down Eighth Street and Sixth Street, taking the trade off of Seventh Street. Even when that trade does come down Seventh Street at present, the noise of the traffic is so great that you can hardly talk to a customer, and it is almost impossible to hold telephone communication with any customer at a distance.

This street has been allowed to become in a worse and worse condition until at present the condition really can be declared deplorable. There are great sunken places in the street at some points; at others there are large humps; at some places by the curbstone the street level is about 18 inches from the top of the curb; and in another place you will find it about 6 inches or less. It is absolutely necessary, even for the preservation of life and limb, that something shall be done.

In going to the District Building to find out the question of dollars and cents, and whether it would be more economical to even try to repave this granite street or to concrete it, we have been informed by those in charge that the street is so worn down that it will cost about $3 per cubic yard to repair it or even resurface it with granite blocks or Belgian blocks, and that it will cost $1.80 per cubic yard to resurface it with concrete. I assume that does not include the foundation stone, which probably would bring it to $2.25 or $2.50 a cubic yard. Therefore, as a question of economy, it would be far cheaper to concrete Seventh Street than it would be to attempt to repair the present blocks on it or to put down Belgian blocks.

If any of you gentlemen have had occasion to go from Union Station up to the Carnegie Library, which is at Seventh and K, and turn around the library building, you will see at that point one of the most congested and dangerous conditions in the city. Every vehicle coming from Massachusetts Avenue and those surrounding districts to Union Station, or vice versa, passes around the corner there for the simple reason that that point is where these rough blocks from Q to New York Avenue stop. You can not get one man in a hundred to go over that part of Seventh Street in an automobile or in any other vehicle, but he will turn that corner. The fact is that from this very cause two deaths occurred at that corner.

The merchants of Seventh Street have been petitioning Congress or appearing before the commissioners for 15 or 20 years to try to get the street concreted. The commissioners have time and time again seen the necessity of it and have promised that they would ask for the appropriation. We would get through our work of convincing the commissioners, but by the time we had shown them the necessity of it the board of commissioners would change and some new commissioners would come in and we would have to do the work over again.

Many of those merchants have been on that street for one and two generations. My own father, for instance, who died last year, was on that street for 47 years, and he was one of the merchants who attempted to get the street concreted. Since his death, I have been trying to do the same thing. I have the same interest in the street. You will find many merchants there who have taken the same interest in the matter. Some of them have died and their children are now seeking to have this improvement made.

Senator SMITH of Maryland. When was the present pavement put down?

Mr. SHREVE. In 1874. It is the same pavement that was laid in 1874 with a few repairs that have been added.

Senator SMITH of Maryland. You do not mean to say that no money has been spent in keeping up the street.

Mr. SHREVE. I say nothing has been done with the exception of the repairs that have been made to the wear and tear of the street, where it has practically worn out the blocks. They are granite blocks, rough and uneven, and really can not be repaired. It is not a question of simply changing one surface for another. It is a question of life and limb, for even around the car tracks—the tracks are some inches above the street in some places—the humps and the lumps make it a danger to pass up and down the streets, outside of the question that the merchants on the street do not want to be longer handicapped as the other merchants of the city were handicapped in the past. We want to be treated just as they have been. We want to be relieved from this deplorable condition.

Senator SMITH of Maryland. You want your street to have equal treatment with the other streets, neither more nor less?

Mr. SHREVE. Yes; no less and no more. I thank you.

STATEMENT OF A. J. DRISCOLL.

Mr. DRISCOLL. Mr. Chairman, I simply want to say that Mr. Shreve seems to have covered the position very well, but along with what he has said I might call attention to the fact that the larger business houses on Seventh Street seem to go as far as New York Avenue and stop there. We contend that that stoppage is due primarily to the condition of the street paving north of New York Avenue.

As it was explained to you, that paving was put down in 1874. I feel that it is safe to say that outside of what little repairing has been done by the street car companies, the commissioners have not put very much money on the street. It is certainly in a terrible condition at the present time. As it was explained to you, it is impossible to use telephones. The merchants' taxes are going up there, and on account of the condition of the street business has departed from it. I think that in itself, Senators, would be a sufficient cause to give us a better pavement in that particular section. It is about the only large business street in the District that is not paved with improved street pavement, and certainly there could be many reasons given and arguments made why the street should be improved.

Senator SMITH of Maryland. You feel that the street has been discriminated against in favor of Sixth Street and Eighth Street to such an extent that it has taken away the trade that should go to Seventh Street and carried it to Sixth and Eighth Sreets?

Mr. DRISCOLL. Yes, sir; I do, for the simple reason that the farmers will come in from the great State of Maryland with their produce, and, instead of coming down Seventh Street, they will divert from Seventh Street and come down Sixth Street or Eighth Street.

Senator SMITH of Maryland. You feel that that is on account of the condition of the street, whereas if it were in better shape they would use it; that they now go down other streets because those streets are in a better condition?

Mr. DRISCOLL. Most assuredly I do, Senator. We have Mr. Shugrue, an old business man on Seventh Street, here, and he will possibly enlighten you with some remarks.

STATEMENT OF JOHN SHUGRUE.

Mr. SHUGRUE. Mr. Chairman and Senators, I have been on that street, in the stove business, for years. The only piece of ground in that whole section that is unoccupied is the site of the Saul Building, which was blown down last summer and which killed two men. It was occupied by myself and son.

Seventh Street has been very much discriminated against. This very day there are 30 idle stores on Seventh Street from New York Avenue to Q and to Florida Avenue and U Street. Seventh Street has been discriminated against very much. For what cause I do not know. There is not another street in Washington that requires the traffic that Seventh Street requires from the steamboat wharves north. There are twenty-odd miles of travel that are almost straight from the wharves. The travel is cut off from Seventh Street because of the condition of the street. Nobody drives on it at all. I drove on it at the risk of my tires this morning just to see the condition. The property holders agree on that. The people are dependent upon their property for a livelihood, and the property is idle, due, I think, to the condition of that street. It is one of the best and oldest business streets in Washington. I have been on it thirty-odd years myself, and, with my journeyman work, I have been probably 48 years on that street. I have known it for the last 60 years.

Senator SMITH of Maryland. Do you mean to say that the fact that the houses are idle is due to the condition of the street?

Mr. SHUGRUE. Yes, sir. There is no other condition on earth that I know of which could cause it.

Senator SMITH of Maryland. Are there not other reasons why streets near by are more desirable streets on which to do business?

Mr. SHUGRUE. They are more desirable to travel on. As I said, Seventh is an old business street. The others are not business streets. It is due to that cause and no other. When I went in business there 35 years ago, I bought the key of a gentleman who went over to Georgetown or I would not have been able to get a store for money. Then people were looking out and trying to get a place to do business. Now, those places are lying idle, the stores are idle, and it is a great detriment to the property holders. They have no revenue to live on, and it is due to that condition. That is about the winding up of the work of the old Board of Public Works. It is the only street that is paved worse than ever before, with the worst cobblestones that I ever saw in the city. There is no street in the city of Washington to-day that is any worse than Seventh Street from New York Avenue to Q. We only ask you gentlemen to consider that it will be helping the city out as well as helping business.

I thank you very much.

Mr. DRISCOLL. I wish to leave with the subcommittee a brief written statement.

Senator SMITH of Maryland. Very well.

The statement referred to is as follows:

M. FRANK RUPPERT,
1021 SEVENTH STREET NW.,
Washington, D. C., January 24, 1914.

GENTLEMEN: We want a square deal. About 15 years ago we merchants of Seventh Street, north of New York Avenue NW., started to plead for a concrete street. In a body we called on Commissioner Lansing H. Beech, who gave us a hearing and agreed we should have a concrete street, as same was very rough and full of holes and diverted business from same. Since then we have pleaded and paid taxes in vain.

I am satisfied we are stepchildren of the District of Columbia, as you can find small cross streets concreted and 50 per cent of the alleys paved with better stone than Seventh Street NW.

The past year several people were killed at Seventh and K Streets NW. and a number injured on account of congested traffic at north side of Mount Vernon Place, all caused by rough, rocky, hilly, and sunken approach of Seventh Street north of New York Avenue, which diverted traffic from Seventh Street westward.

Concreting this street would relieve this congestion and save life and limb.

Mr. DRISCOLL. Gentlemen, I would be glad to bring and members of this committee from their residences at any time in my machine down Seventh Street to the Capitol. If any of you gentlemen will kindly give about 10 minutes more of your time some morning I will bring you from your residence to the Capitol down that street and show it to you.

Senator SMITH of Maryland. We are very much obliged to you.

Mr. DRISCOLL. I thank you, sir.

PROPOSED FIRE-ENGINE HOUSE ON GRANT ROAD NEAR CONNECTICUT AVENUE.

STATEMENT OF DAVID L. SELKE.

Mr. SELKE. Mr. Chairman, the District appropriation bill contains an item appropriating $40,500 for additional fire protection in the territory lying between Connecticut Avenue, Highland Avenue, Calvert Street Bridge, and Chevy Chase. I appear on behalf of the Connecticut Avenue Citizens' Association.

I wish to state, first, that in the second session of the Sixty-second Congress you, Mr. Chairman, were good enough to introduce a bill, Senate bill 6944, which called for an appropriation of something like $45,000, if I remember correctly, providing for the construction of an engine house and equipment on Grant Road near Connecticut Avenue, on a lot now owned and which has been owned for some time by the Government, which was originally purchased for school purposes, and is not used at all.

We asked for that location because the present engine house on Wisconsin Avenue, to which the present appropriation bill contemplates an addition, does not furnish adequate protection to the northern section of this territory. It does not furnish such protection as we think that territory ought to have.

Within the last two years and a half the section lying north of, say, Albermarle Street up to the circle has increased enormously in expensive residences. It was proven by a fire which took place not very many months ago that the engine company coming from Wisconsin Avenue could not reach the farther limits of that territory in time to do very effective service. The location on Grant Road near Connecticut Avenue would not only furnish adequate protection to the section to which I now refer, but, lying almost halfway between that and Cleveland Park, would also give adequate protection to Cleveland Park. The engine would have a very much easier run from Grant Road, going right on Connecticut Avenue, than an engine possibly could have on Wisconsin Avenue to reach that circle.

For that reason we ask that the location of Grant Road near Connecticut Avenue, for which we originally asked, may be designated in connection with this appropriation. We do not ask any increase, or anything of that sort. We only wish to have the location of Grant Road near Connecticut Avenue stipulated in the paragraph making this appropriation, instead of leaving it to the discretion of the commissioners to place it at this other location in addition to the present equipment on Wisconsin Avenue.

Senator SMITH of Maryland. I did not get exactly what you want. Will you state specifically what it is?

Mr. SELKE. We should like to have the paragraph stipulate the location of this additional equipment and engine house on Grant Road on the lot now owned by the Government, instead of placing it where I am inclined to believe the commissioners intend to place it, as an addition to the already established engine house on Wisconsin Avenue.

I should like to read, if I may, a letter written by the commissioners to the chairman of our committee on fire and police protection:

With reference to your request of the 3d instant to be advised of the plans, etc., for furnishing additional and better fire protection for the territory lying between Connecticut Avenue, Highland Avenue, Calvert Street Bridge, and Chevy Chase, the commissioners direct me to inform you that in their estimates for the fiscal year 1915 they have asked for a motor pumping engine and a motor-propelled combination chemical and hose wagon for No. 20 engine company, Tenallytown, D. C.

That is the company I spoke of a while ago.

The commissioners have also asked for a new engine house to assist No. 20 engine house—

The engine company already established—

and this new company, if allowed by Congress, will provide ample protection for the territory for which the Connecticut Avenue Citizens' Association ask an engine house in the vicinity of Connecticut Avenue and Grant Road.

Mr. Chairman, we contend that this additional equipment, located where it is proposed by the commissioners, will not give the section which needs additional protection the protection which it ought to have. During the summer we took the commissioners over the ground to convince them of the need of additional protection for our section, and they agreed that it did need it. There is absolutely no fire protection for the entire distance on Connecticut Avenue proper. I am speaking now of the territory from the bridge to the circle. The only engine house existing in that vast stretch of territory is the one on the Tennallytown Road, on Wisconsin Avenue.

The only thing our association asks is that you may locate this additional engine house on Grant Road near Connecticut Avenue.

Senator SMITH of Maryland. Then, as I understand you, the commissioners agree with you that at present there is not proper fire protection?

Mr. SELKE. Yes.

Senator SMITH of Maryland. But they believe the suggestion they have made here as to the location is sufficient to protect you?

Mr. SELKE. That is what they think; yes, sir.

I should like to have you hear the president of our association, Mr. Arthur E. Dowell, if you will.

Senator SMITH of Maryland. If he would like to say something, we shall be glad to hear him.

STATEMENT OF ARTHUR E. DOWELL.

Mr. DOWELL. Mr. Chairman and Senators, I should like to call your attention briefly to what I think ought to be graphically laid before you, so that the matter will appear to you more clearly.

Here is a map of the section of the country which this association covers. Here [indicating on map] is Connecticut Avenue. Here we see the bridge. Here is the other avenue. Here is Tennallytown, separated from Connecticut Avenue at present by a series of ravines and hills, so that for an engine to reach Connecticut Avenue it has to come up a distance and then go across, or come down a distance and go across.

Senator SMITH of Maryland. Where is the place you propose to locate the new engine house?

Mr. DOWELL. Here [indicating on map] is the lot owned by the Government, within about 100 feet of Connecticut Avenue, at the top of the second hill, which would give them a direct drop down the avenue or up the avenue.

It seems to me the commissioners in their letter have entirely disregarded an important feature of this matter. They refer to the territory between Connecticut Avenue and Highland Avenue and forget the territory east of Connecticut Avenue, between that and the park, which is now all open to subdivision. In that territory, within a very short distance of the proposed new station, the Government itself has been erecting, about this point on Connecticut Avenue, the Bureau of Standards, millions of dollars being involved in that expenditure. The Carnegie Institute is over here. Another building is proposed here. A large school, the Academy of the Sacred Heart, is here [indicating on the map].

As a fact, two years ago there was a fire alarm at the foot of Connecticut Avenue and Newark Street, and a gentleman timed the engine company to see how long it took them to get there. The building had been burning one-half hour when it got there. The one station here is the only protection for all this section.

Senator DILLINGHAM. When you say " here," the reporter can not put down what you mean.

Mr. DOWELL. This is Tennallytown.

Senator DILLINGHAM. Instead of saying " here," please state the location on the map.

Mr. DOWELL. At Tennallytown, I mean; this is the sole station, with one engine, to cover that immense territory. For a second call they have to come down into the city, either into Georgetown on this avenue or across the bridge, where the nearest fire-engine station is on U Street, about Seventeenth and U.

Senator DILLINGHAM. What about the protection of the section between Grant Road and the university grounds, if the station is moved to Grant Street?

Mr. DOWELL. We do not wish it moved.

Senator DILLINGHAM. I understood you did.

Mr. DOWELL. No; we do not wish it moved. The commissioners wish to put additional equipment at Tennallytown.

Senator SMITH of Maryland. That is already there.

Mr. DOWELL. They already have a station there.

Senator DILLINGHAM. I see.

Mr. DOWELL. We wish to have a new station over here, if possible, as it is really the central point of that territory. The Tennallytown station has to take care of all the territory to the west of it as well as east; and it sometimes has been sent out into Maryland on emergency calls, leaving us absolutely without any protection whatever for that entire territory.

As the Government owns the lot which has been pointed out, we think the new station can be placed there for the same amount of money that it will require to add to the on at Tennallytown, and that will give us the protection of two stations. This one can reach any part of Connecticut Avenue and any territory east of Connecticut Avenue with about a mile less travel for the apparatus.

Senator SMITH of Maryland. What is the value of the property the Government owns on which you desire to have this station placed?

Mr. DOWELL. I do not know the value of that property.

Senator SMITH of Maryland. Would any additional property have to be secured at Tennallytown for this additional fire equipment?

Mr. DOWELL. I am not advised as to that. Are you advised, Mr. Selke, whether the Government will have to purchase additional ground at Tennallytown?

Mr. SELKE. I do not know whether they will have to purchase additional ground or not.

Mr. DOWELL. I do not think they will, because I think they have sufficient ground.

Senator SMITH of Maryland. But if the station should be located at the place you indicate it would occupy property already owned by the Government?

Mr. DOWELL. It would be on Government property.

Senator SMITH of Maryland. And you are unable to tell me how much that property is worth, because that would include, in a sense, an additional appropriation? It would include the appropriation of the property which belongs to the Government in addition to the $40,500, would it not.

Mr. DOWELL. That would be included in the total cost; yes, sir. It would be included in the total value of the property.

Senator SMITH of Maryland. The Government property would be exclusive of the $40,500 for this purpose?

Mr. DOWELL. It is exclusive of that.

Senator SMITH of Maryland. You do not know the value of the Government property, you say. What is the size of the property?

Mr. SELKE. It was originally purchased, Mr. Chairman, for school purposes, and is not used at present.

Senator DILLINGHAM. Why has it not been used for school purposes? Is it not needed for school purposes?

Senator SMITH of Maryland. Will it not be used?

Mr. SELKE. It will never be used, because it is not at all suitable for it.

Senator SMITH of Maryland. Is that the reason they did not use it?

Mr. SELKE. I presume so.

Senator SMITH of Maryland. How long since it was purchased for that purpose?

Mr. SELKE. It has been quite a number of years; I do not know how long.

Senator SMITH of Maryland. But about how many years?

Mr. SELKE. I should think fully 10 years.

Senator SMITH of Maryland. Has there been a school erected in the neighborhood?

Mr. SELKE. There has been a little shanty, I think, that perhaps was used for colored children. I do not think it is used for that purpose any more.

Mr. Dowell. Yes; there has been a school erected at Chevy Chase.

Senator Smith of Maryland. In order to fill the want that was then supposed to exist?

Mr. Dowell. The Chevy Chase School supplies the wants of that school just at this time, sir. Since then there has been a school erected in Cleveland Park.

Senator Smith of Maryland. You gentlemen can well understand that it is taking quite a responsibility for us to fly in the face of the commissioners, and when they have recommended one place for us to override their recommendations and put a building in another place. You must appreciate that.

Mr. Selke. I may say here something that I omitted a while ago—that at the time the bill to which I refer was introduced, in the second session of the Sixty-second Congress, it was based upon a conference had by me with the chief of the fire department and with the then commissioners. The location and appropriation were based upon that conference, and the commissioners at that time agreed that that was a proper location.

Senator Smith of Maryland. The then commissioners?

Mr. Selke. The former commissioners. Why it has been changed is beyond our ken.

Senator Smith of Maryland. You gentlemen, as I understand, have given your views to the present commissioners?

Mr. Selke. Yes, sir; very extensively.

Senator Smith of Maryland. And they still adhere to their views?

Mr. Selke. They still adhere to their views, of course.

NATIONAL TRAINING SCHOOL FOR GIRLS.

STATEMENT OF J. NOTA M'GILL, PRESIDENT OF THE BOARD OF TRUSTEES.

Mr. McGill. There are just two items, Mr. Chairman, to which I wish to call attention.

The first is an increase of one in the number of teachers of the $600 grade. Two years ago Congress appropriated $60,000 for the erection of an additional building and a heating plant common to four buildings. We have completed that building and the heating plant. We can not occupy the building until we have an appropriation for at least two additional teachers. The House gave us one at the $480 rate, but did not give us the other that was asked for and recommended by the commissioners, namely, one at the $600 rate. Unless we have two teachers we can not possibly use that building; two officers must always be on duty.

The second teacher we need is one of the $600 grade. I think you will readily see, Mr. Chairman, that it is imperatively necessary that we shall get this additional item. I think it was overlooked in the House through accident, because the committee seemed to be thoroughly impressed with the necessity for providing additional officers to enable us to use the new building.

The other point to which I wish to call your attention is the compensation for the engineer and assistant engineer. You have given us a heating plant which heats all of the buildings. This heating plant carries high steam pressure. In addition to that there are two steam engines, one electric engine, and one steam pump. In the past we could get ordinary firemen to discharge the duty of keeping ordinary boilers in proper working order for $50 and $40, respectively, but we can not get engineers to run this high-pressure plant for any such money.

The commissioners have recommended an increase to $720 for the engineer; but we respectfully ask for $60 more, namely, for $780, because, after most diligent inquiry in every direction, we find that we can not possibly get competent engineers for less than $780.

In the case of the assistant engineer, we likewise ask for an increase in his pay of $180 a year, making it $660. We have to pay a premium on sobriety. Under old conditions we could get men who could do the work which was then required for the money we were allowed to pay; but we can not often get competent, sober, and industrious men for that amount of money. We have these high-pressure boilers going all the time, and the competency of the engineers is a source of great anxiety to our board. At present we have two men who are thoroughly competent and reliable, but they remain only under the expectation and belief that their pay will be increased.

Senator SMITH of Maryland. How many hours are their services required?

Mr. McGILL. The engineer goes on duty at 5 in the morning and quits at 9 at night. The assistant engineer relieves him when he is off duty, which is one day in the week and every other Sunday; and the assistant engineer has to do all of the mechanical work that is necessary around the various buildings.

Senator SMITH of Maryland. What do you mean by "mechanical work"?

Mr. McGILL. We have innumerable fixtures to be cared for all the time—all the steam pipes, the water pipes, filters, ranges, electric wiring, and many other things on the grounds.

Senator SMITH of Maryland. What is the size of that building?

Mr. McGILL. We have four buildings, Senator. Senator Dillingham was out there with us a few years ago and Senator Gallinger is quite familiar with the conditions there. I am sorry we have not had the pleasure of taking you out there. We have three buildings for the girls and one for the male employees. The first, the old building, known as the administration or house building, houses 26 girls and several of the teaching corps. The preparatory building houses 54, I am sorry to say, because that is double the number it ought to have. The new building will house 26.

Senator SMITH of Maryland. That is 106 pupils, then, as I understand?

Mr. McGILL. Yes, sir.

Senator SMITH of Maryland. How many teachers have you altogether?

Mr. McGILL. We have 9 regular teachers.

Senator SMITH of Maryland. For 106 pupils?

Mr. McGILL. Yes, sir. The teachers are pretty well worked all the time. They are on duty very long hours. As one of them said the other day, frequently she begins duty at 5 o'clock in the morning and is working until 9 o'clock at night.

Senator SMITH of Maryland. That is about 1 teacher to every 12 pupils?

Mr. McGill. Yes, sir.

Senator Smith of Maryland. That is what you have now?

Mr. McGill. I have not figured it out, Senator.

Senator Smith of Maryland. You say you have 9 teachers?

Mr. McGill. Yes, sir; I think that is the number.

Senator Smith of Maryland. That would be about 12 pupils to a teacher.

Mr. McGill. Senator, if you will allow me, I will explain the conditions which surround us. It is not a question of a teacher for a fixed number of girls, as in public and private schools, but each officer is head of a particular department and these departments are maintained in each of the buildings. The groups in each building are separate from those in the other building. In the preparatory building we have a housekeeper, a school-teacher, a sewing teacher, and a laundry teacher. In the honor building we likewise have a housekeeper; a school-teacher, a domestic science teacher, and a teacher in charge of sewing and laundry work. All of the girls are required to work in each and every department of the school. They have to divide up their days in the different departments.

In the new building we need an officer in charge of sewing and laundry and another officer as school-teacher.

We can never leave these girls alone. The teachers, as officers, have to be constantly in attendance upon them; and if a teacher goes off duty for any length of time, no matter how short, another has to take her place. We have a substitute teacher, who is on duty the entire year, because, in order to divide up the time among the teachers for their vacational periods, there is always one teacher off duty for a week or two weeks at a time only, but the substitute teacher must take the department of the absent teacher.

These women are hard-worked, and there are no employees under the Government who earn their money harder than they do. It is utterly impossible for us to utilize this additional building without an additional school-teacher at $600. That is all I have to say, sir.

PUBLIC LIBRARY.

STATEMENT OF THEODORE W. NOYES, PRESIDENT OF THE BOARD OF TRUSTEES OF THE PUBLIC LIBRARY.

Mr. Noyes. Mr. Chairman and Senators, the reasons why the library appropriation, in our opinion, should be in conformity with the commissioners' estimates have been fully presented in the hearing before the House Appropriations Committee, and doubtless will receive careful consideration from you; but the cold facts and figures of the printed page are uninviting and unimpressive. I wish, if only for two or three minutes, to try to bring vividly before you the deep personal conviction of the library trustees that in the public interest and in fair recognition of the usefulness of the library and of the benefits conferred on the community by its activities the library provision proposed by the commissioners should be granted in its entirety and held in conference.

Our keen and profound interest in the library has nothing in it that is selfish or that is reckless of other municipal needs. We are convinced that a careful reading of the report of the hearing before the House committee will satisfy you that the library is doing the finest kind of educational work in this community, a work increasing in strength and volume and improving in quality every year.

Senator DILLINGHAM. You are asking, Mr. Noyes, for the items which were estimated for, but omitted in the House bill?

Mr. NOYES. Yes, Senator.

Senator SMITH of Maryland. Then, you are also asking for the additional salaries that have been omitted?

Mr. NOYES. Yes, Mr. Chairman.

Senator SMITH of Maryland. You are asking not only for increases in the salaries of those employed at present, but for an increased number?

Mr. NOYES. Yes; we are asking that the commissioners' estimates be adopted in their entirety. The commissioners' estimates cover both some increases in salaries and some new positions. We feel that if you will consider the facts and figures that were presented in the House hearing you will be convinced that while this work of the library, representing its usefulness and activity, has wonderfully increased, the library maintenance provision (at no time adequate) has been comparatively and practically at a standstill for four or five years; that the resulting condition of a library force overworked and underpaid is unmistakably indicated, in the first place, by an excessive percentage of resignations from the force, ranging from 20 to 53 per cent every year during the last seven years; that inadequacy of maintenance is further indicated by comparisons of every conceivable sort with the library maintenance appropriations of other American cities approximating Washington in size and in the scope of their library work; that while our library, in the expert opinion, as we think, of the Librarian of Congress, is " the most intelligently active for its size and constituency within the entire country "—I am quoting his words—its maintenance appropriation is far less than that of the great majority of the 26 American cities, both larger and smaller, that approximate it in size.

That is the showing in regard to the aggregate library expenditures. There are cities smaller than Washington that spend on their libraries twice what is proposed, even with these enlarged estimates—cities like Minneapolis. They are all enumerated in our hearing before the House committee.

Then we take up the matter of per capita expenditure for libraries, and we show that out of these 26 cities, including Washington, 20 have a larger per capita expenditure for library purposes.

Then we examine into the percentage of library expenditure out of the total of municipal expenditure. The census returns of 1910 are analyzed, wherein the library expenditures of 184 cities having over 30,000 population are compared. The library expenditure of Washington is a smaller percentage of the total expenditure than 172 out of the 184 cities; and of the dozen that have a smaller percentage of library expenditures, some of them have no libraries at all. The percentage of expenditure in Washington is eight-tenths of 1 per cent of the total expenditure. The average expenditure of the whole 184 cities is 1.6 per cent. Washington's average is just one-half of that of these 184 cities. There is not a city in the States represented by the members of this subcommittee the library expenditure of which is so small a percentage of the total expenditure as in Washington; and if it were put in its proper relation to the other expenditures—I mean by "proper" the relation of the average municipality in the United States—it could be doubled without being out of proportion.

Our contention before the House committee was that the appropriation for the library never had been put on an adequate basis, and that therefore the slight percentage of increase that would be proper, once it had been put upon that basis, was not now fairly to be applied; that there was need of a more radical readjustment. The commissioners this year have been convinced of the long delay, perhaps inevitable, in meeting the absolute needs of the library and of the accumulated obligations concerning it, and have recommended a considerable increase in the library's appropriation; and in their remarks before the House committee they indicated the earnestness of their belief that the library's contention in respect to its needs is well founded. The House committee and the House have responded to a certain extent to this recommendation of the commissioners, as far as could be expected and is compatible with a reduction of the commissioners' estimates by about $3,000,000.

Senator SMITH of Maryland. $3,000,000?

Mr. NOYES. $3.000,000; yes, sir—I mean, the total reduction. The House has cut down the commissioners' total estimates by $3,000,000 in making the appropriation; and in doing that there was considerable cutting in the library estimates, as in other respects.

One item that was favorably reported by the House committee, and went out on a point of order in the House, was an increase of the salary of the librarian. The librarian not being able to speak on that subject himself, I wish in a few words to call especial attention to that increase as among the needs of the library.

The librarian is now receiving $3,500 per year for services which in other libraries of the size and usefulness and activity of our own are compensated by salaries of $5,000 or more. In the report of the House hearing a list of those cities, with the salaries. is given. This list includes a number of cities much smaller than Washington, like Springfield, Mass., and others.

The trustees, in their estimates, from year to year have urged that the salary of the librarian should be increased. Our librarian is one of the most progressive and efficient of the leading librarians of the country. We have urged that his salary be increased from $3,500 to $5,000. The commissioners, in pruning the library estimates in order to bring the total estimates within the estimated revenue, have recommended that his salary be fixed at $4,500. This increase the trustees urge most earnestly and emphatically.

In this connection I wish to call your attention to the letter of Dr. Putnam, the Librarian of Congress, printed in the House hearing, which pays a well-deserved compliment to the librarian, and suggests the danger of our loss of him to some other city which pays more adequate librarian's compensation.

We most earnestly urge that you approve all the commissioners' library estimates, and adhere to them firmly in conference.

We very heartily wish it were possible that you could get the time to visit the library, Mr. Chairman, and to convince yourselves at first hand of its activity and usefulness, and the fine part it plays in the educational life of the Capital, as an integral part of the local educational system under the law, and on national lines as the circulating complement of the great reference Library of Congress.

STATEMENT OF GEORGE F. BOWERMAN, LIBRARIAN OF THE PUBLIC LIBRARY.

Mr. BOWERMAN. Mr. Chairman and Senators, I shall make only a few introductory remarks, because I know your time is limited. Lest the committee might think that in view of the fact that the Public Library's present appropriations total but $63,880 and that the library estimates—as approved by the commissioners—total but $90,620, the library is after all a relatively insignificant affair and the work it accomplishes is small and that therefore its needs must be small, I desire to mention a few facts that have not been brought out in the House hearings.

Even though the library has as yet been able to build and conduct but one branch instead of the system of branches needed to make library facilities accessible to the homes of any besides those who live near the central library or its one branch or who come long distances to visit it, yet the library now has enrolled as regular users of its educational advantages just under 47,000 persons. Although this number seems large, yet, judging by the experience of Minneapolis, Cleveland, and Pittsburgh, which have systems of branches, we should have at least 25 per cent of the total population registered as library users, or a total of 88,000 such registered users. To our present registration of 47,000 there should be added at least 5,000 children who secure public-library books from the school duplicate collection without being formally registered at the library, so that not less than 52,000 persons in Washington enjoy some form of public-library advantages, and this on an appropriation of $63,880. Compare with this the fact that the board of education spends about $3,000,000 annually on its enrollment of about 61,000 persons. The educational process of the schools is, of course, more expensive than that of the library, but we believe that the discrepancy of expenditures is too great. We do not argue that the board of education should have less, but we submit that the library should have more. Out of the library's 52,000 users about 15,000 only of school children are reached, whereas the library ought to be able to offer its advantages to the entire school population to help them in their school work and to train them up to be library users when they leave school. The remaining 37,000 users of the library's advantages have passed beyond the school age and the educational resources afforded to them by the library constitute practically the only publicly supported educational advantages they have. We submit that our funds are totally inadequate to do justice to this highly important work of furnishing adult education through the means of the library.

, Another measure of the use of the library is the record of attendance. It is not possible to keep exact records of attendance every day in the year, but records on certain typical days are kept. From them it is estimated that not less than 730,000 persons visit the central library and the Takoma branch in the course of the year. Practically none of such visits are made solely for the purpose of sightseeing, as is undoubtedly the case with a considerable percentage of the 888,493 visits made to the Library of Congress in the fiscal year 1913.

What have we accomplished with our meager and inadequate appropriation? I shall not attempt to answer that question except to refer to the House hearings, especially to the summary given by President Noyes on pages 147 and 148. I do wish to call attention to the fact that although our appropriation for 1913 of $63,000 was 6 per cent less than it was in 1912 ($67,140), yet the library's work as measured by its home circulation of books increased 5½ per cent (from 650,527 volumes to 686,278 volumes) and its circulation of mounted pictures increased 33 per cent (from 54,568 to 72,450) over the previous year. I would also like to call attention to the table printed on page 169 of the House hearings, which shows that although in the nine years from 1904 to 1913 there had been an increase of 71 per cent in library appropriations ($36,280 to $63,000), in the same period there had been an increase of 147 per cent in the library's work as measured by the home circulation of books (278,178 volumes to 686,278 volumes), and that in the same time the percentage of fiction in that circulation had been reduced 26 per cent (from 84 per cent to 58 per cent).

I desire also to emphasize the fact that in adding 5 new positions to the library force the House chose them from the bottom of the list of estimates; that is, the new positions granted were the low-priced ones; and that in one instance—that of the assistant in charge of school work—the salary appropriated for ($900) was $100 less than the commissioners' estimate, which in turn was $200 less than the library trustees thought the responsibilities of the place required. We are, of course, grateful for these increases in our numbers. I wish to point out, however, that this plan—and it is the one that has almost always been followed in dealing with the personnel of the library—of making additions at very low salaries does not strengthen us where we are weakest; that it does not afford us the means of making some very much overdue promotions and thus of stemming the wasteful and disorganizing tide of resignations; does not enable us to tone up our staff by securing from time to time some strong, well-trained people from the outside; does not really enable us to pay such salaries as would place the library on a proper professional basis.

In this connection I would point out that this plan of paying such meager salaries as those appropriated for has resulted in resignations from our staff of trained, professional, educational workers of from 20 per cent to as high as 50 per cent in a single year. The burden of work occasioned by constantly increasing demands of readers and of worry, occasioned by insufficient compensation has had and is constantly having its expected results. Those who can, and they are frequently the best trained and most competent, get positions elsewhere; those who can not become discouraged, the percentage of absences on account of illness is high and complete breakdowns are not infrequent. Occasional illness is serious to the library because the overworked staff is so near the breaking point. Protracted illness is serious to the library because of the loss of service during the period of sick leave and very serious to the individuals because of ultimate loss of pay and the fact that compensation is too meager to enable them to save anything for such "rainy days."

I have in mind a case of one assistant who has been away for several months and lost her place, has had to borrow money from her doctor to pay her sanatorium expenses, and is now having to borrow from her relatives and friends in order that she may go abroad for a period of recuperation. We hope when she gets back we shall be able to pay her a good salary, so that she will not have so narrow a margin as she has had heretofore.

Senator SMITH of Maryland. What salary is she getting?

Mr. BOWERMAN. $1,000 a year, and she has been contributing out of her salary to the support of an aunt, and she has not been able to lay up anything for a rainy day.

Senator SMITH of Maryland. I am not arguing against your asking for an increase of her salary, but at the same time the Government can not take into consideration what its employees have to do for other people. The sole question is whether the compensation is adequate for the service rendered.

Mr. BOWERMAN. In this particular case she is our children's librarian. She is one of the foremost people in that particular branch of library work in the country.

Senator SMITH of Maryland. I am not questioning as to what she should have, but that she has other people to support, that we can not take into consideration. The question is whether she is getting sufficient compensation for the service rendered.

Mr. BOWERMAN. Well, she is not. It does not measure up to the salaries that are being paid elsewhere for equivalent service; and manifestly, even if she had only herself to support out of that salary of $1,000 a year, she could not lay up very much. As she is getting on into mature life, and has for years been a trained professional worker, she ought certainly to have such a salary as would enable her to lay by something.

Senator GALLINGER. In this particular case I think there is no estimate for the increase of salary.

Mr. BOWERMAN. What we have done, Mr. Senator, is this: She is now on our rolls as the children's librarian at the central library. We have in our estimates a position to which I wish to call special attention—the position of director of children's work, at a salary of $1,500; that is, to have supervision of the work at the central library, at the branch libraries, the stations, and in the schools, etc. She fully measures up to that position, is thoroughly competent to fill it, and we should be perfectly justified in transferring her to that position.

Senator GALLINGER. Provided that new position is created?

Mr. BOWERMAN. Yes; that is the idea.

Senator GALLINGER. You would transfer this particular employee to that position?

Mr. BOWERMAN. Yes, sir; when she comes back from abroad we should like very much to pay her $1,500, which is no more than what she is worth; and the library would be the gainer, because she then would not be constantly harassed as she is now. One of the things that contributed to her nervous breakdown is the fact that she has not been able to lay up anything.

Senator GALLINGER. What are her special duties? It says here "Especially children's library." Exactly what does that signify?

Mr. BOWERMAN. That signifies this: She had the choice of all the juvenile books bought for the library. I defer to her completely in the matter of the selection of juvenile books. Out of the vast number of books that are constantly being published she sifts the occasional good book. She has the responsibility of deciding as to the books that should be placed in the hands of the children. She gives counsel to parents and teachers in the choice of books for their children to read, both those secured from the library and those purchased for the family. She trains up her assistants to ideas of best practice in this highly important work. She would supervise this work not only in the central library but at the Takoma branch, at the stations in social settlements, the work in the schools, and in the home libraries, such as we have. She addresses mothers' clubs, teachers' associations, the Twentieth Century Club, etc., and she does a lot of similar work outside of the library; because library work, as we conceive of our duties, consists in part in training the whole community in the choice of the best books and in the reading of the best books, to get rid of the chaff, the rubbish, that is constantly being published, and to get the most good from an intelligent use of books.

Senator SMITH of Maryland. Those are her duties now under the present conditions?

Mr. BOWERMAN. We have interpreted them broadly. She is a person who would never do anything else but interpret her duties broadly. She is really measuring up to the duties of the director of children's work, although she has the minor title and the minor salary.

Mr. Chairman, we believe our estimates as a whole are modest, are moderate, and that we require, in order to measure up to the needs of the situation, our estimates entire, without omitting one single item. If you wish me to, I will mention two or three items of special importance.

In addition to the director of children's work, I would mention the chief of the industrial division. That is a department we have been conducting for a number of years, and it is doing a magnificent work with the people, for the students in the Armstrong Manual Training School and in the McKinley Manual Training School, supplementing their work, and also in furnishing merchants, engineers, and mechanics with the technical literature that they need. But this department has never been properly supported. We have never had a properly trained person to place in charge of this work. We need somebody who has had training at, say, Cornell University or the Massachusetts Institute of Technology, technological training, who will be able to choose books and give special advice to readers in the choice of books. We need an expert of that class. We have had two or three young men, graduates of the McKinley Manual Training School, but now we have lost them because of our inability to pay a proper salary and we have at present a woman in charge. We ought to have a man in charge there, and a man who is an expert in that field.

Senator GALLINGER. Without pretending to have expert knowledge as to library work, it strikes me that you are rather encroaching on the public-school work. You are not only running your library as a circulating library, but you are extending your activities into the schools. Do you think that is wise?

Mr. BOWERMAN. Mr. Chairman and Mr. Senator, I certainly do; and it is the tendency of all the public libraries of the country to hook up the library with the school. In that we have the utmost cooperation from the schools. Dr. Davidson was a member of our board, and he was thoroughly in sympathy with us and encouraged us to do this. We want to have every child while he is in the school to get the library habit, to know that there is a library here, to make use of the public-library books, in order to help him in the school work—and the teachers are constantly sending the children to us and are coming to us for the material to use in the schools—and also so that we may establish the children as readers, so that they will become lifelong library users and carry on their education to the end of life. Unless you make the contact when the children are in school you are likely never to get in contact with them.

Senator GALLINGER. You have a library in pretty nearly every public school in the District now, have you not?

Mr. BOWERMAN. We have not as many as we should like.

Senator GALLINGER. For instance, how many volumes have you in any one of the high schools of the District?

Mr. BOWERMAN. As to that, the high schools have their own libraries. We are loaning specific books to them to meet specific needs, and sometimes we might have two or three hundred volumes there; but they are there only because the people have asked specifically for those books to supplement their own inadequate collections and to meet the particular needs of the teachers and pupils as they arise.

Senator GALLINGER. Suppose you send those books into the schools and your library patrons call for those books; I suppose you want to purchase new books to take the place of those that you have sent into the schools?

Mr. BOWERMAN. On that head, the particular books that the schools are asking for and general readers are asking for concurrently, we try to duplicate. However, we only send to the schools a part of the total stock of a given title likely to be in demand by general readers, so as not to deplete our collections. Thus we are able also to loan copies to people in the general population.

Senator SMITH of Maryland. If these books you speak of are so useful to the schools, is it not reasonable to suppose that the schools themselves would supply their libraries with them?

Mr. BOWERMAN. I am glad you asked that question.

There are certain books that the schools ought to have as a part of their regular equipment—dictionaries and encyclopedias—and books that are textbooks or semitextbooks, which are wanted every year for long periods. There are, however, certain other books that are wanted, in the case of history, for example, when a particular period is under consideration. A certain book will be wanted for only a few days or for a week or so, and in a good many cases all of the schools will not be studying that same period at exactly the same time, so that we will loan a given book first to one school and then when it is sent back it will be sent to another school. On that basis it is an economy to the District of Columbia for the Public Library to have those books and to loan them first to one school and then to another, and, in addition to that, during the other times of the year to loan them to the citizens at large.

Senator GALLINGER. In connection with the question which I propounded a moment ago, when I said that it seemed to me you are extending your activities into the schools, I find that you made an estimate asking for this language to be inserted, "Including the conducting of stations in public-school buildings, playgrounds, social settlements, and in other suitable agencies."

Do you really think that is a function of the public library?

Mr. BOWERMAN. I do, Mr. Senator.

Mr. NOYES. May I interrupt for a moment?

Mr. BOWERMAN. Certainly.

Mr. NOYES. I would call attention to the fact that in the law creating the library, in respect to which Senator Gallinger played a very helpful part; in the organic act, so to speak, of the library it is declared "a supplement of the public educational system of said District."

Senator GALLINGER. Yes.

Mr. NOYES. Of the three classes of the community which clamored and made the popular demand for this circulating library, the school children were at the head. The second class included the workmen of the District, some 20,000, and the third class was the Government clerks. But first of all were the school children; and this library, in pursuance of the very function and purpose announced in the organic act, has made itself an integral part of the educational system of the city and is doing a wonderful work in that connection as a free university of the people.

Senator GALLINGER. Yes; now let me ask, as a practical matter, do you propose to establish a branch library on a small scale in connection with each of the playgrounds? How are you going to do it? If you do it, you will have to have somebody in charge of the books, and new positions will have to be created. Is not that so?

Mr. BOWERMAN. On that question, it is really an economy to have the distribution of books through those agencies.

Senator GALLINGER. We supposed that in establishing playgrounds we were getting the children away from books and away from school work.

Mr. BOWERMAN. I wish you could ask questions of Mr. Martin on that point.

Senator GALLINGER. Well, doubtless Mr. Martin would like to enlarge his jurisdiction, as every official does.

Mr. BOWERMAN. The point I would make is that he is in cooperation with us. This is how it works at the playgrounds. Boys and girls go out and play and they get thoroughly tired on the physical side, and then they will go to the shelter, and they are glad to sit down and read there, and they do that very thing. The director of the playground takes care of the children and has the supervision of the traveling library that is sent there and distributes the books to them for use at the playground and to take home.

The same thing is true of the great work that we are already doing in these schools. My report shows that last year we had a little stock of only 6,000 volumes for our school work. We sent these books out in little collections, traveling libraries of from 30 to 50 volumes each, to 287 schoolrooms in 86 grammar schools. From these little collections—with the teachers handling them and sometimes in the upper grades with pupil librarians in charge of them—there was a total circulation from those 6,000 volumes of 76,339 volumes. I pointed out to the House committee that the city of Galveston, Tex., with a public library of 50,000 volumes, had a total circulation in that city of 73,000 volumes only. This circulation of over 76,000 volumes was accomplished with a comparatively small investment for the books themselves, with services (part time only) of two people, who had charge of the books at the main library and made them up in these groups in response to the demands of the teachers, and with slight expenses for transportation charges. All the remaining work of distribution of these books to the children is performed by the teachers, who are thoroughly in sympathy with the plan and who take to it with very great avidity, because they realize that it aids them in their teaching work. In addition to the children reading these books the parents often read them also. That happens again and again. The parents, particularly in the humbler classes, often really have child minds and want child literature. It happens again and again that a little girl will have her book overdue; it is not brought back promptly, and why not? Why, her mother was reading it—a fairy tale, for instance—or even the father may have been reading it if it were a history or a story. Often we find that the older brothers and sisters who have dropped out of school are reading these books. So we would defend this plan as being an economy in the distribution of these books to the school children in this way.

We also hope that the time is going to come when you are going to allow us something more than the distribution of the books through schoolrooms in the way I have described. There may be in certain outlying districts unused schoolrooms in buildings that are sufficiently large so that we may be able to establish small branch libraries in such school buildings. This is what we have in mind to make a beginning of in a modest way with the increase of this fund from $1,000 to $2,000 that we have asked for. At the present time we are doing something of the kind at the John Eaton School in Cleveland Park, and in Georgetown at the Hyde School, with the help of contributions of citizens, who are furnishing the money to us to enable us to employ the librarians. By this means the station at Cleveland Park is kept open on Wednesday, and the one at the Hyde School is open on Thursday for two hours—once a week at each place. That is being done at a very slight expense, making possible a distribution of books to people who otherwise would not have them at all.

The president of the board suggests that I speak a little about the use at the main library of the children's room. We can get only part of the children to come, because they can not come the long distances, their parents being afraid they will be injured by the cars, so that we are able to get for the most part only the children who live comparatively near. But they come from that limited area and use the room to a large extent, and take books home. In addition, we have lectures. We get Mr. Oldys to come in and give them talks on birds; we give them travel talks, and we tell them stories of classic myths, fairy tales, and other great pieces of literature, and thus direct their reading along right lines, so that they will choose the best books.

Senator GALLINGER. I believe, Mr. Bowerman, that you say you have about 58 per cent now of fiction?

Mr. BOWERMAN. Fifty-eight per cent of fiction. We began with 84 per cent of fiction, and it has decreased now to 58 per cent.

Senator GALLINGER. How in the world did they ever get 84 per cent of fiction in that library? Who made the selections?

Mr. BOWERMAN. Let me explain that. It was not 84 per cent of the entire collection that was fiction, but 84 per cent of the books taken out were fiction. The reason of it was just this, and the reasons we got away from it are these: Few books in the beginning were on open shelves, and there was nothing on those open shelves but fiction. Practically nothing in the way of expert advice was then given, as that feature was not developed at that time. As a result the people who came in followed the line of least resistance and got the books they could get easily, so that perhaps in some cases in desperation, not having help, they took the fiction when, perhaps, they could have been led to take the books of other classes. In the development I have followed out here we have been eliminating the lower grade of fiction, and we have been choosing and purchasing the fiction more wisely. We have been securing the books recommended by the catalogues issued by the American Library Association, and similar guides, and in giving a generous supply of the best fiction and eliminating altogether the poor, weak stuff.

In addition to that we have constantly increased the work (and we wish to develop it still further if you will give us better paid people) of giving more time and attention to the guiding of the reading of people and giving them expert advice. By this means when a man comes and wants to study along a particular line, instead of letting him flounder around and not get anything serviceable, and go away in despair, perhaps, with a book of fiction, we ascertain his needs and find him something exactly suited to those needs. In this way the library, instead of being a literary barroom where he comes to take a fiction tipple, becomes an educational institution where the study side of reading is developed, where people can carry on their education during childhood and during the whole of life. By following this plan we have reduced the circulation of fiction from 84 per cent to 58 per cent, and my idea is to reduce it to 50 per cent or less; and I will be able to do it if you will increase our force of trained people, on the one hand, and also increase our appropriation for the purchase of books, on the other. Take Ambassador Bryce's "South America." At the present time we have 2 or 3 copies. If we had 10 or 15 copies, every single one of those would be in circulation all the time. What would be the result? The large circulation of that moderately expensive book would correspondingly reduce the percentage of fiction circulated in the library's whole circulation. There are many books of non-fiction which are in demand and for which we have very urgent calls that we can not buy at all or that we can not buy until they are old and obtainable at second hand.

Senator GALLINGER. If you turned the appropriation in that direction for a number of years and bought good books and let your supply of fiction remain as it is is now, that would remedy the situation somewhat. It seems to me you have fiction enough for some time to come.

Mr. BOWERMAN. We do not buy any fiction that is not in demand.

Senator GALLINGER. Suppose you did not buy any for several years?

Mr. BOWERMAN. The result would be this: There are certain people with whom you have to use fiction as stepping-stones. The Goldenberg girls, the shopgirls in the store across the way, are people we are very eager to capture and get them into the library to be readers. What is the process? They will come in and get a story book, harmless, and helpful in the way of developing their sympathies; a good deal better book than the so-called family story papers that they would perhaps read if they did not get the book at the library. They come to us and read those books; and then in an ingratiating way, if you will, with the help of skilled people, we can here and there induce those girls to take books of travel or books of biography, and gradually lead them on to these other things. But if we did not have the books of fiction for them, they would turn the cold shoulder on us and not come at all.

Senator SMITH of Maryland. Senator Gallinger's idea is that you have enough of that fiction now that is all right, and that you should for a year or two buy no more fiction, but use the money that you have now for more useful books.

Mr. BOWERMAN. The great books of fiction—Dickens, Scott, Hugo, Dumas, etc.—keep wearing out all the time. We have to keep replacing them. We have to keep a balance. It is good library practice; and on that basis, Mr. Chairman, I am following the practice generally agreed upon by the leaders in the profession, what Dr. Steiner does in Baltimore and what we all of us must do. There has been a good deal of talk—and Mr. Carnegie has made the suggestion—about never buying a book of fiction until it is a year old. Emerson suggested that one should never read any book until it was a year old. If that rule were followed many of them one would never buy at all, because they die before the end of a year. We only select here and there the better ones. Out of the great mass of books of fiction that come to us on approval we take only about 1 in 10, and the rest of the mass is rejected. But we ought not to reject all of them. Take a book, for instance, like V V's Eyes, a book that is a sociological study, a book that has put into concrete form a study of present-day problems. It is very helpful, and it is in great demand. The cultured people of the community want it and they are helped by it.

Senator GALLINGER. It is helpful if it is sound. Because it is a sociological study it does not follow that it is a sound study. There are many modern innovations that are not helpful.

Mr. BOWERMAN. On that basis, we do not decide whether a book is sound in its teachings or not. This is a democratic institution, and we believe if a work comes up to a good literary standard and is not indecent that book is worthy of attention and should be given to the public if it measures up to reasonably good standards.

Senator GALLINGER. My suggestion is an old-fashioned suggestion and is not along the line of modern thought, and I do not intend to follow that line very much. My thought was that about four-fifths of the fiction of the present day is worse than trash, or that it is trash.

Mr. BOWERMAN. Yes.

Senator GALLINGER. And taking even those that they say are the best books that are on the market. I have had occasion myself to review three within the last month, and I would not want to put them into the hands of children. I do not know but the modern child wants that sort of thing and ought to have it; but they are not helpful, they are not ennobling, they are not elevating; and I urge the thought for what it is worth—it may not be worth anything—that you ought to minimize the distribution of books of that kind to as great an extent as possible. Of course people will have them; they will buy yellow-covered literature if they can not get a better class, very likely; but there are so many good books in the world to-day that children, and adults, too, ought to read that I do not think we ought to cater to their taste for fiction. That is simply my old-fashioned thought.

Mr. NOYES. Senator, I think we all agree with you. Individually I know that I do. It is possibly the result of thinking along that line that the percentage of use of fiction by the readers in the library has been reduced from 84 per cent to 58 per cent.

Senator GALLINGER. That is very gratifying.

Mr. NOYES. And that is a very low percentage, as public libraries go.

Mr. BOWERMAN. Yes.

Mr. NOYES. As Dr. Bowerman has suggested, the basic reading in the public library, beginning with those who first read, is along the line of fiction. You know how it is in the development of ourselves as readers; we begin with fiction, with what appeals to the imagination, and we develop into better and better reading; and that is the process which has been going on in our public library, and it is in accordance with the general platform and policy of book reading that you have announced. Of course, we could not run the library as a public library and cut out the fiction altogether.

Senator SMITH of Maryland. How long have you been in reducing the perecntage from 84 to 58?

Mr. NOYES. Nine years, I believe.

Mr. BOWERMAN. Nine years.

Mr. NOYES. And of course the improvement has been in the taste of the readers through the education that they have received through the efforts of Dr. Bowerman and his assistants at the library. It has not been primarily that we have been buying less fiction.

Senator SMITH of Maryland. Then you are buying in proportion less books of fiction than you formerly did?

Mr. NOYES. We are, because we have educated the readers to want less.

Senator SMITH of Maryland. There is not the same demand for books of fiction?

Mr. NOYES. In the very beginning, Mr. Chairman, the chaiman of our books committee was Mr. Spofford, Librarian of Congress, and whatever criticism might be made of his selection of books for the library, the selection of a superfluity of fiction would not be one.

Mr. BOWERMAN. The present chairman of the books committee, Dr. Putnam, now Librarian of Congress, has the same idea. Mr. Chairman, I think I may say that Senator Gallinger and I are in agreement on this. It has been my hobby. A file of my reports will show that I have every year dwelt upon that very point of the reduction in the reading of fiction, I would say that in my opinion Senator Gallinger's estimate that four-fifths of the books of fiction published are trash would be too small. In our experience it would be too small. I think it is probably nearer nine-tenths that are trash.

Mr. NOYES. An awful lot of them are trash.

Mr. BOWERMAN. And I should be the last man to be criticized in the library profession as one who would have too much fiction.

Senator GALLINGER. Yes; I remember that you have made that statement, and we have taken it in good faith.

Mr. BOWERMAN. Yes, sir.

Senator GALLINGER. Now, if the chairman will permit me, I will ask you about another matter. There is here a list of 12 items estimated for and omitted by the House. Will you point out, say, one-half of that number that you think most important?

Mr. BOWERMAN. I would select these as being most important: The director of children's work, $1,500; the chief of the order and accessions division, $1,200; the chief of the industrial division, $1,200; the chief of the catalogue division, $1,500; one additional stenographer and typewriter, $720; one janitor, $480. We need them all; but those are the ones I would point out. They are people we need, and they are all of them, except the stenographer, and the janitor, the more highly paid people I spoke of in my opening remarks as absolutely necessary to tone up the library service. If we could get those positions it would offer us an opportunity for promotions and for strengthening the force.

Senator SMITH of Maryland. You have now a janitor, I assume.

Mr. BOWERMAN. We now have two janitors at the central library, but this is an additional janitor we are asking for. On that point I would say that we have the same number of janitors that we had in the beginning when we had 65,000 volumes, and now we have 165,000 volumes. When we were using only a small portion of our main building we had two janitors, and now that we are using every inch of it we have still but two. The point is that we should like to go over all the books in the library two or three times in each year in order to keep them clean, and we can not do it with the present janitor force. I am envious of the Library of Congress in its ability to keep the library building clean. I should like to be a good housekeeper, too, and keep my establishment as clean as the Library of Congress is kept. I am often ashamed because of the condition of things. For one thing we can not wash our windows often enough.

Senator SMITH of Maryland. Is it necessary from a sanitary standpoint to have this janitor to keep your books clean?

Mr. BOWERMAN. Certainly we ought never, when a person calls for a book, to have it come out with the top of it all covered with dust. That happens, because we can not go over the books often enough. Then we ought to keep the whole building cleaner. I am chagrined whenever a Senator or Member of Congress comes down there—and, by the way, they do not come as often as we should like to have them—to have them look out of a window the glass of which is all covered with flyspecks or covered with dust or splashed and smeared and streaked. I should like to be able to have the entire building perfectly clean at all times.

Let me, in addition to the personnel, mention one or two other points. I wish, Mr. Chairman, it were possible to make all the increases mentioned here; but let me ask you particularly to increase the salary of our engineer. The engineer now gets $1,080. He ought to have $1,200. He is an exceptionally good man.

Senator SMITH of Maryland. Ought not $1,080 get a good man?

Mr. BOWERMAN. I doubt if one could often get a good man to take care of a $375,000 building and a big heating plant such as ours is, and to do all the work that he does. Let me tell you the way in which he is so very valuable. In a moment I am going to lay special emphasis on the desirability of increasing our fund for contingent expenses.

Senator SMITH of Maryland. We do not want to hurry you, but we have others to come after you, and so I will ask you to be as brief as possible, if you please.

Mr. BOWERMAN. I will do so, Mr. Chairman. One way in which we have been able to get along for all these years with as small a contingent fund as we have is that that man is a specially competent man in the way of making minor repairs. We get a small quantity of material for 15 cents or 25 cents, and he will not infrequently do a job that would cost us $30 or $40 if we had to have it done outside. He is always on the job. He is the most faithful and efficient man that I have ever had any experience with. He is not much on the literary side, but in the matter of being able to solve a problem of building administration, of a steam plant, he can usually put his finger on the difficulty without our having to send for a high-priced man to come and find out what is the matter and then make the repairs. He will usually find it out and then make the repairs himself. We have been recommending for about seven years that his salary be increased to $1,200, and I most heartily hope that it will be done, because he thoroughly earns that now.

Senator GALLINGER. There is one practical difficulty about that, and that is to differentiate between a man such as you describe this man to be, and a man who is not quite as competent. The result is that when we increase one item of that kind we will find 20 other engineers in other branches of the Government service who are getting $900 or $1,000 a year, who will think that they ought to have their salaries raised also. We have found that difficulty every year in dealing with these matters.

Mr. BOWERMAN. This man has been with the library from its beginning, and I would not know how to do without him, he is so much a fixture of the library.

Senator GALLINGER. Why, you would get another man, that is what you would do.

Mr. BOWERMAN. I have talked about him, describing him to other members of the library profession. I remember talking with one librarian who has been called up from one position to another until now he gets $9,200 as librarian of the Brooklyn Public Library, and who has been librarian successively of five large libraries, and he told me that in just one of those libraries did he have the kind of man I have described this man to be. He says they are very scarce; that you seldom find a man with the cleverness to do all these things, and that he is a very great acquisition.

In addition to personnel, Mr. Chairman, we also want more money for books; that is evident. We need them in order to buy the expensive books we so much need, to make it more and more an educational institution. But I want particularly to urge you to increase our contingent fund, as estimated, from $8,000 to $9,000.

The reasons for increasing the library's contingent fund as estimated are as follows: Our contingent fund of $8,000 is exactly the same as it was before the Takoma Park branch library building was erected, so that we now have to heat and light and repair and get supplies for two buildings on a fund that was not too large for one. This year we had a flood that ruined our elevator and cost us nearly $600. If we should have any other unusual drain on that fund it might be necessary to close up one or both buildings, and, of course, we do not want to do that. Second, the main building is now 11 years old and it costs us each year more for repairs. We ought to spend at once a considerable sum on it to keep it in good shape. For instance, the mortar is getting chipped out, and it ought to be pointed up. The putty is all off most of the windows, and it lets the rain in. There are a whole lot of those little things that we can not do that ought to be done. We simply haven't the money to make certain necessary repairs and improvements. Third, every year the increasing activities require more stationery, more materials, more supplies, and more light. Coal and practically all supplies are increasing in price. Fourth, the House amendment permits us to buy what we very much need, a motor delivery vehicle, but the permission will not help us unless we have the funds with which to get it. Unless the fund is increased as estimated we would be unable to avail ourselves of the permission, and we want very much to do it. We need it in the development work—this school extension work that we are trying to do at the present time. We simply can not do it unless our fund is increased.

On the question of the auxiliary boiler, since we appeared before the House committee we have had a serious time with our boiler. The expense was disproportionately high, because the repairs had to be made at night, when we have had to pay double time for the workmen on the repairs. The boiler had to be allowed to cool down, and we had to do the work after midnight, and we had to pay the men for making these repairs double price for night work. If we had two boilers we could let one of them cool down and run on the other while repairs were being made. Some of these times we shall have a breakdown that will force us to close up the library for several days, and, of course, we do not want to do that. We should like very much to have that auxiliary boiler.

I should be very glad to answer any questions. I thank you very much for the opportunity you have given me of making my statement, and I should like it very much if you could come down there so that we could visualize for you the work that we are doing there with very insufficient funds.

Senator GALLINGER. Mr. Bowerman, simply to verify my suggestion as to the danger of increasing this appropriation for the engineer—and doubtless he is a valuable man—I want to call your attention to the fact that the chief engineer at the Washington Asylum and Jail, which is an institution occupying several buildings, gets but $900 a year. At the Home for the Aged and Infirm the chief engineer gets but $1,000. That is down in Blue Plains. At the National Training School for Girls the engineer gets $600. At the Tuberculosis Hospital, which, you know, is quite an institution, the engineer gets $700. So it is all along the line. With the exception of the engineer at the Municipal Building, which is a great building, you will hardly find a case where the engineer gets over $1,000 a year, and in most cases he gets considerably less. That is not an argument against your suggestion, but to show you what difficulties we may run into, and what difficulties we do run into when off-hand we increase the salary of any one person who belongs to a class.

Senator SMITH of Maryland. The point Senator Gallinger makes is that this man is getting more than other men in similar positions elsewhere.

Mr. NOYES. In our House hearings we contrasted the pay that our assistants get—trained librarians—some of them getting only $480 a year, with the compensation in other branches of the Government, and we called attention to the fact that the clerks in the departments get a minimum pay of $720 a year. Of course if the outside scale is going to be applied as to engineers, we will be glad to have all our employees put on the same scale; and if that be done, the minute that contrast is made all along the line—and I admit that the contrast in respect to the engineer is to our disadvantage—if it were made all along the line there could not be any stronger support furnished for the contention that the salaries paid in the library are inadequate.

Senator GALLINGER. In all of these lower grades beyond a question they are inadequate. I do not believe any person in the year 1914 ought to be asked to work for $480 a year. I do not know how on earth a man can live on such a salary. If I had my way, I would increase the salary of every one of that class.

Mr. BOWERMAN. They live by their families contributing to their support. I made some calculations, as shown in my report. I invited members of my staff to hand in schedules showing how nearly their salaries went to paying their own expenses, and I found that with all of them, without exception, who were paid under $600 their families were contributing to their support, and a considerable number of them above that were, not being able to live and to have a proper vacation. These people are professional people, and they were not able to pay their expenses to go to the American Library Association meeting, as they ought to in order to keep in touch with the profession. They were simply unable to do that. Those figures show very conclusively that it can not be done.

Senator GALLINGER. You speak of having a proper vacation and you are arguing that the activities of this library ought to be extended into the schools. What do you think of the suggestion recently made by the United States Commissioner of Education that the school children ought not to have any vacation at all; that they ought to be compelled to work 12 months in the year; that they would be better off?

Mr. BOWERMAN. Newark has taken up that. It has something to be said for it in this respect. Let them have, if you please, nine months of literary training, and then let the other three months be devoted to school gardening, to handicraft training, to training in play, and that will keep them out of mischief. Also, during that time bring them to the library and let them spontaneously develop by reading books of their own selection.

Senator GALLINGER. That is a vacation at the expense of the Government.

Mr. BOWERMAN. I had reference, of course, to employees, not to those who are wards or are being instructed. On the question of a proper vacation, I had reference to the fact that the employees were not able to go away to a mountain resort or to the seashore and take a real recuperative vacation.

Senator SMITH of Maryland. Of course, that is outside of what we are discussing; but I was startled this morning to read that Mr. Claxton believed in no vacation for children.

Mr. BOWERMAN. I do not think that he meant that the children should be kept inside of a schoolhouse all the time.

Senator SMITH of Maryland. Perhaps not.

Mr. BOWMERMAN. I think he meant that they should have this handicraft training—training in gardening, and all that.

I think that is all I have to present, Mr. Chairman.

PURCHASE OF PATTERSON TRACT FOR NEW PARK.

STATEMENT OF CARLILE P. WINSLOW AND CHARLES J. BELL.

Senator SMITH of Maryland. The item you desire to speak to the committee on is in regard to the proposed Patterson park?

Mr. WINSLOW. I understand that there is a recommendation of the commissioners which was not included in the bill from the House, which is under consideration by your committee, and as one of the trustees of the estate owning this property, Mr. Charles J. Bell being also one of the trustees, I should like to address you on that matter.

Senator SMITH of Maryland. I understand that you are representing the owners of the property; is that it?

Mr. WINSLOW. Yes.

Senator SMITH of Maryland. The owners of the property who want to sell this land for a park; is that it?

Mr. WINSLOW. No, sir; the owners of the property which the Commissioners of the District of Columbia have recommended should be condemned for a public park.

Senator GALLINGER. Let me inquire as a preliminary. is this that open field north of the White House Station?

Mr. WINSLOW. No, sir; the property in question lies northeast of the Union Station.

Senator SMITH of Maryland. About 1½ miles northeast of the Union Station?

Mr. WINSLOW. North of Florida Avenue.

Senator GALLINGER. Yes; I know where it is now. That involves an area of approximately 82 acres, I think. Is it built on to any extent?

Mr. WINSLOW. It is not built on at all, excepting for an old family house that has been up on the hill there for a hundred years, or something of that sort.

The condition of the property is roughly shown on this topographical survey [presenting map] which was made by the Coast and Geodetic Survey many years ago. This is New York Avenue and the railroad tracks are here [indicating]. This is Florida Avenue and the Union Station is down here [indicating]. Here is this tract of land [indicating]. You can see from this that the southern portion of the tract is practically all flat, lowland, and then it starts to rise to a hill back on the northern end of it, on which the old house stands and where the woods are found. The area involved is approximately 82 acres, and the commissioners' recommended figure in their recommendation was $375,000, which amounts to a little over 10 cents a square foot for the entire tract. In my position as a trustee on that property, I feel that if the matter goes to condemnation proceedings a jury will undoubtedly return a larger amount for the value of that property than that figure given by the commissioners, and in substantiation of that view I should like to call your attention to just a few points.

About 10 or 11 years ago property lying to the west of the Patterson tract, and now occupied by the tracks of the Pennsylvania and the Baltimore & Ohio railroads, was sold for 13 cents per square foot. This was property on the same elevation as this hill that at present stands here—high ground. It was subsequently graded by the railroads in putting their tracks in, and they paid 13 cents per square foot. At that time they had the right to purchase or condemn, and they saw fit to pay that price, so that it seems quite evident that they must have considered the property fully worth 13 cents, or they would have gone to condemnation proceedings.

Property down here at the southwestern corner of the tract, lying a little north of Florida Avenue, and also used by the railroads, brought $1.55 per square foot. I am not certain whether that was under sale or condemnation. I think it was a sale. Several years later this southwestern corner of the Patterson tract abutting on Florida Avenue and the railroad tracks was sold, under condemnation proceedings and an award by a jury, at $1.30 per square foot.

Senator SMITH of Maryland. How much land was there in that tract?

Mr. WINSLOW. A half an acre, or a little over. About 1910, on New York Avenue extended, a strip of 10½ acres was condemned, which formed the northwestern boundary of the tract, and they took from the west side to the east side of New York Avenue. The jury award for the value of that 10½ acres was approximately 8½ cents per square foot. That strip of land lies right along the railroad tracks, and the great majority of it is high land, away up.

Senator SMITH of Maryland. What do you mean by the "strip of land"; that you speak of, or that you have now?

Mr. WINSLOW. No, sir; this other. Eight and one-half cents per square foot for that strip along there [indicating on map]. Now, in so far as the values of property can be determined from the tax assessments, I have determined these values by assuming the assessed valuation as two-thirds of what the tax assessors consider the value. The whole tract is assessed at a valuation of a little over 12 cent per square foot, as compared to the commissioners' recommendation of 10½ cents per square foot.

Senator GALLINGER. It is paying taxes on 10½ cents?

Mr. WINSLOW. Paying taxes on two-thirds of 12 cents.

Senator GALLINGER. Eight cents?

Mr. WINSLOW. That has been carried since 1908, paying taxes on that figure.

The property lying north of Fairview Avenue, which is directly north of this tract, is valued at 9 cents per square foot in the proposed new assessment for 1914. That is a section of property which is low land, which will be below grade of the proposed New York Avenue which will be put in, and is also behind the hill of this property, which slopes down from here [indicating], and in my opinion is less desirable than the greater portion of this tract. It is less desirable than any of this portion [indicating].

This property which is occupied by the railroad is valued at something like 16 cents per square foot. The property to the south of Florida Avenue, which is valued at from 40 to 60 cents per square foot, and in some cases as high as a dollar per square foot——

Senator SMITH of Maryland. That is a small area. I suppose all of those properties are like the one you spoke of a while ago—of half an acre?

Mr. WINSLOW. Yes.

Senator SMITH of Maryland. Is it not a different proposition where there is so much of it, and that you are supposed to buy a large quantity of land for a less rate than you can buy a small quantity for, for a specific purpose?

Mr. WINSLOW. There is square No. 710, which lies directly south of Florida Avenue here [indicating], and cater-cornered over here [indicating]. That is a square comprising some 220,000 square feet, I think.

Senator SMITH of Maryland. How many acres would that make?

Mr. WINSLOW. Roughly, 5½ acres. It is valued at $1.35 per square foot.

Senator GALLINGER. That rather surprises me. I chanced to be passing on Clifton Street the other day, between Thirteenth and Fourteenth Streets, where a house lot was being sold, directly opposite the Barber estate, and it sold at auction for 60 cents a square foot.

Mr. WINSLOW. This flat portion and that square I referred to was valued on the industrial possibilities rather than the residential. It is close to the railroad development, and lying about one block this way is the freight house of the Baltimore & Ohio Railroad.

Senator SMITH of Maryland. That is a different proposition, you know. That made the value there.

Mr. WINSLOW. And there is a car line along Florida Avenue, and there is also one along New York Avenue coming out to this [indicating on map]. There is a property lying about two blocks this side, between Trinidad Avenue and Bladensburg Road, that is valued at from 16 cents to 36 cents per square foot, and in some cases as high as 90 cents.

Just one other point in this connection: At the time this strip was condemned for the extension of New York Avenue there were approximately 92 acres which were valued, from the taxation, at $484,000, approximately. The jury in bringing in its award on this condemnation allowed benefits to the property practically equal to the damages, so that the owners of the estate received, I think, for that 10 acres only approximately $200, the rest having been considered as benefits; so that on that assumption the remaining 82 acres were worth within $200 of as much as the original 92 acres were worth. Now, that original 92 acres was——

Senator SMITH of Maryland. I do not think you can base it on that. I do not think you can claim that there were only a few hundred dollars taken from the 92 acres, and what remained was on the 82 acres, simply because of the benefits; and you do not know what the amount of the benefits is. You are taking one side of the case altogether in only allowing $200.

Mr. WINSLOW. It seems to me that if the property was valued at a certain amount—and I figured that it was that, $480,000—and it was equally valuable after that part was taken, that is where it would stand.

Senator SMITH of Maryland. That value is not made by the property itself. The property does not make that value. It is what has already been done by the 10 acres that was taken from it. I can not see that that is a fair proposition, that it should only take $200 from it if 10 acres is taken from it.

Senator GALLINGER. As I understand the matter, you are here to represent that provided the Government concludes to appropriate this land for park purposes a larger amount ought to be allowed than is estimated?

Mr. WINSLOW. Yes, sir.

Senator GALLINGER. You are not here to argue that the Government ought to buy it?

Mr. WINSLOW. No, sir; and I should like to state that neither the owners nor the trustees of the estate have in any way taken steps looking to have this property condemned.

I notice here a note which says that this tract is already largely used for recreation purposes by the residents of that section, and which goes on to suggest that unless it is acquired it will probably be built on. It seems that it is pretty nearly a park now.

Mr. CHARLES J. BELL. Mr. Chairman, I should like to explain that. The trustees, after consultation with the owners, gave to the people there that right.

Senator SMITH of Maryland. Without charging anything for it?

Mr. CHARLES J. BELL. They have never gotten a dollar out of it. I may say for Mr. Winslow, who is not only one of the trustees but is also the son of one of the ladies who owns this tract, that they have been very much opposed to the Government taking the property. They have a much bigger idea of the future value of that property than perhaps I might have. When they look at the land selling at $1 and $2 a foot all around it they naturally think that this property is going to increase to that price. It may or may not do so, but they feel, and I feel, that it is certainly a great injustice to assess the value of this land at $480,000 and then condemn it, saying that it is worth only $375,000, and that if the condemnation proceedings are to go on and the Government does acquire that land for park purposes the upset price should be raised considerably, and then it is for a jury to condemn. Otherwise we would be put in this position, of the appropriation being so much money—and no jury in the District, I believe, would cut the price down so low—so that we would have a cloud over the property. We have been in negotiation with the railroads for the sale of a portion of it. You know what the times have been in the last two or three years, and the railroads have deferred action; but if the Government does not take it we do not want to be tied up; we do not want to feel that we can not make a sale to the railroads for what they may need now or may need in the future.

Senator GALLINGER. In view of the experience we have had in condemnation matters in the District, I do not think the owners need become alarmed on the ground that a jury will not give them all it is worth.

Mr. CHARLES J. BELL. That is the situation, Senator. If you limit the appropriation, we are simply tied up with a cloud on the value.

Senator SMITH of Maryland. Do you think you would rather have a jury condemnation than to have the amount set here, $375,000?

Mr. CHARLES J. BELL. Far rather; yes, sir.

Mr. WINSLOW. That amount, as I understand it, was set not to purchase, but to condemn, so that the jury would not come in there.

Senator GALLINGER. I believe I am correct in the assumption that nobody has appeared before our committee advocating the purchase of this tract?

Senator SMITH of Maryland. No, sir.

RANDLE HIGHLANDS FIRE PROTECTION.

STATEMENT OF MR. J. H. BROWN.

Mr. BROWN. Mr. Chairman, I have only a few words to say. I represent the committee of citizens from Randle Highlands, and we want to ask that our fire protection be not taken from us. We understand there is some proposition in the bill as it came from the House to do such a thing. We have all frame buildings over there, and we feel that we need fire protection. There is a good sized village or town there now, and I am just here to ask that our fire protection over there be preserved. We feel that we need it, and while we feel that we have been fortunate in the last year in not having a fire, we do not know when we will have one, of course; and if our fire protection is taken away from us it will make the distance probably a couple of miles to the next nearest fire engine house which could come to our aid.

Senator GALLINGER. Is there an engine house at Twining City?

Mr. BROWN. No, sir. Randle Highlands is just above that.

Senator GALLINGER. I understand Twining City is just across the bridge. Is there a fire station there?

Mr. BROWN. No, sir. There is one at Randle Highlands, which is just above it.

Senator GALLINGER. I understand that.

Mr. BROWN. But there is none at Twining City. Anacostia, from some parts of Randle Highlands, would be probably two miles.

Senator GALLINGER. So that if a fire should occur in Twining City your fire apparatus would be called into requisition?

Mr. BROWN. That is right. It is right there, near it.

Senator SMITH of Maryland. Where is Twining City?

Senator GALLINGER. Twining City is just across the highway bridge at the end of Pennsylvania Avenue east.

Senator SMITH of Maryland. What is the population of Twining City?

Mr. Brown. There are several thousand people there.

Senator Gallinger. Not in Twining City proper?

Mr. Brown. Maybe not. I could not answer that exactly.

Senator Gallinger. I do not know; it is quite a village. Beyond that place, about half a mile, is this fire station, is it not?

Mr. Brown. It is less than half a mile. It is a quarter of a mile. In that section there are quite a number of houses that need fire protection, and, as I say, if this protection is taken away, engines would have to come from Anacostia, and a frame building would be consumed before the fire engine would get there.

Senator Gallinger. Are there any buildings under construction at Randle Highlands?

Mr. Brown. Yes; there are several under construction there now, and we are building and getting along, with the understanding that we have this fire protection; and after we have got it, to have it taken away from us seems rather hard.

Senator Smith of Maryland. The place is improving and being built up?

Mr. Brown. Oh, yes, sir; it is being built up.

Senator Smith of Maryland. How long has this fire protection been there?

Mr. Brown. For about a year, now. We have a new engine house there.

Senator Smith of Maryland. There is a new engine house there now?

Mr. Brown. Yes, sir; a new building.

Senator Smith of Maryland. There is a large new school building there, too?

Mr. Brown. Yes; a $64,000 school building. The land for both the school building and the engine house was donated, with the understanding, of course, that the fire protection would be there.

Senator Smith of Maryland. The land was given for that purpose?

Mr. Brown. For that purpose; yes, sir.

Senator Smith of Maryland. And you think that any of these new buildings now being constructed probably might not have been constructed if they had not had the assurance of fire protection?

Mr. Brown. It might be so.

Senator Smith of Maryland. Yes.

Mr. Brown. That is the way we feel, living there, that our suburb will not grow as fast if we do not have fire protection.

Senator Smith of Maryland. Did you have hearings before the House committee upon this subject?

Mr. Brown. No, sir.

Senator Smith of Maryland. Is it by action of the commissioners that this removal is being made?

Mr. Brown. There is no estimate to change it; no, sir.

Senator Smith of Maryland. I find this was simply put on in the committee in the House, and there is no estimate back of it to change the engine house, and no place is selected for it?

Mr. Brown. No, sir; this change is not estimated for. I did not know of it until a little while ago.

Senator Gallinger. You did not learn of it until after it passed the House?

Mr. Brown. No, sir. Some of the citizens might have, but I had no knowledge of it myself.

Senator Smith of Maryland. Have you any idea why it was done?

Mr. Brown. Not the least in the world.

Senator Smith of Maryland. It seems very singular that it should be put there and now taken away. The appropriation is made for it?

Senator Gallinger. Oh, it is built. The station is there and completed, and this large school building is there, completed and occupied.

Mr. Brown. That is right.

Senator Gallinger. I believe the argument has been made that we spent more money on the school building there than we ought to have spent; but the population there is growing. I think it is a good thing to keep that fire station there.

Senator Smith of Maryland. Does anybody else desire to be heard in regard to this?

Br. Brown. Mr. Tucker is one of the committee, and he is here.

STATEMENT OF V. M. TUCKER.

Mr. Tucker. Mr. Chairman, I just wish to say this, in connection with that fire station: That I have recently built a place there, myself, right near the school building, which cost me $4,500, and there has also been another nice building put there by another man from Maryland, besides mine. That is right near the school building, on that street; and we have, as has been stated, a good many new buildings in course of construction there. I am a salesman, myself, of the realty company, and that has been one of my strong talking points, that we have a nice fire department there, put there at a cost of $26,000 by the Government, independent of the cost of the land.

Senator Smith of Maryland. The land was donated for that specific purpose?

Mr. Tucker. For that purpose, and that purpose alone, that the station should be maintained there. Also, we gave the site for this fine school building.

Senator Gallinger. We made that a prerequisite, that the land should be donated for the engine house and the school building. Otherwise we probably would not have given consideration to it.

Senator Smith of Maryland. Possibly if the school building had not had fire protection, you might not have built it and property close to it?

Mr. Tucker. Yes, sir; that is true. We ask that it be kept there.

(The following petition concerning fire protection at Randle Highlands was presented by Mr. Brown:)

Hon. John Walter Smith,
   Chairman Senate District Committee, Washington, D. C.:

We, the undersigned citizens of Randle Highlands, petition your honorable committee to save our fire department for us. The ground on which the engine house is erected was donated to the District of Columbia with the understanding that a fire department would be established and kept in force. It would be a hardship on us to be deprived of fire protection, as we have practically our all invested in homes, and to have them destroyed by fire would be a great loss and hardship on us.

We appeal to the Senate, through you, to strike out the clause in the District appropriation bill which takes away our only fire protection.

This fire department not only takes care of this section of the city, but in case of a fire in the northwest section, the fire engines on Capitol Hill go to assist in extinguishing the fire and our fire department at Randle Highlands goes to Capitol Hill to protect the property east of the Capitol.

B. T. Woodward, R. Reichard, Wm. H. Dorell, John A. Mazzulle, Geo. M. Martin, T. D. McLane, Mrs. J. M. Brooks, Mrs. N. Y. Hoffman, Geo. V. Blakeney, Mrs. G. V. Blakeney, Mrs. B. I. Stansbury, Mrs. C. W. Stansbury, Mrs. W. B. Caton, Wm. B. Caton; W. H. Sneedy, A. S. Phelps, J. Chilton, Mrs. E. A. Harrison, Mrs. E. L. Beardsley, G. L. Roberts. Ida M. Hohn, W. H. Groves, Harry A. Buss, Mrs. M. A. Graham, Mr. J. W. Graham. Miss E. French, John Hohn, R. Melling, Thos. J. Jones, N. R. Snyder, Mrs. Geo. H. Blakeslee, Mrs. Geo. M. Martin, Miss French, S. M. Dixon, R. J. Tiller, Paul E. M. Kinney, L. J. McIlvaine, Jas. M. Brooks, C. A. Baeder, Geo. J. Frenchs, S. E. Snyder. Mrs. L. B. McAllwane, Mrs. R. E. Schimmett, Mrs. Grace Blakeslee, J. H. Brown, A. H. Blakeslee, W. C. Van Horn, A. L. Van Horn, M. Keene, H. O. Blakeslee, N. E. Harrover, Mrs. M. A. Taylor,·Mrs. W. H. Groves, Mrs. T. H. Matthews, O. A. Stansbury, W. H. Baxter, Ella Browning, J. S. Browning, T. W. Maccubbin, J. C. Beveridge, L. M. Mullican, S. M. Dixen, Suzanne Tiller, W. I. Smith, Mrs. Theo. New, Barbara E. Lanham, Mrs. G. J. French, Mrs. E. M. Cavan, Mrs. J. Henry Brown, Mrs. R. F. Bradbury, Mrs. N. F. Ladd.

STATEMENT OF HON. FRANK W. MONDELL, A REPRESENTATIVE IN CONGRESS FROM THE STATE OF WYOMING.

Mr. MONDELL. Gentlemen, the item I desire to speak of is on page 84 of the bill. I am not a member of the subcommittee on the District of Columbia of the Committee on Appropriations of the House; therefore I had nothing to do with the making up of the District of Columbia bill. I disagreed with the majority of the committee with regard to quite a number of items in the bill: that is, I thought the committee had not allowed some items that it should have allowed and that it should have been a little more liberal with regard to other items. However, the difficulty was not so much with our committee as it was from the fact that the District Committee in the House seems to be very jealous, and properly so, of its prerogatives, and inclined to raise points of order on items in the bill. Therefore our committee exercised great care in not making provision for anything that might be subject to a point of order, otherwise some of the estimates made by the commissioners might, in my opinion, have been allowed.

But what I wanted to talk to you about particularly is section 8. You will discover, if you will read the record of the proceedings, that section 8 of the bill, which violates the half-and-half principle as between the District and the United States Government in the matter of appropriations, passed the House wihout any discussion whatever. I do not want your committee to remain under the impression, if you have any such impression, that the manner in which the matter passed the House, or the House committee, in any way reflected the views of a large number of Members on both sides with regard to the provision; and it is because I feel somewhat responsible for the fact that the point of order was not raised, for the fact that a motion was not made to strike out, that I feel justified in appearing before you and taking your time for a moment.

Senator GALLINGER. The point of order against that provision would have been sustained, necessarily, would it not?

Mr. MONDELL. I can not say as to that, Senator. I have my doubts. My own opinion is that it is subject to a point of order, as it, in my opinion, does not come within the Holman rule, which provides that an item may contain new legislation if it reduces the expenditures of the Government. But this item does not do that; it increases the revenues. And of course there is a very considerable distinction between the reduction of the expenditures and an increase of the revenues. But I am not sure that the chairman of the Committee of the Whole would have agreed with me. At any rate, I had intended to make the point of order. If the point of order was overruled I had intended to move to strike out. If we failed on that motion I had intended to move to reconsider; so that my intentions were the best in the world. I had been giving the bill more attention than anyone on our side, had been making frequent observations with regard to it, offering amendments from time to time. A number of the gentlemen on our side, without my realizing it, were rather expecting me to look after these features of the bill, which they did not approve and which they knew I did not approve.

Senator GALLINGER. You had been pretty active in the debate in opposing all proposals to violate the half-and-half principle?

Mr. MONDELL. I had discussed that matter half a dozen times. So, in view of the fact that I had intended, and that Members knew that I had intended, to make the point of order, and if it was overruled to make the motion to strike out and then to make the motion to recommit, and the fact that I was unavoidably absent from the Chamber for a very brief time, that the item was reached much sooner than any of us had expected, and I did not take that action, and other Members, expecting me to do it, were also absent. I feel that I should make this statement to you. I wanted to make that explanation so that if anyone made that suggestion you might understand the situation, that it was not because the House agreed to that provision, and that there was no opposition to it, that it passed. It was simply because those of us who were very much opposed to it unfortunately for the moment were out of the Chamber, and the item was reached very much sooner than anyone had expected. If there is anyone to blame at all in the matter I am to blame.

Senator SMITH of Maryland. Otherwise you would not have been out of the Chamber, if you had thought it was going to be reached?

Mr. MONDELL. Certainly not. Now, feeling somewhat guilty in the matter, I wanted to make this statement and have you clearly understand that the House did not test the matter, because those who had been expecting to make the test were out for the moment. Of course I have no means of knowing what the outcome would have been, except that I do know that there are many Members on both sides of the Chamber who do not agree with that provision. I am very much obliged to you gentlemen.

Senator SMITH of Maryland. Not at all. We are very glad to have heard you.

(At 1.45 o'clock p. m. the subcommittee took a recess until 3 o'clock p. m.)

AFTERNOON SESSION.

The subcommittee met, pursuant to the taking of recess, at 3 o'clock p. m.

EXTENSION OF AVENUE OF THE PRESIDENTS.

The CHAIRMAN (Senator Smith of Maryland). Mr. Shoemaker, we would be glad to hear you, sir. We want to give you gentlemen all the time that is necessary, but time is rather valuable, and we would like you to be as concise and short as you can.

Mr. SHOEMAKER. We understand, Senator, that your time is valuable, and we will try to be as considerate as possible. Can you give me an idea how much time we may have?

Senator SMITH of Maryland. How many of you are there to be heard?

Mr. SHOEMAKER. There are several.

Senator SMITH of Maryland. Go ahead, and be as brief as possible.

STATEMENT OF LOUIS P. SHOEMAKER.

Mr. SHOEMAKER. Mr. Chairman, it affords me pleasure, as presiding officer of the Brightwood Citizens' Association, to appear before you on this occasion. I am sorry that I have not a copy of our recommendations, but we will leave copies with the clerk, who will transmit them, of course, to the members of the committee.

The first matter of importance out there with us is Sixteenth Street, or the Avenue of the Presidents; and by the way, while I am speaking of it, and in case I might forget it later, there is some advocacy for the change of that name. It has been changed from Sixteenth Street to the Avenue of the Presidents. I want to say to you gentlemen that we believe that the strong sentiment prevailing in the District is in favor of the name "Avenue of the Presidents," and we desire very much that you shall do all you can to preserve that name.

Senator SMITH of Maryland. The House has changed it back to Sixteenth Street.

Mr. SHOEMAKER. Yes, sir. I suppose that is a question that will come before this committee. If it does not come directly before this committee it will come before some other committee.

We recognize Sixteenth Street as a great, leading thoroughfare, and many of you are entirely familiar with it. It is with diffidence that I allude to its importance. It is 160 feet in width and goes directly north from the White House to the District line. There is a strong advocacy in favor of the appropriation that we ask for this street; first, because 15 years ago the Brightwood Citizens' Association took a keen interest in the importance of opening this thoroughfare, and we secured through the instrumentality of Mr. Berliner here, and Mr. Blagden and Mr. Blair Lee, and others, the dedication of all the land from Piney Branch Road to the line north, to the width of 160 feet, and the title to that land has rested in the Government from that date; and we were assured then, so far as the gentlemen in power could assure us, that if that land was dedicated the street would be opened at a very early date. We have waited patiently, and the street has not been opened.

Senator GALLINGER. It has been partially opened.

Mr. SHOEMAKER. It has been partially opened. I am referring to its being opened to the District line. A great deal of money has been spent along the line of the street, and I might call your attention to the fact that I am advised that when Sixteenth Street was opened as far as the Piney Branch Road, or a little beyond, there was necessity for an enormous extent of condemnation proceedings.

These proceedings were had, and as I recollect it, $600,000 was taken out of the treasury of the District in that one single year to pay the cost of opening that street up as far as Mount Pleasant or a little beyond. This enormous expense was incurred because the old Sixteenth Street was a narrow thoroughfare, and it was the policy of the Government to establish this great thoroughfare, and we were in sympathy with it, and they proceeded to put in this great Sixteenth Street, and that necessitated the enormous condemnation proceedings to which I have just alluded. But the reason for it is that we feel we have an equity and a right, if I may use that expression, to ask the United States to appropriate a little every year for the purpose of carrying along this improvement, inasmuch as we have dedicated the land all the way, free of cost to the Government, excepting below, where it had to be condemned; and I think Senator Gallinger's recollection will bear me out in that statement, that in that one year, when $600,000 worth of property had to be acquired by these proceedings, it was wholly paid by the District government. The United States did not contribute a penny to the cost of that ground.

Now, there is another reason. The distance between the Rock Creek Park and the old Georgia Avenue or Brightwood Avenue—the name of which was changed over our protest and without our consent by a very worthy Senator, I believe—is not very great, but there is a somewhat rural territory out there, and in the whole history of the District from the beginning, 100 years ago, down to the present time, there has been opened by this Government not a single thoroughfare which leads from the boundary of the city to the boundary of the District. Georgia Avenue, formerly Brightwood Avenue, was opened pretty nearly 100 years ago. It has been used for travel, crowded with electric cars, with pedestrians likely to be run over at any time, without even footways along it except to a very limited extent, so that with all the traffic of farmers who come in from Maryland, it is all concentrated right on this old road, 100 years old. Now, we are earnestly appealing to you here to grant this appropriation of at least $35,000, I believe it is.

Senator SMITH of Maryland. It is $26,952.

Mr. SHOEMAKER. $26,952 to put it up to the Military Road. Of course we want, and we desire, very much, and we believe that the public interest demands that the street should be extended all the way to the District line; but we have followed a certain course here under the administration of your worthy predecessor, and with reference to whom we have been successful, really, in getting so many public improvements, in asking for a little bit every year, crawling, as it were, and we have pursued that course with reference to Sixteenth Street.

Senator SMITH of Maryland. How far would this $26,952 take it?

Mr. SHOEMAKER. Not more than half a mile—2,000 feet, I am told. Now, I stop there. When you reach the Military Road you will find that the Military Road is in a valley, and there is a hill, of course, beyond, and a hill to the south. The policy of the commissioners is to build a bridge or viaduct over that place. Consequently they ask for $25,000 or $26,000 more to build this viaduct, and I am afraid that in connection with this appropriation we ask for the commissioners will say, "We do not want this extension there unless we can get the viaduct."

Senator GALLINGER. The road stops at a certain point now, and it will stop a little farther on if it is extended.

Mr. SHOEMAKER. Sixteenth Street?

Senator GALLINGER. Yes.

Mr. SHOEMAKER. Yes; but Sixteenth Street stops on a grade, on high ground; and when you get to the Military Road, the Military Road is down here [indicating].

Senator SMITH of Maryland. But I understand that the additional length of road that you want to construct with this $26,952 that is provided for here is still on level ground, is it not?

Mr. SHOEMAKER. Oh, no. That is the point I make. The Military Road is here, in the valley [indicating]. There is a hill there and a hill here [indicating].

Senator GALLINGER. This takes it to the Military Road?

Mr. SHOEMAKER. Yes; this takes it to the Military Road; but it is not practicable to get into the bed of the Military Road, because there is a hill over here on Sixteenth Street [indicating].

Senator GALLINGER. It will not make it any worse than it is now if the appropriation is made, will it?

Mr. SHOEMAKER. We shall be very glad to have the appropriation and have that improvement.

Senator GALLINGER. Are we to understand that the commissioners are opposed to this appropriation now of $26,952?

Mr. RAMSEY. I do not know that they are, sir. They had the original estimates there, up to the last day, and then it was stricken out, through some influence I do not know about.

Mr. SHOEMAKER. Independent of the allusion I made a moment ago, there is another objection, and that is that there is no other thoroughfare out there for these people, and to accommodate the general public. The taxation has been enormously increased. These gentlemen who are here will bear me out in the statement that their taxation has been increased two-thirds.

Senator SMITH of Maryland. In what way?

Mr. SHOEMAKER. By the new assessment.

Senator SMITH of Maryland. By a new valuation of the property?

Mr. SHOEMAKER. By the new assessment of the property; what they consider the value of the property. If we are to have this continual increase of taxation, pray let us have public improvements commensurate in proportion to it, so that we can reach the land. Here is Mr. Berliner, who will tell you that he has no highway to his property to-day. He can not reach it by way of Sixteenth Street or by way of Georgia Avenue, and on the west of that is Rock Creek Park. But the taxation has been increased two-thirds.

Mr. BERLINER. It is doubled.

Mr. SHOEMAKER. We hope that you will give very great consideration to this improvement of Sixteenth Street. We have other projects we should like to include, but I am confining myself to that at present.

May I allude to an improvement over on Rock Creek while I am speaking? It will not take but very little longer.

Senator SMITH of Maryland. Is that in any way in this connection here?

Mr. SHOEMAKER. Yes, sir.

Senator GALLINGER. What is it? Has it been estimated for?

Mr. SHOEMAKER. Yes, sir; this is in regard to Audubon Terrace. It was here last year and is here this year. This is on the slip pasted on page 22. It is No. 69.

Senator GALLINGER. It is pretty well down on the list.

Mr. SHOEMAKER. I am sorry to say that it is. We will have to appeal to you to lift it, that is all.

Before I leave the matter of Sixteenth Street. I ought to say that, as I stated a moment ago, I am here as presiding officer of the association, and I have no personal interest in this Sixteenth Street matter at all. I have not any property anywhere near it that is liable to be improved by it. I appeal to you in view of these national improvements, and I believe if Sixteenth Street could be opened it would be of great benefit and advantage. not only to property owners out there, but to the general public as well.

Now, if I may have a few moments in reference to Audubon Terrace, I will not detain you long. I hold in my hand here a map of a tract of land of probably 200 acres. It lies between Connecticut Avenue over on the west and the Rock Creek Park on the east. This property has been in our family for many years. I am speaking now, perhaps, from the standpoint of personal interest. We have been paying taxes on it for about 100 years, my father and my grandfather and my great grandfather before me, my earlier progenitors living here before the city of Washington was laid out. These lines are the lines drawn on the ground by the Congress, and correspond with the city-street plan [indicating on map]. Here is Rock Creek down here, and here is Connecticut Avenue over here [indicating], and we have dedicated Albemarle Street all the way through from the District line to the Broad Branch Road or Rock Creek Park. The improvement of that street was made to the extent of two squares, and Senator Gallinger has heard me talk of Albemarle Street a number of times, I am sure; but it is not proposed to go any farther with it on account of the grades in through here [indicating], and the commissioners have now dropped Albemarle Street and have recommended Audubon Terrace, coming down on the hillside here [indicating]. That will be a new thoroughfare leading from Connecticut Avenue to Rock Creek Park; and I want to say in reference to that, notwithstanding the fact that we have dedicated all the land and we have no scheme whatever of subdivision with reference to it, people are going in there and buying up an acre of land here and there, and establishing homes, and a number of them have gone in there to-day.

Senator GALLINGER. Why did the commissioners abandon Albemarle Street?

Mr. SHOEMAKER. On account of the grade; the very severe grade.

Senator GALLINGER. That street has .been discussed here very often. On Albemarle Street we have spent a great deal to carry the improvement as far as it has gone, and the Government of the United States has not spent anything in the way of public improvements in the whole history of the District. We appear here and ask you to comply with the request of the commissioners to grant this appropriation to open up this driveway from Connecticut Avenue right down into Rock Creek Park, coming somewhere near Pierce mill, and we would suggest to you that from the Klingle Ford Road all the way north to the Childrens' Country Home, a distance of a mile and a half, there is not a single thoroughfare to-day, and there never has been a single thoroughfare opened up to Rock Creek Park. This is a logical place for a street running east and west, and therefore we ask that this appropriation for the improvement of Audubon Terrace be granted, in the public interest, so that they can get over to Rock Creek Park.

Senator GALLINGER. Let me ask just one question. I think I am not faulty in my recollection that some years ago the House changed their policy regarding the opening up of new streets—suburban streets—so as to require that the District of Columbia should pay the entire cost. Is not that correct?

Mr. SHOEMAKER. Yes, sir. The street extension act as it was passed provided, at the end of the act, that no cost for the opening of these streets should be at the expense of the United States, but it should be all at the expense of the District of Columbia. We are now seeking the improvement of these streets that have been dedicated.

Senator GALLINGER. They have not been opened?

Mr. SHOEMAKER. We want to have them opened.

Senator GALLINGER. Has not the House raised the issue that the District shall pay all the cost of opening the streets?

Mr. SHOEMAKER. Not to my knowledge.

Senator GALLIGER. Suppose we find that to be the case; would you still be in favor of this improvement, if the District was obliged to pay the entire cost of opening the street—not of improving it, but of opening it?

Mr. SHOEMAKER. You know we have to take what we can get here.

Senator GALLINGER. Yes.

Mr. SHOEMAKER. And I do think it is a great mistake and a great injustice to the people of this district that the Congress of the United States should dedicate a great national street plan, and take dedications from the people in accordance with that plan, and then not be willing to pay its proportion of the cost of opening the streets.

Senator GALLINGER. I am not arguing in favor of the policy, but I am looking the matter squarely in the face, and it is my recollection that of late years we have never been able to get the House to agree to any appropriation for the opening of a new street.

Mr. SHOEMAKER. We have to consent to the policy of Congress here, and in answer to your question, I would say that if that is the policy, nothwithstanding the injustice, we will have to accept it. notwithstanding we have to suffer a greatly increased taxation.

Senator GALLINGER. We will look carefully into the matter.

Mr. SHOEMAKER. You will observe now that notwithstanding all these recommendations we have made in respect to the things that we really need, the things we would like to ask for, I have confined my remarks to that great national thoroughfare, Sixteenth Street, showing that we are advocating something in the interests of the public, and not in my interest or somebody else's interest; but this is a public demand, and we have not gone into details with you at all.

Senator SMITH of Maryland. Was not this up at the last session of Congress?

Senator GALLINGER. Yes, it was; and we did not think the time had quite arrived to make an appropriation for it.

Senator SMITH of Maryland. The proposition last year was for a longer extension.

Senator GALLINGER. Mr. Shoemaker, I am going to ask you one question about this Audubon Terrace: First, why do you call it a terrace?

Mr. SHOEMAKER. It is along on the brow of the hill.

Senator GALLINGER. Why do you want that improved?

Mr. SHOEMAKER. It is on the street-extension plan. It is a very proper thoroughfare leading over to the park.

Senator GALLINGER. It enters the park?

Mr. SHOEMAKER. Yes; it enters the park.

Senator GALLINGER. From Connecticut Avenue?

Mr. SHOEMAKER. Yes, sir; and there is no other road, as I stated a moment ago, for a distance of a mile and a half leading across there.

Senator GALLINGER. Where is it located?

Mr. SHOEMAKER. You know where Albemarle Street is? It is just south of Arbemarle Street. It leaves Connecticut Avenue and curves to the south, right about where Albemarle Street intersects Connecticut Avenue.

Senator GALLINGER. And there is no entrance to the park throughout that entire stretch of country, is there, until you come down to the Zoo Park?

Mr. SHOEMAKER. None except Tilden Street. It comes down to the old Pierce Mill.

Senator GALLINGER. Yes; I know where that is.

STATEMENT OF MR. EMILE BERLINER.

Mr. BERLINER. Mr. Chairman and gentlemen, I simply want to point out to you some facts. I have made some computations and find that when an important street like Sixteenth Street, or the Avenue of the Presidents, is extended 1 mile, you can at once, the following year, collect $10,000 more in taxes. That is the first year, and as the years follow the extension of every important street like that, that additional money coming in from taxation will increase, so that inside of four years you will not only have the money back which you have spent on that, but——

Senator GALLINGER. That is, the District Government will get this increased revenue.

Mr. BERLINER. Yes; the District; and this government will not only get the money back, but there will be an increased amount of $15,000 or $20,000 more coming in by virtue of the extension.

Senator SMITH of Maryland. It will increase the assessable basis?

Mr. BERLINER. Yes, sir.

Senator SMITH of Maryland. The money, of course, comes to the District, and does not come to the United States Government?

Mr. BERLINER. Yes; it comes to the District, of course.

Senator SMITH of Maryland. At the same time, that ought not to be ignored.

Senator GALLINGER. I would say they are building very rapidly there, and a beautiful class of buildings, out to the extreme point of the present extension of Sixteenth Street. It is being built up with great rapidity. I think I am correct about that.

Mr. BERLINER. Away beyond that.

Senator SMITH of Maryland. From the remarks I have just made, I do not mean it to be understood that because the Government does not get any benefit from it the District should be deprived of the benefit of an increased taxable basis, but I merely make that remark, that the benefit of the assessable basis would inure to the District of Columbia.

Mr. BERLINER. And at the same time it would inure to the benefit of the city, of which the Government gets the benefit; and the improvement of the great streets is of the greatest importance to the District, and in four years the money would come back.

Senator GALLINGER. Sixteenth Street, now know as the Avenue of the Presidents, constitutes the most beautiful drive in the city, as I look at it.   .

Senator SMITH of Maryland. I think possibly that is one of the reasons I spoke of that they want the District to do it, because it gets the benefit of the increased assessable basis.

STATEMENT OF MR. A. E. McLAUGHLIN.

Mr. McLAUGHLIN. Mr. Chairman and gentlemen of the committee, I desire to file with you this short statement, unless the committee wishes to hear it read.

The CHAIRMAN. You may read it.

Mr. McLAUGHLIN. I desire to repeat what I stated on a previous occasion when this question was being considered and to add thereto that assessments in this locality have gone on increasing like streams to a rivulet flow. Why continue to increase assessments and not use some of this ample revenue to make this much-needed public improvement. If improvements justify increased assessments in this locality, and the assessor seems to think that they do, then why not continue the improvements?

JUVENILE COURT.

STATEMENT OF J. WILMER LATIMER, JUDGE OF THE JUVENILE COURT.

Senator GALLINGER. You begin on page 56 of the bill?

Judge LATIMER. Yes, sir. I should like first to say to the committee that when the juvenile court was reached by the subcommittee of the House Committee that had it in charge, I was ill, at home, and they said they could not postpone the consideration of it until I could be present, and Mr. Baldwin, who is here this morning, kindly consented to go down and speak, and I was able to tell them only what I could say to him through my wife over the telephone.

I am not here to ask the subcommittee to do anything more than I believe any member of it would do if he knew the conditions in our juvenile court. The court was organized seven years ago, and the growth has been simply tremendous, as is indicated from one thing merely, and that is the collections under the nonsupport law, which have jumped from $6,000 the first year to $52,000 this last year.

The court is not only a juvenile court, but it is an adult court. Nearly half the cases there are adult cases. The result is we have to hold separate sessions, a court for adults and a court for children.

Senator GALLINGER. The adult cases come under the head of non-support cases?

Judge LATIMER. That is it; yes, sir. If I may, I will take up the items just in the order in which they appear in the appropriation bill.

JUVENILE COURT SALARIES.

The first item is for an increase in the salary of the deputy clerk. We have only two clerks, a clerk and a deputy clerk; the clerk at $2,000, and the deputy clerk at $1,200, up to this time. The deputy clerk is a bonded officer. He handles all the money, and is a bonded clerk and has a serious responsibility in handling all that money, and he works from early in the morning until late at night. He comes early in the morning and works until late at night. I think that in simple justice he should have $1,500. That is less than the clerk in the police court gets. He gets $1,600, and another clerk gets $1,500; so that I think that is a reasonable request. I will not linger on it. I am only going to speak now of the increases over the House bill.

PROBATION SYSTEM.

The next item is for an increase in the salary of the chief probation officer from $1,500 to $2,000. I found, in studying the conditions in other cities and comparing them with ours, that the chief probation officer in Washington was very much underpaid, and the result was that we could not get a man of the grade we needed to take charge of the other probation work and direct the probation officers under him and direct the important work which the chief probation officer ought to do. He ought to be a man of education and executive ability and a man of some presence; a man who can meet people. In Chicago and in New York he is paid $3,000, and in some other cities $2,500, and in cities nearer the size of Washington $2,400 and $2,250. We asked the House to give us $2,500, and they did not increase it at all, and we have now come down to $2,000. The chief probation officer we have had there has just resigned, and I have just appointed a man who has had large experience in the St. Louis office, and I told him that while I could not promise him an increase we were asking for an increase, and I think the prospect of an increase was what led him to come here. He comes the first of the month.

In addition to what we are asking for the chief probation officer, we are renewing our request, as in the estimates, for one more probation officer at $1,200 and one more at $1,000. We do that because

Senator GALLINGER. That is a most remarkable proposition.

Judge LATIMER. Most of the boys seem to be satisfied to have the judge try them, and they do not ask for a jury.

RENT OF COURT QUARTERS.

When our estimates were submitted we supposed that we would continue in the same building during the ensuing year, and therefore we asked for the same amount for rent. The court occupies a building in a square owned by the Government and where the Hall of Records is going to be placed, and we were notified by the Treasury Department that we would have to vacate some time next summer and that we had better look elsewhere. Of course we can not look elsewhere for quarters with the amount that we have for rent. We are provided with $20 a month for rent, and we can not go anywhere and get anything like what we have for ten times that.

Senator GALLINGER. Did I understand you to say that you have been notified that the Government is going to build on that site in the near future?

Judge LATIMER. Yes; and we will have to vacate next summer or in the early fall. Whatever appropriation we get must be gotten now, at this session of Congress, or it will do us no good. We will be out on the street. Therefore I have asked for $2,400. Somebody asked me where we were going to get for $200 a suitable place, and I must answer that I do not know. I did not think Congress could appropriate any more than $200 a month, and we will have to get the best we can for that. When you realize that you have men and women and children there, and that you have to have separate retiring rooms, and rooms for the judge and the jury, and detention rooms, rooms for the parents and for the children, judge's room and prosecuting attorney's room and probation officers' rooms—a private room for each one so that they can talk to their children privately—you will see that it takes considerable space.

Senator GALLINGER. Even if you were not to be ousted, your present facilities are very inadequate?

Judge LATIMER. Very inadequate. I would not want to stay there very long. I would be asking for an increase, anyway; but we have got to leave there.

Senator GALLINGER. You think you should have $2,400 for rent?

Judge LATIMER. I do not see how we can find anything for less than that, and I do not know what we can find for that. Some persons would look at that and say, "That is ten times what you had last year," not observing that the rent is a merely nominal amount now.

Senator GALLINGER. You did not call that to the attention of the House committee?

Judge LATIMER. I did not know about it at that time. I had not received that notice; and when I did receive the notice I did not know whether to ask for an appropriation for a new building or what to do. Because of that change we have had to ask for a change in our miscellaneous expenses. We have got to move, and that is expensive; and we have got to equip a new place, and we have asked for $1,500 for furniture, fixtures, and equipments, and repairs to the courthouse and grounds, and cost of moving, and such items as that.

Senator GALLINGER. Of course, you do not want to repair this courthouse, so called, if you are going to leave it.

Judge LATIMER. No; that is simply following the language of the old act. There probably will be alterations to be made in the new place.

Senator GALLINGER. That is how much?

FURNITURE, EQUIPMENT, ETC.

Judge LATIMER. $1,500. I have furnished to the members of the committee a list of the equipment that we need, exclusive of the two typewriters and the adding machine. We have been using an adding machine, loaned by the manufacturer, for two or three years, and they keep calling on us to pay for it; and we have had it there some two years, and I do think that we ought to pay for it.

Then there is the miscellaneous item for fuel, ice, gas, and laundry work, etc., for which we have asked $3,500. The result of that is that with the additional probation officers and additional fuel that will be necessary in a larger building, we are not going to be able to make both ends meet.

Senator GALLINGER. It is estimated at $1,500.

Judge LATIMER. We have to have this because of additions in the force and changing our place. If we have a larger building, it is going to take more coal, for one thing.

A summary of how the money was expended last year will show that over one-third of the appropriation under this item was required for car tickets and fuel—two items alone.

Senator GALLINGER. That includes the increase in force and also the removal to some other place?

Judge LATIMER. Yes; we have already got some increase in force, and there will be some increase of expenses. I think that the amounts that are stated there are as low as they could be put in order to at all equip us for the work. Our estimates were $23,440. That was about $9,000 more than we had last year, and they gave us $22,000 of it. The amount of increase is caused by the fact—which has developed since—that we have got to move. $4,000 of that is due to this one fact alone.

In conclusion, I merely want to say that we are very much interested in the work and are very anxious to do it well; and it is very discouraging to us not to have the facilities to do it, and we can not hope to do it unless we can get this $7,500. That is all we are asking over the other.

NEW COURT QUARTERS—AGAIN.

Senator GALLINGER. If we should increase these estimates here, we would never be able to hold them in conference, unless we absolutely know that you will have to abandon your present site.

Judge LATIMER. We do know that. I have been notified officially.

Senator GALLINGER. You have been?

Judge LATIMER. Yes.

Senator GALLINGER. Well, your statement is sufficient on that point.

Judge LATIMER. The chief clerk of the Treasury Department notified my predecessor, before I got there, that he had better be looking for other quarters, and then I telephoned to him and verified it.

Senator GALLINGER. The committee will take this into consideration and do the best we can.

Judge LATIMER. If you will hear Mr. Densmore, chairman of the legislative committee interested in the work, we would appreciate it.

STATEMENT OF J. B. DENSMORE.

Mr. DENSMORE. I am going to permit Mr. Baldwin to make the statement for the juvenile court advisory board. I just happen to be the chairman of the legislative committee. The other members are Mr. Macfarland, Mr. McKelway, Miss Janet Richards, Mrs. Wallace Radcliffe, and Miss Aline Solomon. Some of these people you know better than you do me. They wanted me to state to the committee that they regretted that they could not be here this afternoon to tell you how badly they wanted the appropriations for this juvenile court. I am sure they would if they were here. They are very greatly interested. I have had two or three meetings with them, and if you are not familiar with the organization and purposes of the juvenile court advisory board, I will say that it was organized by the citizens of the District—of the city of Washington—for the purpose of taking some of the burden off of Judge Latimer's shoulders in such matters as this, for instance, except in matters where the judge explains the personnel or the requests for the increase in his court in making up the personnel of his court. There are two things the judge mentioned that I want to call your attention to.

NEW FURNITURE AND FIXTURES.

In a meeting that we had with the judge last week, in view of a call upon this committee, I suggested and the committee also suggested that the judge increase his estimate for furniture and fixtures from $900 to $1,500. Really, if he moves out of where he is now he can not buy anything at all with $900, and he has not any furniture there now. He has not anything in the entire place that is worthy of the name. To the mind of anybody who is familiar with the purposes of juvenile courts, the equipment of this as a juvenile court in the National Capital is a ghastly joke. It is awful.

Senator GALLINGER. Hardly that. It was a serious matter.

Mr. DENSMORE. I appreciate that.

Senator GALLINGER. It was started in a small way, with the expectation that it would grow. Everthing grows in Washington.

Mr. DENSMORE. Yes; and I suggested and the committee suggested an increase in the estimate, and also in his miscellaneous expense contingent fund, necessitated by the expense of moving and the increased amount of fuel that will be necessary. Those are the only two items that I wanted to mention.

Senator GALLINGER. At the start we gave the judge a very small salary, but we have increased that largely.

Mr. DENSMORE. I am satisfied that Congress will, and really they should, give attention particularly to this juvenile court here, to which other juvenile courts in the country will look to see what is at the Capital, just as they do in the case of other courts. Every

State court attempts to pattern after the United States courts; the State legislatures attempt to pattern after the legislation of Congress here in Washington. I think that it would be of importance in building up juvenile courts, which is, of course, a mighty vital necessity all over.

STATEMENT OF MR. WILLIAM H. BALDWIN.

Mr. BALDWIN. I have been asked to appear here as chairman of the Juvenile Court committee. The judge asked me to explain the matter to the House committee when he was not able to be there, which I did, and I was pleased with the courteous reception I got and with the interest they showed there, and I am sure they wanted to do all that they thought that they could. I am sorry that they did not make the increases that were recommended, and the matter has been explained to you in detail by Judge Latimer, and what I want to do is to speak of the character of the work in which this committee of representative citizens is interested. It is different from other judicial work. A lot of it is work that is constructive; that does not depend on what the hard decision of the law is; but it is a question of what we are going to do with these social problems that are presented, and it is because of that that the court ought to be properly taken care-of here.

ADDITIONAL PROBATION OFFICERS (AGAIN).

With regard to the additional probation officers, they are absolutely necessary, as the Judge has said, and I want to speak of one thing here that he did not mention. When he came in as judge there were about 450 boys and perhaps a few girls under probation, and he found that, while the court under its necessity had been getting along and trying to take care of all of those with three probation officers, it was just like trying to provide a dinner for a thousand people with one cook. You could not do it. The whole dinner would spoil. What did the Judge do? He let go 300 of those boys, not because they did not need to be on probation, but because it was spoiling all the rest of them; no one was being properly taken care of. So he reduced the number to 165, of sheer necessity. They asked me in the House committee what became of the rest of those boys. I said they went, like sheep, out through the city. I do not think you should let those go in this way.

Another thing happened because of the interest that Judge Latimer had awakened after he came in. This question is not new. The juvenile court has needed more probation officers all the time, ever since the work began. Because of the interest aroused by Judge Latimer, the good ladies of the Society of the Daughters of the American Revolution came to the front. They are quite capable, and they raised some money for an additional probation officer, so that while the government has three probation officers, and the records show only three, they have really got four, one of whom is being paid by the ladies of the Daughters of the American Revolution; and, Senator, I would almost as soon think of having them pay for my winter overcoat as having them pay for a probation officer doing the work for which the United States Government is responsible. I do not think you want that. That probation officer has been added by the House. They gave one more, but still another is just as much needed now in addition to the one the House has provided for here, as that additional one was needed whom these ladies provided last year. I do not think you want that done again. You should take care of the court in an adequate way, in order that this work may be done properly.

Judge Latimer has alluded to the condition in Cleveland. I have been interested in this matter of nonsupport, as you know, and I was really instrumental in getting through this nonsupport bill in 1896, under which more than $240,000 has been collected by men under suspended payments, as an addition to the financial resources of this community, not wholly as a result of the law here, but of the court. These cases are being taken up and this is being worked through there, and these men are being watched, and this additional clerk is badly needed. One clerk got into trouble some time ago and something was lost; I do not think it was taken, but he was not competent to do it properly. I was out at Cleveland four or five years ago and Judge Adams of the juvenile court there, one of the best juvenile courts in the country, asked me to sit with him. I was quite interested in these things, and he found out I could help some about those things particularly, and he said, "Come in; I want you to sit with me."

I found one poor woman there whose husband was a structural iron worker and had deserted her in Canton, and the judge had something about the size of a sheet of legal cap, about that big [indicating] made up by a probation officer, and he commenced to question this man, going by this memoradum. He said, "You lived at such and such a place, and you deserted your wife, so and so, and so and so happened?" "Yes." And so he went along, the man answering yes, until he got down to about the end of the page, and he said, "I will give you a year in the workhouse, and you will just leave right away. You need that." I asked him after that, "How could you do all that? A lot of that was hearsay evidence." He said, "Well, he admitted enough to convict him, and the rest was evidence which was looked up by the probation officer." The judge had all that done for him, he had all the facts before him, and they were prepared not by some belligerent woman who would come in and make statements which could not be verified, but by one of his own probation officers.

The chief probation officer there is a man named Lewis, who was formerly connected with the American Steel & Wire Co., a man who has a wide acquaintance among the labor people, among the people of Cleveland, and who is a bright, keen man. He would make a very good juvenile court judge himself. I was quite interested in talking with him, and finding the grasp that he had of these cases. He was an arm of the court, upon whom the judge relied. They have their new courthouse in Cleveland, and what have they done? They have cleared out the whole ground floor and turned Judge Adams loose in there, with capacious chambers, which gives a chance for these boys when they come in to have the care of these probation officers, and it is a great help to have their quarters in that way.

What I want to say about these probation officers here is that they are really the right arm of the court. Cases under the non-support law are tried in the juvenile court, and they are getting just as good treatment in the juvenile court here as if they had a separate domestic relations court; but they have to have the separate facilities.

There has been a good deal of fault found, and Judge De Lacy was blamed unjustly for that, because children were present in the court where these nonsupport cases were tried and heard a great many things they should not hear. How could you help it in that old building there. I have gotten a good many replies from a great many cities in the United States. I have sent around printed questions and schedules asking, "What happens here?" and "How do you get along?" They all say they make these inspections and investigations. You take a man who has been a rounder for 10 years, or something like that, and if the judge gets things wrong in his case and makes a mistake it does not make much difference about him; but you take one of these boys and get things wrong with him and he is hurt; and, more than that, he has got it in for you. You have a problem there that is going to last sometimes for years.

Another thing about probation here. You may get these men to take it somewhat philosophically, but if one of these 150 boys who is on probation under the probation officer is not getting proper attention and he is fooling the probation officer, that is a different matter.

Judge LATIMER. And he tells all the other boys.

Mr. BALDWIN. Yes; he tells all the other boys, and the judge has not control of it. Now, if you can go and look up that case thoroughly and then say to the boy, "You have done that," and you know all about his case, so that the probation officer is on top, then it is all right. I do not know anything worse for the discipline of the school than to have the school on top.

Senator GALLINGER. Where are these children mostly placed; are many of them placed outside of the city?

Judge LATIMER. The children that are under probation are very few of them outside of the District. They are kept here in their own homes, as far as possible. If we have to take them away from their parents, they are placed in some institution in the District.

Senator GALLINGER. Do you place any of them in private homes?

Judge LATIMER. After they have been in the institution a while they are placed out in the country.

Mr. BALDWIN. Let us go into that. Suppose one of these boys does not have proper supervision, and he goes wrong, and the judge finds that he is not doing right and puts him in a home; how much more does it cost? I tell you that is an item of expense there, and it is too bad; but it happens. It is bad policy financially to have these people go wrong and get into institutions where they ought not to be at all. They ought to be properly taken care of, and that is what Judge Latimer wants these probation officers for.

Judge LATIMER. I understand that it costs $250 a year to support a boy in the reform school. It would cost $1,000 for four boys, and for $1,000 we can get a probation officer who will undertake the reformation and care of 50 boys.

Mr. BALDWIN. These are facts; and it does not take much work on this problem to make it very clear that the increase ought to be granted which is asked for in this item. I have been, perhaps, more interested in the probation officers' work in the court here; but in regard to the moving expenses which were spoken of, you will find that item mentioned in the hearing before the House committee. You will find it stated there that that amount was needed. Judge Latimer said he did not know just what was needed. I know we said that we would just leave that until we came to it. Now we have come to it, and that accounts for this increase over what the House granted. Just for the same reason that it is necessary to have an adequate number of probation officers, it is necessary to have adequate accommodations for the court, so that he can marshal these people where he wants them. The main object is to have these boys not mixed in with old offenders, and have them as if they were in prison, but to save them from that; so that that is what we want now, and I do not think this appropriation is enough to do that, with what we will probably have to handle; but the judge has been modest about asking for it, and, if you give him that, I can assure you that this committee will do their best to help him figure it out and get what they can under it.

I was reluctant to add to the other things the work I have been trying to do here the work of this committee, but I believe it is important, and the citizens who are members of it here, who are good, representative citizens, like Mrs. Radcliffe and Miss Janet Richards, who are deeply interested in it—I do not know of anything she has shown as much interest in here—have taken it up in this earnest way because they believe in the importance of it and because they believe in what it will do for the people of Washington, if only these young people can be properly taken care of by Judge Latimer.

Senator GALLINGER. In the absence of the chairman, I will take the liberty of assuring you that the committee will look into this matter sympathetically. If I had my way, I would double your appropriation.

Judge LATIMER. I should also like to add that the officers of the juvenile court would welcome a visit from any of the members of the committee any day when we are in session, which is every day in the week, in order that they may see for themselves our conditions and the work we are doing.

PUBLIC SCHOOLS.

STATEMENTS OF E. L. THURSTON, SUPERINTENDENT, AND HENRY P. BLAIR, CHAIRMAN OF THE BOARD OF EDUCATION.

OFFICERS—DIRECTOR OF PRIMARY INSTRUCTION.

Mr. BLAIR. The first thing that we ask for which the House did not see fit to give us should be included in the first paragraph. We ask to add among the officers a director of primary instruction at a minimum salary of $2.200. That takes her from the place below, under teachers.

Senator GALLINGER. Yes.

Mr. BLAIR. That is Miss Elizabeth Brown, who has been in the school service for a number of years; and you know her father's connection with the public buildings and grounds work of the city; and there seems to be no reason in any way why the director of primary instruction should not be classified with the director of intermediate instruction. It means a slight difference in her salary basic of $200, and ultimately would lead to a slightly increased longevity for her. We think that the placement ought to have been made, but it has not been made. She is charged with the supervision of all the work in the four lower grades in the system, and it is exactly the same thing that the director of intermediate instruction does in the four upper grades of the system, the place now held by Mr. Stewart.

CLERKS—SECRETARY'S OFFICE.

Then, in connection with the next item which is practically for the secretary's office, when Dr. Davidson came here, after some inquiry, the question of the business end of the schools being one of the most important things and one of the things requiring greatest attention, Dr. Davidson with the auditor for the District made a very considerable study of accounting systems and business systems in the various schools in the East and in the West, and as a result we have installed what, in the opinion of the auditor, will be the best system of school accounting in the United States, and we need the clerical force with which to properly operate and handle that system.

Mr. Tweedale has estimated that we ought to have 12 clerks in that office, but we have not asked, and do not ask, for anything of that character. We ask to have a salary given to us of $1,800 for the head of the office, and to have one $1,200 clerk given us, and to have one $1,000 clerk given us, in addition to what we already have in the office. The House has not changed the provisions of the existing law, so that we have the additional obligation still cast on us, and I would almost be willing to say that it would be a physical impossibility to operate that office with the clerical force that we now have. The man who is to-day getting a thousand dollars in that office is a man whose services are worth $2,000 to $2,500 anywhere. We can probably hold him at $1,800, and we are very anxious to have that new salary in order that we may keep him. Those changes were all estimated for in the estimates which we submitted.

ATTENDANCE OFFICERS.

With respect to the attendance officers, we are caring for 2,500 pupils with three attendance officers. We have asked for an increase of salary for the chief attendance officer, and we have asked for two additional attendance officers at a salary of $900, and a minimum salary of $650. That would give us, then, five attendance officers to handle a school system of approximately 50,000 children, of whom about 2,500 come under the care of the attendance officers during the year. Last year 2,700 children were under the care of the attendance officers, between 900 and 1,000 children being looked after by each officer.

Senator GALLINGER. Do these attendance officers look after the delinquents?

Mr. BLAIR. They look after the pupils under the compulsory-education law. They look after delinquents, whatever the form of delinquency may be.

ASSISTANT DIRECTOR OF PRIMARY INSTRUCTION.

The next item we have asked, on page 33, is that the assistant director of primary instruction, which is a position similar to the one occupied by Miss Brown in the high schools, may take the salary of Miss Brown. After Miss Brown's promotion to one of the officers of the system is granted that should follow; and if her promotion is not granted, it would not be appropriate at this time.

DIRECTORS OF DOMESTIC ART, DOMESTIC SCIENCE, AND KINDERGARTENS— SALARIES.

On lines 18, 19, and 20 we have asked that the directors of domestic art, domestic science, and kindergartens shall receive the same minimum salary that the directors of music, drawing, and physical culture now receive, together with the same longevity increase, which would follow. It increases the longevity. For some reason, in the original law the requirements for the directors of those three subjects—domestic art, domestic science, and kindergartens—are precisely the same as the requirements for the directors set out in the eighteenth, nineteenth, and twentieth lines of the bill, and yet for some reason their longevity was half that of the other directors; and this is simply that they may have the same longevity as the other directors, the basic salary being the same in both cases.

Senator GALLINGER. Those classes of teachers were left out, as you perhaps know, simply because we could not get them all at the time.

Mr. BLAIR. I think that was the reason.

Senator GALLINGER. We did the best we could.

Mr. BLAIR. And we are asking for them from time to time so as to equalize that proposition.

PRINCIPALS OF NORMAL, HIGH, AND MANUAL-TRAINING SCHOOLS—SALARIES.

We have asked in our estimates, in lines 14 and 15, on page 33, an increase in the basic salary of the principals of the normal, high, and manual-training high schools. Their basic salary now is $2,000, and by longevity increase they go to $2,500. We have asked to change the basic salary from $2,000 to $2,500 and let the longevity remain as it is. One of the reasons for that, and the chief reason, is that the situation now is that if we are obliged to go in competition for a high-school principal—any high-school principal—we are practically unable to make the position attractive to anyone outside of the system, and it would, broadly speaking, involve a loss of salary to any high-school teacher within the system if they were promoted to the position of high-school principal. It illustrates one of the inequalities of the system that has worked out.

Senator GALLINGER. Would not the increase in the salary of this principal necessarily increase the longevity?

Mr. BLAIR. It would, ultimately. It would not at the present time. It would happen to operate at the present time in this way, if I remember correctly. I think it is about $400 that it would change at the present time; and, then, there are seven of them, and the longevity would increase at $700 a year for five years after that was done. So that to-day, if we had a vacancy in a high-school principalship and we wanted to promote one of our group B $2,200 teachers, that teacher would have to sacrifice $200 the first year in order to become principal of that high school, and for two years would receive a less salary than he had received for teaching. Ultimately he would be able to get $300 more. It is one of the inequalities which we have left to the last, really, of the salary scale as it has worked out in actual practice. It is remarkable that we have had so few of them; but we have been gathering them up one at a time and that is one that remains.

. The teaching scale on pages 33 and 34, and librarians and clerks, running through to longevity pay, on page 35, is satisfactory and practically in accordance with the board's estimates.

LONGEVITY PAY.

The item of longevity, on page 35, seems to have created some misapprehension, perhaps, in the minds of the committee, and certainly in the minds of the Members of the House. We are able to estimate longevity pay now with reasonable accuracy. Of course, we have between 1,700 and 1,800 teachers, and we can not absolutely tell who is going to die and who is going to resign a year before that happens; but a year ago the board's estimate for longevity was $407,915, and the House thought that we were mistaken about it and appropriated only $375,000. The urgent deficiency carries an item of $32.000 to cover the longevity deficit for the current year.

Senator GALLINGER. That would make a total of how much?

Mr. BLAIR. A total last year of $407,000. I want to call your attention particularly to the fact that that was our estimate a year ago. That is, the deficit that we are asking now, at this time, and there will be very little difference in the amount appropriated over what we actually need.

Our estimate for next year is $462,935, and the House has cut us down to $435,000, basing that, so far as we know, on absolutely no information other than what we have given.

Senator GALLINGER. Why this increase?

Mr. BLAIR. From $407,000 to $462.000?

Senator GALLINGER. Yes.

Mr. BLAIR. The classification of teachers means practically that for 10 years there is a steady line of increase in this item, and it is undoubtedly going to increase somewhat for that length of time. The act has been in operation for 7 years. The longevity, of course, as you know, carries in the different classes, the longest period of increase covering 10 years, so that if our body of teachers had remained static there would have been an increase for 10 years. Now, it is modified by resignations and by deaths. Those resignations come naturally in the lower classes. A teacher who is getting $1,800 to

$2,200, which is the maximum in the high schools, is not likely to retire from the system. The teachers in the grade schools who are getting the maximum salaries are not likely to retire. Their life is substantially fixed as teachers. These modifications come in the lower grades, in large measure, and it would seem that for a period of substantially 10 years there might be an increase in this item.

Senator GALLINGER. Let me ask you if this estimated amount has been figured out upon any basis that can be relied upon?

Mr. BLAIR. With the utmost caution and with the utmost care, based on the teachers in the system at the time the estimate was made, with some allowance for the probable changes; and it is a curious fact, as I have just illustrated, Senator, that on the same basis the year before we came within a very few hundred dollars of the amount that is actually needed, and the auditor's office has agreed with us in the figuring of this longevity each year. The only thing I am afraid of is that some time there will come a debate on this, and these appropriation acts as made will be cited as evidence that we did not know what we were estimating for; and yet the contrary is the truth. We have estimated with great accuracy for the past two years, and have asked for what we needed for this longevity item.

NIGHT SCHOOLS.

We asked for a little more money in respect to the night schools, and the House committee has given us $2,500, and we are going to try to get through with that. On page 36 it is the same way with respect to the contingent expenses for the trade schools.

Senator GALLINGER. Did the appropriation of last year enable you to keep the night schools open?

Mr. BLAIR. We are able to keep them open about 60 days. They open in October, and with allowance for vacations—they have a little longer vacation at Christmas, because many of the people work—we are able to keep them open into March. We need a longer time, really, but we are making headway with that, and perhaps the appropriation is commensurate with that actual growth.

JANITORS AND CARE OF BUILDINGS.

At the top of page 37 we estimate an increase for the superintendent of janitors from $1,200 to $1,800, and we feel that that very efficient and worthy employee, who has been with the school system for a great many years, is entitled to that increase. He has charge of these janitors who have the care and custody of property that is worth some $12,000,000—which cost us some $12,000,000—and he has under him a large number of employees, and he is efficient, and he is at work early in the morning and all day long.

Senator GALLINGER. Does he have charge of this entire janitor force?

Mr. BLAIR. He is supervisor of the entire janitor service.

Senator GALLINGER. It does not seem possible that one man could give supervisory attention to that work.

Mr. BLAIR. It is pretty difficult. We would like an assistant for him, but we do not think of that until we have adequate pay for him. If we lost him it would be a great loss and a difficult one to supply.

In line 8 we have asked an increase in the salary of the engineer having charge of the J. Ormond Wilson Normal School and the Ross School to $1,000. That is to equalize the salary of the engineer in charge of that plant and to make it correspond to the salary of the engineers in charge of similar plants. We have two or three plants of about the same size as the Ross and the J. Ormond Wilson Normal School plants where the engineers receive $1,000. The M Street High School and the Douglas and Simmons Schools, on page 38. are illustrations of that, and I think there is one other school of the same character.

FIREMAN AT JEFFERSON SCHOOL.

On page 37 we also ask for a new fireman down at the Jefferson School. That is in line 10. The situation there is that we have a new heating plant put in, and in the present situation we are practically requiring that janitor to be on duty all the time. He ought to have a fireman to relieve him, and he ought to have a fireman to enable him to take care of that large and new plant. This is to give us that fireman at that salary.

Senator GALLINGER. That is a large school, as I remember it.

Mr. BLAIR. The Jefferson is a big school; an old school down southwest. It is three stories high, and I think there are only two schools in the system which are larger, and perhaps there is only one. I think the Thompson is the only grade school that is larger. The Lincoln gets the largest session room pay.

ASSISTANT ENGINEER, ARMSTRONG MANUAL TRAINING SCHOOL—INCREASE OF SALARY.

On page 38 we have asked, at the Armstrong Manual Training School, that the salary of the assistant engineer at $720 may be put at $900, and that we may have a new fireman at $420. That is a new plant that takes care of this, and is a large and valuable plant. It is the same kind of an establishment, as you are aware, that the white training school is, and we need that amount to take care of that plant.

Senator GALLINGER. That is not as large a building as the McKinley Manual Training School?

Mr. BLAIR. No, sir; it is not as large a school.

There is no other change in the janitor schedule. They were changes due to the enlargement of schools, and the House has incorporated them in accordance with the changes that have been made in the schools. That carries us through pages 38 and 39 and down to page 40.

MEDICAL INSPECTORS.

In connection with the medical inspectors, we have asked this year for three graduate nurses, one of whom should be colored, to act as public-school nurses, at $900 each. That was the amount that was indicated by the health officer as the minimum salary at which we could expect to get efficient nurses. A study of that problem of medical inspection and graduate nurses has convinced me that the graduate nurses are almost an essential part of medical inspection.

A very interesting paper in the Annals of the American Society of Political Science indicates that the employment of graduate nurses increases the efficiency of medical inspection in the schools by about 50 per cent—between 50 and 60 per cent. This is merely a beginning in that direction, and it does seem as though we ought, here at the Capital, to be making some headway along that line. That is the reason we have asked for it. It is a very important thing.

Senator GALLINGER. I suppose the attention of the House committee was called to it?

RENT OF SCHOOL BUILDINGS.

Mr. BLAIR. Yes, sir. The next item—the item for rent of school buildings—is a very important one to us, and we need the full amount that we have asked for. This year's rents amount to $17,000 in full that we have provided for, but we have filed an estimate showing the necessity for next year of $20,000 for rent, which is the amount we estimated and asked for, and a portion of that is found in the new storehouse. One of the things for which the school authorities were most severely criticized in a recent investigation was the character of the storehouse we were occupying on L Street, and we have moved, the first of this month, into a large and semifireproof storehouse on Eckington Place, the rental of which is in excess of what the former rental was; and that, together with the other items that we feel we are going to need during the next year, makes up the $20,000, and we need that entire item. The House has given us $1,000 of it, but we need the entire amount, and if we do not get it we shall be very much cramped in doing the things we need to do.

REPAIRS AND IMPROVEMENTS OF SCHOOL BUILDINGS.

At the top of page 41 appears the usual item for repairs and improvements, which we estimated at $100, and put into a special item, $90,000 additional, covering structures that were practically already up, and needed these items to be put to them. You will find it in the printed note at the top, "Altering and remodeling school buildings," and we set out those items in detail showing the character of the work, and the work that was necessary, the places at which it was necessary, and the cost. There was filed with the committee, I think, a separate item explaining the cost. The committee struck out entirely the estimated paragraph which is on the right of the page, and added $15,000 to what we asked for repairs and improvements. Practically, with the exception of the remodeling of the Franklin Building, to which there seems to be some opposition in the House, every one of these things is necessary to make the school properties which are now in use efficient and serviceable for the use for which they are intended. If the estimate for the Franklin Building, which as I recall it was $20,000, and which is stated at some point, was left out, we would have the $70,000 that remain to do the specific things that are set out in that item and render them serviceable.

Senator GALLINGER. It would answer the same purpose to insert whatever increase is allowed, if anything, in the estimate at the top of the page, and not insert a new item?

Mr. BLAIR. I think probably it could be done in that way if we get an increase in that item.

COOKING SCHOOL AND MANUAL-TRAINING SHOP.

The next item in connection with which we need some addition is " one cooking school and one manual-training shop." That is on page 41. We asked for $300 in connection with each of these, and the House would give us neither, so that we are in a situation where we should like to have this. We estimated one other kindergarten at $350, one cooking school at $300, and one manual-training shop at $300, making $950, and the House has given us none of those items. It gave us four kindergartens, just what we have this year, and we really need five and have estimated for five, and we need this cooking school and the manual-training shop in addition. We really ought not to be deprived of those. The new buildings are going up, and the work is there among the children for all three of those schools or shops.

LIVERY EXPENSES, SUPERINTENDENT OF SCHOOLS.

If I may digress a little bit, at the top of page 42 a curious thing has happened in the effort to secure an automobile for the superintendent of schools, and that is that entirely by inadvertence—but nevertheless it has been the result—he has been deprived of the allowance that was formerly made to him of $25 a month for livery, so that the superintendent has not only failed to get his automobile, but he has failed to have any allowance made to him in the last appropriation bill for livery or garage, and we would like very much to have an additional $300 put into this paragraph at the top of page 42, allowing for the livery of horse or garage for the superintendent of schools, as well as for the superintendent of janitors. It is merely restoring what he has had ever since the schools were founded, but which has gone out in this effort to get for him an automobile.

Senator GALLINGER. What is the use of a garage if he has not an automobile?

Mr. BLAIR. The present superintendent has an automobile of his own, and the superintendent of janitors has bought an automobile, and if this language was not permitted to remain there there might be some question as to whether he could make the payment.

Mr. THURSTON. Senator, there has been a confusion in this paragraph the present year. Last year the phrasing read. " For livery of horse, superintendent of janitors," the words " or garage " having been struck out. The result of that is that the superintendent of janitors, who has his own machine, has been compelled to pay for that machine this year. It all resulted from the attempt to straighten out that item.

Mr. BLAIR. It was one of those things that in the pressure and hurry was lost both for the superintendent of schools and for the superintendent of janitors; and, of course, in each instance there exists, for the superintendent of schools as well as for the superintendent of janitors, the necessity to cover the entire system.

TEMPORARY PERSONAL SERVICES—MOTOR TRUCK.

We have abandoned the item of " Temporary personal services," which was included in our estimates, and we have entirely abandoned—unless the committee finds it wise to take up the item—every effort to get our motor truck for delivery, although the economy of those things can be proven without any question whatever.

STOREHOUSE FOR SUPPLIES.

On page 42, in connection with the storehouse, preservation of textbooks and supplies, and work at the storehouse, we have at the present time a $1,200 clerk and a $600 clerk for foreman or caretaker, or whatever you may choose to call them, in charge of the supplies of the school system, and we need, estimated for, and asked for, one assistant at $800 in addition to the two that we now have at $1,200 and $600; and it is vital in order to handle the supplies at that point and get them properly distributed that we should have this other employee.

ASSISTANT CUSTODIAN OF TEXTBOOKS AND SUPPLIES.

Senator GALLINGER. You have inserted " one assistant, $800," on line 15?

Mr. BLAIR. Yes; one at $800. The accounting system between the office and the storehouse will make additional work at that point, besides the manual, physical labor.

PURCHASE OF TECHNICAL BOOKS.

On page 43, to avoid any misunderstanding and any question as to the right of purchase, we ask to have inserted after the word " apparatus " the words " and technical books." There has been some question raised as to the right to spend any portion of this appropriation, and we have been refused the right to do it, for technical books. The result is that the things that are essential, some of the basic books that ought to be there in connection with both the physical and chemical laboratories we are unable to purchase out of the appropriation because of the technicalities of the law.

Senator GALLINGER. You do not ask any increase?

FIXTURES, ETC., CHEMICAL LABORATORY.

Mr. BLAIR. Not in the physical department, but in the chemical laboratory we do ask an increase. Because of the poverty of the old laboratory, we ask an increase of $900 to put it on the same basis as the physics department. We need that very much; perhaps not for a year or two, but if we could have it so as to bring the chemical laboratories up to the same standard as the physical laboratories we could get along very much better.

NEW CENTRAL HIGH SCHOOL.

I do not know whether it is necessary to go into this Central High School proposition. I want to say that the board is absolutely in favor of it. The wisdom of Congress has been demonstrated by the subsequent developments in our school system, and the estimates of the principal of the Central High School, who of course is interested in this proposition; of the principal of the Business High School, who has a school which is already crowded; of the principal of the Technical High School, who knows his conditions at his school; and of the principal of the Eastern High School, who is anxious to have a new school, all of them unite in this, that when we get this 2,500-pupil school built and equipped and ready to open we will practically be in a position where the high-school population of the District will fill the building, and more than fill it.

Senator GALLINGER. It certainly will by the time it is built.

Mr. BLAIR. The estimates show that.

Mr. THURSTON. At the present rate of growth it will fill it in about four years.

Senator GALLINGER. Now, with reference to that matter, no change is suggested in the bill as it stands.

Mr. BLAIR. We are very well satisfied with the bill so far as it affects the Central High School proposition, and would like to have it left just as it is. The other items on that page are in accordance with the existing law. That is another item to be urged, in respect to the Central High School. It is in accordance with existing law, and we are a little at a loss to understand why it should be attacked.

SCHOOL BUILDING WEST OF SOLDIERS' HOME.

At the top of page 44 the bill carries a building which we urged and asked for at Park View, the site west of the Soldiers' Home, and which this year demonstrates the fact that we are going to be two years behind time with the school that is needed there to-day. That was put in by the Senate committee last year.

Senator GALLINGER. And lost in conference.

BUILDINGS AND GROUNDS.

Mr. BLAIR. And lost in conference. There appears on a slip at the right, $400,000 of additional estimates, which we put in and asked. May I say just a word, Senator, on this? I do not want to talk too long.

Senator GALLINGER. Go ahead. That is a very important matter, and we want to hear whatever you have to say on this matter.

Mr. BLAIR. In the estimates of a year ago the board of education estimated and asked for about $770,000 worth of new buildings. For reasons which I do not entirely understand, but which were no doubt entirely satisfactory to Congress, we got about $162,000. In other words, we lost approximately $600,000 worth of things that we felt at that time were vital. That was three years ago. The following year we estimated about $770,000, and we got a little less than $600,000. So, adding the two years together, we had lost approximately, over our estimates, more than $800.000 of our estimates.

This year we came up carrying the large high school proposition and the M Street Colored High School proposition, which in themselves amount in this bill to $450,000, and still carrying those we kept our estimates down to $1,155,000. The House has been kind and liberal to us, without any question, but the items which appear in our estimates in the order in which they appear are in exactly the same situation as to the needs of these schools to-day as that Park View school was a year ago. The Eastern High School at the February promotion, which occurs this week, will send probably 25 pupils to some other high school, because we can not take of them at the Eastern High School. The pressure is tremendous at that point for a high school, and except for the fact that we have this other big project here, I do not believe that Congress would hesitate a second in giving this appropriation. The figures show that the school is full to-day, and that a site must be purchased and a building must be erected very shortly.

EASTERN HIGH SCHOOL BUILDING.

Senator GALLINGER. Has the board made an estimate of the limit of cost of the Eastern High School?

Mr. BLAIR. We have not reached that point. It is not expected that the Eastern High School will be of what has been termed a monumental character, as the Central High School is, but it is a fact that for a combination high school in the eastern section of the city there will be a very large school population. It ought to be not as large as the Central or Technical High Schools, but it should easily be one of 800 or 1,000 pupils, or perhaps larger than that.

Senator GALLINGER. Has the board given any consideration to the possible use of the old building?

Mr. BLAIR. Of the present high school?

Senator GALLINGER. Yes.

Mr. BLAIR. We have discussed it, Senator, in a general way. It is possible that with the development of the vocational training idea, we may have occasion to use that Eastern High School. One tendency of education seems to be to take the child under the sixth grade and carry him on four years into what might be called a junior high-school course, and it may be that that old Eastern High School building will furnish the center for that vocational movement, if that comes to be developed. The population in this section of the city would probably be well served by a school of that character, and it may be that when the time comes we would want to establish such a school and locate it at that point.

Mr. THURSTON. I might say also, Senator, that two grade buildings on the same general site as the Eastern High School are crowded to the limit, and that additional space for regular grade classes may be needed right at that point.

Mr. BLAIR. We can not predict that which is four or five years from now, and it may be that, as Mr. Thurston has suggested, the grade proposition will solve the question of the Eastern High School building. But we have that in mind, and also we have the same thought in mind in regard to the Central High School building, which would be vacated ultimately.

Senator GALLINGER. These items which have been estimated for and not placed in the bill you suggest are of importance in the order in which they appear?

Mr. BLAIR. With possibly the change of the Powell and the Cook Schools. That is, with the exception of the necessity for the Powell

School being greater than that for the addition to the Cook School, the items stand in the order in which the board regards them as of importance and necessity.

CONTRIBUTIONS OF PUPILS.

We have a little bit of legislation at the bottom of that page which created a good deal of discussion, and it illustrates one of the peculiarities of the public service in Washington that so far as the board was concerned, the necessity for this character of legislation first appeared in the debates at the House end. It had never been brought to our attention. Perhaps one of the things which it is intended to reach is the voluntary contribution made by the school children at Thanksgiving time to a public-school fund for the benefit of children who can not get the things that are necessary to wear in order that they may come to school and who are kept at home for that reason.

Senator GALLINGER. Some of those children did make contributions—children of the poorer class?

Mr. BLAIR. I do not know that they did. It is entirely a voluntary contribution, so far as I know, made at Thanksgiving time, taken the day before Thanksgiving Day, and it is entirely voluntary. It is made in envelopes, which are sealed, and any child can pass in an empty envelope just as well as an envelope with a dollar bill in it.

Senator GALLINGER. I think probably I did not catch your first statement. For what purpose were those contributions made?

Mr. BLAIR. Those contributions were made for what we call the school children's fund, and the money is turned over to the Associated Charities.

Senator GALLINGER. For the school children?

Mr. BLAIR. For the benefit of the school children as they may need it. The truant officer reports, for instance, that some boy is absent because he has no shoes. Shoes are purchased for him from this fund.

Senator GALLINGER. That would seem to be a pretty worthy object. I supposed from casually reading the debates before the House that it was a contribution made by the children, including these destitute children, for some testimonial to some officer or teacher.

Mr. THURSTON. What we have told you is absolutely all, so far as we have ever known. The contribution is made through the use of envelopes, one envelope being given to each pupil, and that pupil being expected to return that envelope sealed. Whether there is anything in it is known only to the child who returns it. The fund is turned over to the Associated Charities and is reported separately. Whenever it is found out that a child can not attend school for the want of shoes or other clothing, the case is turned over to the Associated Charities to investigate the matter, and the return comes back to the superintendent of schools, so that we know positively in regard to it. Not only shoes are bought, but car tickets are furnished for children who have to come to a special school, or in the case of a child of a very poor family who can not walk, who has to have some contrivance to help him. Sometimes the fund is used to purchase material—cloth—that is made up in our sewing classes and used to help out in very poor families. In some cases it is used for extremely

these old school buildings, and we have allowed things of that sort to be done. One of the divisions up northwest has just received permission to use the school building for a minstrel show in order to equip their playground. Under this provision here we could not have granted that permission; and yet because they have that minstrel show at that point it does not mean that the children in some other quarter of the city where they can not afford to have a minstrel show will be in any way affected. Under this clause we would have had to refuse to allow the use of that building for that particular purpose.

Senator GALLINGER. I presume there has never been any compulsion, or even suggestion, from the board of education in regard to these little contributions that have been made?

Mr. BLAIR. On the contrary, the whole attitude of the board has been just the other way.

Senator SMITH of Maryland. And you say that there is nothing done that would discriminate or hurt anybody's feelings in any way?

Mr. BLAIR. No, sir; nor anything that would hurt anybody's feelings or hurt any child's feelings. The constant attitude has been that if anything of that sort was known it would injure the whole business.

Senator SMITH of Maryland. It strikes me that this is a matter that ought to be handled at a closer range. It strikes me so.

OFFICE SPACE, FRANKLIN SCHOOL BUILDING.

Mr. BLAIR. There is one other matter I want to call the attention of the committee to. The next item is at the top of page 45. We feel that that is a restriction that we would like to have removed, if it might be. It says we shall use no greater amount of floor or room space in the Franklin Building for office purposes than is now used until there shall be further action by Congress, and that we must use what we do not use for office purposes for teaching purposes.

The facts about the Franklin Building are that from the start of the school system that has been regarded as school headquarters. The superintendent has been located there. I went to the public schools here in the seventies, and he was located there then, and he is located there to-day. There has been some growth and development in the size of the school system in that length of time, and it takes more room to-day. We have installed this modern business method and equipment, and we need the room there that we are now using. Congress indicates that they do not want that made into a headquarters building, or there is no occasion to use any more room for office purposes. There will be no encroachment by the board of education; but if we do need it for our offices, for the orderly conduct of our business matters and orderly access to the things that are essential in the way of records, etc., we do not feel that we ought to be curtailed in that way. For years the normal school was there, and in connection with the normal school we had certain practice schools in that building. The normal school has gone to the J. Ormond Wilson Normal School, and the practice schools have gone with it, and we are using the practice school that is adjacent to the J. Ormond Wilson Normal School, and it seems a character of limitation on the board that is entirely unnecessary. We have encroached very little on the school space. We have taken the normal school and the

Now, we should like very much to see it go out. We feel, as was suggested in the House debate, that this is rather a matter for the board of education, and that if Congress undertakes to legislate in any way in respect to a matter of this sort, it may work to the very serious detriment of the school system. The board of education has been aware of no complaint about this, and the authority given by the board from time to time during the years that I have been in the service there I know has been very carefully guarded, and although there is a desire on the part of the children to do more in the direction of these social activities than they are allowed to do, yet the board has always restrained it to what seemed to it wise for the necessity and upbuilding of each particular school, and we really feel that it would be wise if the board could be trusted with a matter of such intimate personal school administration as this is. But if that is not to be done, then we should like to have the concluding clause, or the last two lines, made to read, beginning with the word "promotion," as follows: " For the promotion of school athletic, school playgrounds, school gardens, commencement exercises, and other exclusive school activities approved by the board of education."

Senator GALLINGER. Commencement exercises?

Mr. BLAIR. Commencement exercises. That strikes out a little of the clause that is already there. It would read " school gardens, commencement exercises, and other exclusive school activities approved by the board of education."

Senator SMITH of Maryland. Do you not think this is a matter that ought to be left to the board of education, anyway, without legislation?

Mr. BLAIR. We feel very much that way.

Senator SMITH of Maryland. It seems to me if the board is not able to regulate these things, they are not fit to be there.

Mr. BLAIR. We all feel that way about it.

Senator SMITH of Maryland. Those little things that come up are not matters for legislation. but are matters of propriety. to be attended to by the board.

Mr. BLAIR. May I illustrate that very thing? This clause reads, as drawn, " and commencement exercises of high schools." Now, we are having a little grade commencement. in which the children who have to stop at the end of the eighth grade are given a commencement diploma, so that they have something to show if they have to go out at the end of the eighth grade.

If that clause remained. the ribbons that are necessary to tie up those diplomas would have to be purchased by the teachers out of their own pockets or else they would have to go without. That item does not amount to anything in a division, and it does not come on anyone who does not want to do it. We have had these things, and they may or may not have been wise. We have had entertainments occasionally in schools, which have been permitted in order that they might buy pianos. We have 160 buildings, and I could take the Senators to some buildings where I am sure you would not want to hear the piano played, and the chance of their getting new pianos is pretty poor in many of them. We have $900 a year for pianos. and we generally have one or two or three new buildings to equip of recent years. and then the rest of that appropriation has to go to supplying

city. Some of our pupils are admitted free here, and we would like to have more of them admitted. Our community is a very rapidly-growing one. We do the very best we can through our local school facilities, but in providing facilities for children we can not possibly take care of all of them. We would like the freer use of the schools of the District.

I am going to ask a few citizens to speak briefly on this matter. I wish to inform the committee that we would have had a much larger delegation but for the death of one of the prominent citizens of Alexandria County, whose funeral takes place this morning. A good many of the county officers could not be present on that account. I am going to ask Mr. W. W. Douglas, a prominent citizen of one of our near-by towns, to speak briefly on this matter.

STATEMENT OF W. W. DOUGLAS.

Mr. DOUGLAS. Mr. Chairman and gentlemen of the committee, it is quite unexpected to me to be called on this morning to say anything, but those whom we had expected to be present and to speak have been detained in the manner suggested by Supt. Hodges.

I wish to offer simply a few suggestions in regard to this question. In the first place, while we do not subscribe entirely to Representative Johnson's view on the contribution of taxes to the support generally of Washington City, we believe that the present arrangement is a proper one and should continue, and that while people outside of Washington do not commonly care whether they contribute to the support of Washington City or not, assuming it to be correct, and that the condition exists, and I believe it is going to continue to exist, we feel that the children of those taxpayers who are contributing the one-half to the support of the city of Washington should have some recognition in the public schools here. By the way, this would not be so true, perhaps, of other elements going to make up the expense of Washington City. The streets, for instance, leading to this building, owned by the United States Government, are paid for in half by the people of Washington and half by outsiders. But the Government itself has no children to send here to school in Washington, and any child outside of the confines of the District of Columbia who attends here may fairly be charged against the one-half that the General Government is contributing to the expense of these schools.

Even so, you may offset the expense of this and any other matter against property owned here in the District of Columbia, but the property itself sends no children to school, as in the case of the half which is contributed by the General Government toward the expense of running schools here. There are no children to offset that, unless there might be some few children in adjacent territory who would be admitted. What is true in that respect of Virginia is true equally of Maryland.

Senator GALLINGER. Why would it not be equally true of New Hampshire?

Mr. DOUGLAS. Undoubtedly, except that geographically the distance is such that it would be impossible for them to attend; but a scholar from New Hampshire can come here and rent a room for a dollar a week and claim residence, and that admits him to all the rights of the school. Undoubtedly it is true of New Hampshire or

Utah. It is simply a question of only the small territory from which it is possible for children to come in on trolley lines in the morning and attend school during the day to return to their homes in the evening. If they come here and occupy a room and sleep here over night they are admitted to the schools free. That I say is one very strong reason why the children living immediately adjacent to the city should be admitted to the public schools.

Senator DILLINGHAM. Upon what terms are they admitted now, if at all?

Mr DOUGLAS. Mr. Hodges can answer that question better than I. They are admitted to schools, as I understand, under most onerous and excessive charges for tuition. I understand that the children of the high school are paying $90. Is that the case, Mr. Hodges?

Mr. HODGES. Yes.

Mr. DOUGLAS. I am sorry that I did not come prepared to answer the question. It is only within a minute that I was notified I would be expected to address the subcommittee.

Senator DILLINGHAM. That is a matter which can be ascertained.

Mr. DOUGLAS. The tuition is $90 a year. Now, I come to the suggestion I want to make to the gentlemen of this subcommittee.

Senator GALLINGER. Are the taxes the parents pay deducted?

Mr. DOUGLAS. Only in the event that the taxes are sufficient to cover the entire bill. I may pay an annual tax here of $89 a year, and yet if the tuition of my child in the high school is $90, that child is debarred from the school unless I pay the entire $90, and I am not even given credit for the $89 that I do pay.

Senator SMITH of Maryland. One could buy a dog tag and make up the balance. [Laughter.]

Senator GALLINGER. How would it do if we should provide that credit should be given for the amount of taxes paid, and if they did not reach the maximum they should pay the difference between the amount of taxes and the maximum.

Mr. DOUGLAS. That would be a step in the right direction, but before we consider that I have one further suggestion to make which to my mind is most material. It relates exclusively to Alexandria County, so far as I am advised. Perhaps it may pertain in a lesser degree to Maryland, but in Alexandria County one-seventeenth of the taxable area is owned by the United States Government, and I believe the nearest estimate we can get of it is that about one-twelfth of the fair value of the ground is owned by the Government. One-seventeenth of the area and one-twelfth in value; that is, not counting the value of the improvements on other lands, is owned by the United States Government, upon which the United States Government contributes not one red cent toward the support of Alexandria County. That area is carved out from the heart of the county, the most valuable ground, the highest tax-producing section of the county, and yet we get absolutely nothing from it.

Nor is that all. On that area of ground, as we all know, is located Fort Myer, with some six or eight hundred horses there, which are exercised practically the year round on the roads of our county that are built and paid for by the taxpayers exclusively.

I would not attempt, gentlemen, for one moment to set up here a claim that the Government having come into Alexandria County should pay one-half of the taxes there, nor yet that it should pay even one-twelfth because it owns that property. but I do say the question before you should be considered in view of what they get and in view of their damage. And you, gentlemen, must understand that that little county, figuratively speaking not larger than my hand, is paying forty-odd thousand a year for the upkeep of its roads. Yet those cavalrymen—all the cavalry and artillery, and at times wagon trains—go out on those roads, and not only go on the roads but they ride on our sidewalks with impunity because they wear the United States uniform.

Senator GALLINGER. That is true the country over, wherever there is a military post.

Mr. DOUGLAS. Undoubtedly it is true wherever there is a military post, but that military post imposes such burdens on the taxpayers of the adjacent territory that if the Government can grant some little amelioration or alleviation of those burdens they ought to do it. That is precisely the point, gentlemen. I say, the small consideration of admitting our children to the schools here would be only a very small compensation for the loss of taxes and for the extra expenses incurred by reason of the Government occupation of the Arlington Reservation.

Gentlemen, I wish to make one suggestion more. I make it on my own responsibility, however, without having consulted the superintendent of schools or any other gentleman. We have in our county excellent schools of lower grades, and if this committee and Congress saw fit, why not so adjust this matter that the children of the high schools could be admitted here? We have excellent lower-grade schools, schools graded from the first to the eighth grade, and our children can come out of our eighth grade and enter the high school here. The physical conditions of Alexandria County are such that we are, I believe, the most densely populated county in the State of Virginia, but the children are scattered over such a territory that it would be impossible for us to maintain a high school, even if we had the money; that is to say, to get enough children together at one point. Without obligating any of the gentlemen present this morning or anyone in Alexandria County, or compromising the question, I simply offer as a suggestion that if the children may be admitted to the high school here without charge we can take care of the lower grades, because we have in each community enough children to maintain from the first to the eighth grade, but we have not and could not get together enough children, if we had the money, to maintain a high school.

With these suggestions there are other gentlemen present whom I should like to have you hear, and I respectfully present to you with gracious kindness to Alexandria County that it is but just and fair that the United States Government should in return for what it receives at the hands of the people of the State of Virginia at least admit our children to the public schools of Washington.

Senator GALLINGER. What would the citizens of your county say to a proposition to abandon the Fort Myer Military Reservation?

Mr. DOUGLAS. And turn it into taxable property?

Senator GALLINGER. Yes.

Mr. DOUGLAS. As one citizen, I will not assume to say a leading citizen, but as a man largely interested in property over there, I should be very glad, indeed, to see it.

Senator GALLINGER. In other parts of the country the people are clamorous for the establishment of military posts.

Mr. DOUGLAS. Yes; they are clamorous to retain the posts there; but let me tell you that the most valuable ground in Alexandria County for building purposes lies right over here to the right of the reservation. That ground was sold 20 years ago when Fort Myer was not nearly so large as it is now for from 10 to 15 cents a square foot and it can be bought for 3 cents to-day, while 2 miles farther back the ground is worth three and four times as much. The reason is that people will not go down there and locate where soldiers when off duty are straying around through the country. It is a well-known fact that our Army gathers together many of the very best men in the United States. I am not speaking of the officers; I am speaking of the privates. It is also undeniably true, gentlemen, that they get some of the very scum of the earth. That is a fact. You can not rub it out. People do not want to locate their homes there. I left my home this morning with my wife and servant in the kitchen alone. If they had lived within half a mile of Fort Myer I could not have gone away feeling perfectly satisfied.

Gentlemen, I want to say right here the Government reservation and particularly the military end is not a precious boon to Alexandria County, and if it could be removed to-day and that section built up as other sections have been built up it would be a godsend to Alexandria County, and the taxation would run so high that we could have as good a high school as the District of Columbia has in it.

Gentlemen, I do not want to consume more of your time. There are other gentlemen to be heard. I thank you very much for your attention.

Mr. HODGES. Mr. Chairman, Mr. George H. Rucker, the clerk of the circuit court, will now address the subcommittee.

STATEMENT OF GEORGE H. RUCKER.

Mr. RUCKER. Mr. Chairman, I did not come prepared to make a talk. I am very largely interested in Alexandria County. I can not agree with some in thinking that the Government interest there is detrimental to us by any means, but many of our people located out there under the old law, and it is working quite a hardship to them, especially a great many people who are employed in the District of Columbia—street car conductors, motormen, men working in stores who have a family and are not able to live here and raise their children unless they go in some dark alley in the District of Columbia, and they have come out there and bought their ground and made a small cash payment and are now paying monthly on their homes.

I think those men are just as anxious to have their children educated as any man, and unless those men are afforded the opportunity to educate their children in the high school here they can not be educated there Owing to the sparsely settled country it would be impossible to build up a high school and maintain it if we had the money. I hope at least that those who are employed in the District of Columbia, who are making their money here and are spending it here, will be allowed to permit their children to come here and attend the high school. We can take care of all branches up to the eighth grade as well as they can be taken care of anywhere else.

There is a sort of a community of interest between Alexandria County and the District of Columbia. Alexandria County is a sort of health garden for the people employed here, and they ought to be allowed to go over on our hills and build their homes and still not be deprived of the privilege of educating their children here. I hope you gentlemen will at least give us that r v ege that we had.

Senator SMITH of Maryland. Pardon me fpri ûhe minute. It is your idea that people doing business in the District of Columbia should have free tuition?

Mr. RUCKER. That is it exactly.

Senator SMITH of Maryland. I understand you do not claim that people who are Virginians and only Virginians and who pay no taxes in the District of Columbia and who have no interest in the District of Columbia, either by occupation or otherwise, should be permitted to send their children to school here.

Mr. RUCKER. I do not. That is exactly my position.

Senator SMITH of Maryland. For the reason that if that was the case, then there would be no incentive whatever to have any schools in Virginia.

Mr. RUCKER. Exactly.

Senator SMITH of Maryland. Because the children would come to school in the District of Columbia, and that would evidently be unfair.

Mr. RUCKER. That is my position exactly.

Mr. HODGES. Mr. Chairman and gentlemen of the committee, I would like to introduce to you Mr. A. H. Dadmun, secretary of the Navy League. He is a citizen of Alexandria County.

STATEMENT OF A. H. DADMUN.

Mr. DADMUN. Mr. Chairman and gentlemen, I have two children coming to the Washington schools. It cost me $111 in fees last year, and the fees this year are $180.

Senator SMITH of Maryland. For how many children?

Mr. DADMUN. For two children, $90 each. The rate has been raised this year.

Senator SMITH of Maryland. What is the school rate?

Mr. DADMUN. It is $90. The normal school is $140, or something like that. The woman who sews for us has two children in Washington schools. Her husband earns $40 a month and gets his house. She goes out six days in the week sewing, and works until 11 o'clock at night to earn money in order that she may educate those children. Three other families near her moved from their wholesome country life into a miserable little flat in Washington last year because they could not afford to pay the tuition fee.

We ought to have a high school if we could; but two children out of three who come to high school here are exempt from this tuition fee because of the discriminating clause, whereby the children of Government employees have their tuition free. If it were not for that discrimination, in my personal opinion we could all get together and perhaps have a high school out there. But, you see, here are two-thirds of the families already exempted. You have discriminated against the people who are not Government employees. I do not think the spirit of our institutions and of the Constitution itself favors discrimination. You discriminate against me, although I spend all my money in Washington, virtually, for foou and for clothing. I pay $64 a month office rent, and practically spend my entire income in Washington. Yet you discriminate against me because I am not working for the Government.

Now, either charge us all—Government employees and all—the same tuition, so that we can unite and get a high school, or else do not discriminate. It may be legal, but I do not think it is right, to tell the Government employee, " You will not have to pay this fee," and to tell the other man, who is spending all his money in Washington, " You must pay this fee."

I have a private project, which I hope you will keep in mind. If the memorial bridge goes across the foot of Sixteenth Street, put an agricultural high school on the experimental farms. Have a high school for the Washington boys right on that Arlington experimental farm, and open it to the people of Virginia. But that, of course, is away ahead. However, keep it in mind. There is where I should like to send my girls for a vocational education to earn their own living. But, meanwhile, while we can pay for the education of our children up to the eighth grade, it seems to me we should be relieved from the high-school fees, because the fees are very large. They are beyond what is the actual cost. I should like to send one of my children to the normal school, but $140 a year and car fares, too, seem too much for me. You will acknowledge that we are paying a good fee now for a school education.

Senator DILLINGHAM. What is your position?

Mr. DADMUN. I am secretary of a patriotic society—the Navy League.

Senator GALLINGER. Let me ask you a question. I had something to do with this law when it was enacted, but I did not have my way about it. I will say frankly that we made the best compromise we could with other gentlemen with whom we had to deal, as you are aware. I ought to know without asking the question, but do I understand that when a man is in Government employ, paying no taxes in the District of Columbia, but living in Alexandria County, his children have free tuition?

Mr. DADMUN. Yes.

Senator GALLINGER. They get free tuition simply from the fact that the parent is employed by the Government?

Mr. DADMUN. Yes. It is a discriminating law.

Senator GALLINGER. So the Government employee, getting presumably a good salary from the Government, gets this added privilege of educating his children, while the man employed in civil life in the District and living over the line does not get it?

Mr. DADMUN. Yes.

Mr. DOUGLAS. I should like to interject at this point that if I am not in Government employ, but a taxpayer in the District, my children have to pay tuition in the high school unless my taxes equal the amount of the tuition, but the child of Mr. Jones or Mr. Smith, who draws his pay from the Government, does not pay tuition; he gets it free.

Senator GALLINGER. That is precisely the point I suggested a moment ago.

Senator MARTIN. Let me ask you, Mr. Dadmun, whether your business is entirely in Washington City?

Mr. DADMUN. Yes, sir; it is.

Senator MARTIN. You simply have your residence on the other side of the Potomac? You go to Alexandria County to sleep, but your daily occupation is in the District of Columbia?

Mr. DADMUN. Yes, sir; entirely.

Senator GALLINGER. What is your position?

Mr. DADMUN. I am secretary of a patriotic society, the Navy League.

Senator GALLINGER. You are employed by the society?

Mr. DADMUN. Yes, sir.

Senator GALLINGER. And paid by the society?

Mr. DADMUN. Yes, sir; paid by the society. I will state that their settling in Washington was largely through my personal influence, and it meant bringing our account here and spending our money here.

Senator MARTIN. You work here and spend your money here?

Mr. DADMUN. I spend all here.

Senator MARTIN. You go to Alexandria County to sleep?

Mr. DADMUN. Yes, sir.

Senator MARTIN. But you are aiding in building up the city of Washington, and not the county of Alexandria?

Mr. DADMUN. Yes, sir.

Senator SMITH of Maryland. Would there not be difficulty, however, in undertaking to discriminate in favor of those who spend their money here? You say you spend all your money here, but have not the people who sent their children to school spent their money here? Is not that taken for granted?

Mr. DADMUN. There would be difficulty, I acknowledge, about that.

Senator SMITH of Maryland. So far as I am individually concerned, I am unwilling to throw any restriction in the way of the education of children; but of course there has to be a stopping place where one community should cease to educate the children of another community. The point is to be able to get at it.

Mr. DADMUN. I will state that the fees charged pupils in the high schools are doubtless larger than in most other cities. I corresponded with the authorities of Cleveland, Boston, Philadelphia, Baltimore, and a few other cities. Though I have not the figures here, I found that the tuition fee which we nonresidents are paying is much higher than in the other principal cities of the country.

Senator SMITH of Maryland. The tuition in the normal school, I understand, is $140, and in the high school $90.

Mr. DADMUN. I am not sure that it is $140, but it is in that neighborhood.

Senator DILLINGHAM. The rate of tuition per annum in the normal schools is $140.40.

Senator SMITH of Maryland. Can you tell us what the corresponding charges are in other cities?

Mr. DADMUN. For the academic course in Cleveland, Ohio—I am trusting my memory—it would be one-half of that, and for the scientific course it is about the same. I find that for the scientific course in other cities the cost is practically the same. Here in Washington it is $90 in the technical high school, but for the academic course the fees usually are very much less.   The fee in the normal school is, I think, the highest that is charged anywhere.

Senator DILLINGHAM. The rates of tuition in the District of Columbia are given here in this pamphlet as follows: Normal schools, $140.40; secondary schools, $90; elementary schools, $31.50; night schools, $6.30.

Mr. DADMUN. I want to say to you, gentlemen, as a taxpayer in Alexandria County I feel that I am not taxed nearly enough.   I do not want to be placed in the position of trying to shirk a burden; but, speaking for myself, it seems to me to be too much to pay $180 tuition for two children.

Senator SMITH of Maryland. That is, in the high school here?

Mr. DADMUN. Yes.   I see others who deny their children this education and others are moving to town.   I see my poor little sewing woman simply taking her life's blood and shortening her life in order to give her two children an education, and that makes me come here this morning.

Senator GALLINGER. Are her children being educated in Washington?

Mr. DADMUN. Yes; because there is no high school in Alexandria County.

Senator GALLINGER. They are old enough to enter the high school?

Mr. DADMUN. They have gone through all the grades they can get through in Alexandria County.

Senator GALLINGER. In this connection I will suggest what the custom is in my own State. and I presume in the State of the Senator from Vermont it is similar.   In my own city of Concord, a small city of 25,000. we have an admirable high school.   There are a great many towns—they are called townships, perhaps, in the West--surrounding Concord, where there is no high school and where they could not support a high school.   Those children come into Concord and pay tuition, but probably not as much as the schools of Washington exact. But we have not this complication in regard to Government employees, which I think is a matter we may well seriously consider.

Senator DILLINGHAM. I will suggest. in connection with what the Senator from New Hampshire has said. that in Vermont there are many towns which can support a high school and many surrounding towns which are unable to do it. and we have a provision by which the children of the surrounding towns may come to the central town on the payment of a certain rate of tuition. which is not more than half what it really costs, and that in many instances is paid by the town from which the children are sent.   In most cases the statute authorizes the towns, I think, from which the children are sent to pay the tuition.

Senator GALLINGER. It seems to me that the rate of tuition here is very high.

Senator DILLINGHAM. It is very high.

Mr. DADMUN. I was just going to ask, Senator. if those children paid tuition individually, or whether it was paid by the town or county.

Senator GALLINGER. I think it is paid by the parents.

Mr. HODGES. Mr. Chairman, I should like to introduce to you one of our prominent attorneys, Mr. Frank Lyon.

STATEMENT OF FRANK LYON.

Mr. LYON. Mr. Chairman and gentlemen, I will state, first, that I am what might be considered a considerable taxpayer in Alexandria County. I am a considerable taxpayer in Washington City, and my children have up to this time reaped the advantage of the provision. So personally I have no complaint, except I think rank injustice is done that my children should be able to attend the Washington high school simply because I pay taxes in the city of Washington. I thought the day.had passed when taxation was a basis of education.

.I do not agree with the statement that has been made here to the effect that there is objection to having the employee of the United States admitted without charge. I do not want my voice to be raised against anyone being educated in the Washington schools because the parent is employed by the Government. I think the child should have that education, but I think the exemption of every taxpayer in Washington who pays taxes beyond a certain amount is not based upon reason or sound public policy.

I rent what houses I have in Washington. I do not pay the taxes, except indirectly. My tenants pay the taxes. It is recognized that school rights based upon taxation is contrary to the principle of free schools and, I believe, does not accomplish the result Congress intended. I state that, however, generally. It does not affect me personally.

I think the matter should be looked upon from a much larger point of view. This is a great Government here. Half the taxes are paid by the people of Virginia and the other States. I think any child ought to be able to come to the seat of government and receive an education. The children of Members of Congress come here to Washington, and they are educated in the public schools. Why should that be done? What is the reason for it? There is none. Their parents do not pay taxes here; they have their being and their business back in the home district. It is not that I am opposed to it, but I ask, Why should you confine the proposition merely to the people who pay taxes in the District of Columbia? Why should it be made to apply to a man because he happens to live there, though he does not pay any taxes, to a Congressman who brings his children here and does not acquire residence, or to employees of the Government? The National Government divides this expense. Half of it is paid by the people outside, and not by the people of the District of Columbia. And why should not the people outside get the benefit of the schools here? Alexandria County is simply a bedroom for the people who work in Washington City. There is no business in Alexandria County. Absolutely, there is almost nothing there. They have a few railroads that run through the lower end of the county, and there are a few little enterprises located along the edge, but the people come here from there. and by 9 o'clock in the morning it is generally said that there is no man left in the county.

This District is the heart of the territory. and you might as well draw a line around the heart and refuse nourishment to the arteries and veins as to forbid the people from coming here for an education. Here is where the people of Alexandria County make their money, and here is where it is expended, and here is the natural place where the schools should be located. It seems to me that that is the point of view from which this question should be considered, and it seems so, sir, when you consider the number of children who would attend the public schools. I do not know just how many there are. The superintennt can state the number.

Mr. HODGES. Four or five hundred.

Mr. LYON. There are four or five hundred, but here are 40,000 or 45,000 children in the schools, and it is a small thing for the National Government to be engaged in to discriminate against a few people, 1 per cent, whose business is in the District of Columbia and who spend their time here, and to exclude their children from the schools.

Senator MARTIN. What would you think of a provision to the effect that the schools here should be open to the children of persons who are employed in the District of Columbia?

Mr. LYON. I think that would be a most excellent advancement over the present proposition.

Senator MARTIN. The children of Government employees are now admitted free, but suppose the children of all the people who are actually employed in the District of Columbia were admitted.

Mr. LYON. I think that would be an equitable disposition of the matter.

Senator MARTIN. You think that would regulate conditions fairly?

Mr. LYON. I think that is so far superior to what we have at present that if Congress shall indorse it we will be most glad to receive it. But, of course, I think the other would be the true solution.

Senator DILLINGHAM. Have you thought out any definite amendment of the law that you would suggest?

Mr. LYON. Yes, sir; I would allow all children to come to the Washington schools free. That is what I would do.

Senator SMITH of Maryland. If you will pardon me, your argument is that the United States pays one-half the expenses anyhow, and that the people who pay taxes in the District of Columbia ought to be willing to allow the children outside to come to school here free, inasmuch as they pay only half of it?

Mr. LYON. Yes, sir. I think we ought to have a great national school here and it should be open to all children who would come to Washington and attend it. Children do come to Washington who have absolutely no connection here. I have had my own relatives come from North Carolina and reside in the city of Washington for the sole purpose of getting the advantage of these national schools, which are upon such an excellent basis.

Senator GALLINGER. Do you think if your theory were put into a law that there would be any schoolhouses in Takoma Park or Chevy Chase, beyond the boundary line, or in any of these outlying districts?

Mr. LYON. Senator, that has been the rule in the District of Columbia for the 25 years I have been here, with the exception of the last three or four, for practical purposes.

Senator GALLINGER. Do you think they would have any schoolhouses practically in those districts?

Mr. LYON. I think we have had excellent schools in Alexandria County.

Senator GALLINGER. I am not speaking of Alexandria County. I am speaking of the effect on the outlying districts that I have named.

Mr. LYON. I do not think they are as good schools as we ought to have, but we have the graded schools for our children until they are educated in the elementary branches.

Senator GALLINGER. I can not imagine that they would have any schoolhouses there if they had only to cross the border and get into the Washington schools. Our Washington schools, as you know, are very much crowded. We find it very hard to take care of our present school population. That we should open our schools to the country without restrictions of any kind is a rather startling proposition.

Mr. LYON. They are open to the country now. Dozens of families are moving here from Alexandria County. They take a Washington flat at $20 or $25 a month, and they are sending their children to these schools. They are open in that sense to children coming from all over the country.

It seems to me it is very small for the Government to exclude these children; and now I will refer to what Mr. Douglas said about the property owned over there by the Government. He said in area it is one-seventeenth, and it is very much more valuable than Mr. Douglas would place it. I would say, from my knowledge of the county, that the value of that land would equal one-fourth or one-fifth the value of other land in Alexandria County. People do not like to live close to a military reservation, and you can hardly get people to live within half a mile or a mile of the national cemetery there. Men do not like to handle real estate close to a military reservation. I know the property is of very high character, but those are conditions we have to meet.

I hope the committee will look at it from that point of view. When people are knocking at your door for their children to be allowed to enter your schools you should not turn them away. I have seen children not able to go to school here because the National Government closes the door and charges as much as $140 to get into the school. It seems to me it is beneath the Government to do it, and I think excluding these children is indefensible from any point of view.

Mr. HODGES. I will now ask the subcommittee to hear a few words from Mr. Crandal Mackey, our county attorney.

STATEMENT OF CRANDAL MACKEY.

Mr. MACKEY. Mr. Chairman and gentlemen of the committee, I want to say at the threshold of my remarks that I feel no personal interest in this matter. I own enough real estate in the District of Columbia and pay enough taxes to send my seven children to school here and the children of a few other families if I wished to do so.

I want to enlarge, however, on one thought of Mr. Lyon. It does not take any definite period of time to become a citizen of the District of Columbia. A man who moves here with an intention in his subjective mind, becomes ipso facto a citizen of the District of Columbia the second that he lands here. There was no legislation within the memory of any of you gentlemen discriminating against the citizens of the United States until just a few years ago. Then Congress passed a law which was a reasonable law; that if one is employed in the District of Columbia or if he resides here or if he pays taxes here he can send his children to school. The county of Montgomery practically, almost, circles this District. You are surrounded by the

County of Alexandria, Va., and Montgomery County, Md. The people living in those counties are employed almost exclusively in the District of Columbia—in the markets, in department stores, by various companies. The large population surrounding this District is mainly employed in the District. The head of the family spends his time here during his entire working hours. If not so employed, he comes here to purchase goods and he comes here for his pleasure.

There was no demand in Congress that these people should be discriminated against when the law was passed by Congress a few years ago permitting only a man who was employed here or who pays taxes here to send his children to school free. This movement against the children in the outlying territory emanated from the school authorities. It did not emanate from Congress. The corporation counsel then prepared a bill, the effect of which was absolutely to exclude everybody except the rich, except those who paid taxes sufficient to the amount of the tuition that would be charged. That law has been strictly construed. In this city there is a large pay roll, for example, in the depot of the Quartermaster's office. Those men work in the Arlington National Cemetery. The pay roll is made up at Seventeenth and E or F Streets. They come there to draw their pay. The board of education of the District of Columbia, under the advice of their counsel, then counsel Mr. McNamara, ruled that those people could not send their children to school in the District of Columbia.

The same is true of employees of the Agricultural Department. The pay roll is made up there. They come there to get their pay. Yet those people are discriminated against because they live in Alexandria County. The statute, I say, is strictly construed to exclude any who can possibly be excluded. The law provides that you must pay an amount of tax equal to the tuition charged, but the man who lives in the District of Columbia does not pay an amount of tax equal to the tuition charged to send his children to school. I live on a hill with 15 or 20 neighbors. The head of each family is employed here in Washington, to my personal knowledge. I am the only one, though several of them are property owners in the city, who pays enough taxes to send his children to school here, and I am the only one who could afford to pay the tuition if I had to pay it. That is unjust.

There never has been an argument advanced for a national university here that does not equally apply to the public schools of the District of Columbia. It is just as fair to spend money on public schools, free and open to every one in the United States, as it is to establish a national university free and open to the people of the United States. How is it fair? How is it just? Because the people who will go to this national university will not be the sons of motormen and car conductors and clerks in department stores. They will be people who can afford to pay the tuition.

Senator GALLINGER. But the national university is still in the dim distant future.

Mr. MACKEY. Yes, sir.

Senator SMITH of Maryland. Pardon me one minute, but you made a remark just now which indicated opposition to free tuition on the part of the school authorities. Is it your opinion that the taxpayers of the District of Columbia are offering no opposition?

Mr. MACKEY. I never heard of any in my life. I talked to Mr. Oyster when he was president of the school board and to Mr. Cox, who was an active member of the school board, and those gentlemen, with the other members of the board, wanted a law drawn that would exclude from the schools the children living in outlying territory.

Senator SMITH of Maryland. Then, you do not think the opposition comes from the taxpayers of the District?

Mr. MACKEY. There is not a newspaper in the city of Washington that ever said so, and there is no human being who ever said so. There was never anything said by any person in either branch of Congress to that effect, as far as I know, until the matter was brought up by the school board, and the corporation counsel was urged to draw a bill that would exclude from our schools here the children of every poor man who owned one building lot in the city of Washington with the intention some day of building a home upon it. Many of our people have been paying $100 or $200 under the old law simply to send their children to school, but this proposed law practically wipes them out. This law says: " If you own a lot worth a thousand dollars, you can not send your children to school. If you own a lot worth $5,000, you can not send your children to the high school. You must be a man worth so much money and pay so much in taxes."

It is the most vicious kind of class legislation, the plainest exposition of predatory wealth, I might say, to say to a man: " We will establish a standard of money, and the man who has the most money can have the most school facilities."

Senator GALLINGER. On your theory, do you not think the District of Columbia ought to allow all automobilists from all over the country to come and use its streets without the payment of a license fee?

Mr. MACKEY. Yes, sir. I will assert that every automobilist in the country who comes to Washington uses our roads in Alexandria County. I do not think one ever comes here who does not go to Arlington or to some part of Fort Myer or to some part of Alexandria County and use up the roads of our county.

Senator GALLINGER. That is a Government road, though.

Mr. MACKEY. Part of it is, but it never became a Government road until a few years ago. There is not a road in our county that is not torn up and destroyed by the Cavalry and Artillery at Fort Myer, and we make it good.

Senator GALLINGER. Unfortunately, you do not make your roads very good. [Laughter.]

Senator SMITH of Maryland. You give us the best you have, however?

Mr. MACKEY. Yes, sir.

Senator SMITH of Maryland. They use the same roads you do.

Mr. MACKEY. To show there was no crying demand for the present statute, when objection was made in the Committee of the Whole it went out. It went out of the bill in the House in Committee of the Whole. It was inserted next day when the two most prominent opponents of the bill were absent, without any discussion, because they were absent.

Senator MARTIN. Mr. Mackey, do you feel that the reasonable necessities of the people outside of the District of Columbia would be met if all those who are employed in the District of Columbia were permitted to send their children to the schools here?

Mr. MACKEY. I think so, Senator.

Senator MARTIN. In other words, it seems to me that being employed here makes a certain sort of citizenship here.

Mr. MACKEY. Yes, sir.

Senator MARTIN. If a man spends his time here in the day, labors here, works here, builds up the city here, earns his money here, and spends his money here, he is really more a citizen of Washington than he is a citizen of Alexandria County, except in a legal sense. I mean, in reason and common sense he is more a citizen of Washington than he is of Alexandria County. I think you will have to get at some basis of equity about it.

Mr. MACKEY. Or if he pays taxes here, either, Senator.

Senator MARTIN. I can not exactly give my assent to that. I doubt whether paying taxes ought to be a standard for education. Those who do not pay any taxes need education more than the men who does pay taxes.

Mr. MACKEY. Yes, sir; but it has been made a standard in the House bill.

Senator MARTIN. I should be very loath, myself, to advocate the education of people because they had property and paid taxes, and exclude people who had no property and could not pay taxes. I would rather admit those who had no property, and make the men who had property pay. I do not think paying taxes is a fair standard by which this matter should be settled.

Mr. MACKEY. The standard you suggest would be far more liberal, Senator, than the payment of taxes. Under that plan the fact that you were employed here would give you the right. That is what the old law said, except that it went further and said that if you paid taxes here at all you were eligible.

Senator MARTIN. What I am trying to do is to find some plan which can be justified by reason and fairness. It occured to me that occupation here, living here in the daytime and working here, in a certain sense made citizenship here. It is pretty hard to justify admitting children living in other jurisdictions to the schools here, in my mind—and I say that with much hesitation, because of course my sympathies are with the people of Virginia and Maryland, but we must recognize the whole country, and adopt some plan that meets the sense of reason and the sense of justice of the whole country. It is pretty hard to argue that the schools should be open to everybody when we know that very few can get here. It is only in these two counties. If they could all get here equally from California and from New Hampshire and from Maine, just as they can from Alexandria and Montgomery Counties, it would be a good rule; but they can not.

Mr. MACKEY. Yes, sir.

Senator MARTIN. I am trying to find some rule that will meet the requirements of justice from the point of view of the disinterested people all over the United States. It seemed to me that perhaps working here, being occupied here, pursuing a profession or a vocation here during the working hours of a man's life, and spending here the money he earns during those working hours might make such a man more a citizen here than a citizen of the place where he simply goes to sleep.

Mr. MACKEY. Senator, from my knowledge of the situation, I think that would admit practically 90 per cent of the people who are now excluded.

Senator MARTIN. That is what I am trying to get at—whether that would admit people who are really suffering for the want of schools.

Mr. MACKEY. Yes, sir.

FURTHER STATEMENT OF W. T. HODGES.

Mr. HODGES. Mr. Chairman and gentlemen, we are very grateful for the hearing this morning.   Unless some of our men here want to talk, I am not going to call anybody else.

I should like to talk for just a minute about what I, as the county superintendent, think about the matter.   I have studied local school conditions in my county probably more closely during the past five years than any other man, and I want to ask, if Mr. Mackey's contention is correct, that 90 per cent are taken care of by the proposed plan, what shall become of the other 10 per cent?

To use a personal illustration, when my oldest child gets old enough for high school I shall have to pay his high-school tuition; so will the minister of my church, or any other church over there, who does not happen to work in the District of Columbia.

The point of the matter is this: Dr. Davidson, the former superintendent of schools, and I talked about this thing a good deal, and what we thought would be most desirable from the standpoint both of the District school authorities and the school officers of Alexandria County would be to admit free to the high schools in this city everybody in our territory, but to shut out equally all from the elementary schools, because probably we could take care of those; but we can not, with the existing circumstances, give them a high-school education.

I am not giving this as the sentiment, however, of the whole committee.   This is merely my private opinion of the matter.   Whatever you do for us, try to give us some relief, and give us a proper use of the educational facilities of the schools here.

We thank you very much.

FURTHER STATEMENT OF CRANDAL MACKEY.

Mr. MACKEY. We can not agree with what Prof. Hodges has said just now, Mr. Chairman.   High-school education alone would not benefit the poor people at all.   They take their children out of school when they get to be 15 or 16 years of age and put them to work.   We figured up last year that there would be only about seven children in our county who would want to go to the high school.

Mr. HODGES. About 70, I think.

Mr. MACKEY. Was it 70?

Mr. HODGES. Yes, sir.

Mr. MACKEY. There are a great many more, ten times a many, who go to the elementary schools; but my experience with people of ordinary means is that when the children go through the elementary school they must take them out and put them to work.

Senator GALLINGER. Most of them graduate, then?

Mr. MACKEY. Yes, sir.

Senator SMITH of Maryland. There is no question but that there is a greater demand for educating children below the high schools than there is in the high schools. Of course, the high school is all right, but a great many people can not afford to let their children go on that far. The children have to make their own living. I think anything that would shut out the elementary education would be a hardship.

Mr. MACKEY. Senator Martin's suggestion would bring practically all of these children into the high school.

Mr. HODGES. I am not arguing the matter, gentlemen, but I will simply say that the State of Virginia expects us to give everybody an education. We are trying to do it, particularly in the elementary schools; but we see no prospect of doing it in the high schools, with conditions as they are.

FURTHER STATEMENT OF W. W. DOUGLAS.

Mr. DOUGLAS. Mr. Chairman, I simply wish to say that if the children do not get an education in the lower grades in Alexandria County—and some do not—it is the fault of the parents and not of the taxpayers nor of the school officials. We have the low grades there, and we can handle that part of the problem. When the day comes when we can not handle it we had better go out of business as a political organization. The high school is the critical point with the children there. That we can not handle.

Senator SMITH of Maryland. Of course if you can educate those in the elementary classes, and have sufficient means to do so, that settles it as far as that goes.

Mr. DOUGLAS. We can do that.

FURTHER STATEMENT OF FRANK LYON.

Mr. LYON. Mr. Chairman and gentlemen, I have been talking with some of the gentlemen over here and we certainly indorse thoroughly what Senator Martin has suggested as the only practical and logical thing that could be addressed, we think, to the Senate or to the House. We realize the importance of it. It will give us, if not all we want, at least possibly all we are entitled to, and in any event it will give us so much more than we have now that we trust Senator Martin's views will be looked upon with favor.

Senator MARTIN. I will say to Mr. Hodges that the difficulty would be to give a reason to disinterested people for an arbitrary division of this sort.

Senator SMITH of Maryland. I assume that if Senator Martin's idea should be adopted not all of the children would come here. A great many of them would go to the elementary schools in your own county.

Mr. HODGES. Certainly; by all means. I was speaking merely from the standpoint of our own county.

STATEMENT OF C. H. GREATHOUSE.

Mr. GREATHOUSE. If I may take half a minute to answer the question of the Senator from New Hampshire, we have good schools in Alexandria County for children under 10 years old. From that age up, including many who do not go to high school, we have not.   The reason is—and you would see it very readily if you lived there—that little children can not walk the distance to the city schools.   Under t e old rule we certainly have had excellent schools for young children.

Senator GALLINGER. In our State the government provides transportation for children who live a considerable distance from the schools.

Senator MARTIN. They are doing that somewhat in Virginia. That will come.   We are doing it largely in Virginia now.

Mr. GREATHOUSE. .The observation of the chairman, that we should not pay anything in the way of education, goes to the heart of this matter.   If you are going to tax us for anything, would it not be much better to tax us for the privilege of coming here and using your streets, and take off this tax on our children coming in to go to school ?

(The subcommittee thereupon adjourned.)

WEDNESDAY, FEBRUARY 11, 1914.

The subcommittee met at 10.30 a. m.

Present: Senators Smith, of Maryland (chairman), Lea, and Gallinger.

Senator Martin, the chairman of the committee, sat with the subcommittee.

PAVING OF SEVENTH STREET.

Charles S. Shreve appeared.

The CHAIRMAN (Senator Smith, of Maryland). Mr. Shreve, you wish to submit something further on the improvement of Seventh Street ?

Mr. SHREVE. Yes, sir.

Senator SMITH, of Maryland. The estimate appears in the margin on page 23 of the bill, and you will proceed.

ADDITIONAL STATEMENT OF CHARLES S. SHREVE.

Mr. SHREVE. Mr. Chairman, there was an appropriation of $30,000 asked for by the District Commissioners for paving Seventh Street from New York Avenue to Q Street with asphalt. It is now paved with granite blocks. You gave us a very full and patient hearing. Since that time we had a meeting at Carroll Institute Hall where we had over 150 very prominent business men of the city present, all of whom expressed themselves as seeing the necessity of the immediate paving of Seventh Street in view of its deplorable condition.   There were present representatives of the Chamber of Commerce, the Board of Trade, all the citizens' associations, and the Retail Merchants' Association.   Those organizations have given us letters which we wish to file.

When Mr. Rea called me up this morning I immediately tried to get into communication with Mr. Berberich, that he might send me those letters and we might file them.   I should like to ask the permission, just as soon as I can secure those letters from Mr. Berberich, that they may be inserted in the record.

Senator GALLINGER. How numerous are the letters? We do not want to unnecessarily load down the record.

Mr. SHREVE. They are very short letters.

Senator SMITH of Maryland. We will look at the letters, and if we find them all right and not too cumbersome we will put them in the record; otherwise we will not do so.

Mr. SHREVE. They will not burden the record at all. Otherwise we would not ask to have them put in.

Senator SMITH of Maryland. You were before the subcommittee on this matter a few weeks ago?

Mr. SHREVE. Yes, sir. There is nothing, really, that I could add to what was said before. I know that you gentlemen are very busy and I will not ask to take up any of your time.

Senator GALLINGER. I understand that the traffic has very largely passed from Seventh Street?

Mr. SHREVE. It has.

Senator SMITH of Maryland. Quite a number of people appeared before us and stated that, owing to the condition of that street, it has been almost abandoned and that the travel has gone to other streets not so accessible.

Senator GALLINGER. Precisely.

Mr. SHREVE. I want to add one word; I will not take up your time, you gave me such a patient hearing before. There are several of us who, including ourselves, our fathers, and even grandfathers, have been born and raised in that neighborhood and have been in business there in succession for over half a century. We have many thousands of dollars invested there outside of our business. The only thing that appeals to us now is that we realize that we can not have the same privilege or chance that other merchants have in the city. If the present condition continues we will have to pick up and get away, though old Seventh Street is dear to us; it is our home street, and we would like to stay there.

Senator SMITH of Maryland. The fact is you feel that you are——

Mr. SHREVE. Discriminated against.

Senator SMITH of Maryland. Discriminated against.

Mr. SHREVE. Inadvertently, but it has happened.

Senator SMITH of Maryland. You feel that you have not had fair play. or

Mr. SHREVE. Yes, sir.

SCHOOL PUBLICATIONS.

Watson Davis, editor of the Easterner, official school publication of the Eastern High School; Bertram Y. Kinzey, editor in chief, and J. Wilder Tomlinson, business manager of Hand and Mind, a magazine published by the students of the McKinley Manual Training School: Richard L. Yates, editor of the Review; Francis C. Stestson, editor of the Western; H. H. Dutton, business manager of the Western; Edwin H. Felt, editor of the Tech News; Frank Loeffler, business manager of the Tech News; Miss Thelma Miller, editor of the Balance Sheet; Hilda Malcolm, circulation department of the Balance Sheet; and Henry F. Vanderlip, business-manager of the Balance Sheet appeared.

Senator SMITH of Maryland. Mr. Davis, whom are you here to represent?

Mr. DAVIS. I am here to represent the Easterner, the official school publication of the Eastern High School.

Senator SMITH of Maryland. In what capacity are you connected with that publication?

Mr. DAVIS. As editor in chief.

Senator SMITH of Maryland. The matter upon which you wish to be heard appears on page 46 of the bill.

Mr. DAVIS. Yes, sir; it deals with that part of the act which reads:

No part of any money appropriated by this act shall be paid to any person employed under or in connection with the public schools of the District of Columbia who shall solicit or receive, or permit to be solicited or received, on any public-school premises, any subscription or donation of money or other thing of value from pupils enrolled in such public schools for presentation of testimonials or for any purposes other than for the promotion of school athletics, school gardens, and commencement exercises of high schools.

As that provision reads it would cut out our school papers and we would have to suspend their publication. Those who are here with me represent some of the other school papers. Not only would it cause to be suspended the public-school papers, but also all other school activities other than school athletics, school gardens, and the commencement exercises of high schools. All activities such as dramatics, debating, and the High School Rifle Club would be suspended, because the provision would do away with taking contributions, and without money such activities can not be supported.

Senator SMITH of Maryland. Your paper is edited and kept alive by contributions from the students?

Mr. DAVIS. Yes, sir. About three-fourths of the money for supporting the paper comes from advertising solicited from outside, and the other fourth comes from subscriptions solicited in the school.

I suppose you can not doubt that these school papers are good things. They work in cooperation with the English course of the high school, and I assure you that I at least have gotten as much good out of handling the school paper as from a year of English in the high school.

Senator SMITH of Maryland. Your objection to the provision in the bill is on account of the effect it would have on the paper of which you are the principal editor?

Mr. DAVIS. Yes, sir.

Senator LEA. Are the subscriptions solicited by teachers rather than by students?

Mr. DAVIS. The teachers give their sanction to it, but the soliciting is done entirely by the students.

Senator GALLINGER. Do you solicit outside, or simply in the school? You solicit advertisements, of course, outside?

Mr. DAVIS. We solicit advertisements outside, and also some subscriptions from alumni; we try to get them interested in the paper.

Senator GALLINGER. You do not put any pressure in any way upon scholars to subscribe?

Mr. DAVIS. No, sir.

Senator GALLINGER. It is a voluntary matter?

Mr. DAVIS. It is absolutely voluntary. Of course, we tell them how good the paper is.

Senator GALLINGER. How large an amount do you usually secure?

Mr. DAVIS. In money?

Senator GALLINGER. Yes.

Mr. DAVIS. It takes about $415 to print the paper.

Senator SMITH of Maryland. For how long?

Mr. DAVIS. For the year. The Easterner gets out five issues. The last issue is a sort of yearbook. Other school papers have larger schools to cater to and get out more copies, and consequently they cost more money; they cater to a larger number.

Senator GALLINGER. How many pupils are there now in the Eastern High School, approximately?

Mr. DAVIS. Four hundred and fifty.

Senator MARTIN. Who made complaint about this matter? How did it come to be taken up by the House committee?

Mr. DAVIS. I suppose we started the matter. We sent a letter through the Board of Education. I do not know whether that letter reached you or not.

Senator MARTIN. You did not send a letter objecting to the practice? You are in favor of allowing money to be solicited?

Mr. DAVIS. Surely.

Senator MARTIN. Who objected and considered the practice to be a bad one? Did the teachers in the school object, or who objected to it?

Mr. DAVIS. No, sir; no one in the high school considered it to be a bad practice that I know of.

Senator MARTIN. How did the matter get before Congress?

Mr. DAVIS. I do not know. I suppose some Representative thought it was an evil to be remedied.

Senator MARTIN. I do not think a Representative would have known that the practice was going on or would have heard of it unless some one had brought it to his attention.

Senator SMITH of Maryland. I understood the other day when some of the trustees were here that it did not come from them. Was not that your understanding, Senator Gallinger?

Senator GALLINGER. That was my understanding. It has been suggested (I do not know what force there may be in it) that at the time Supt. Davidson was about to leave the city there was a very strong movement inaugurated here to retain him, and the suggestion was made that they might increase his salary by contributions from the schools. I have no doubt if it could be ascertained definitely it would be found that that was the basis of this proposed legislation. That would have been an unfortunate proceeding. Supt. Davidson himself put a stop to it just as soon as news of it reached him.

Senator SMITH of Maryland. That was wrong, of course.

Senator GALLINGER. During the years I have served on this committee, which have been a good many, there has never been any objection to these matters presented to the committee before.

Senator SMITH of Maryland. My recollection is that in talking with Mr. Blair the other day he stated that it did not come from them at all.

Senator MARTIN. I should think if the school trustees did not want the pupils to engage in soliciting for this purpose they could make any regulation they pleased to stop it.

Senator GALLINGER. I think Senator Smith made that suggestion to Mr. Blair the other day. Of course there need not be any law on the subject. It is entirely in the hands of the school trustees to regulate those matters.

Senator SMITH of Maryland. I think the matter should be left to the school trustees to manage. Is there anything further you would like to say to the subcommittee, Mr. Davis?

Mr. DAVIS. Nothing except that the penalty imposed in case this provision were passed would be rather severe upon poor teachers. It would be the loss of their salary for a whole year. I think the penalty is all out of proportion to the crime.

Senator SMITH of Maryland. If there is no law there will be no penalty.

Mr. DAVIS. Of course not.

Senator SMITH of Maryland. Does anyone else present wish to be heard?

Senator GALLINGER. It seems to me that we are very well informed on the subject.

STATEMENT OF J. WILDER TOMLINSON.

Mr. TOMLINSON. Mr. Chairman and gentlemen, I should like to make a single suggestion. I am the business manager of Hand and Mind, a school magazine published by and for the students and alumni of the McKinley Manual Training School. From my connection with the business department of the paper I may add that we are making a business department that the students are taking an interest in. They are trained in practical business so that when they get out of school and go before a business man they will not be flustered and will not be ignorant of business methods. We are training them in a systematic way; they have a certain system to follow, and in that way it is a great help to the students.

STATEMENT OF FREDERICK L. SIDDONS OF THE BOARD OF COMMISSIONERS OF THE DISTRICT OF COLUMBIA.

Commissioner SIDDONS. Mr. Chairman, I wish to express the regret of the Commissioners that they were not able to be here at your call. We had a call from the House Committee on Appropriations. and the other Commissioners will be here just as quickly as they can leave the room of the House committee. In the meanwhile, I will go on with the items which we desire to bring to your attention.

Senator SMITH of Maryland. What is the special item to which you wish first to call to our attention?

REMOVAL OF ENGINE HOUSE AND TRUCK NEAR CAPITOL.

Commissioner SIDDONS. I will call the attention of the commitee first to one of two matters in connection with the fire department. The items begin on page 52 of the bill. First of all there is an item that the commissioners did not include in their estimates. The importance of the item was not made known to them, but it is important, and I will explain it. This item was omitted from our estimates transmitted to Congress.

For house, site, furniture, and furnishings for truck company No. 1 of the fire department of the District of Columbia, including cost of necessary instruments for receiving alarms and connecting said house with fire-alarm headquarters, $55,000.

I am compelled to call that item to the attention of the committee, though it was not included in the estimates, and for this reason.

No. 1 truck house, North Capitol Street, between B and C Streets, has been purchased by the United States Government in connection with the enlargement of the Capitol Grounds.

This truck company is one of the most important in the fire department inasmuch as it is relied upon to provide hook-and-ladder protection for the United States Capitol, the Senate and House Office Buildings, Congressional Library, Union Station, Government Printing Office, etc., and is also required to respond to alarms of fire from the congested business center of the city.

It is proposed to locate the new house in as close proximity to the old quarters as possible, and therefore it is recommended that it be built in the vicinity of North Capitol and D Streets.

The buildings in the square occupied by the present truck house are in process of demolition and the truck house is now the only building standing in the square. The truck house must be demolished before the work of parking can be completed and a new house for this truck should be provided before the old house is destroyed.

Senator GALLINGER. Where do you propose to locate the new building?

Commissioner SIDDONS. I do not think, Senator that that has been absolutely determined, but in the general vicinity it is now serving.

May I say with respect to the present site, it is now the property of the Federal Government through the condemnation proceedings, and the District received and there has been covered into the Treasury from that condemnation for the site the sum of $18,124. The building is still allowed to remain standing by the Federal authorities, pending the selection of a new site. I am compelled to ask the consideration of the committee to an insertion in the bill of the item I have read, if it can be done, though it was not included in our estimates.

Senator SMITH of Maryland. It is a substitute for the building that is to be torn down?

Commissioner SIDDONS. Yes, sir; it is a substitute for the building to be torn down.

Senator GALLINGER. It is the truck house adjoining the office of the Senate stables?

Commissioner SIDDONS. That is the truck house. Two places are taken over, one a fire house and the other a truck house. The fire house has been taken care of by the Superintendent of the Capitol Building in a satisfactory way. He has provided a site, I believe, but the truck house we lose absolutely. It is important for this territory that there should be a site somewhere in the neighborhood.

Senator SMITH of Maryland. Was this matter submitted to the House committee?

Commissioner SIDDONS. It was not. I regret to say that its importance was not called to our attention until the bill had passed the House.

Senator SMITH of Maryland. You have an estimate of the cost?

Commissioner SIDDONS. $55,000.

Senator GALLINGER. I have wondered, Mr. Commissioner, that that item did not appear in your estimates, because it was evident that you were going to lose the present building.

Senator SMITH of Maryland. Why did you not appear before the House committee?

Commissioner SIDDONS. I can not give you a very satisfactory explanation, Senator, except to say that in the estimates submitted by the fire department to the commissioners for their consideration, in making up the total estimates of the District there were some four sites at least recommended, and this was apparently included in them, but they did not emphasize to the commissioners the need for this particular site made necessary by the conditions I have explained, and in our consideration of the four or five proposals that they did submit to us we selected but one which the House accepted and which is in the bill, the site out in the Tenleytown region, and that is very necessary.

Senator SMITH of Maryland. That has no bearing on this site.

Commissioner SIDDONS. None whatever. This is for the protection of this immediate neighborhood. We felt that we must submit it to you, although it had not been included in our estimates transmitted to Congress.

Senator GALLINGER. It is in the nature of a supplemental estimate, is it not?

Commissioner SIDDONS. It is, Senator.

RANDLE HIGHLANDS FIRE PROTECTION.

The next item to which I called the attention of the committee in the fire department items is on page 53. I submit this item with some diffidence, Mr. Chairman and gentlemen, and I do it because the fire department urgently ask it. My diffidence is born of the fact that the action taken by the House was original with the House. It proposes practically the dismantling or the abandonment of what is known as No. 2 Chemical Company, which technically is located at Twenty-eighth and Pennsylvania Avenue SE. It is a fire-engine house close to the home of Mr. A. E. Randle. I am informed that through his influence the building was originally built by authorization of Congress. When before the House committee some questions were asked us about the need of the chemical house. The committee visited it. The result was that they introduced the language which you find in the bill before you, which contemplates an abandonment of that house.

The fire department have urged very strongly upon me that the matter should be called to the committee's attention, because they say that the chemical house and the chemical apparatus are only useful in the suburbs, where there is no available water supply, and to abandon this particular house, they insist, would cripple very much the service in that suburban portion of the District, the Anacostia district.

Senator SMITH of Maryland. It is your judgment that it should remain?

Commissioner SIDDONS. I do not venture to express a personal judgment of the matter except to say that had I been consulted as to the locations of that place as it is now when it was established by act of Congress, I should never have dreamed of recommending the location there. That does not mean that I would not have another fire house somewhere in that general territory, but not at the particular point where it was located.

Senator SMITH of Maryland. It has been established and the money has been spent?

Commissioner SIDDONS. The building has been up for some years, sir.

Senator SMITH of Maryland. Is not that section growing?

Commissioner SIDDONS. It grows.

Senator SMITH of Maryland. Does it not need protection?

Commissioner SIDDONS. At that particular point there is very little development.

Senator GALLINGER. There is a schoolhouse in that vicinity?

Commissioner SIDDONS. There is a schoolhouse very close by. It also attracted the attention of the House committee and its location there, but I am not speaking of the schoolhouse; I am speaking of the fire house. It is within less than a square of the schoolhouse.

Senator GALLINGER. I think, Mr. Commissioner, one matter that somewhat influenced the committee in the location of both the engine house and the schoolhouse was that Col. Randle gave the land, and hence it cost the Government nothing for it. As to whether the buildings were wisely located, of course, that is perhaps a question, but they are there and it would seem not to be in the line of economy to dismantle either the schoolhouse or the engine house.

Then, Mr. Commissioner, when some gentlemen were here asking that this item should not remain in the bill I inquired of them whether or not there was an engine house at what we call Twining City just this side of Randle Highlands. They said there was not, and that is quite a village.

Commissioner SIDDONS. Yes, sir.

Senator GALLINGER. There are hundreds of houses there, and it seemed to me that even if a mistake had been made as to the exact location of this engine house, it would be unwise to dismantle it under existing conditions and allow the property there and at Twining City to be without any fire protection. I do not see the wisdom of it.

Commissioner SIDDONS. The Commissioners, Mr. Chairman and gentlemen, personally make no specific recommendation but in deference to the urging of the fire department we have laid the matter before you.

Senator SMITH of Maryland. I suppose it is a matter of judgment.

Commissioner SIDDONS. The matter of the proposal did not originate with the Commissioners, but it did originate very definitely with the House in its Committee on Appropriations.

FORAGE.

The fourth item for the fire department is at the top of page 53. The amount appropriated in the bill for forage is $32,250. The Commissioners ask for $43,146. If the decrease is concurred in by the Senate a deficiency in this appropriation will be unavoidable.

During the fiscal year 1915 the fire department estimates that it will have to maintain 235 horses. Under the present price of forage it costs $15.30 for forage per horse per month. The estimated deficiency therefore will be $10,896. We suggest a consideration by the committee of restoring the estimates transmitted to Congress in the sum of $43,146.

Senator SMITH of Maryland. Is your estimate of $15.30 for the forage alone or for the attention also?

Commissioner SIDDONS. It is for forage. Mr. Chairman, the price of forage has very greatly increased in the last year or two. May I say that the House perhaps was influenced in reducing our estimate by this consideration. They remembered that we are gradually changing from horse-drawn vehicles to motor-drawn vehicles. Each bill contains an appropriation to carry out that general plan, but the House committee may have overlooked the fact that after an order is placed for motor-driven carriages a period of from six to eight months elapses before they are delivered, and the necessity for maintaining the horse-driven vehicles continues until we have actually received the new vehicles. The Commissioners thought it possible that the House might have overlooked that consideration, because if it were a fact that we could get the motor-driven vehicles as soon as ordered there would be a good reason for making some reduction in the estimate we submitted.

Senator SMITH of Maryland. Will there not be some reduction anyway? If it takes six months to get the motor-drawn vehicles, will you not require less horses at the end of that time?

Commissioner SIDDONS. We will, sir.

Senator SMITH of Maryland. What amount of appropriation have you been getting for this purpose?

Commissioner SIDDONS. I do not think it appears here, but I should say that the bill for the current year carries the same sum as the pending bill as it left the House.

Senator SMITH of Maryland. $32,500?

Commissioner SIDDONS. Yes.

Senator SMITH of Maryland. You are asking for an increase?

Commissioner SIDDONS. We are asking for $43,146.

Senator SMITH of Maryland. Notwithstanding, you say there will be a decrease in the number of horses?

Commissioner SIDDONS. Yes; but bear in mind that the fire department estimates that there will be during that period 235 horses to be taken care of.

Senator SMITH of Maryland. Have you the same number of horses that you had when your estimate was made?

Commissioner SIDDONS. I think it is about stationary, because there has been an increase in the service.

Senator SMITH of Maryland. Was there a deficiency in the last appropriation that you had?

Commissioner SIDDONS. I can not answer that question a the present moment.

Senator GALLINGER. There are some motor-driven vehicles for the fire department now in commission, are there not?

Commissioner SIDDONS. Oh, yes, sir; and the pending bill provides for additional vehicles.

Senator SMITH of Maryland. It should not take any more for the coming year than you already have, inasmuch as you have now a less number of horses and will have a still less number.

Commissioner SIDDONS. I can only say to you, Mr. Chairman, that the estimate of the fire department is that they will have during the fiscal year 235 horses to take care of, and at the price per month for forage of $15.30 it will require the amount estimated.

I discussed with the chief of the fire department the question of the decrease in the number of horses and he explained that, notwithstanding that, the estimate here is the estimate of the number that will be in service despite the fact that we are gradually, under the authorization of Congress, displacing horse-driven vehicles by motor-driven vehicles.

Senator SMITH of Maryland. What is the next item?

Commissioner SIDDONS. I have but one other item to submit.

Senator MARTIN. Just one moment please, Mr. Commissioner. How do you explain that in the appropriation for 1913 there was only $934 deficiency? Forage is no higher now that it was last year?

Commissioner SIDDONS. My advices are that it is, sir. We had the question up during the late summer or early fall in making new contracts for forage.

Senator MARTIN. It could not possibly make so large an increase as that in the appropriation.

Commissioner SIDDONS. Perhaps not. I can not give you the details.

Senator LEA. That would be a 30 per cent increase.

Senator MARTIN. Yes. I buy those things in a small way and I know that the price is no higher now than it was last year.

Senator SMITH of Maryland. I do not think that the price of either corn or hay is any higher.

Senator MARTIN. I do not think it is any higher than it was last year. I do not see how there should be any necessity of an increase unless it was in the increased cost of the supplies, because you certainly diminish the number of your horse-drawn vehicles. Your increased need is made up with motor vehicles.

Commissioner SIDDONS. That is true, Senator, but those are the figures furnished us, and, as I said, the question of the price of forage is the initial reason for asking for the increase.

Senator MARTIN. I think the man who made the estimate ought to have given some reason for it.

Commissioner SIDDONS. I may be able to submit the details to the committee if they would like to have them. We only want to avoid a deficiency. We want to prevent if we can any deficiency, and in order to accomplish that the appropriation must be sufficient. However, I will endeavor to get more definite figures on that point and submit them to the committee.

Senator SMITH of Maryland. Mr. Commissioner, do you remember how much has been appropriated, independent of this, for the electrical equipment of the fire department that takes the place of the horse?

Commissioner SIDDONS. There is a fire engine, motor driven, and a combination chemical and hose wagon, motor driven, and two tractors, motor driven. We lift the body of an old car and place it upon the tractor and have a motor-driven vehicle.

Senator SMITH of Maryland. Do you know how many horses that would do away with?

Commissioner SIDDONS. For the fire engine, I should say three; for the combination chemical and hose wagon, I think two; and as to the tractors, motor driven, it depends upon whether they are to be placed on a fire engine or a hose wagon. If on a fire engine, I should say that each would displace three; if on a hose wagon, it would displace two horses.

Senator SMITH of Maryland. That would be 11, then, if it was 3?

Commissioner SIDDONS. Yes, sir.

Senator SMITH of Maryland. Eleven less horses would be required when that was put in service?

Commissioner SIDDONS. Yes, sir; but I ask the committee to bear in mind that it takes us some six to eight months to get them after the contract for them has been executed.

Senator SMITH of Maryland. They have not been purchased yet?

Commissioner SIDDONS. Oh, no; of course, not yet.

Senator SMITH of Maryland. The appropriation has not been made yet?

Commissioner SIDDONS. We are just inviting bids now.

REPAIR SHOP, FIRE DEPARTMENT.

The last item, which I simply submit for consideration, is this: The estimates of the commissioners included provision for a force of men for the new repair shop of the fire department. I can give you the proposed personnel and the estimate of salaries, if you wish.

Senator SMITH of Maryland. Very well.

Commissioner SIDDONS. The repair shop in question is one now rapidly approaching completion, and in order to get the advantage of that shop contemplated by the authorization we need a force of men for it. We submitted an estimate to the House, and I can give the items here if desired. The House, however, evidently did not consider that it was necessary and omitted it.

Senator GALLINGER. We have those items on a slip.

Commissioner SIDDONS. You have them on a slip; yes, sir. I simply call that matter to the committee's attention.

That is all I care to submit to the committee with respect to the fire department.

PUBLIC WEIGHING.

I will ask the committee's consideration next of a matter relating to the superintendent of weights and measures. I have before me the bill as it was introduced in the Senate, having passed the House, and what I am now going to call your attention to I can better do with reference to that bill.

The item I now want to speak about is this: Under existing law the commissioners may farm out or contract for the public weighing on the public scales of the District of Columbia; and for some years, under existing authority of the Congress that has been the practice.

Increasing difficulty is being found in securing a contract for the performance of this public function, public weighing on public scales, and the commissioners favor that being done by their own employees instead of by farming it out, as is permitted though not required by the existing act of Congress. In order that we may employ our own weighmasters and pay them out of the fees that are received for the weighing, this proviso is proposed to be inserted on page 29, line 18, of the bill which I have before me. With your permission, I will read the proviso:

That on and after August 1, 1914, fees received for the use of public scales shall be paid to the collector of taxes and covered into the Treasury to the credit of the appropriate trust fund account, miscellaneous trust fund deposits, District of Columbia; and the commissioners of the said District are empowered to use so much as may be necessary of said fees for the payment of compensation, to be fixed by the said commissioners, of the weighmasters authorized by the act approved March 19, 1906, entitled "An act authorizing the Commissioners of the District of Columbia to make regulations respecting the public hay scales," and the said commissioners are hereby authorized to appoint and pay such weighmasters. Any balance of said fees remaining at the close of each fiscal year shall be covered into the Treasury to the credit of the United States and the District of Columbia in equal parts.

That proviso, if adopted, would enable the commissioners to employ weighmasters. The one receiving the largest compensation would be paid $600 a year. The other weighmasters at some of the other public scales would receive from $25, as a minimum, to $75 per year for their services at those scales.

Mr. SMITH, of Maryland. Per month, do you mean?

Commissioner SIDDONS. No, sir; per year.

Senator SMITH, of Maryland. $25 to $75?

Commissioner SIDDONS. Twenty-five dollars as a minimum and $75 as a maximum, with the exception of public scale No. 3, I think, where most of the weighing is done, in which case the proposed compensation the commissioners have in mind is $600 a year. The rest would receive from $25 to $75 per year compensation for weighing at the various public scales. The object is to do away with the contract system, the contracting out of the public weighing on the public scales. We are now finding some difficulty in getting people to contract for it.

Senator GALLINGER. Do you think it would be a matter of economy.

Commissioner SIDDONS. I wish to say, frankly, Senator, in response to that question, that under the practice that has prevailed for the last three or four years, of contracting out the weighing at public scales, the net result has been more advantageous to the extent of three or four hundred dollars per year than probably would be the case if you should adopt the proviso we are recommending, though there is now reason to believe that we can not do as well in the future under the contract system. That is, the net amount will not be so great as it is now. It is not a large amount, you see—three or four hundred dollars a year, net, probably, to the revenues. Under the system proposed, of employing our own weighmasters, a large part of that net profit might be wiped out; it probably will be; but we feel that the work is essentially a public function, and personally the present Board of Commissioners want to get away from farming out any public function.

It may be that a little later we shall submit for the consideration of Congress somewhat similar provisions with regard to the measuring of lumber, and I think the matter of boiler inspection, as the present system does not meet with our approval. The fees that are charged by the boiler inspector go entirely to him. No accounting is made to the District Commissioners, and the practice generally is one that the present Board of Commissioners does not favor. I think the function should be performed by employees of the District.

We are not asking you for any appropriation. We are only asking you for authority to apply these fees to the extent necessary for the very modest compensation which it is proposed to pay to weighmasters employed directly by the District of Columbia.

POLICE MATRONS.

I will ask the committee's attention to some items in the police department estimates, if I may do so. These are items which the chief of police has urgently asked the commissioners to present. They do not cover all of the items omitted by the House, by any manner of means.

The first item relates to police matrons. Under existing law we have three police matrons, one at each of three different stations. The growth of that character of business, and the need of police matrons—who, as of course you know, deal with the female prisoners brought in—justifies us, we think, in asking for an increase of three more, making a total number of six. We included that in our estimates to Congress. The House omitted the increase asked for. We respectfully renew the request for that increase. You will find in the estimate we asked also that these matrons be clothed with police powers, which they do not now enjoy.

It is reported to me by the chief of police that the three matrons we have now have been exceedingly useful in the detection of criminals without at all interfering with their duties at the police stations. If Congress will give us first the three additional ones we ask for, we also ask in our estimates that they be clothed with police powers.

Senator GALLINGER. The House inserted language giving that power to the three matrons provided for?

Commissioners SIDDONS. Yes.

Senator GALLINGER. The language of the bill as it comes to us is, "To possess police power of arrest."

Commissioner SIDDONS. Yes; then that is covered, and it remains only that we ask your consideration of the increase of three, making a total of six.

REPAIRS TO STATION HOUSES.

We asked in our estimates for $7,000 for allowance for repairs to station houses. There are a number of station houses that are in need of repairs. The House allowed $5,500. The feeling is that that would not be sufficient to make all of the repairs that are needed. Of course they are in the older houses.

Senator GALLINGER. The amount allowed by the House is the same as last year?

Commissioner SIDDONS. Yes, sir. They rejected the increase of $1,500 that we asked for. We request your consideration of that increase.

Senator SMITH of Maryland. Do you think the repairs will be greater this year than they were last year, Mr. Siddons?

Commissioner SIDDONS. They will be greater in this respect, Mr. Chairman—that repairs that have long been needed ought to be made. We can not make all of the repairs so needed within the $5,500. We ask that the increase be made that we estimated for, a $1,500 increase.

Take the No. 3 precinct station house on K Street, what we sometimes call the White House precinct. There are repairs needed in that station house, and there are repairs needed in one or more of the others. For instance, we need lighting in one or two of them. The upper stories of one or two of the station houses—two, at least, that I have personally seen—have nothing but the old gaslighting, although they are wired. We want to be able to electrify them and give them electric lighting in the upper portions of the station houses. I think all of the first floors of the station houses have electric lights. The buildings are wired throughout, I think, in every case. We want to put the electric lighting through them in the upper rooms occupied by the reserves, for instance.

Senator SMITH of Maryland. Then this would include not only repairs, but the improvement, in that particular, of additional light?

Commissioner SIDDONS. It will permit us to do that. It is in the nature, perhaps, of a permanent improvement, and not strictly repairs; but repairs are needed, too.

I should like to repeat to the committee that the commissioners would be very happy indeed, if the committee indicates its desire to have them do so, to take the committee around to all of these places, to these station houses, for instance, if you care to go.

Senator SMITH of Maryland. We are very much obliged. I do not know whether the committee will exercise that privilege or not.

CONTINGENT EXPENSES, POLICE DEPARTMENT.

Commissioner SIDDONS. May I ask your consideration of a matter under the item of miscellaneous and contingent expenses for the police department? Our estimate was for $35,000. The House allowed us $30,000, which, if I recall, was an increase of $500 over the amount carried in the current appropriation bill.

The increase of $5,000 that we asked for was to cover the item which was mentioned to your committee before, the item of transportation for the police, estimated to amount to $5,000. That was discussed here when we had the honor of appearing before you before; and we urgently renew the request for this increase, in order that we may provide transportation for the policemen who are sent about the District on official duty.

Senator SMITH of Maryland. That would be included in the increase from what the House has allowed you to $35,000?

Commissioner SIDDONS. It would, sir.

Senator SMITH of Maryland. And really it would be only an increase, as I understand, of $500 over the current amount given.

Senator GALLINGER. No; $5,500.

Senator SMITH of Maryland. I understand; but the $5,000, as I understand, is an extra item of expense, for transportation.

Senator GALLINGER. Certainly.

Senator SMITH of Maryland. Which really makes $500 over and above what you got before, excluding the $5,000 for which you asked for the transportation of the police.

Commissioner SIDDONS. Yes. The House gave us $500 more than the current appropriation bill. We asked for $5,000 more.

Senator SMITH of Maryland. But you include in that an expense of $5,000 which you now have not, as I understand?

Commissioner SIDDONS. Yes, sir. May I read what the chief of police says?

An increase in this fund is absolutely necessary by reason of the recent law which charges this department with the enforcement of the law relating to delinquent husbands, which increases the expense for transportation of the numerous cases of arrests that are made, in view of the fact that this department must now pay all the expenses incident to members of the force appearing before United States commissioners in other jurisdictions where criminals have been arrested for this jurisdiction. The number of arrests under the excise law has increased considerably, thereby requiring an additional expenditure for the feeding of prisoners. There has been a large increase in car fare expended in the prevention and detection of crime, which does not apply to the general force. The upkeep of the motor cycles employed in the department has become an item of advanced expense, and some of these machines are old and have reached the unserviceable period, where they will have to be replaced if this important adjunct to the service is to continue.

Then he goes on to speak of other matters not of so much importance.

I may have been in error when I said to the committee that the $5,000 increase is to take care of that additional transportation. I prefer that the committee shall consider what was said before, on our previous hearing, on the $5,000 estimate which was submitted. The $5,000 here asked for is rather to carry on the increases which are indicated by the chief of police. I was in error in putting it on the other ground.

Senator SMITH, of Maryland. Then, you do not include the $5,000 for the transportation of police?

Commissioner SIDDONS. No; I say I was in error in that, Mr. Chairman. Our statement in regard to that item was made in the previous session of the committee. This is an increase made necessary by what I have just read to you from the statement of the chief of police.

Senator SMITH of Maryland. This is exclusive of police transportation?

Commissioner SIDDONS. Yes, sir.

ADDITIONAL DRIVER FOR MOTOR VEHICLE, POLICE DEPARTMENT.

The House gave to the District the motor vehicle for the use of the detective bureau that it asked for, but only provided, as the chief informs me, for one driver. There ought to be, he says, 2 drivers, which would make a total of 20 drivers in the Department instead of 18, and an additional expense of $720 per annum for the driver. This new motor vehicle is for use at detective headquarters. The House has allowed it, but apparently made provision for only one driver. That machine is in use day and night, and it would require too much work for one driver; and the chief asks that he be given two in connection with that new motor vehicle.

Although there are some further suggestions made by the chief of police, I think I shall not venture to call the committee's attention to any excepting those I have mentioned on that subject.

POUND AND STABLE, HEALTH DEPARTMENT.

I now ask your attention to one or two items in connection with the health-department estimates.

We asked for $2,200, as I recall, Mr. Chairman and gentlemen, for the completion of the pound and stable, including the necessary equipment and paving. The estimate did not cover the conversion of any portion of the stable into a garage; yet had the appropriation been made it would have been possible to have accomplished that end in a more or less satisfactory manner in connection with the construction work. The provision of a motor vehicle, however, as provided for in the appropriation bill as it passed the House, renders it almost imperative for this item to be put by the Senate on the bill, or that some appropriation be made for the conversion referred to. Looking ahead to the possible more general use of motor vehicles, whatever changes are made should have that in view. Our explanation of the need of this $2,200 is covered on page 552 of the hearings before the House committee.

Senator GALLINGER. This is for the new pound that is now under construction?

Commissioner SIDDONS. The completion of the pound and stable; yes, sir. You will see the item on page 55, on the margin, Senator.

Senator GALLINGER. Yes; we have it.

Commissioner SIDDONS. That is felt to be very necessary, especially in view of the fact that if you approve the allowance the House has made for a motor vehicle there we shall have to have a place to house it, and we want to make the repairs to this stable so that the stable will be useful for that purpose.

Senator GALLINGER. Was a stable authorized at the time the pound was authorized, Mr. Commissioner?

Commissioner SIDDONS. I think later, sir.

Senator GALLINGER. The pound is being constructed somewhere south of the Capitol, is it not?

Commissioner SIDDONS. I think so, sir.

Senator GALLINGER. Taking the place of the old pound that was up on New York Avenue, or somewhere in the northwest. Let me ask you one question on that subject You speak of this stable in connection with the pound as being necessary to house the motor wagon. Is that it?

Commissioner SIDDONS. Yes; the one allowed by the House.

Senator GALLINGER. But the motor wagon has not been allowed. You have estimated for it?

Commissioner SIDDONS. Not allowed?

Senator LEA. It is on the next page.

Senator GALLINGER. That is for the sanitary and food-inspection service. That is not in connection with the pound.

Commissioner SIDDONS. I do not mean that the motor vehicle is to be used in the work of the pound, but we want a place to house it, and we think we can house it there very well.

Senator GALLINGER. Then it is the motor vehicle for the health department that you desire to house at the pound ?

Commissioner SIDDONS. Yes, sir; that is it, Senator.

Senator GALLINGER. That clears up the matter.

Commissioner SIDDONS. And the probable addition from time to time of motor vehicles makes the provision for their care and shelter very necessary. We are looking forward a little bit in this respect, although we shall have this one vehicle immediately to take care of if you should approve the House allowance in that particular.

CONTAGIOUS-DISEASE SERVICE.

In relation to the contagious-disease service, beginning on the bottom of page 52, the health officer says that the estimate submitted by the commissioners for this service was $30,000. Was $25,000 allowed by the House, or $24,000 ?

Senator LEA. $25,000 was allowed by the House.

Commissioner SIDDONS. And $24,000 last year, or an increase of $1,000. We ask an increase of $5,000. The health officer submits this statement on that point:

The most important reason for the increase being the pressing need for closer supervision over tuberculosis in the District of Columbia and the desirability of relieving the sanitary inspection force of work in connection with the contagious-disease service.

I invite the committee's attention to the discussion that is found on page 526 of the hearings before the House committee. To relieve the sanitary inspector's force of this work would be to increase the efficiency, not only of the contagious-disease service, but also of the sanitary inspection.

FIRE PROTECTION FOR SMALLPOX HOSPITAL.

I ask the committee's attention to the matter of fire protection for the smallpox hospital. We included in our estimate an appropriation of $1,800 to extend the water mains for that purpose. The reasons for that are set forth at length, beginning on page 532, in the hearings before the House committee, and I will not repeat them now; but it is important that such provision be made.

I might say that the smallpox hospital has at times a number of persons in it. There are times when there may be no one in it, but at the present time we have a number. There is some smallpox in the District, and we have a number of patients over in that hospital. We have no adequate fire protection at all. We ask an increase of $1,800 to connect up these water mains.

Senator SMITH of Maryland. You now have no fire protection whatever ?

Commissioner SIDDONS. No efficient fire protection. The fire department would have to travel a long distance with hose to get there at all. We ask that these water mains be extended so that we can get close and immediate fire protection to that isolated building. As I say, the reasons are set out at length in the hearings before the House committee.

Senator GALLINGER. Is not that hospital situated in the vicinity of the Washington Asylum?

Commissioner SIDDONS. Yes, sir; not at all far from that.

Senator GALLINGER. I should think they could get the fire protection from the Washington Asylum, if they have the requisite hose, without any trouble.

Commissioner SIDDONS. If you will turn to the hearings you will find that was gone into. The House committee, I believe, interrogated us quite closely on this subject. I think, Senator, you will find on page 532 the full statement. If you care, I will read from it. I do not want to burden the record.

Dr. Woodward said to the House committee:

We have the ordinary Potomac water for domestic purposes, but there is no fire plug in the immediate vicinity of the hospital. You will notice the report made by the fire marshal, or the chief engineer of the fire department after an investigation by the fire marshal. The report says:

"To use any of these plugs would require long leads of hose, and in all probability the fire engines using the farthest plugs would be compelled to line in."

He then says:

"I would further recommend that a small reel carrying from 200 to 400 feet of hose be procured for use at the crematorium and quarantine station—something that two men can handle—and the plug opposite the quarantine station could be used until the arrival of the fire department. If the water main to hospital is installed as recommended, then I would recommend a similar reel to be procured for the use of hospitals and buildings in the immediate vicinity."

Then there is much more discussion of it, Senator, beginning there, which explains the reason.

There are a number of other items pressed upon us by the fire department, but I shall not urge them further before the committee. You have our original estimates; you have the hearings of the House committee, and we have only ventured to call your attention to the items omitted by the House that the commissioners feel are vital. Others that we recommend and that have been omitted are important, but we are not disposed to ask the Senate committee to review the action of the House except in such matters as we consider very vital; and those for the departments that I have discussed this morning are the items that I desire to call to the committee's attention.

Mr. Chairman, two of the patrol drivers of the police department solicited the commissioners for permission to appear before the committee and ask an increase in the salaries allowed them. The commissioners did not themselves ask for the increases. Indeed, they very generally avoided asking for increases in many cases where they felt increase to be necessary, but they did so for reasons that they thought were desirable. I should be very glad, however, if you care to do so, if you would let these men present their claims for increase. We have not the slightest objection to their doing so, and have no objection to the increase if the committee should see fit to give it to them, though we are not asking the increases.

Senator SMITH of Maryland. Is there anything further you wish to state?

Commissioner SIDDONS. Nothing for my departments.

STATEMENT OF HARRY N. ENGLEHART AND JOSEPH COUGHLIN.

SALARIES OF PATROL DRIVERS, POLICE DEPARTMENT.

Senator SMITH of Maryland. Mr. Englehart, you are one of the drivers in the police department?

Mr. ENGLEHART. Yes, sir.

Senator SMITH of Maryland. Your salary now is how much?

Mr ENGLEHART. $60 a month, $720 a year, sir.

Senator SMITH of Maryland. What are you asking for?

Mr. ENGLEHART. We are asking for $75 a month and, if possible, to be put in the classified service; to be recognized as regular officers is what we mean.

Senator SMITH of Maryland. What have you to say in justification of your claim?

Mr. ENGLEHART. We work 12 hours a day, sir, one week and 12 hours a night trick. Every second Sunday in the month we are subject to duty of 24 hours. We come on at 8 o'clock Sunday morning and we stay there until 8 o'clock Monday morning. At no time during our trick of duty are we allowed a meal hour—something that every branch of labor the world over is entitled to. We are subject to inspection; we have to stand inspection as well as a regular officer. Our summer uniforms cost $14.65. Then there is our car fare and our running expenses at home, all coming out of that $60.

Senator SMITH of Maryland. You mean car fare going to and coming from your homes?

Mr. ENGLEHART. Yes, sir; besides the uniforms we are compelled to buy out of our $60. We are all family men, every one of us, with the exception of one, and we feel it, more especially those who have children.

Senator GALLINGER. What do you say your hours are?

Mr. ENGLEHART. We work from 8 o'clock in the morning to 6 in the evening one week—that is the day trick—and then, the night trick, we work from 6 in the evening until 8 the next morning. Every second Sunday in the month we work 24 hours right on, straight, without any relief whatever.

Senator SMITH of Maryland. Do you work every day in the week?

Mr. ENGLEHART. Yes, sir.

Senator SMITH of Maryland. And every Sunday, or every two Sundays?

Mr. ENGLEHART. Every second Sunday we work 24 hours without any time off whatever.

Senator DILLINGHAM. What are your duties?

Mr. ENGLEHART. We are chauffeurs in the police department, driving patrol wagons.

Mr. COUGHLIN. We are in quite a lot of danger in performing our duties. We have to assist the officer in charge of the automobile patrol in handling prisoners, and we are not protected by any pension for long service or for injury received in the line of duty.

I have spent seven years now in the service. Senator Gallinger, here, secured a $10 increase for us eight years ago; and, as you know, the cost of living has increased since then. We appreciated very much at the time what the Senator did for us. It is a big hardship, however, to make out with what the Senator allowed us eight years ago.

As I say, we are not protected by a pension for long service or for injury received in the line of duty. We have been kicked by horses. We are often knocked down by the prisoners. We are not protected at all as other members of the police force are in that line, and we would not have a dollar if we were thrown out of work to-morrow.

We are not entitled to a trial for any charges of misconduct or any little violation of the police regulations. We have not the privileges the other men of the police force have to protect us in our positions, unless by an act of kindness the honorable commissioner would grant us a trial; but we would not be entitled to a trial, as all other members of the police force are. We could be dismissed upon just the say so of one inspector—just the feeling of one inspector—without the privilege of a trial, unless we have some good kind-hearted commissioner to give us the benefit of it.

We have to understand the engines used in propelling these automobiles. We have to clean and wash the automobile patrols. They are kept out in a cold stable, gentlemen. It is not heated up or furnished with any conveniences in that line. We have to wash the cars and keep them looking as neat as possible between runs, and we really have not time to wash the cars and keep them the way we ought to keep them on account of the number of runs that come in for us. We have to respond to runs for two stations since the automobile was adopted in the police department last Congress. We have to respond to all fire calls for both stations and all box-station arrests and all emergency runs, such as burglars in people's houses, and carrying people to the hospitals at a high rate of speed.

Senator SMITH of Maryland. How much of your time are you in actual service? You are waiting a good deal of the time, are you not?

Mr. COUGHLIN. Not very much, Senator.

Senator SMITH of Maryland. Do you mean to say you are always on the go?

Mr. COUGHLIN. We are, practically all the time. Of course, it comes in bunches.

Mr. ENGLEHART. Since July 1, gentlemen, we have been performing what they call double duty. When we had the horses, every station had a horse and wagon; but since July 1 we have only had six automobiles, and these six automobiles cover 11 stations, besides police headquarters.

Senator SMITH of Maryland. Do I understand, then, that there are six of the drivers in the same condition that you two are? There are six of you occupying the same position, are there?

Senator LEA. Eighteen.

Mr. ENGLEHART. Eighteen of us.

Mr. COUGHLIN. There are two extra drivers, Senator, in order to give us a chance to get our leave.

Mr. ENGLEHART. We carry two extra drivers, and then the major has one.

Senator SMITH of Maryland. This would include 18 men, then?

Mr. ENGLEHART. Yes, sir. There are 18 on the regular roll now.

Mr. COUGHLIN. You see, where the 18 come in is that the major has one, and there are two extra drivers.

Senator SMITH of Maryland. I understand.   Then this would apply to 18 drivers?   Is that right?

Mr. COUGHLIN. Yes, sir.

Senator SMITH of Maryland. The increase you ask would apply to 18 drivers?

Mr. ENGLEHART. Yes, sir; counting those on the vans.   They are rated as patrol wagons, too.

You see, the reason we mention the classified service, for one thing, is that in case we should respond to a fire call or a raid call, or something like that, probably we would have four or five men in the wagon answering the call, and if any one of them should meet with an accident and be injured, if the disability should become permanent, they would be retired on a pension, you understand, but we would be retired with nothing.   It is a plain case.

Mr. COUGHLIN. We would not even have a physician.   We can not meet our debts or bills in case of sickness to our children.

Commissioner SIDDONS. These men are not, of course, members of the police force, and therefore do not enjoy the benefits of the pension system.

Senator SMITH of Maryland. I understand.

Commissioner SIDDONS. The work has been largely increased, though with the motor-driven wagons they make much greater speed.   Each patrol wagon connected with the station now serves two stations, where formerly there was a horse-driven wagon for each station. · They cover, therefore, a great deal more territory. Of course they can do it more rapidly because of the different power that propels them.   Their hours are long.   Their work, I think, is arduous.   I think they have to sleep in the stable which houses their machine.   The surroundings are not very comfortable.   They have also dilated upon certain other features that differentiate their case from those of other people in the police department.

Senator GALLINGER. Did you have these same long hours before the motor vehicles were installed?

Mr. COUGHLIN. Just the same, Senator, only there were 26 drivers then.   There was a reduction of 8 made by the last appropriation bill.

Senator GALLINGER. Yes; I recall that.

Mr. ENGLEHART. The only thing that has been added onto it is that, as the honorable commissioner stated, we do a double duty. We do the work of two stations instead of one.

Mr. COUGHLIN. We will be glad if you can do this for us.   We highly appreciate the privileges given us, and anything that you gentlemen can do for us we will highly appreciate.

HEALTH DEPARTMENT—ADDITIONAL INSPECTORS.

STATEMENT OF DR. PERCY D. HICKLING, REPRESENTING THE COMMITTEE ON PUBLIC HEALTH OF THE WASHINGTON BOARD OF TRADE.

Dr. HICKLING. Gentlemen of the committee, I represent the chairman of the committee on public health of the Washington Board of Trade.   We have from time to time been interested in the enactment of laws for the promotion of the health of the citizens.

These bills have become laws, and it is necessary in order to enforce them that the health officer be given the proper number of inspectors, and recently, in going over the matter, the committee has found that the health officer is really embarrassed in the enforcement of just and righteous laws that are now on the statute books for lack of proper inspectors, and the honorable commissioners have transmitted to Congress an estimate for a minimum number of inspectors to carry out and enforce these laws, and the House committee has omitted the inspectors which are necessary. On page 52 there is a side note as to the inspectors. It is believed in the committee on public health, and has been indorsed by the president, after going into the matter, that these inspectors are absolutely necessary, and that the health of our citizens and conditions in the city which can be abated by proper laws will suffer for the lack of proper enforcement, and we urge that these inspectors be restored to the bill.

Senator SMITH, of Maryland. You are asking for nine additional inspectors, as I understand it?

Dr. HICKLING. Yes.

Senator SMITH, of Maryland. Or rather, 11 additional, and you take off 2, which makes an increase of 9 over the present force?

Dr. HICKLING. Yes, sir.

APPARATUS AND SUPPLIES FOR BACTERIOLOGICAL LABORATORY.

The second important matter which I am authorized to call your attention to is under the appropriation for the health department as authorized by the honorable commissioners, which is on page 54, in a side note. Of these special items that we have considered and desire to call your special attention to, the first is the bacteriological laboratory. The work of the health department depends largely on these laboratory facilities, and as to its usefulness to the officials of Washington and to the poor of Washington, these examinations should be made. It is almost impossible to make them without the greatest kind of expense in private practice.

The fees are very large, and the men who make those examinations are very few. They are necessary for the poor very often more than for the rich, not only for their own benefit, but to protect the community; and for that reason other cities have found it necessary to equip not only bacteriological but chemical laboratories at the health office, and these estimates are needed, and badly needed, for the protection of the community, and we can not urge you too strongly to consider this matter. Of course there is a great deal that I could say in detail, but I do not want to take up your time. We have gone into these matters, and they are absolutely essential.

Senator GALLINGER. Let me ask you, in reference to bacteriological work, as to whether or not the Public Health Service is at your command at all?

Dr. HICKLING. It is not; no, sir.

Senator GALLINGER. Might it not be well utilized to some extent?

Dr. HICKLING. The question of that has been raised time and time again; but they are doing a special work, and they have special laboratory facilities for that work.

Senator GALLINGER. They have a very large force of men there, which it would seem to me might be utilized for work that is of joint interest to the Government and to the District.

Dr. HICKLING. They have been very kind, I know, in making special examinations, not only for the health department but for physicians, but it is only in a special line, and what is needed is the routine work. In other words, a physician should be able to go to the health department and get a specimen examined and a report made upon that, for the cure of an indigent patient, just as he would, if he was able to pay for it, to go to a private laboratory. These men need it, not only for the health of the citizens of the poorer class, but many of these conditions, of course, are contagious in their nature. The whole prophylaxis of venereal diseases is often most important. Again, as to venereal disease, very often a man does not know that he has it; he has no means of finding it out, no method of finding it out, and he lets it go from bad to worse, and he is a menace not only to himself but to the community. I have in mind syphilitic conditions which are now only ascertainable by the Wasserman reaction. It is most important that they should be discovered, and it is almost impossible to do that without these examinations.

Senator DILLINGHAM. Is there no service of that kind now for the poor as well as the rich?

Senator GALLINGER. The health office supplies that as well as it can. The argument of Dr. Hickling is that they have not a sufficient equipment.

Dr. HICKLING. There is an equipment at the health office, and it has been used from time to time as a help, but instead of being increased it has been from time to time modified, and the increase is absolutely needed; and not only the health department recognizes it, but the honorable Commissioners of the District of Columbia have recognized the importance of it, and brought it to the committee.

Senator SMITH of Maryland. Do not the hospitals take care of these people to a great extent?

Dr. HICKLING. They take care of them, but there is practically no hospital in the city that has facilities for making these examinations, and they want to depend on the health department for them.

Senator GALLINGER. You are in medical charge of the Washington Asylum Hospital, as I recall it?

Dr. HICKLING. Yes.

Senator GALLINGER. That is the hospital for the indigent poor. If you require an examination, you have to go to the health office?

Dr. HICKLING. We should go to the health office, but we can not do it, because they have not sufficient facilities. We have been having these examinations made by the courtesy of Dr. White, of the Government Hospital for the Insane, but that is not a regular thing and it is not a dependable thing.

Senator GALLINGER. It rather surprises me to see that you rather limited the opportunities this year, instead of extend— I think we have slightly increased the facilities of this year to year, granting the health officer an additional to time an inspector and, I adding to the ap bacteriological and chemical atories; but it rapidly as I should have like have it done

Senator DILLINGHAM. For personal i to ask this question. Take re of family. Suppose that he suspects tuberculosis and wants the sputum examined. Is there no way in which he can have that done?

Dr. HICKLING. Yes; he can go to the health office and the health office will make an examination. That is just what we want done in the case of syphilitic and gonorrheal conditions, and other conditions. The question of pellagra is an active one that needs laboratory help. Then we have the question of amoebic dysenteries, in which laboratory help is needed which is not open to us. In other words, we do get good laboratory reports on diptheria and on tuberculosis, but with those two exceptions we do not get—the general profession do not get—laboratory reports from our health department in other directions, which are needed.

Senator SMITH of Maryland. For the want of proper facilities?

Dr. HICKLING. Yes, sir.

Senator SMITH of Maryland. You do apply to the same sources; but your claim is that they have not the facilities to give you the reports that you want?

Dr. HICKLING. Yes; and, as I understand it, if these items are added to the appropriation bill they will be able to give us those facilties. That is my understanding of it. This is on page 54.

Senator GALLINGER. Will you kindly designate, for the information of the committee, the portion of these items which you consider the most important, on page 54, on the slip pasted on the right-hand side of the page?

Dr. HICKLING. Under the head of the bacteriological laboratory?

Senator GALLINGER. Yes.

Dr. HICKLING. That for the purchase and installation of new apparatus, $2,000. That is essential to make these additional examinations.

Then the next item is for the replacement of apparatus.

Senator GALLINGER. Let us skip that now.

Dr. HICKLING. I do not know about the condition as to that.

The next item, "For maintaining and keeping in good order, and for the purchase of reference books and scientific periodicals, $300," is most moderate, indeed. This work, of course, is the product of laboratories, and it is only by keeping in touch with foreign laboratories and research laboratories of this country that a health department can keep up with the times.

CHEMICAL LABORATORY.

Senator GALLINGER. The next item is, "Chemical laboratory: For the equipment and maintenance of the chemical laboratory and the purchase of reference books and scientific journals, as follows:

"For the purchase and installation of new apparatus and equipment, $1,920.

"For the replacement of apparatus and equipment, $755.

"For maintaining and keeping chemical laboratory in good order and the purchase of chemicals, filter paper, absorbent cotton, gauze, and so forth, reference books and journals, $500."

Dr. HICKLING. I do not know the conditions there.

Senator GALLINGER. As a matter of fact, the most important items in that list would be for the purchase and installation of new apparatus for both bacteriological and chemical laboratories?

Dr. HICKLING. Yes; they are absolutely necessary.

HOSPITAL FOR INEBRIATES.

Dr. HICKLING. Now, there is another item that I want to most urgently call attention to. The Committee on Public Health have had this question of a hospital for inebriates actively before them, and it has been before this committee. This is on the side note on page 75, at the bottom, "Hospital for inebriates."

Senator GALLINGER. That is an old friend.

Dr. HICKLING. Yes. The point is this, gentlemen: The inebriate question has been rather pushed from pillar to post; that is, we have two extreme views, and it depends really on the personal experience of the observer which side of the fence he is on. If he has had an inebriate in his family, he believes that these patients should be sent to an insane asylum. They are not insane. They do not belong there. If he has not, if he looks on it from the outside, he thinks they deserve to be sent to the workhouse. They do not belong to the workhouse. Then very often, as a compromise, they are sent to a general hospital, and they do not belong there; they are no use there. So that the poor inebriate is pushed from pillar to post, and made worse instead of better. Now, the inebriate is not a criminal; he is not a sick man in the sense of needing hospital treatment to cure him; he is not insane, as the term is used now to admit them under the law to the Government Hospital for the Insane. But he is an inebriate, and he needs proper treatment to cure him. That proper treatment is not only medical, but sociological and industrial.

Senator SMITH of Maryland. Have you no inebriate hospital here?

Dr. HICKLING. Absolutely nothing, sir. In fact, our inebriates are pushed from court to court. They are a large criminal element which could be treated, and under modern ideas could be cured and restored to citizenship instead of being made worse.

Senator SMITH of Maryland. Senator Gallinger, is not that rather exceptional that in a place of this size there should be no inebriate hospital?

Senator GALLINGER. I have not investigated that. Some States have such hospitals and some have not. I think some of the smaller States have not any hospital of the kind.

You speak of curing these men. Have you any data which would suggest to the committee the proportion of cures of that class of men?

Dr. HICKLING. I have not. It is too soon to say, from these institutions. They are rather recent. The special inebriate institution is rather a recent thing, and to say that a man remains away from alcohol for a year does not mean to say that he is cured, by any means.

Senator GALLINGER. No.

Dr. HICKLING. But the returns from these institutions are most encouraging.

The plan proposed, as I understand it, and which the commissioners have in view with this appropriation, is as follows: By the way, the bill not only includes inebriety, but that most distressing condition which is getting most common amongst us now, that of the morphine and cocaine habits—drug habits. The bill first defines these habitués as committing a misdemeanor. They have now a right to be an inebriate, and they have a right to be a cocaine fiend or an opium dope fiend; but this fixes it. It provides that they shall be taken in custody only when through the effect of this drug, or through this excess of alcohol, they become a menace to the community, or they become unable to support themselves.

Senator GALLINGER. At that point let me ask you, is it a fact that notwithstanding our very stringent laws, some recently enacted, governing the sale of cocaine and drugs of that character, they are being sold largely in the District of Columbia?

Dr. HICKLING. Yes, sir; that is, the law has been passed.

Senator GALLINGER. No; I ask are these drugs being sold largely? Can these people still get them with any degree of freedom—the class of people that use them?

Dr. HICKLING. Judging from the cases that we have at the Washington Asylum Hospital, and, generally, I should say that it is more frequent than ever. We are getting more of the cases, and more opium and cocaine fiends. How they get it we do not know. We notify the inspector and he takes it up, but we do not know the result. Certainly they are on the increase in the District of Columbia.

Senator GALLINGER. So that the drugs are being sold surreptitiously, notwithstanding the law?

Dr. HICKLING. It would seem so. I can not make a charge of that kind, but the number of cases we see under the influence of these drugs is certainly on the increase, according to our statistics.

Senator GALLINGER. We have tried to make it mighty difficult for anybody to get that class of drugs without a prescription from a physician.

Dr. HICKLING. Yes. The law seems all right.

Now, we do not propose to take these cases as a temperance measure. We merely take the man when he is unable to take care of himself, when he becomes a charge on the community. We take care of him now. The purpose of this inebriate hospital is merely to take care of him properly instead of improperly, as we do now, when he becomes a care upon the community.

Senator GALLINGER. What appropriation is asked for this.

Dr. HICKLING. $25,000.

Senator GALLINGER. Because of your great familiarity with this, I should like to ask you about those buildings which are not now occupied, which are in close conjunction with the Washington Asylum. There are five or six hundred thousand dollars' worth of brick buildings there, which were abandoned when we sent the people from the workhouse to Occoquan.

Dr. HICKLING. Yes.

Senator GALLINGER. Could not one of those fine brick buildings be easily reconstructed and made into an inebriate asylum?

Dr. HICKLING. I do not know. I am not familiar enough with construction to be able to say. On that point, however, if you will permit me, I will state there have been a number of appeals submitted to Congress, going from the extreme of providing nothing in the way of an appropriation for their care, merely putting them down there in the old female workhouse and utilizing that the best they can, merely asking for law and not for money, to another extreme, of putting up a half a million dollar institution with probably half as much required for maintenance. Those are the two extremes of the bills that have been introduced in Congress during the last few years. Now, of course, you can take care of them as comfortably as is done at the Willard, or you can make them feel, as I believe they should be made to feel, something in the way of their position. I do not believe in providing too much in the way for the care of these inebriates. My plan is to first treat them medically. We can cure them of the desire for drink. There used to be a time when they thought if we could only kill the desire, they would be all right. We have drugs now that do kill the desire; but while it has been a great benefit and a great help, it is not the whole story by any means. They do not stay cured, but they are cured for the time being.

Senator SMITH of Maryland. Are there private institutions here to which inebriates go who have means to pay? Are there any of that kind?

Dr. HICKLING. There is no private inebriate asylum. The genearl hospitals, some of them, occasionally take in inebriates.

Senator SMITH of Maryland. What I mean is, are there any institutions to which a man who has means to pay can go, and pay for treatment?

Dr. HICKLING. As an inebriate asylum?

Senator SMITH of Maryland. Well, is there any such place where they treat inebriates? I do not know whether you would call it an asylum or not.

Dr. HICKLING. Providence Hospital will take them for $20 or $25 a week and put them in a ward which they have for these alcoholic cases. Georgetown University Hospital has a special ward in which they will take these cases. Most of the other hospitals refuse to take these cases unless special appeal is made. Of course, the indigent cases we are doing the best we can to take care of at the Washington Asylum, but that best is far from satisfactory.

Senator SMITH of Maryland. A person of means can get treatment by paying for it?

Dr. HICKLING. He can not get treatment for inebriety. He can get over his debauch and straighten up, but that is not the end of the treatment, by any means. If you will bear with me just a moment more. We have several principles in the treatment of these inebriates. First, to get them over their debauch; second, to kill the appetite for their drink; third, we find that they need exceptional supervision during the period where they are able and willing to work. This bill provides that they shall be put to use at some profitable occupation, such as they are able to do. It also provides that they shall be compensated for the work; the compensation to be divided into three unequal parts, the first part to go to the maintenance, so that in time this institution should become self-supporting, the second part to go to their dependent families, depending upon the number of claims made upon them, and, third, the surplus, if any, to go to themselves when they are discharged on the parole system, such as this bill provides for or this idea calls for.

Commissioner SIDDONS. May I interrupt just a moment, Mr. Chairman? Has the committee any more questions that they wish to put to me, or may I be excused?

Senator SMITH of Maryland. I do not know of anything, unless you have something else.

Commissioner SIDDONS. No; I have submitted all that I had, and with your permission I will retire.

Senator SMITH of Maryland. Does any gentleman of the committee wish to ask the commissioner anything further? It seems not.

(Commissioner Siddons at this point withdrew from the hearing.)

Senator GALLINGER. Dr. Hickling, your great familiarity with health matters enables you to give the committee, as you are doing now, very important information. Let me ask you this: Do you not think it would be a good plan for the Commissioners of the District of Columbia or some other officials to take up this whole question of the condition at the Washington Asylum, which is a disgrace to any civilized community?

Dr. HICKLING. Most assuredly, I do.

Senator GALLINGER. And try to work out this problem, first, of giving proper care to paupers in this District, which they do not now have at that asylum; and, next, whether you might not in conjunction with that, having this property lying here on the borders of the Eastern Branch, get just such an institution as you are now advocating without asking Congress to go outside somewhere and buy a piece of land and build a new asylum of this kind. I will ask you whether in the near future there might not be a comprehensive scheme worked out that would not only take care of poor people in a much better way than they are cared for now, but also provide for an institution something like that you are now advocating?

Dr. HICKLING. The only thing that occurs to me now is the delay. It is not the intention, as I understand, with this money to buy a tract of ground elsewhere and put up a large building. My understanding is that this ground which we now have will in some way be utilized. Whether it is to be on the ground of the new municipal hospital, as advocated by the Board of Charities, or whether it is to be down in the reservation where the Washington Asylum now is, I do not know, but rather than jeopardize the scheme I would consent to its going anywhere. It seems to me that any legislation would do, and the only thing is that we need it badly and need it quickly. This matter has been before Congress for years in various shapes and forms, and the condition has not been relieved, and it is growing worse every day, and we need it and need it badly. We need something.

Senator GALLINGER. During the years that I acted as chairman of the Committee of the District of Columbia I was much troubled over the situation at the Washington Asylum Hospital, but it seems to be an impossible thing to remedy what to my mind were disgraceful conditions. There we have two or three brick buildings which cost the Government, as I said a moment ago, somewhere in the vicinity of $500,000 or $600,000.

Dr. HICKLING. Those buildings cost $200,000 each.

Senator GALLINGER. More than that, and they are standing idle.

Dr. HICKLING. There are three buildings there.

Senator DILLINGHAM. Where are they?

Dr. HICKLING. They are right out Pennsylvania Avenue, east.

Senator GALLINGER. Then there are those ramshackle buildings that you are trying to utilize for the poo , where they are all huddled in there in the condition in which they are, which is most disgraceful; and I have not yet been able to see why, by some wise and comprehensive scheme, we might not utilize those existing buildings, either for the asylum proper or for an institution such as you are advocating. But as long as that matter remains there in the condition it is in, even if we should provide a new building for inebriates, we still are leaving the poor, much larger in numbers, in a condition that is not to the credit of the Government. I think those poor people who are really suffering from all kinds of diseases are entitled to first consideration, rather than the man who gets drunk.

Senator SMITH of Maryland. Speaking of the buildings in which they are now located as being inadequate and not fit to locate them in, how many are there there of these paupers?

Senator GALLINGER. Dr. Hickling can probably answer that.

Dr. HICKLING. We have a 200-bed hospital there now in wooden buildings. Only the old almshouse is a brick building, and the others are all frame buildings. We handle about 3,000 patients a year, coming and going, according to our last annual report.

Senator SMITH of Maryland. Why are not these present brick buildings utilized for taking care of them?

Senator GALLINGER. They are not adequate now. The interiors would have to be changed over, and on my own motion I had Mr. Woods make an investigation of those buildings, and he made a report, and I think that probably it can be found somewhere, showing that it would not be a very expensive experiment; but the commissioners then in office were opposed to the whole scheme and blocked it.

Senator SMITH of Maryland. Would those buildings, of which you speak, be adequate for the poor and for inebriates too?

Senator GALLINGER. I think so; to a very large extent so. Of course you might have to still occupy some of the buildings that are now occupied.

Senator LEA. Have you any data on this?

Dr. HICKLING. We now have more charity patients than Providence Hospital, Garfield Hospital, Georgetown University Hospital, and George Washintgon University Hospital all put together. In fact, so far as numbers are concerned, the truth is that I have somewhat hesitated at asking an appropriation for a hospital for inebriates so long as we have our poor people in so much larger numbers than those that are suffering from inebriety.

Senator DILLINGHAM. Do you not think they all ought to be provided for?

Senator GALLINGER. I think so, if we can get an appropriation.

Dr. HICKLING. The point is that we are providing in some way for our sick poor, but for the inebriates we are not making any appropriation which leads to their uplifting and cure.

Senator SMITH of Maryland. How long have you been advocating a building of this kind?

Dr. HICKLING. Ever since I have been at work on it. For years I have done everything I could in that direction. We have had a number of bills introduced in the House and Senate, and there are a number of questions in them. In my statement to-day I have been avoiding the detail.

The question of where it should be located has embarrassed us considerably, and the question of whether it shall be an elegant or a poor place. Those things have all come in, and have only had the misfortune to block the whole scheme. Now we need something, and we need something quickly.

Senator GALLINGER. Is there any reason why a hospital of this kind should not be located on that 34 acres where the Tuberculosis Hospital is?

Dr. HICKLING. That is the note here that the commissioners recommended.

Senator GALLINGER. Would it not be better for it to be located in the country than anywhere in the city?

Dr. HICKLING. From my own personal judgment, from what I know of the situation, that is the proper place for it.

Senator GALLINGER. We have there about 34 acres, 3 or 4 miles out.

Dr. HICKLING. It is just beyond the Soldiers' Home. That is where the Tuberculosis Hospital now is.

Senator GALLINGER. We have on that 34 acres nothing but the Tuberculosis Hospital.

Dr. HICKLING. The plan has been to build a great municipal hospital there, but that has not made much headway, and probably will not in the immediate future.

Senator GALLINGER. How many tuberculosis patients are being treated out there?

Dr. HICKLING. I do not know very much about the details of that institution.

Senator GALLINGER. It is a fine hospital.

Dr. HICKLING. A nice hospital and in a nice place.

Senator GALLINGER. That was built five or six years ago, was it not?

Dr. HICKLING. Yes. The point is that these inebriates are now being left to the courts and the jails and the workhouses and the hospitals, and we are absolutely ignoring them, so they are absolutely prevented from anything like a chance for recovery. If this appropriation recommended by the commissioners could prevail and the institution could be located on the ground already owned by the District at Fourteenth and Upshur Streets, on a part of which the Tuberculosis Hospital is now located, and where some have proposed to build a Government hospital or city hospital, it would be ideal. There would be no question about that, and it would do the greatest amount of good that $75,000 could possibly do to the District of Columbia, I think, at this time.

Senator GALLINGER. We have this large tract at Fourteenth and Upshur Streets, three or four miles out.

Dr. HICKLING. It is a beautiful spot, and we have there this one fine hospital, which cost $100,000.

Senator GALLINGER. If I recall, that is an admirable place for an inebriate asylum. It is much better than to have it in the city.

Senator SMITH of Maryland. It is the judgment of Dr. Hickling that that is an ideal place.

Dr. HICKLING. Yes, sir.

Senator SMITH of Maryland. Your judgment is that even if this other property was improved as a place for the poor, that would be better than this ground where the Washington Asylum Hospital now is?

Dr. HICKLING. Yes, sir. There are many reasons why it should not be put down where the Washington Asylum Hospital now is.

Senator SMITH of Maryland. I think it would be better to put the inebriates outside of the city.

Senator GALLINGER. Very much better, from all considerations.

Dr. HICKLING. Mr. Fenning, who is here, who is a member of our committee, wants to speak to you on a question connected with the bill, if you will hear him.

Mr. Singleton, who is the vice president of the Washington Board of Trade, is also present, and he says that he has something that he would like to say to you about the inebriate asylum, which will take about two minutes.

STATEMENT OF WILLIAM H. SINGLETON.

Mr. SINGLETON. I appear here for the Board of Trade in support of our commitee, but with your permission I want to say a word about this inebriate asylum, from another angle.   I am also a member of the executive committee of the Prisoners' Aid Department. Our business is to look after the first offenders down in our courts, and take charge of them, or if we do not, pay their fines and send them back home.   A great deal of our business is done with inebriates, and our greatest trouble is to know just how to manage those cases. This is a matter that is up to our Prisoners' Aid Department, and we have urged on Congress the necessity of aid, and I wanted to take just a minute to support what Dr. Hickling has said toward having an inebriate asylumn here to take care of those cases.

STATEMENT OF DR. CHARLES M. EMMONS.

Dr. EMMONS. I represent the East Washington Citizens' Association, and we ask permission to object to the location of the inebriate asylum on the present grounds of the Washington Asylum Hospital for this reason, that we have requested permission to use that reservation, which contains about 100 acres, for an Eastern High School site, as we have disapproved of any idea of a scheme to buy a site when we have an elegant site of that kind right at hand.

Senator SMITH of Maryland. A smooth site, right at the Washington Asylum Hospital?

Dr. EMMONS. Right at the Washington Asylum Hospital, where the present jail and these old dilapidated hospital buildings are.

Senator SMITH of Maryland. Your suggestion about making it a school site would presuppose the destruction of the present buildings?

Dr. EMMONS. It would, and we feel that the present buildings could not be converted into the proper form of hospital for inebriates.

We disapprove also of the suggestion made to place it where the Tuberculosis Hospital is, because you have only 35 acres there, and that is not any too much for the present and future use for treatment of tuberculosis cases.   We disapprove of it for this reason, Senator: You are going to get a good many incipient cases that will require at least that much ground for their treatment.   But there is another reason that is as strong.   The State of Massachusetts has found that in the treatment of these inebriates they have required a farm of from 100 to 200 acres of ground.   They send their cases there for from one month to two years, under their method of treatment. The District now has at Blue Plains an elegant location for the erection of this building, in the present almshouse site at Blue Plains, with a farm attached to it of 100 or more acres. If you put them on 35 acres, you will not be able to work those inmates. This matter should come up in the shape of an independent bill and be considered as an independent proposition, making provision for the management of this institution, and the manner of the commitment to it.

Senator GALLINGER. We have two large institutions at Blue Plains now, have we not? We have an almshouse there and a hospital attached to that, and we have the building for the aged and infirm there.

Dr. EMMONS. Yes, sir; and you have the industrial school on the other part of it.

Senator GALLINGER. Yes.

Dr. EMMONS. But you have in the neighborhood of 125 acres of ground unused, and you have also there a new hospital with a capacity of 35, with a physician and nurses. There is no reason in the world why this institution should not be placed there. They need it.

It was stated there were no efforts to take care of these unfortunates. I want to state that at the present time the Salvation Army has now established an institution and is taking care of 25 to 30 of these cases. They have a farm out in Maryland and are using that as an adjunct to that institution, so that while there is no municipal institution of this kind the people themselves are waking up to the necessity.

I am in thorough accord with the effort to get a municipal hospital, but we do not want it located on the present Washington Asylum grounds, and we would suggest that you locate it at Blue Plains, where you have ample grounds in which to work these men after you place them there. The employment of these men is a part of the treatment of these cases, and you can not do that on your 35-acre tract.

STATEMENT OF FREDERICK A. FENNING.

MEDICAL INSPECTORS AND NURSES FOR PUBLIC SCHOOLS.

Mr. FENNING. If the committee please, I desire to call the attention of the committee to but one single feature in the Book of Estimates, and that is one recorded on page 40. I refer to the estimate of the honorable commissioners for an appropriation for three graduate nurses in connection with the medical work of the public schools. I appear before the committee as the chairman of the committee on public schools of the Washington Board of Trade, and wish to call attention to the fact that some years ago when the commissioners, in their wisdom, and the Congress, in its wisdom, made an initial provision for medical work in connection with the public schools, it was believed that there was a need for such service. The fact that such a need did exist has been shown by the work that has been done by the medical inspectors, few in number, who have been employed in connection with the school service, and that has been recognized by the continuance of the appropriation by the Congress from session to session. If that work is to be carried on to the full extent that it, should, and if the work is to expand in the manner that seems to be necessary, there must, of course, be the adequate workers and the adequate means with which to work, and so the board of education and the commissioners—and in this the board of trade heartily concurs—have asked Congress for an appropriation for three female nurses to assist in this work.

The reasons and the practice prevailing in other jurisdictions, were presented to the House committee, and what was said there may be found in the report of the hearings at that time. Dr. Davidson, the then superintendent of the public schools, and Dr. Woodward, the health officer of the District, spoke in extenso on that subject. Briefly, they outlined the reasons; that a female nurse could get in closer communication and in closer contact with children and with teachers, and in many cases pave the way for the necessary attention of the physician and save him the time that might be required to get the information which the nurses could get very much more expeditiously; and the other reason was that in those cases in which the pupil is sent home by order of one of the school physicians, the nurse would be enabled, by follow-up methods—that being the term referred to by Dr. Davidson—to keep in touch with the child and see that the parents were led to do that which the physician had recommended, with the view of bringing the child back to his school at the earliest possible time.

Senator GALLINGER. The representations made to the House were not made this year, were they?

Mr. FENNING. Yes. You will find them in the report I have just been referring to.

Senator GALLINGER. I knew they were made last year, but I did not know that they made those recommendations this year?

Senator SMITH of Maryand. They are on pages 260, 262, and 554.

Mr. FENNING. We believe that the work that has been done in this connection is but a part of the work with which we are familiar that has been done throughout the country during the recent wave that has swept over the country—the wave of public sentiment for the conservation of the great social body—and the work that has been done of that kind has commenced with the child from the time of its very birth; and this is but a portion of the work that seeks to take care of the child during very important years of its life. We hope that the committee in its wisdom will see fit to put back into the appropriation bill the appropriation recommended by the commissioners. I thank you very much for this opportunity.

Senator GALLINGER. We have in the last two bills undertaken to do something of this kind, so far as the Senate is concerned, but you know what happened to it, of course.

Mr. FENNING. Yes, sir.

STATEMENT OF DR. WILLIAM C. BORDEN.

Dr. BORDEN. I came here as representing the department of medicine of George Washington University and as chairman of the executive committee of the hospital. In our hospital we are caring for some of the sick of the District, and we have an appropriation at the present time of $5,000 a year for that purpose.

Senator SMITH of Maryland. Yes.

Dr. BORDEN. We asked, through the Board of Charities, that this appropriation be increased to $6,000 for the coming year, for the reason that in the past the appropriations allotted to us have never been sufficient to pay for the patients sent to us. I may say that the same situation obtains in Georgetown University Hospital, I believe, as Dr. Kober will state.

For the past five years we never have had an appropriation in any year sufficient to cover the cases sent to us, at a dollar a day, and in the last two years we have treated patients in excess of the amount allotted to us by the District by $1,257.80. The amount we receive is very small—a dollar a day—and it costs us really more than that to care for the patients; and if this $6,000 was allowed us and we did not have patients enough to consume that amount, of course we would only get paid for those we actually took care of. It would only be equity to give us the money for what we really did.

Senator SMITH of Maryland. They pay you for what you do if you do not exceed the amount; and if you do exceed the amount, you hold the bag; is that it?

Dr. BORDEN. If we exceed the amount we have to pay it out of our own pockets. That is what we have done for the last five years, and we are now behind on the care of these patients approximately $5,000. I have not the exact figures.

Senator SMITH of Maryland. There is a fixed charge of $1 a day?

Dr. BORDEN. Yes, sir. In the past two years we have treated patients at a cost in excess of the amount allotted to us of $1,257.80.

Senator GALLINGER. Is the class of patients that you care for increasing in your hospital? That commenced with an appropriation of $3,000, if I remember correctly, and we have been raising it a little each year.

Dr. BORDEN. Yes, sir; the appropriations have been increasing.

Senator GALLINGER. I think it was first $3,000 and then $4,000 and then $5,000; and it suggested itself to me to ask the question that I did, whether or not the patients are increasing, more and more being sent to your hospital?

Dr. BORDEN. That is the reason we asked more this time —in order to meet this increase in the number of patients.

Senator GALLINGER. They have kept the Georgetown University Hospital and the George Washington University Hospital on all fours, giving them the same appropriation?

Dr. BORDEN. Yes.

Senator GALLINGER. You say Dr. Kober will speak for Georgetown University Hospital?

Dr. BORDEN. Yes, sir. I think that is all I have to submit, Mr. Chairman. Here is a letter in regard to the matter, if you wish it.

Senator GALLINGER. You had better file that.

Dr. BORDEN. Thank you very much.

(At 1 o'clock p. m. the subcommittee took a recess until 2.30 o'clock p. m.)

The letter submitted by Dr. Borden is as follows:

condition that is not to the credit of the Government. I think those poor people who are really suffering from all kinds of diseases are entitled to first consideration, rather than the man who gets drunk.

Senator SMITH of Maryland. Speaking of the buildings in which they are now located as being inadequate and not fit to locate them in, how many are there there of these paupers?

Senator GALLINGER. Dr. Hickling can probably answer that.

Dr. HICKLING. We have a 200-bed hospital there now in wooden buildings. Only the old almshouse is a brick building, and the others are all frame buildings. We handle about 3,000 patients a year, coming and going, according to our last annual report.

Senator SMITH of Maryland. Why are not these present brick buildings utilized for taking care of them?

Senator GALLINGER. They are not adequate now. The interiors would have to be changed over, and on my own motion I had Mr. Woods make an investigation of those buildings, and he made a report, and I think that probably it can be found somewhere, showing that it would not be a very expensive experiment; but the commissioners then in office were opposed to the whole scheme and blocked it.

Senator SMITH of Maryland. Would those buildings, of which you speak, be adequate for the poor and for inebriates too?

Senator GALLINGER. I think so; to a very large extent so. Of course you might have to still occupy some of the buildings that are now occupied.

Senator LEA. Have you any data on this?

Dr. HICKLING. We now have more charity patients than Providence Hospital, Garfield Hospital, Georgetown University Hospital, and George Washintgon University Hospital all put together. In fact, so far as numbers are concerned, the truth is that I have somewhat hesitated at asking an appropriation for a hospital for inebriates so long as we have our poor people in so much larger numbers than those that are suffering from inebriety.

Senator DILLINGHAM. Do you not think they all ought to be provided for?

Senator GALLINGER. I think so, if we can get an appropriation.

Dr. HICKLING. The point is that we are providing in some way for our sick poor, but for the inebriates we are not making any appropriation which leads to their uplifting and cure.

Senator SMITH of Maryland. How long have you been advocating a building of this kind?

Dr. HICKLING. Ever since I have been at work on it. For years I have done everything I could in that direction. We have had a number of bills introduced in the House and Senate, and there are a number of questions in them. In my statement to-day I have been avoiding the detail.

The question of where it should be located has embarrassed us considerably, and the question of whether it shall be an elegant or a poor place. Those things have all come in, and have only had the misfortune to block the whole scheme. Now we need something. and we need something quickly.

Senator GALLINGER. Is there any reason why a hospital of this kind should not be located on that 34 acres where the Tuberculosis Hospital is?

Dr. HICKLING. That is the note here that the commissioners recommended.

Senator GALLINGER. Would it not be better for it to be located in the country than anywhere in the city?

Dr. HICKLING. From my own personal judgment, from what I know of the situation, that is the proper place for it.

Senator GALLINGER. We have there about 34 acres, 3 or 4 miles out.

Dr. HICKLING. It is just beyond the Soldiers' Home. That is where the Tuberculosis Hospital now is.

Senator GALLINGER. We have on that 34 acres nothing but the Tuberculosis Hospital.

Dr. HICKLING. The plan has been to build a great municipal hospital there, but that has not made much headway, and probably will not in the immediate future.

Senator GALLINGER. How many tuberculosis patients are being treated out there?

Dr. HICKLING. I do not know very much about the details of that institution.

Senator GALLINGER. It is a fine hospital.

Dr. HICKLING. A nice hospital and in a nice place.

Senator GALLINGER. That was built five or six years ago, was it not?

Dr. HICKLING. Yes. The point is that these inebriates are now being left to the courts and the jails and the workhouses and the hospitals, and we are absolutely ignoring them, so they are absolutely prevented from anything like a chance for recovery. If this appropriation recommended by the commissioners could prevail and the institution could be located on the ground already owned by the District at Fourteenth and Upshur Streets, on a part of which the Tuberculosis Hospital is now located, and where some have proposed to build a Government hospital or city hospital, it would be ideal. There would be no question about that, and it would do the greatest amount of good that $75,000 could possibly do to the District of Columbia, I think, at this time.

Senator GALLINGER. We have this large tract at Fourteenth and Upshur Streets, three or four miles out.

Dr. HICKLING. It is a beautiful spot, and we have there this one fine hospital, which cost $100,000.

Senator GALLINGER. If I recall, that is an admirable place for an inebriate asylum. It is much better than to have it in the city.

Senator SMITH of Maryland. It is the judgment of Dr. Hickling that that is an ideal place.

Dr. HICKLING. Yes, sir.

Senator SMITH of Maryland. Your judgment is that even if this other property was improved as a place for the poor, that would be better than this ground where the Washington Asylum Hospital now is?

Dr. HICKLING. Yes, sir. There are many reasons why it should not be put down where the Washington Asylum Hospital now is.

condition that is not to the credit of the Government. I think those poor peo e who are really suffering from all kinds of diseases are entitled topfirst consideration, rather than the man who gets drunk.

Senator SMITH of Maryland. Speaking of the buildings in which they are now located as being inadequate and not fit to locate them in, how many are there there of these paupers?

Senator GALLINGER. Dr. Hickling can probably answer that.

Dr. HICKLING. We have a 200-bed hospital there now in wooden buildings. Only the old almshouse is a brick building, and the others are all frame buildings. We handle about 3,000 patients a year, coming and going, according to our last annual report.

Senator SMITH of Maryland. Why are not these present brick buildings utilized for taking care of them?

Senator GALLINGER. They are not adequate now. The interiors would have to be changed over, and on my own motion I had Mr. Woods make an investigation of those buildings, and he made a report, and I think that probably it can be found somewhere, showing that it would not be a very expensive experiment; but the commissioners then in office were opposed to the whole scheme and blocked it.

Senator SMITH of Maryland. Would those buildings, of which you speak, be adequate for the poor and for inebriates too?

Senator GALLINGER. I think so; to a very large extent so. Of course you might have to still occupy some of the buildings that are now occupied.

Senator LEA. Have you any data on this?

Dr. HICKLING. We now have more charity patients than Providence Hospital, Garfield Hospital, Georgetown University Hospital, and George Washintgon University Hospital all put together. In fact, so far as numbers are concerned, the truth is that I have somewhat hesitated at asking an appropriation for a hospital for inebriates so long as we have our poor people in so much larger numbers than those that are suffering from inebriety.

Senator DILLINGHAM. Do you not think they all ought to be provided for?

Senator GALLINGER. I think so, if we can get an appropriation.

Dr. HICKLING. The point is that we are providing in some way for our sick poor, but for the inebriates we are not making any appropriation which leads to their uplifting and cure.

Senator SMITH of Maryland. How long have you been advocating a building of this kind?

Dr. HICKLING. Ever since I have been at work on it. For years I have done everything I could in that direction. We have had a number of bills introduced in the House and Senate, and there are a number of questions in them. In my statement to-day I have been avoiding the detail.

The question of where it should be located has embarrassed us considerably, and the question of whether it shall be an elegant or a poor place. Those things have all come in, and have only had the misfortune to block the whole scheme. Now we need something, and we need something quickly.

Senator GALLINGER. Is there any reason why a hospital of this kind should not be located on that 34 acres where the Tuberculosis Hospital is?

Dr. HICKLING. That is the note here that the commissioners recommended.

Senator GALLINGER. Would it not be better for it to be located in the country than anywhere in the city?

Dr. HICKLING. From my own personal judgment, from what I know of the situation, that is the proper place for it.

Senator GALLINGER. We have there about 34 acres, 3 or 4 miles out.

Dr. HICKLING. It is just beyond the Soldiers' Home. That is where the Tuberculosis Hospital now is.

Senator GALLINGER. We have on that 34 acres nothing but the Tuberculosis Hospital.

Dr. HICKLING. The plan has been to build a great municipal hospital there, but that has not made much headway, and probably will not in the immediate future.

Senator GALLINGER. How many tuberculosis patients are being treated out there?

Dr. HICKLING. I do not know very much about the details of that institution.

Senator GALLINGER. It is a fine hospital.

Dr. HICKLING. A nice hospital and in a nice place.

Senator GALLINGER. That was built five or six years ago, was it not?

Dr. HICKLING. Yes. The point is that these inebriates are now being left to the courts and the jails and the workhouses and the hospitals, and we are absolutely ignoring them, so they are absolutely prevented from anything like a chance for recovery. If this appropriation recommended by the commissioners could prevail and the institution could be located on the ground already owned by the District at Fourteenth and Upshur Streets, on a part of which the Tuberculosis Hospital is now located, and where some have proposed to build a Government hospital or city hospital, it would be ideal. There would be no question about that, and it would do the greatest amount of good that $75,000 could possibly do to the District of Columbia, I think, at this time.

Senator GALLINGER. We have this large tract at Fourteenth and Upshur Streets, three or four miles out.

Dr. HICKLING. It is a beautiful spot, and we have there this one fine hospital, which cost $100,000.

Senator GALLINGER. If I recall, that is an admirable place for an inebriate asylum. It is much better than to have it in the city.

Senator SMITH of Maryland. It is the judgment of Dr. Hickling that that is an ideal place.

Dr. HICKLING. Yes, sir.

Senator SMITH of Maryland. Your judgment is that even if this other property was improved as a place for the poor, that would be better than this ground where the Washington Asylum Hospital now is?

Dr. HICKLING. Yes, sir. There are many reasons why it should not be put down where the Washington Asylum Hospital now is.

it only cared for 1,257 patients. Last year we were obliged to take care of nearly 3,000 patients—to be exact, 2,939 patients—in the same institution, showing that the existing hospitals had not met the real needs. We could not have accomplished this if we had not converted some of the old buildings that were formerly used as an almshouse into hospital purposes. The appropriations for the improvement at the Washington Asylum Hospital amounted to $28,200 in 12 years, whereas nearly a million dollars was expended for the other hospitals.

The situation has not been met in any way, beause we practically take care of three times the number of patients in the so-called city hospital that we were obliged to prior to the appropriations made for the expansion of other pospitals.

We feel that it is a great injustice to the inmates of that institution to be treated in that particular hospital. First of all, the environments are exceedingly unfavorable; it is located within the shadow of the jail, and formerly of the workhouse, and the deserving poor naturally shrink from being treated in such close proximity; we have, indeed, great difficulty to persuade the people to avail themselves of the hospital facilities. It is the only hospital in the city where patients can be sent with any certainty of their being admitted. It is a municipal hospital in name but not in fact. These conditions, I am sure, were well appreciated by the joint committee of Congress as early as 1898, and they made some very definite recommendations. These recommendations were based upon expert opinions. Dr. Henry M. Hurd, the superintendent of Johns Hopkins Hospital, and Dr. John B. Chapin, superintendent of the Pennsylvania Hospital, were called in by the joint committee to assist in the solution of the problem, and I should like to read what they said on that subject in November, 1907:

This institution is connected with the almshouse and workhouse and consists of 5 wards, accommodating about 70 patients. * * * The wards or pavilions are wooden structures, erected in recent years, and are considered an improvement on former buildings. They are lacking in conveniences, have insanitary water-closet arrangements, the furnishings are poor, and the number of nurses insufficient for the proper attendance upon the sick. In our opinion it has been an erroneous and unwise judgment to erect or maintain a hospital for the worthy poor who are sick in the shadow and amid the environments and association of an almshouse. While we sympathize with the efforts of officers, physicians, and others concerned to make the best use of the limited facilities placed at their disposal, yet if we are to use plain language we must declare the present standard of care and provision for the sick but little above that of the primitive country poorhouse of an earlier day.

Then they recommended as follows:

It is recommended and proposed that a municipal hospital be erected to receive all patients, inmates of Garfield, Providence, or any other hospital in the District and inmates of the Washington Asylum or almshouse who may be proper subjects for such an institution; that is, those who have been under treatment in the hospitals of the city at public charge and have become chronic or are, in the opinion of the physicians, incurable patients.

The proposed municipal hospital should be a well-constructed building, with modern appointments * * * and medical service equal to the best in the District, with plain and becoming furnishings, on grounds entirely separate and disassociated from the almshouse, jail, and house of correction. This would remove objections made by the worthy poor to treatment in an almshouse hospital.

Practically this recommendation was indorsed, or at least approved, by a joint congressional committee, who took, as I have already stated, the necessary steps to bring about remedial con-

ditions; that is, they appropriated sufficient money to improve hospital facilities.

They also made an appropriation, or at least an appropriation was secured June 6, 1900, of $100,000, for the purchase of ground upon which to erect a municipal hospital, and the commissioners acquired title to 35 acres of ground at a cost of $80,000.

An appropriation of $5,000 for the preparation of plans was also made. When these plans were forthcoming, the general scope of the undertaking and the prospective cost seemed somewhat appalling, and it was concluded that possibly the object could be accomplished by providing additional accommodations in the existing hospitals for the care of the worthy poor.

That object, for the reasons I have indicated, was not attained. Instead of spending the money for plain wards for the sick poor, the money was largely expended for expensive operating rooms and for private suites for high-grade patients. At all events, the very fact that we have to take care of three times the number of patients now in the Washington Asylum Hospital indicates that the real needs have not been met and the conditions have not been remedied. We deem it our duty to make a strong plea in favor of the beginning of an institution that will at least care for the present population at the Washington Asylum Hospital. The need is very pressing, because there can be no question that it is not fair that these people should be taken care of in buildings that are inadequate and were considered unfit for even an almshouse, and that is what we are doing now.

In addition to the five frame buildings that we have we have converted two of the old almshouse buildings into hospital accommodations.

Senator GALLINGER. Is it not a historic fact that one reason why the findings of that joint board or committee were not carried out resulted from the fact that immediately upon that project being launched an appropriation of $3,000,000 was asked from Congress?

Dr. KOBER. I think not, Senator. I have no idea, because it was before I entered the board.

Senator GALLINGER. Yes.

Dr. KOBER. Mr. Wilson probably can tell us better. If such an appropriation was ever contemplated, I think it could not have been countenanced by the Board of Charities. The whole plan, as I remember, contemplated the ultimate erection of a hospital for 1,000 patients, but only so much of it was to be built as was actually needed at that time and additions were to be made as the city expanded.

Senator GALLINGER. I have a pretty vivid recollection of some of those things, and I want to read something from the House hearings. I read from page 373, where Mr. Page was questioning Mr. Edson, who is on the board with you:

Dr. KOBER. Yes.

Senator GALLINGER. I read as follows from the House hearings: "So that there was a proposition made for an expenditure of $3,000,000, and it absolutely frightened Congress, and that has been one reason, I guess, why there has been nothing further done." No denial was made of that.

Senator SMITH of Maryland. How long ago was that?

Dr. KOBER. It must have been about 1901, Mr. Chairman.

Senator GALLINGER. It was in 1901, or thereabouts.

Dr. KOBER. We know, and have very positive ideas, that the expenditure of $300,000 is all that will be needed to meet the present needs, and for several years to come, for the accommodation of these people now at the Washington Asylum. That is our idea, whatever the notions of the Commissioners may have been in regard to the cost of a city hospital in 1901.

Senator GALLINGER. Of course you would frankly admit to this committee, would you not, that the $300,000 would be only a beginning?

Dr. KOBER. Why, Senator, you probably will remember that we built for tuberculosis purposes a hospital that will accommodate 120 patients; a building that is exceedingly creditable and will bear inspection. That building was erected and partly equipped for $100,000; so that we feel that for $300,000 a hospital can be built that will accommodate 250 patients. Such an estimate appears safe, judging by our past experience.

Senator GALLINGER. That would not meet the necessities of the District at the present time, would it, if we propose to care in that way for all those being cared for by congressional appropriations?

Senator SMITH of Maryland. I understood you to say that there were 3,000 of these people.

Senator GALLINGER. I assume that if a new hospital was built the plan would be to draw all of these patients from the various hospitals that we are now appropriating for. You would not have a municipal hospital and still have us make these appropriations for the individual hospitals, to care for the poor, would you, Dr. Kober?

Dr. KOBER. There is no such intention, Senator, because our main object is to properly house and care for the inmates now at the Washington Asylumn Hospital. After this is accomplished, if more accommodations are needed for the indigent sick of the city, they should likewise be erected on the site purchased for that purpose, in harmony with the general project of a city hospital. There is no disposition to vacate a bed in a single private hospital of this city. It would be extremely unwise, and with the constant growth of the city there will be enough to do to provide increased facilities for care of the sick poor. We deem it our special duty to the less resourceful people who can not speak for themselves, to present the case as strongly as possible. We believe that it is a disgrace to the city for the sick poor to be taken care of within the shadow and the environment of the jail.

Senator SMITH of Maryland. I understand, Doctor, that that is not the only objection. I understand that the quarters and facilities for taking care of them are inadequate.

Dr. KOBER. It is both.

Senator SMITH of Maryland. Yes.

Dr. KOBER. In every way the location is a most undesirable and unfortunate one; friends of the inmates in the hospital have to walk about six to eight squares to get to the hospital.

I have just recently prepared a condensed history of the medical charities of the city, and I will be glad to send you copies. This hospital question is by no means of recent origin. The medical profession, for example, as early as 1820 urged the erection of a decent city hospital. They finally succeeded in 1831 in convincing Congress that if they could not do better, they could convert the old jail, then located in Judiciary Square, into a city hospital. Congress first appropriated $10,000, and afterwards $20,000 more, to convert this old jail into a city hospital. This hospital rendered excellent service until 1861, when the Government took charge of it and used it for military purposes. Unfortunately, the building was entirely destroyed by fire in November, 1861. The situation gave rise then to the establishment of Providence Hospital, and Congress for the first time in its history appropriated, probably as an emergency measure, money also for building purposes and an annual subsidy. Since then the appropriations have increased from year to year, new hospitals have sprung up, and new requests for appropriations have been met

The board does not object to the present contract system, because it provides definitely for specific payments for specific services; but the board deems it extremely unwise that any appropriations should be made to private corporations and hospitals for building purposes as the title does not rest in the United States Government. The board feels that whatever may be needed in the way of additional buildings for the indigent sick in the city should be erected on ground owned and controlled by the Government. That is the position of the board, and I think it was the position, clearly, of Congress up to 1861.

Senator SMITH of Maryland. It seems to me, from what I am learning in these various investigations, that one of the troubles in establishing an efficient hospital here has been the lack of concentration as to what is best to be done. There seems to be a division as to what is best. Is it not a fact, Senator Gallinger, that there has been a division of opinion as to what is the best means?

Senator GALLINGER. There has been a pretty acute controversy between the Board of Charities and some good people in the District which has been heard a good many times before. Dr. Kober is going over the same ground that has been presented here many times in the past. The Board of Charities wanted to practically destroy all the hospitals of the city and have a great municipal hospital, putting out of commission such institutions as the Emergency Hospital and the Columbia Hospital. That has been their policy, and it has been resisted by the friends of these hospitals. The result is that we are just where we are now. It may be wise to make the appropriation of $300,000 for a new hospital for the poor, but that is an entirely different proposition from the scheme heretofore advocated, which would have cost many times that amount.

Senator SMITH of Maryland. In other words, they can not agree.

Senator GALLINGER. There has not been any agreement. There has been a very acute disagreement on these matters between influential people in the District and the Board of Charities. There is this to be considered, that the policy of the board has been to build a very large municipal hospital out in the country 3 or 4 miles and doing away with the Emergency and Columbia Hospitals. However, those hospitals were saved by appropriations made for them last year.

Senator SMITH of Maryland. How can they get patients there with any degree of comfort?

Senator GALLINGER. They say they can; but I think many of them, especially emergency cases, would die on the way, and for that reason I have resisted the effort. I may be wrong, but it has not seemed to me good policy. We did buy that tract of land. I do not know whether it was simply in contemplation to build a great hospital on that tract of land or not, but it is to my mind absolutely incontrovertible that if we bought it for that purpose we made a mistake in going away out there beyond the Soldiers' Home to establish a hospital.

Senator SMITH of Maryland. It seems to me that a hospital for emergency purposes ought to be one which can be gotten at readily.

Dr. KOBER. In reference to that, the board has had no idea of putting an emergency hospital on the site that was selected for a municipal hospital. The board had some very definite ideas as to what an emergency service should consist of, namely, of four distinct emergency stations, just like so many police stations, in four different sections of the city.

Senator GALLINGER. That is for first aid.

Dr. KOBER. That is for first aid.

Senator GALLINGER. In other words, you are going to destroy the great Emergency Hospital which has been here for many years—I do not know how many—and establish four stations for first aid, and then your patients would have to be gotten to a hospital somewhere afterwards.

Senator SMITH of Maryland. Can you not concentrate the whole business?

Senator GALLINGER. Well, Senator, I think the matter is now fairly well adjusted.

Dr. KOBER. As I conceive it, an emergency hospital should receive patients and render efficient service right there, and keep them long enough until it is safe to send them to their homes or to a city hospital or to a private hospital, whichever the patient may select. Patients would not be transported if the transportation would in any way injure their welfare—that would not be the purpose of an emergency station or hospital. In speaking of the present and prospective emergency hospital, I will say that it is a very deserving institution. I have been identified with its early history, and I have still a good deal of sympathy on account of the good work accomplished. But is it good economy to put three or four hundred thousand dollars into one hospital in a certain section of the city for emergency purposes pure and simple?

If that is wise economy, then it is equally proper to put the same amount of money in the north and the east and the west, because no emergency hospital, however well equipped, can do the service for the entire city. The most efficient service is rendered when it is located in convenient geographical sections of the city, just as the fire and police service is now rendered as promptly as possible.

Senator GALLINGER. We have other emergency hospitals in the city, largely supported by private contributions, and in this bill we are making contributions to them. The Eastern Dispensary, which is an emergency hospital, is doing most excellent work, is it not?

Dr. KOBER. Yes, sir.

Senator GALLINGER. We make a slight contribution to aid them. They own their building. It is a great big question, Mr. Chairman, that we have had to deal with. Neither House of Congress has been willing to make the appropriation that the Board of Charities has

DISTRICT OF COLUMBIA APPROPRIATION BILL.

insisted upon to build a great hospital out in the country. I, myself, think that the hospital situation here is in rather a fragmentary shape, and that some wise man or some wise committee or some wise Congress might solve the problem and make it much better than it is. The Washington Asylum Hospital is anything but a credit to the city. But I do believe, as I suggested a couple of hours ago, and as I think I suggested to the Board of Charities last year, that that $600,000 worth of brick buildings down there that are lying idle might well be utilized to meet the conditions that are existing at the Washington Asylum Hospital. The Board of Charities has not apparently agreed with me on that point. Maybe they are right and possibly I am wrong. The mere fact that it is in reasonable proximity to a jail I do not think is a valid objection to a hospital for the poor classes. I do not think that that should affect them. The distance is considerable between the two. I think that argument is not really one that we ought to very seriously consider.

Dr. KOBER. I regret, naturally, to differ with the Senator.

Senator SMITH of Maryland. As I understand it, Doctor, the matter that we are specially treating now is that you want this appropriation of $5,000 increased to $6,000; and the other thing you speak of is that you have been treating those patients at a cost price that far exceeds the amount that you have been receiving?

Dr. KOBER. Not only that, but we are taking care of about 35 patients a day, and we are paid practically for only one-third of those patients.

Senator GALLINGER. I will say that so far as my knowledge goes, I think the Doctor is entirely justified in asking for that increased appropriation for Georgetown University Hospital, and that we might well make it greater. Then, if we could differentiate between the George Washington University Hospital and the Gerogetown University Hospital, the appropriation ought to be made larger at Georgetown than at George Washington, because they are treating more patients in Georgetown than they are in George Washington, are they not?

Dr. KOBER. Yes; because we have a larger plant. But I should not like to see any distinction made between the two educational institutions.

Senator GALLINGER. We carry them along together.

Senator LEA. Why is it proper to carry them along together? One is very much larger than the other.

Dr. KOBER. I think the Senator is quite correct as a matter of abstract justice. The principle of specific payment for specific service ought to govern.

Senator LEA. That would seem to me to be the right criterion.

Senator SMITH of Maryland. The one that does the most work ought to get the most pay.

Senator GALLINGER. Yes. They were both very modest in asking the aid of Congress, and I think they frankly resisted some suggestion that had been made along that line until a few years ago, when somebody representing the George Washington Hospital, and likewise some one representing the Georgetown Hospital, came in and asked for the modest sum of $3,000. We granted it, and it has grown from that up to $5,000; but they never have been paid at either hospital for the entire number of patients they have cared for, and the Georgetown

it only cared for 1,257 patients. Last year we were obliged to take care of nearly 3,000 patients—to be exact, 2,939 patients—in the same institution, showing that the existing hospitals had not met the real needs. We could not have accomplished this if we had not converted some of the old buildings that were formerly used as an almshouse into hospital purposes. The appropriations for the improvement at the Washington Asylum Hospital amounted to $28,200 in 12 years, whereas nearly a million dollars was expended for the other hospitals.

The situation has not been met in any way, beause we practically take care of three times the number of patients in the so-called city hospital that we were obliged to prior to the appropriations made for the expansion of other pospitals.

We feel that it is a great injustice to the inmates of that institution to be treated in that particular hospital. First of all, the environments are exceedingly unfavorable; it is located within the shadow of the jail, and formerly of the workhouse, and the deserving poor naturally shrink from being treated in such close proximity; we have, indeed, great difficulty to persuade the people to avail themselves of the hospital facilities. It is the only hospital in the city where patients can be sent with any certainty of their being admitted. It is a municipal hospital in name but not in fact. These conditions, I am sure, were well appreciated by the joint committee of Congress as early as 1898, and they made some very definite recommendations. These recommendations were based upon expert opinions. Dr. Henry M. Hurd, the superintendent of Johns Hopkins Hospital, and Dr. John B. Chapin, superintendent of the Pennsylvania Hospital, were called in by the joint committee to assist in the solution of the problem, and I should like to read what they said on that subject in November, 1907:

This institution is connected with the almshouse and workhouse and consists of 5 wards, accommodating about 70 patients. * * * The wards or pavilions are wooden structures, erected in recent years, and are considered an improvement on former buildings. They are lacking in conveniences, have insanitary water-closet arrangements, the furnishings are poor, and the number of nurses insufficient for the proper attendance upon the sick. In our opinion it has been an erroneous and unwise judgment to erect or maintain a hospital for the worthy poor who are sick in the shadow and amid the environments and association of an almshouse. While we sympathize with the efforts of officers, physicians, and others concerned to make the best use of the limited facilities placed at their disposal, yet if we are to use plain language we must declare the present standard of care and provision for the sick but little above that of the primitive country poorhouse of an earlier day.

Then they recommended as follows:

It is recommended and proposed that a municipal hospital be erected to receive all patients, inmates of Garfield, Providence, or any other hospital in the District and inmates of the Washington Asylum or almshouse who may be proper subjects for such an institution; that is, those who have been under treatment in the hospitals of the city at public charge and have become chronic or are, in the opinion of the physicians, incurable patients.

The proposed municipal hospital should be a well-constructed building, with modern appointments * * * and medical service equal to the best in the District, with plain and becoming furnishings, on grounds entirely separate and disassociated from the almshouse, jail, and house of correction. This would remove objections made by the worthy poor to treatment in an almshouse hospital.

Practically this recommendation was indorsed, or at least approved, by a joint congressional committee, who took, as I have already stated, the necessary steps to bring about remedial con-

ditions; that is, they appropriated sufficient money to improve hospital facilities.

They also made an appropriation, or at least an appropriation was secured June 6, 1900, of $100,000, for the purchase of ground upon which to erect a municipal hospital, and the commissioners acquired title to 35 acres of ground at a cost of $80,000.

An appropriation of $5,000 for the preparation of plans was also made. When these plans were forthcoming, the general scope of the undertaking and the prospective cost seemed somewhat appalling, and it was concluded that possibly the object could be accomplished by providing additional accommodations in the existing hospitals for the care of the worthy poor.

That object, for the reasons I have indicated, was not attained. Instead of spending the money for plain wards for the sick poor, the money was largely expended for expensive operating rooms and for private suites for high-grade patients. At all events, the very fact that we have to take care of three times the number of patients now in the Washington Asylum Hospital indicates that the real needs have not been met and the conditions have not been remedied. We deem it our duty to make a strong plea in favor of the beginning of an institution that will at least care for the present population at the Washington Asylum Hospital. The need is very pressing, because there can be no question that it is not fair that these people should be taken care of in buildings that are inadequate and were considered unfit for even an almshouse, and that is what we are doing now.

In addition to the five frame buildings that we have we have converted two of the old almshouse buildings into hospital accommodations.

Senator GALLINGER. Is it not a historic fact that one reason why the findings of that joint board or committee were not carried out resulted from the fact that immediately upon that project being launched an appropriation of $3,000,000 was asked from Congress?

Dr. KOBER. I think not, Senator. I have no idea, because it was before I entered the board.

Senator GALLINGER. Yes.

Dr. KOBER. Mr. Wilson probably can tell us better. If such an appropriation was ever contemplated, I think it could not have been countenanced by the Board of Charities. The whole plan, as I remember, contemplated the ultimate erection of a hospital for 1,000 patients, but only so much of it was to be built as was actually needed at that time and additions were to be made as the city expanded.

Senator GALLINGER. I have a pretty vivid recollection of some of those things, and I want to read something from the House hearings. I read from page 373, where Mr. Page was questioning Mr. Edson, who is on the board with you:

Dr. KOBER. Yes.

Senator GALLINGER. I read as follows from the House hearings: "So that there was a proposition made for an expenditure of $3,000,000, and it absolutely frightened Congress, and that has been one reason, I guess, why there has been nothing further done." No denial was made of that.

Senator SMITH of Maryland. How long ago was that?

Dr. KOBER. It must have been about 1901, Mr. Chairman.

it only cared for 1,257 patients. Last year we were obliged to take care of nearly 3,000 patients—to be exact, 2,939 patients—in the same institution, showing that the existing hospitals had not met the real needs. We could not have accomplished this if we had not converted some of the old buildings that were formerly used as an almshouse into hospital purposes. The appropriations for the improvement at the Washington Asylum Hospital amounted to $28,200 in 12 years, whereas nearly a million dollars was expended for the other hospitals.

The situation has not been met in any way, beause we practically take care of three times the number of patients in the so-called city hospital that we were obliged to prior to the appropriations made for the expansion of other pospitals.

We feel that it is a great injustice to the inmates of that institution to be treated in that particular hospital. First of all, the environments are exceedingly unfavorable; it is located within the shadow of the jail, and formerly of the workhouse, and the deserving poor naturally shrink from being treated in such close proximity; we have, indeed, great difficulty to persuade the people to avail themselves of the hospital facilities. It is the only hospital in the city where patients can be sent with any certainty of their being admitted. It is a municipal hospital in name but not in fact. These conditions, I am sure, were well appreciated by the joint committee of Congress as early as 1898, and they made some very definite recommendations. These recommendations were based upon expert opinions. Dr. Henry M. Hurd, the superintendent of Johns Hopkins Hospital, and Dr. John B. Chapin, superintendent of the Pennsylvania Hospital, were called in by the joint committee to assist in the solution of the problem, and I should like to read what they said on that subject in November, 1907:

This institution is connected with the almshouse and workhouse and consists of 5 wards, accommodating about 70 patients. * * * The wards or pavilions are wooden structures, erected in recent years, and are considered an improvement on former buildings. They are lacking in conveniences, have insanitary water-closet arrangements, the furnishings are poor, and the number of nurses insufficient for the proper attendance upon the sick. In our opinion it has been an erroneous and unwise judgment to erect or maintain a hospital for the worthy poor who are sick in the shadow and amid the environments and association of an almshouse. While we sympathize with the efforts of officers, physicians, and others concerned to make the best use of the limited facilities placed at their disposal, yet if we are to use plain language we must declare the present standard of care and provision for the sick but little above that of the primitive country poorhouse of an earlier day.

Then they recommended as follows:

It is recommended and proposed that a municipal hospital be erected to receive all patients, inmates of Garfield, Providence, or any other hospital in the District and inmates of the Washington Asylum or almshouse who may be proper subjects for such an institution; that is, those who have been under treatment in the hospitals of the city at public charge and have become chronic or are, in the opinion of the physicians, incurable patients.

The proposed municipal hospital should be a well-constructed building, with modern appointments * * * and medical service equal to the best in the District, with plain and becoming furnishings, on grounds entirely separate and disassociated from the almshouse, jail, and house of correction. This would remove objections made by the worthy poor to treatment in an almshouse hospital.

Practically this recommendation was indorsed, or at least approved, by a joint congressional committee, who took, as I have already stated, the necessary steps to bring about remedial con-

ditions; that is, they appropriated sufficient money to improve hospital facilities.

They also made an appropriation, or at least an appropriation was secured June 6, 1900, of $100,000, for the purchase of ground upon which to erect a municipal hospital, and the commissioners acquired title to 35 acres of ground at a cost of $80,000.

An appropriation of $5,000 for the preparation of plans was also made. When these plans were forthcoming, the general scope of the undertaking and the prospective cost seemed somewhat appalling, and it was concluded that possibly the object could be accomplished by providing additional accommodations in the existing hospitals for the care of the worthy poor.

That object, for the reasons I have indicated, was not attained. Instead of spending the money for plain wards for the sick poor, the money was largely expended for expensive operating rooms and for private suites for high-grade patients. At all events, the very fact that we have to take care of three times the number of patients now in the Washington Asylum Hospital indicates that the real needs have not been met and the conditions have not been remedied. We deem it our duty to make a strong plea in favor of the beginning of an institution that will at least care for the present population at the Washington Asylum Hospital. The need is very pressing, because there can be no question that it is not fair that these people should be taken care of in buildings that are inadequate and were considered unfit for even an almshouse, and that is what we are doing now.

In addition to the five frame buildings that we have we have converted two of the old almshouse buildings into hospital accommodations.

Senator GALLINGER. Is it not a historic fact that one reason why the findings of that joint board or committee were not carried out resulted from the fact that immediately upon that project being launched an appropriation of $3,000,000 was asked from Congress?

Dr. KOBER. I think not, Senator. I have no idea, because it was before I entered the board.

Senator GALLINGER. Yes.

Dr. KOBER. Mr. Wilson probably can tell us better. If such an appropriation was ever contemplated, I think it could not have been countenanced by the Board of Charities. The whole plan, as I remember, contemplated the ultimate erection of a hospital for 1,000 patients, but only so much of it was to be built as was actually needed at that time and additions were to be made as the city expanded.

Senator GALLINGER. I have a pretty vivid recollection of some of those things, and I want to read something from the House hearings. I read from page 373, where Mr. Page was questioning Mr. Edson, who is on the board with you:

Dr. KOBER. Yes.

Senator GALLINGER. I read as follows from the House hearings: "So that there was a proposition made for an expenditure of $3,000,000, and it absolutely frightened Congress, and that has been one reason, I guess, why there has been nothing further done." No denial was made of that.

Senator SMITH of Maryland. How long ago was that?

Dr. KOBER. It must have been about 1901, Mr. Chairman.

Mr. WILSON. Not at all. We are perfectly willing that they shall be sold. But that is the custom. We never buy horses for our institutions, and we use a good many on the farms.

Senator LEA. They now belong to the District?

Mr. WILSON. Yes, sir; but I want, before leaving that, to say this, that while there is a slight economy in this, we do not urge it primarily because of economy.

Senator SMITH of Maryland. If I understand it, you would do away with two men to start with?

Mr. WILSON. We would do away with one man to start with. The reason we only do away with one is that we have a night service, and while we have only three vehicles, one would be on duty in the night and three in the daytime. But even then we would drop one man.

Senator SMITH of Mayland. It takes five men now, does it?

Mr. WILSON. Yes.

Senator SMITH of Maryland. To equip these five vehicles that you have?

Mr. WILSON. We have five now.

Senator SMITH of Maryland. Why would it take four to run three vehicles?

Mr. WILSON. Because of the night service. We want the three to do all the work of the five horse-drawn vehicles, and the service must be maintained night and day.

Senator LEA. Three will take charge of the three vehicles in the day, and you will have one in the nighttime?

Mr. WILSON. Yes.

Senator SMITH of Maryland. Do you not now have enough?

Mr. WILSON. We have five men now.

Senator SMITH of Maryland. But you have five vehicles?

Mr. WILSON. Those five vehicles are not all in service at the same time. We can not man over four; but we have different types of vehicles. For instance, on the days when we transport the insane, which we do two or three days a week only, as a rule, we use a large vehicle that would not be suitable for an ambulance to transport the sick. One is a general-utility vehicle, which we use to haul the aged people to the home for the aged and infirm and for things of that kind. Another is used at the Government Hospital for the Insane to bring over the people who come to the courthouse here in the city for their hearings. They are accompanied by the attendants, and they are returned if they are committed to the hospital after a hearing.

Senator GALLINGER. Will this ambulance allow you to dispense with one of the drivers provided for in the House bill?

Mr. WILSON. The employee we dispense with is the man who is called hostler. We would like to keep four men—three for the day and one for the night. One additional reason for that is that in 10 years this service has increased about 50 per cent, and we have had no increase of employees. We occasionally to-day get a driver from the police department to help out in case of sickness. We are very much cramped, but we would dispense with the hostler.

Senator GALLINGER. Why has the service increased 50 per cent? The population has not increased to that extent. Are the people getting poorer all the time, or what is the trouble?

Mr. WILSON. No doubt a great deal more is being done for our people now than 10 years ago. For instance, the Tuberculosis Hospital, with a population of 100, did not exist and practically no tubercular patients were cared for.

Our home for the aged and infirm has been established; and then we have Occoquan, 25 miles down the river, so that there has been a great increase in the service that has much more than corresponded to the increase in population. It is undoubtedly, however, in response to public sentiment and public conviction on these subjects. I frankly say, that in proportion to the population, we are in most communities to-day doing very much more for these classes than ever before.

Senator SMITH of Maryland. There is no doubt that there is more charity in proportion to the population than there was 10 years ago.

Senator GALLINGER. Undoubtedly that is so. When he said it had doubled, I thought the proportion was very large.

Senator SMITH of Maryland. He said that it had increased 50 per cent.

Mr. WILSON. That is what I meant to say, anyway.

Senator GALLINGER. Probably you did.

Mr. WILSON. One word I want to say about efficiency. You know in a general way the extent of the District, and it is not as it ought to be in this day, proper to send a horse-drawn vehicle in all kinds of seasons and weathers for a sick person 3 or 4 miles away, or even 2 miles. The service is not as efficient as it ought to be. Our city, you know, is scattered, and these horse-drawn vehicles are slow, and we ought to give a more prompt service than we can with horses. I want to emphasize that.

Senator GALLINGER. I assume that the transportation to the workhouse at Occoquan is now mostly by water?

Mr. WILSON. No; it is by rail, thus far; and it will not be by water soon, because we can not get a boat that is quick enough without spending a good deal of money; and then we would have to have two boats—one for hauling the material, brick and stone, and the other for passengers. It is too slow, at present.

If there is not other question on that, we will pass along to the next item. Is it your desire that I should mention any item that the House has inserted in the bill, or only those that have been omitted by the House?

Senator SMITH of Maryland. You had better touch only those that have been omitted. Have you made any inquiry as to the cost of these ambulances?

Mr. WILSON. Yes; I went over that very carefully with such advice as I could get in the fire and police departments, where they are using those vehicles.

Now, if you please, we will pass to the top of page 63 of the bill. The first item there is for the maintenance fund of the Washington Asylum and Jail. That is the large general institution that you have been speaking about, and this appropriation for maintenance we ask $38,000, which is for the hospital department of that institution, and regardless of what the future may bring for the hospital situation, next year we need this increase, or it means a deficiency. We do not like to have deficiencies, though Congress does appropriate for them, because in this institution we are practically forced to receive these people.

This year there is a deficiency.

Senator SMITH of Maryland. Even with that $35,000, there is a deficiency?

Mr. WILSON. With the $35,000.

Senator SMITH of Maryland. How much is the deficiency?

Mr. WILSON. There is a deficiency of about $2,500, as near as we can now know, having gone but half of the year. There is a tendency to increase of population.

Senator SMITH of Maryland. Is there more work to be done now? Is the work increasing?

Mr. WILSON. It does increase steadily. As Dr. Kober has indicated, there is some increase every year. It is inevitable with the growth of the city. That is true in almost every city.

HOSPITAL FURNISHINGS, ETC.

On page 63 there is an estimate which we have urged, regardless of the future hospital situation, "For hospital furnishings, including sterilizers and accessories for operating room and microscope for laboratory, $2,000." If you care to hear especially about anything in this item, of course Dr. Kober, the chairman of the medical charities committee, can fully explain it. He understands it much better than I would as a layman.

Senator SMITH of Maryland. We would like to know why you want this extra $2,000.

Dr. KOBER. I wish to state, Mr. Chairman, that we are trying, as long as we are situated at the Washington Asylum, to render the service as efficient as possible, and the articles that this money is to be expended for are practically worn out, and there is a want, a lack, everywhere of apparatus and facilities for doing good work. Nowadays a patient can scarcely be treated intelligently without having microscopes and laboratory equipment, in order to make accurate diagnosis, and to aid in the treatment, as far as possible. Sterilizers and equipment for the operative room will naturally wear out, and they are needed now, where 25 years ago they were not regarded as essentials, while to-day it is considered almost criminal to have surgical operations performed without having every possible safeguard.

Senator SMITH of Maryland. This is for the city hospital?

Dr. KOBER. For the Washington Asylum Hospital. It is a very modest appropriation, absolutely needed to equip our service with those things that are essentially needed, and to replace the worn-out articles.

Senator SMITH of Maryland. Have you had any appropriation lately for that purpose?

Dr. KOBER. Not recently; no, sir. As I said a while ago, we have had only $28,000 for actual improvements in that institution since 1901, and that has been judiciously invested in improving and bettering the old buildings and the establishment of additional hospital facilities.

Senator GALLINGER. They have had a microscope of some kind in that institution, have they not?

Dr. KOBER. It is practically worn out, and I have loaned them two microscopes from Georgetown University to do the work. That is the real fact.

Senator SMITH of Maryland. In other words, you have had to borrow from other institutions in order to do the work at this hospital?

Dr. KOBER. Absolutely.

Senator SMITH of Maryland. What is the next item?

LAUNDRY PLANT IN JAIL.

Mr. WILSON. The next item to which we would like to invite your attention is on the same page: "For installing laundry plant in jail, including dry box, washing machine, and other appurtenances, $1,500."

We are glad to say, in reference to that item, that if you should include that we would next year omit one of the engineers in the list of employees above, and in that connection I want to say that the item immediately following, in lines 22 and 23, granted by the House, for connecting up the heating plant, allows for dropping two of the engineers, and they have already been dropped from the bill by the House. The reason we can drop the two this year and the other one not until next year is that the laundry service must go on, and we could not have it ready by July 1 unless that money could be made available very early, or made immediately available, and in case of the heating plant we will have the time to connect this piping, etc., before the cold weather. Hence two of the employees have been dropped already, and if you grant this for the laundry the purpose will be to enlarge the laundry that is now in the jail and discontinue the laundry now in the old female workhouse building.

I do not want to take up your time with that, Mr. Chairman, but possibly a word may be proper as to the general situation at this Washington Asylum and Jail. Two years ago the jail, which up to that time had been administered under the Department of Justice, was transferred to the commissioners and combined with the Washington Asylum, and the warden of the jail and half the guards of the jail were eliminated from the bill, most of the prisoners going to Occoquan, and the one superintendent taking charge of the combined institution, consisting of the hospital and jail. This enlargement of the heating plant which was provided for a year ago has enabled us to get down to three heating plants, where we formerly had five, and the piping that the House has already provided in this pending bill will connect up another plant and dispose of two engineers, and the only isolated plant that we will then have is in the laundry, which was formerly in the old female workhouse, about a quarter of a mile distant from the jail, and if we could combine the two laundries, we would save enough, in getting rid of the employees, in two years to save the entire cost of the installation, without mentioning the substantial saving that would come in the economy of coal.

Senator GALLINGER. What employees would you get rid of?

Mr. WILSON. One assistant engineer. Two have been dropped, and we drop one more—not in this bill. We need the laundry every day; the laundry work is so heavy. And we need the present force until the change has been made.

Senator GALLINGER. But after this year you will drop one more?

Mr. WILSON. We will drop one more.

HOME FOR AGED AND INFIRM.

On page 64, under the title "Home for Aged and Infirm," there are quite a number of employees for whom the board recommends an increase of compensation, and I want simply to say that we believe that all merit it. We gave these matters very careful consideration. The board visits all of these institutions prior to the time of sitting, when they hear the superintendents relative to the making of these estimates, and I will not take them up in detail except to mention two instances. The first is that of the superintendent, in whose salary we recommend an increase from $1,200 to $1,500.

I think, if Dr. Kober will listen to this, we may say without question that while all our employees we try to get efficient, from the standpoint of economy this superintendent is probably the most efficient man we have in the service. He has taken that institution down there when it was almost in a wilderness and has made it what it is at a very little cost to the Government. He has a peculiar faculty of taking the old, abandoned school buildings, most of which are wooden, and taking them down there and in the course of time, working his men on rainy days, converting them into most substantial outbuildings.

Senator GALLINGER. He built a barn there?

Mr. WILSON. He has built dairy barns, and outhouses, and silos, and all sorts of things. I think you will admit that that is the best farm in the District. Of course, there are not very many farms in the District.

Senator GALLINGER. It is very well managed. I have visited it.

Mr. WILSON. Of course, by comparison with the compensation of others, his compensation is meager.

Senator GALLINGER. These employees all get their board and lodging?

Mr. WILSON. Yes; that is so in all of the institutions.

Senator GALLINGER. Including the superintendent?

Mr. WILSON. Yes; that is a general statement, including all.

Senator GALLINGER. Of course, the superintendent has a house?

Mr. WILSON. Yes.

Senator SMITH of Maryland. The chief engineer gets his lodging?

Mr. WILSON. Yes.

Senator SMITH of Maryland. And has he a family?

Mr. WILSON. No, sir. The present chief engineer is not married, but he might keep his wife there if she were an employee. We try not to get a man with family in institutions.

Senator SMITH of Maryland. When you do get one, do you board his wife, too?

Mr. WILSON. That may be. If it is a man like the superintendent who has a house. But with the exception of the superintendent, we seldom can take a married man, except his wife may act as matron or teacher. But we can not take children.

Senator SMITH of Maryland. But the engineer and the assistant engineer get their board?

Mr. WILSON. They all get their board, and they are all single men, or they do not have their wives with them.

Senator SMITH of Maryland. I understand all these men who are connected with this home get their board.

Mr. WILSON. Yes. There is a blacksmith and woodworker there who gets $540, and we have asked to have his pay increased to $720. The superintendent regards that as most important, because the man he has he will lose unless he gets an increase of pay. That man, who is called blacksmith and woodworker, is a general all-around mechanic. He is superintendent of construction, but I told him we did not want to recommend any such a title as that, because the place was so built up that the committee would think he ought to be through constructing; but there is constant improvement on a reservation of 300 acres.

Senator SMITH of Maryland. Is there much work for a blacksmith there?

Mr. WILSON. We have a great number of horses. It is a farm of about 300 acres, altogether.

Senator SMITH of Maryland. How many horses have you?

Mr. WILSON. We have there usually about 15 or 16 horses.

Senator SMITH of Maryland. On a 300-acre farm?

Mr. WILSON. Yes. There is a great deal of hauling from the city. We get the stuff much cheaper if we will haul it than if we have to have them deliver it to us. Then the men have to be taken back and forth. However, we will not need so many horses in future years, as the rough land becomes more reclaimed.

Senator GALLINGER. Can you not get water transportation to that reservation?

Mr. WILSON. I think likely in the course of a year or two the commissioners will very seriously consider recommending the purchase of a passenger boat that would serve that institution in conjunction with Occoquan and the proposed new reformatory, provision for which you have already authorized. But you see, it is rather expensive for one institution, because it means three or four additional employees for the crew of the boat.

The item for repair, in line 20, was estimated at $3,000, and it has been $3,000 prior to last year, as I recall it, and it was cut by the House. We believe that the money could be well spent. They are rather cheap structures, and if they are not kept in good repair they deteriorate rather rapidly. Much of the original woodwork was too cheap. This man of whom I spoke to you is reconstructing a good deal of the outside woodwork, the floors and porches, with concrete, and he gets this old steam piping, and he makes nice iron railings out of it.

Senator GALLINGER. How many people have you in this institution?

Mr. WILSON. Usually 300; from 280 to 300. Then there are the employees in addition.

Senator GALLINGER. You have more in winter than in summer?

Mr. WILSON. Not very greatly more.

At the foot of that page there is an item for the purchase of two electric generators, $4,570. Those are duplicates for which we ask. The present generators have been in use for seven years and are very badly worn, and are likely to break down. Mr. Hamilton, who is president of the Capital Traction Co. and a member of our board, says that when generators of that type have been used for seven years we ought to be providing for duplication. We make our own power and electric light, and we would regard that provision as only fruga .

Senator GALLINGER. I suppose it would be a protection in case of a breakdown?

Mr. WILSON. Yes; because it would give us a little light. On page 65 I think there is another item, the National Training School for Girls. There were several items cut, but I understand that the president of that institution, Mr. J. Nota McGill, was before you.

Senator GALLINGER. Yes.

Mr. WILSON. Then, it is unnecessary for me to mention that.

FREEDMEN'S HOSPITAL.

Then we pass to page 66, and on line 12, under Freedmen's Hospital, we recommend that the amount available for contracts be increased from $34,000 to $38,000. That is the hospital for the colored patients now maintained by the Government and conducted under the direction of the Secretary of the Interior and the District indigent patients are cared for there under contract. We recommend the amount of $38,000.

Senator SMITH of Maryland. How many have you there?

Mr. WILSON. The daily average number of patients at Freedman's Hospital is 192. That includes what are know as the United States patients as well as the local patients. This hospital is maintained by the Federal Government, and will care for people coming from any part of the United States, and it gets a very large number of colored people from the near-by States, here.

Senator SMITH of Maryland. You have 192 patients and you get $34,000?

Mr. WILSON. That is for both classes combined.

Senator SMITH of Maryland. I say, that is the total number?

Mr. WILSON. Yes.

Senator LEA. Some of these pay, as I understand.

Mr. WILSON. No; but in addition to this appropriation you provide in the sundry civil bill for the maintenance of United States patients.

Senator SMITH of Maryland. How much is that?

Mr. WILSON. I do not recall that. It is not under our supervision.

Senator GALLINGER. It is quite a large amount.

Mr. WILSON. In round numbers it is probably $50,000.

Senator SMITH of Maryland. $50,000 in round numbers?

Mr. WILSON. Yes.

Senator SMITH of Maryland. And this amount is $34,000.

Mr. WILSON. Yes.

Senator SMITH of Maryland. That makes $84,000; and you have 192 patients.

Senator GALLINGER. The appropriation contained in this bill is for indigent patients?

Mr. WILSON. For indigent patients under contract.

Senator GALLINGER. Under contract. What do you pay in that hospital per diem?

Mr. WILSON. $1.10 for adults, 65 cents for children, and 40 cents a day for infants with mothers in maternity cases.

Senator GALLINGER. Why do you pay $1.10 there and $1 at Georgetown University Hospital?

Mr. WILSON. The explanation is simply a historical one. We were paying $1.10 a day for the treatment of patients and $1.20 for maternity cases and emergency cases when Georgetown came into the field and came before the congressional committees and themselves volunteered to take the patients at $1 a day.

Senator GALLINGER. What do you pay at the Emergency Hospital?

Mr. WILSON. $1.20 a day. There are other items that you probably understand, for special work, emergency treatments and ambulance service.

Senator GALLINGER. What is the expense of treatment at the tuberculosis hospital?

Dr. KOBER. To be exact, it is $1.40 a day. This is somewhat high on account of the comparatively small number of patients. The overhead charges are always about the same, whether you have a hundred or two hundred patients. For instance, our average was about 94 patients last year. The expense for food was only 59 cents per head, but the overhead charges were 47 cents. Naturally the overhead charges would be about the same, whether we had 100 or 200 patients. The State institution in Maryland must have about 200 patients.

Senator SMITH of Maryland. We have now more than that.

Dr. KOBER. I have been there and visited it, and it is a most excellent institution.

Senator SMITH of Maryland. Have you been there recently?

Dr. KOBER. I think it was two years ago I was there.

Senator SMITH of Maryland. We have built a place over 500 feet long since then to care for 200 patients. Those other buildings were shacks, and the patients were put 20 in a shack.

Mr. WILSON. On the same pages, between lines 17 and 18, we estimated for a new washer at the Columbia Hospital for the laundry at $500. That is needed, and we recommend it.

For the Children's Hospital, on line 20, we recommend the amount being increased from $14,000 to $15,000, because they have earned as much as that in recent years, and we have not had the money to pay for all.

Senator SMITH of Maryland. You have done that?

Mr. WILSON. They have earned the $15,000 and a little more for the past two years.

Senator GALLINGER. What per diem do you pay at that hospital?

Mr. WILSON. Sixty-five cents for children. On page 69 I think there is no other item until we come to the two institutions which we have already considered this morning—that is Georgetown University and George Washington University. You notice those in the middle of page 67. These are the institutions concerning which Dr. Borden and Dr. Kober spoke, and we suggest an increase from $5,000 to $6,000 in each instance.

TUBERCULOSIS HOSPITAL.

On the same page, on line 21, under the Tuberculosis Hospital, we recommend that two cooks at the Tuberculosis Hospital be increased from $180 to $240. There is an increase of one in number, which the House allowed, and I ought to say that that was to restore one omitted last year, I think inadvertantly. In naming the cooks they have provided now for the usual number.

Senator SMITH of Maryland. You are now paying $180 a year?

Mr. WILSON. Yes.

Senator SMITH of Maryland. For two cooks?

Mr. WILSON. Yes.

Senator GALLINGER. $180 a year for each?

Mr. WILSON. For each.

Senator GALLINGER. And you have one cook at $360?

Mr. WILSON. Yes, and two at $180 each. For $180, of course, we are getting scullions rather than cooks. For $240 we would be able to get one that could take charge in the absence of the cook herself, and we would be glad if you would consider that.

Senator GALLINGER. How would it be in that particular, inasmuch as an additional cook is allowed, to have it made, one at $360, one at $240, and one at $180?

Mr. WILSON. I think that would be reasonably satisfactory.

Senator SMITH of Maryland. I think that $240 is not an extravagant price. That is less than $5 a week. It is a great problem now, to get servants.

Mr. WILSON. Yes; and in a tuberculosis institution particularly difficult.

Passing on to page 68, if you will be good enough, on line 6, under the head of general maintenance fund for that institution, we ask that the amount be increased from $30,000 to $32,000, and we can say with reference to that that the service is of a very high order, and we can also say that it will mean a slightly decreased cost per capita, because our population is increasing. Last year the daily average was 93. The current year, up to December 31, it was 97.

Then you have provided, by little metal structures, 15 additional beds, and the population to-day is 109, so that that will mean less per capita cost than for the current year, even with the increased appropriation.

Senator SMITH of Maryland. What is the increase in three years?

Mr. WILSON. From 93 to 109.

Senator SMITH of Maryland. What did you get when you had 93?

Mr. WILSON. My recollection is that in the last year it was $28,000.

Senator GALLINGER. Last year it was $30,000.

Mr. WILSON. Then it was $30,000 when we had 93 patients. It is still $30,000, and we have 97 patients, and we want it to be $32,000 for the next year. In the middle of this year we have had 109 patients, so that, looking to next year, it ought not to be less than 109. We want to keep that service, as you know, at a high standard, because when patients go there they ought not to come away from there as sources of infection, and we have no law by which we can restrain them if they want to come away.

Senator SMITH of Maryland. Will you kindly tell me what is the total cost of running that hospital, with the patients you have? Have you got that, including everything?

Mr. WILSON. Per capita and per day; I have it exactly; and that amount subdivided for each item.

It was $1.40 per day, and I have it divided, showing the salaries, the food, and the fuel, and we will be glad to put that in the record, showing it for each institution.

(The table referred to is as follows):

Laundry and laundry and cleaning supplies.	Purchase of vehicles and repairs to same	rent.	Taxes.	Insurance.	Miscellaneous.	Total.	
$0.0040	$0.00				$0.0197	$0.6358	1
.0081					.0127	.5137	2
					.0169	.6500	3
					.0138	.7939	4
.0152					.0288	1.2212	5
.0098					.0403	1.4601	6
		037		$0.0102	.0508	1.7856	7
		055	$0.0088	.0031	.0676	2.1674	8
.0756		017		.0030	.0297	2.0409	9
.0118		072		.0019	.0157	1.4537	10
		005			.0827	1.3655	11
.0049		015		.0021	.0230	.9281	12
					.0751	1.4007	13
.0064					.0340	1.0464	14
.0075	.00				.0032	.6447	15
	.00				.0146	.7720	16
					.0045	.3274	17
.0168		07			.0115	.6848	18
.0095					.0114	.7580	19
.0063					.0083	.5221	20
.0036					.0008	.4123	21
		03			.0257	.2973	22
			.0349	.0070	.0368	.9114	23

Senator SMITH of Maryland. $1.40 a day?

Mr. WILSON. Yes. But that amount will be less this year because of the increase in the population.

Senator GALLINGER. The total in the House bill for the next year is $56,000. They estimated for $58,000, and the House gave them $56,000, which is an increase of $1,180 over last year.

Senator SMITH of Maryland. Is this tuberculosis hospital for incipient cases, or for cases of all kinds?

Dr. KOBER. For all kinds. Unfortunately, the number of incipient cases is quite limited. Indeed, it is rare to find in any of these institutions more than 10 per cent of the cases in the incipient stage. The majority are either in a moderately advanced or in an advanced stage. The percentage of recoveries is therefore comparatively small; but such a hospital subserves a very important function in this, that it takes care of the advanced cases who, if they remained in their homes, would be a distinct menace to their families, and also a very great burden. The greatest danger undoubtedly is from the consumptive himself, right in his immediate family. The husband may contract it from the wife, or the wife from the husband, or the children from the parents, or vice versa, by that close contact; so that if we accomplish nothing else than the isolation of those patients we will be doing good.

Senator SMITH of Maryland. I consider taking them away and preventing them from spreading the disease, and the education that they get in taking care of themselves and looking out for others to be worth more than the cures you make. Yes, you teach them how to take care of themselves and how to take care of other people, and the main thing is to take them away from spreading the disease in the various localities from which they come.

Dr. KOBER. Yes.

Senator SMITH of Maryland. Do you take children up at this hospital?

Dr. KOBER. A limited number. There are no provisions for their care elsewhere, except for bone and joint cases. There is also a summer camp mostly for tuberculous children on the same ground which is maintained by a local chapter of the Red Cross Society.

MUNICIPAL HOSPITAL.

Mr. WILSON. Mr. Chairman, the next item omitted was on page 68, between lines 10 and 11, which was an estimate of $60,000 for the preparation of plans and specifications, necessary grading of site, and so forth, for beginning the work for hospital buildings on the hospital site at Fourteenth and Upshur Streets. That is an item concerning which you have already heard Dr. Kober at length, and I presume you do not want me to discuss it. I would only like to say this, that, regardless of what the future general hospital policy might be, I hope in some way in the very near future that improved accommodations will be available for our people down at the Washington Asylum Hospital. The estimate here submitted, $60,000, with authority to contract for an expenditure of not to exceed $300,000, could not possibly anticipate any numbers beyond those now needing care and not cared for in other institutions, and of course the future policy as to buildings and maintenance is in the hands of the Congress entirely.

Senator LEA. My objection to that at this time would be that I think there is no comprehensive hospital plan under way, and to spend that amount of money for plans and specifications without having a comprehensive plan would be a mistake.

Mr. WILSON. If I might say this without touching the Municipal Hospital question technically, the site that we have, 35 acres, is near to Mount Pleasant, and accessible by two car lines. On it is a tuberculosis hospital, and it is designed for minor contagions, such as diphtheria and scarlet fever, on one plat, which is on Thirteenth Street, and on the other plat of 20 acres we would propose to build these buildings, and then we would recommend that in the future, in so far as Congress is willing to build buildings for general city work, aside from strictly emergency purposes, they should be on their own site, which is admirably located, and while it is now on the north side of the city, it is yet in the city, and if you will look at the map you will see that it is in the inevitable center of population of the District of Columbia. It is now 20 minutes from Pennsylvania Avenue on the Fourteenth Street car, and the same from the Ninth Street car, which passes it on the other side. This is, in brief, our plan, regardless of how much of a public hospital or how many private hospitals you have. It is the poor people down there that we are interested in, and we do not resist the improvement of the buildings at the present site. You must know that there are many other things involved there that other people are interested in.

The commission for the beautification of Washington wants that site vacated for park purposes, and it is suggested as a site for an eastern high school, and so on, and the Board of Charities does not desire to inject itself into that particular problem. I am sure we recommend, as we did, in the past that those buildings be modified and equipped properly if they are to be used for hospital purposes.

Dr. KOBER. I may add, that the plans that were authorized and secured 10 years ago, on competition, really gave a very definite outline as to what ought to be done there sooner or later to develop the hospital features in the city of Washington.

Senator LEA. You have those plans now?

Dr. KOBER. Yes, sir; the block plans were secured under a prize competition, and give a very definite idea as to the arrangement of the different pavilions or hospital units. So for example, on the west side of Thirteenth Street, the departments for contagious diseases would be located; one of these units, the tuberculosis hospital has already been erected, and on the east side of Thirteenth Street pavilions for medical, surgical, obstetrical, gynecological patients; and buildings for administration purposes have been definitely planned. It was laid out on a very comprehensive scale, not only for 10 years, but for the needs of the city incident to its expansion for many years to come; and its magnitude possibly appalled Congress, on the assumption that it involved the immediate expenditure of several million dollars. Now, of course, there is no necessity for such large expenditures. There is no need for the investment of over $300,000 to relieve the present situation, and additional units can be provided as they are needed. Each building is a separate pavilion and will be connected with the administration building by a common corridor, and the line of units could readily be extended as they are needed.

A definite plan for the future is therefore in existence; it was prepared by Frank Miles Day, of Philadelphia, who was the successful competitor.

Senator GALLINGER. Of course new plans would have to be made for your $300,000 hospital?

Dr. KOBER. No, sir; I think not, except for the preparation of working plans. Mr. Miles Day will receive, under the terms of the award, 5 per cent on the contract price for all buildings that are put up, just as he did for the preparation of detailed plans and specifications for the Tuberculosis Hospital. In other words, he did not receive a prize for his general plans, but was to be the architect of whatever buildings are put up, and he received 5 per cent on the contract price for his detailed plans of the Tuberculosis Hospital, which was the first unit erected, and he would probably receive a like rate on the different buildings that are built hereafter.

Senator GALLINGER. I meant that these old plans that contemplated this very large building would not be applicable.

Dr. KOBER. No, sir; they would not be applicable except the general outline, but all the different units will be put up in accordance with his original block plans.

Senator GALLINGER. Mr. Chairman, in justice to Dr. Kober and his associates on the Board of Charities, with whom I have differed very acutely sometimes—but we have always been good natured about it—I want to say that this proposition appeals to me to a much greater extent than some former propositions that have been made. This seems to be rather a clearing-house proposition——

Dr. KOBER. Sure.

Senator GALLINGER. To take care of most of the poor people who are in this very bad instiutution, as I call it, the Washington Asylum and Jail.

BOARD OF CHILDREN'S GUARDIANS.

Mr. WILSON. On page 68, on line 16, the amount for the general expenses of the board of childrens' guardians, we recommend an increase, $3,100 to $3,500. We urge that as very important, Mr. Chairman, because it is the item that is used for traveling and incidental expenses relative to the visitation of the 1,700 and more children that this public board has as a public guardian, about one-half of whom are placed in communities outside of the District of Columbia, and it would be unfortunate if they could not be visited.

On the next three lines, lines 17 to 19, I simply want to make a general statement. We suggested a very radical change there, and I am very sorry Mr. Hamilton of our board is not here, because he, as chairman of the committee, made a very exhaustive inquiry into this whole work last year, and the committee concluded it was exceedingly deficient. We were placing children in homes beyond our means to reach them by way of visitation, and because of the lack of help for that purpose, and I understand that in all probability some of the agencies here interested in social work are likely to appeal to you in behalf of that item as well as others in that schedule, because people are becoming more and more interested in these things in the community at large. As a result of this inquiry, when the board made up its estimates beginning of line 17, page 68, with the words "placing officers." in lieu of all up to and including line 19 except the clerk at

$720, the board recommended one placing and investigating officer at $1,200, whom they expected to be the chief placing officer, and nine placing and investigating officers at $1,000 each. That is an entire reorganization and an increase of four employees.

Senator LEA. That is $5,120.

Mr. WILSON. An increase of $5,060. We thought, in lieu of all those officers, the investigating clerk, placing officers, visiting inspectors, whose duties were all more or less similar—they are a little different but they are more or less similar; for instance, one visiting officer will investigate an application that is filed for receiving a child into their care as being destitute and another investigating officer will investigate a home in which the child has been or is to be placed.

Senator GALLINGER. Is Mr. Mann the agent of this board?

Mr. WILSON. No, sir; Mr. Mann is president of the board. Mr. Cisco is the agent.

Senator GALLINGER. Are these children placed outside of the District?

Mr. WILSON. About one-half of them. In practically all instances where they expect to get more or less permanent homes they are placed outside of the District. In the District are the boarding homes of those who are temporarily wards and are likely to be returned to their own parents by the court within a comparatively short time.

Senator GALLINGER. How do you get jurisdiction over these children?

Mr. WILSON. The Board of Children's Guardians?

Senator GALLINGER. Yes.

Mr. WILSON. Through the agency of the juvenile court. They receive no child except for a period of one week, pending investigation, without a court commitment.

Senator GALLINGER. The judge of the juvenile court comes here and asks us to give him an additional placing officer.

Mr. WILSON. A probation officer, is it not?

Senator GALLINGER. Yes.

Mr. WILSON. Their work is somewhat similar, but this placing officer has different duties. I will be glad to explain the difference. The probation officer deals with the child that is not a public ward, but is under the supervision of the court. These placing officers deal only with the children that are taken from their parents and become public wards, or in making investigations with a view to submitting evidence toward that end to the court. Is that clear?

Senator GALLINGER. That is satisfactory. How many do you say you have?

Mr. WILSON. Upward of 1,700 at the end of last year.

Senator GALLINGER. That is splendid work, of course.

Mr. WILSON. That is important work; and, frankly, our board feels that it is not possible, because of physical limitation in numbers of employees, to give it the supervision that it ought to have.

Senator GALLINGER. You think that after a child is placed, the family should be visited from time to time to see how the child is behaving and how it is getting on?

Senator SMITH of Maryland. And how it is being treated?

Senator GALLINGER. Yes; and how it is being treated?

Mr. WILSON. Yes.

Dr. KOBER. That it is properly placed and properly treated; and also to secure free homes. The more free homes we can find for those children among proper people, the more economical the administration will be.

Senator GALLINGER. Did you present that to the House committee?

Mr. WILSON. We did, with, we thought, considerable emphasis. Mr. Chairman. We are sorry we have not convinced them.

Senator LEA. How many of these children are white and how many are colored?

Mr. WILSON. About two colored to one white. The percentage varies slightly from time to time. The last item we considered was on page 68. I have concluded my general statement on the Board of Childrens' Guardians, unless there is some question.

MAINTENANCE OF FEEBLE-MINDED CHILDREN.

Senator LEA. On line 21 is the item "For maintenance of feeble-minded children (white and colored), $20,000."

Mr. WILSON. $22,000 was the estimate. That is just to avoid a deficiency.

Senator GALLINGER. What do you say to the proposition that was embodied in a bill that passed the Senate once or twice providing for the building of a home for feeble-minded children in the District—a bill that I introduced?

Mr. WILSON. We are heartily in favor of that, and we are this year recommending it in the form of legislation.

Senator GALLINGER. I have reintroduced that bill this year.

Senator SMITH of Maryland. Is there no home for feeble-minded children here?

Senator GALLINGER. No, and it is a crying shame, too.

Senator SMITH of Maryland. You have been getting $18,000 previously for this item?

Mr. WILSON. Yes, sir; and the estimate was $22,000. There will be a deficiency. We can not control the number.

Senator SMITH of Maryland. How many feeble-minded children have you?

Mr. WILSON. We have at present a little over 80. The number varies from week to week, but we have only a little over 80 children now that are being cared for in institutions outside of the District of Columbia.

Senator SMITH of Maryland. Is that all you have? What does it average, I mean?

Mr. WILSON. It is always over 80.

Dr. KOBER. These children are cared for in New Jersey and Pennsylvania, and we have to pay just what they ask, a regular contract price. I think it is nearly $300 a year.

Mr. WILSON. About $250 a year.

Senator LEA. For 80 children that would be $20,000, then.

Mr. WILSON. No; I said the number was upwards of 80. If I may, I will put in the record the number and the cost, giving the accurate figures. I would necessarily be inaccurate if I attempted to state it now.

Senator SMITH of Maryland. All right. They have given you $20,000.

(The following statement was submitted by Mr. Wilson:)

Feeble-minded children under care of Board of Children's Guardians.

School.	Number.	Amount.	Total.
Training school at Elwyn, Pa.	42	$250	$10,500
Training school at Falls Church, Va.	25	250	6,250
Training school at Vineland, N. J.[1]	2	250	500
Do.	2	300	600
Boarding homes.	15	180	2,700
	86		20,550

[1] When children were first sent from the District to Vineland the rate was $250. When the rate was afterwards raised, it was agreed that the two children already there should be kept at the rate of $250, but that all children admitted from that time on should be paid for at the rate of $300 per annum.

Mr. WILSON. The next item is on page 69, line 4. We have estimated for $60,000 there instead of $45,000, which was what we had last year.

Senator SMITH of Maryland. They increased that to $50,000.

Mr. WILSON. There is a deficiency of $20,000 this past year, which Congress granted, entirely owing to the number of children. I think possibly it would be for your advantage if I were to put in a memorandum here giving the number in homes and institutions, and as they distribute it.

Senator SMITH of Maryland. We would like to have it, because we can not judge of it unless we know what you are doing. We only know by the number of children.

Mr. WILSON. Do you want that put in the record?

Senator LEA. Yes; you had better put it in the record.

Senator GALLINGER. How do you reach your estimate of $20,000; from the basis of what you have fallen behind from time to time?

Mr. WILSON. Yes. I meant to say that last year your deficiency bill actually carried about $20,000.

Senator GALLINGER. For last year?

Mr. WILSON. Yes; I meant that.

Senator SMITH of Maryland. You do not remember how many of the children you have here, do you?

Mr. WILSON. Yes; at the date when this memorandum was made up, two weeks ago, we had in all, permanent and temporary wards, 1,712 children, and it is given here in detail as to where they are, and those on expense for board, those on expense for visitation only, and those in institutions. I will undertake to verify these figures, and put them in the record, and give you the details.

(The statement referred to by Mr. Wilson is as follows:)

Board of Children's Guardians.

Expense of maintenance of wards:
June 30, 1913, wards on expense—
In institutions—
Permanent wards... 127
Temporary wards... 89*
—— 216
In boarding homes—
Permanent wards... 243
Temporary wards... 39
—— 282

Total.. 498

Permanent wards on expense................................... 370
Temporary wards on expense................................... 128

Total.. 498

The board pays for board, care, and maintenance of clothing of children in boarding homes from $10 to $12 per month each, In a very few cases of crippled and defective children requiring special care a per capita of $15 per month is paid. The average payment to boarding homes for the fiscal year 1913 was $10.85 per capita per month.

The cost to the board for the maintenance of children in institutions varies from $100 to $156 per capita per annum. The average per capita cost of maintenance of wards in institutions during the fiscal year 1913, per month, was $11.29.

The large increase in expenditure for board and care of wards for the fiscal year 1913 was caused:

1. A necessary increase of payment to boarding homes because of the increased cost of living.

2. An unusual increase in the number of children committed to the board by the juvenile court.

3. The natural increase of the number of physically defective children under care of the board and who can not be placed in private homes to become self-supporting.

4. The closer attention given to the physical welfare of the children and to the care and preservation of their teeth.

5. Providing a better and more serviceable outfit of clothing for children placed in private homes and off expense to the board: first, because such clothing is due a self-respecting child, and, second, because persons taking these children into their families take the quality and completeness of the outfit of clothing the child has when it comes to them as an index of what the board requires of them as to clothing its wards.

At the close of the fiscal year 1913 the board had under its guardianship 1,515 permanent and 197 temporary wards, a total of 1,712, distributed as follows:

On expense to the board:
In institutions—
Permanent wards.. 127
Temporary wards.. 89
—— 216
In boarding homes—
Permanent wards.. 243
Temporary wards.. 39
—— 282
At no expense to the board (for maintenance):
In institutions at expense of District of Columbia—
Permanent wards.. 161
Temporary wards.. 60
—— 221
In institutions, with relatives, on indenture, apprentice or other family arrangement without expense for maintenance—
Permanent wards.. 984
Temporary wards.. 9
—— 993

1,712

INDUSTRIAL HOME SCHOOL FOR COLORED CHILDREN.

Mr. WILSON. In reference to the industrial home school for colored children, which is on the same page, page 69, we recommended there an increase in the salary of the blacksmith and wheelwright, in line 32, to $540. His present salary is $480. We would urge that, and particularly we would emphasize an item which would come in on line 23, after cook and laundress for $240 each, a new item for temporary labor, $500. You will find that all our institutions with the exception of this one have a small fund for temporary labor. Under the general statute the District of Columbia government can not spend money for services only when it is specified and in terms so authorized, and it is very desirable that at particular seasons we should have a little extra labor on the farm. While we have boys, nearly all the boys are under 12, and of course they are wayward or they would not be there, and they are not very useful; and we have a 100-acre tract. We would urge strongly that item for temporary labor, $500, as a matter of economy, if nothing else.

Senator GALLINGER. There was a time when I had in mind accurately the location of these various schools, but I am not sure about this one. Is this industrial home for colored children up Georgetown way?

Mr. WILSON. No, sir; that is the one for the white children. This is at Blue Plains, in the southeastern corner of the District. You have visited it.

Senator GALLINGER. Oh, yes; I have visited it.

Mr. WILSON. The next item is in the last line on that page—for maintenance, including purchase and care of horses, wagons, and harness. The House has given us $9,000. The estimate was $9,500, and the appropriation, including the deficiency for three years past, has been between $9,000 and $9,700, and it is to avoid a deficiency that we made that estimate. That is a new institution, comparatively, and the maintenance fund was never adequate, but Congress always allowed a deficiency. These children are committed by the courts in every instance.

Now, I think we come to next page, 70, line 3, "Repairs and improvements to buildings and grounds, $2,500." The House has given us $1,500, which is a very substantial increase. The reason for that apparently large estimate is that we have never had there a sufficient repair fund. We have had as much as $500. The original buildings cost $100,000, and we have not had the money necessary to keep them in proper repair. The outside woodwork, particularly the blinds and the porches and the stairways, are in very bad need of paint. The board personally went over the property, and they made the estimate.

Senator SMITH of Maryland. How old are the buildings?

Mr. WILSON. About 7 or 8 years old. The buildings have been entirely repainted since they were built.

Senator SMITH of Maryland. What was the cost of the buildings?

Mr. WILSON. $100,000.

Senator SMITH of Maryland. Are they of brick or wood?

Mr. WILSON. They are brick buildings.

Senator SMITH of Maryland. Has there been much cost for repairs?

Mr. WILSON. No, sir. Until the last year the amount was only $500. It is very inadequate.

Senator GALLINGER. I visited that school some years ago, shortly after it was built, and repairs were then needed. I had the impression that it was not a very good structure.

Senator SMITH of Maryland. A building 7 or 8 years old of course would need repairs.

Mr. WILSON. They are comparatively substantial, in the main, brick buildings; but they look pretty bad unless they are kept in repair, because they get rough usage. Wayward boys of 12 years of age will abuse buildings. We confess to abuse, but we are limiting it to the extent of our ability.

Senator LEA. This change in the amount in line 7 is due to the different amounts you have estimated?

Mr. WILSON. Yes, sir, entirely. That is the total.

There is another item that we asked for that was omitted—at line 3, on page 70—for rebuilding a barn, $1,500. Now, the only barn that we have for that farm is an old structure that the contractor that put up the original building built. There was not money enough left, and there never was an appropriation to provide a sufficient amount.

Senator SMITH, of Maryland. For rebuilding barn, that is?

Mr. WILSON. Yes.

Senator SMITH of Maryland. It must be in bad shape. It costs no more than $1,500 to build a fairly good barn. We can build one for that in our country, can we not, Senator Lea?

Senator LEA. You can in Tennessee—a new one.

Mr. WILSON. It means practically a new building.

Senator GALLINGER. Have you farm stock in connection with this school?

Mr. WILSON. Yes; we keep some cows and some horses. We farm the greater part of that 100 acres.

Senator SMITH of Maryland. How much stock have you?

Mr. WILSON. We have from 6 to 8 horses, according to the season. We have 8 cows and 20 to 30 hogs. We get our horses from other departments of the District government, and we need about 8 in the summer, and we let the number go down in the winter, so that we will not have to feed them, to about 6.

Senator SMITH of Maryland. It seems to me $1,500 would build you a new barn.

Mr. WILSON. It is practically that. It is an all-inclusive kind of a building we have in mind. We have no place for our farm implements, or to put any crops. We would arrange in that barn to put such crops as we would make there in the season.

Senator SMITH of Maryland. Who made this estimate of a cost of $1,500?

Mr. WILSON. The board made it, after inspection. Dr. Kober has built a great many buildings, and he could speak better than I can on that.

Senator LEA. I do not know how it is here, but in Tennessee $1,500 would build a very substantial barn, and a barn big enough to take care of all the crops you could raise on 200 acres, and all the stock you would have on that farm.

Dr. KOBER. This is about 6 miles from the center of the city, and all the building materials have to be taken down there from the city, and labor there is very much higher. If that is done by contract, on a small job of that kind they want apparently to be on the safe side. At all events, we have not gotten a place there in the form of a barn for the price required. It might be said, too, of the buildings in general. One reason why the buildings require a good deal of repair is because they have outside porches, and are exposed to the elements, and rough usage has already been indicated.

Senator GALLINGER. How is the acreage of this farm divided between the Home for the Aged and Infirm and the Industrial Home for Colored Children? We are providing a farmer and the kind of help that would be required in both instances. How is it divided?

Mr. WILSON. Approximately two-thirds to the Home for the Aged, and one-third to the school.

Senator GALLINGER. What is the acreage of the farm?

Mr. WILSON. Approximately 300 acres. I am speaking in round figures, of course. At that point also we have submitted another estimate. In the interest of economy we would urge this for the erection of a residence for the superintendent, $5,000. This is an isolated institution, and the only buildings are the original cottage buildings, and each cottage cost about $12,000 and accommodates some 20 to 24 boys. At the present time one of these is occupied by the superintendent and his family, and for his offices and general purposes; and for $5,000 we undertake to vacate that large building entirely for school purposes, which would add 20 to our population. That, of course, would add to our cost, but these 20 boys are now being cared for in private homes and institutions, and of course we must pay board for them if they are not there.

Senator SMITH of Maryland. Do you require this house that he occupies?

Mr. WILSON. We do. We could fill it immediately with children that are now an expense to the District because they are paid for in private homes or in institutions, because of not having the room down there to receive them.

Senator LEA. Would not $5,000 build quite an elaborate cottage, just for the superintendent's home?

Mr. WILSON. Our board members have gone over that, and they feel that $5,000, if you built of brick, and this being some six miles from the city, you would not get more than a substantial 8-room brick building, with possibly two additional rooms for the office and those general purposes that you would not have need for in a private home. We have no administrative building, in general, such as you would have in an institution like this down here.

Senator SMITH of Maryland. You have no administration building?

Mr. WILSON. No; We have a school building and a building to house the employees.

Senator LEA. Of course, I have no knowledge of the cost of building here. The cost of everything differs with the environment; but in Tennessee a man on a $1,200 salary does not live in a $5,000 house.

Mr. WILSON. I think it would be a fair statement to say that a Government clerk here, getting $1,200, in buying a house would quite frequently buy one that would cost as much as $5,000; sometimes less, but, I think, more frequently more. A $5,000 house is a very modest home here.

Senator SMITH of Maryland. That includes, of course, also the cost of the ground, which in the city is a very decided cost.

Mr. WILSON. Yes, sir.

Senator SMITH of Maryland. This is for nothing but a building.

Mr. WILSON. Nothing but the building alone and the equipment.

Senator SMITH of Maryland. What do you mean by the equipment?

Senator LEA. Do you call furniture equipment?

Mr. WILSON. Yes, sir.

Senator SMITH of Maryland. I assume it is furniture.

Mr. WILSON. Everything except some private belongings. We do not want people to have their private property mixed in there. All the public property is inventoried.

Senator SMITH of Maryland. I presume everything of that kind is already supplied?

Mr. WILSON. Yes, sir.

Dr. KOBER. Our city architect has given us those approximate figures, and they are largely based on the increased cost of transportation and the increased cost of labor, because this place is 6 miles away, and there is no street car to get to it.

Senator GALLINGER. The street car line goes within a couple of miles?

Dr. KOBER. Yes. It is fully 2 miles from the street car line.

Senator GALLINGER. That is why I made my inquiry about transportation by water. It seems to me that if you could get transportation by water to Blue Plains and Occoquan you would very much reduce the cost of transportation.

Mr. WILSON. The next item is on page 70, lines 13 to 19. The board has recommended some six increases in pay of employees, and we regard them all as equally necessary. This school is a well-conducted institution, with a moderate salary roll that has not been revised to any considerable extent for a great many years.

Senator LEA. The total increase is $760.

Mr. WILSON. Yes, sir. The increases are only $5 to $10 a month, in most instances.

Senator GALLINGER. This is the institution where they raise and sell flowers?

Mr. WILSON. Yes, sir; on Wisconsin Avenue.

Senator GALLINGER. Do you know how much revenue they derived last year from the sale of flowers?

Mr. WILSON. Yes, sir. It was $4,290.52.

Senator GALLINGER. It is a very interesting place.

Mr. WILSON. I was going to mention that, if the committee would be good enough to bear in mind on the item for repairs and improvements in line 23, repairs and improvements to buildings and grounds. We have asked that that appropriation be increased from $1,700 to $2,000. We have had $2,000 for a greater portion of the time for a number of years back. The amount was reduced to $1,700 by the House committee one year, not as a result of any particular hearing, as I understood. A number of items like that were reduced. We feel that we need that pretty badly out there. It is a large institution. The buildings—most of them—are old, and they have, as the Senator said, five substantial greenhouses which are subject to the attacks of weather and which sometimes suffer severely, as for instance in the storm that we had last year. The income we had from that place last year was $4,290, and we will do a little better this year, if we have ordinary good fortune.

Senator SMITH of Maryland. What did you do with that money?

Mr. WILSON. That is turned in. It is a part of the school fund as provided here in the maintenance fund, and is disbursed by the Government disbursing officer.

Senator LEA. It is covered into the Treasury?

Mr. WILSON. No, sir; it is used in the maintenance of the school.

Senator SMITH of Maryland. That was not used?

Mr. WILSON. It was used in connection with this care and maintenance. The law so provides, and it is a part of the general maintenance fund, and that is one reason why the maintenance at that school is lower.

Senator SMITH of Maryland. How many have you there?

Mr. WILSON. About 130. The other school for the colored has only 60; and you will notice that the total maintenance is only $16,000. That is plus the earnings.

Senator SMITH of Maryland. That is plus the earnings, and what is appropriated above for other purposes.

Senator LEA. Do you mean $16,000 plus the earnings?

Senator SMITH of Maryland. Yes; plus the salaries.

Mr. WILSON. Plus the salaries.

Senator LEA. What were the earnings?

Mr. WILSON. Last year a little over $4,000.

Senator LEA. That makes a large amount per capita.

Mr. WILSON. For the Industrial Home School the cost is 65 cents a day. For the colored it is 77 cents, but there are a much smaller number.

Senator GALLINGER. This Industrial Home School is an admirably managed school. I have examined it.

Senator SMITH of Maryland. How many pupils have you?

Mr. WILSON. 130 to 135. The number does not vary very much.

Senator SMITH of Maryland. That is over $200 a year per pupil.

Mr. WILSON. Yes, sir. Our child-caring institutions of that character—if we can get them around $200 and give a high service, we are doing pretty well.

Senator SMITH of Maryland. That may be, but it is considerably over $200 per capita.

Senator LEA. It is $256, I think.

Senator SMITH of Maryland. What is the next item?

MUNICIPAL LODGING HOUSE.

Mr. WILSON. On page 71 I think there is nothing until you get to the "Municipal Lodging House, wood and stone yard."

On line 13, after the word "superintendent," we recommend that the words "who shall also act as foreman" be stricken out and substitute therefor the words "Foreman, $480." This is the institution that cares for the homeless men, the tramps, who formerly slept in the police stations until they established this place. It is a 24-hour day service, and it is a real hardship if the superintendent has no one but the cook, and really the employees' roll is a modest one, to say the least. It has been a great hardship this year. This was cut out a year ago, and I happen to know that where the cook is provided for there at $360 the superintendent secured a man under that and used him for foreman, and he paid out of his own pocket $15 a month to a woman who did the cooking.

Senator GALLINGER. What is the significance of the title to the next item, "Municipal lodging house and wood and stone yard"? Does it mean that the inmates do some stone work?

Mr. WILSON. They saw some wood. In recent years they have not handled stone at all. That is a misnomer.

Senator SMITH of Maryland [reading]. "Municipal lodging house and wood and stone yard: Superintendent, who shall also act as foreman, $1,200."

What is this estimate now, "foreman, at $480"?

Mr. WILSON. That is an estimate for a new foreman, at $480, and we omit the words "who shall also act as foreman."

Senator LEA. You did not have that before?

Mr. WILSON. Yes, sir; up to this current year.

Senator GALLINGER. How many people do they lodge there in the course of a year? Have you those statistics?

Mr. WILSON. It has been running about 6,000 to 8,000 individuals in the course of a year. The population varies from 10 or 12 up to 60, and it needs constant supervision, as you know, so that it is pretty hard for one man to be 24 hours there. We hope that you will restore that.

Senator LEA. The next item is at the bottom of page 72, is it not?

WORKHOUSE.

Mr. WILSON. On page 72 I see nothing until we come to the workhouse, and I would say there, making the general statement again, that under the salary list of the workhouse we have made a number of suggested increases, and I went over the matter with the superintendent only this morning, and he said he regarded them all as of substantially equal importance; that holds down to line 13 of page 73. If there is anything more in detail the committee desires to know, I have notes as to the duties of each employee.

On page 72, beginning at the bottom of the page, the workhouse salary list begins and continues on pages 72 and 73, and unless the committee has some question, I merely make the general statement that we regard all of these increases we recommended as of equal importance.

FIREMAN ON STEAMBOAT.

On line 14, page 73, we would ask that you insert, after "engineer of steamboat, $480," the item "fireman, $480." That is for a fireman on the steamboat. On the old steamboat we did not need a fireman. The prisoners were able to do all the work; but we have gotten now, under the appropriation of last year, a new steamboat. It is good sized tug, which cost some $20,000, and with heavier machinery, and is a very different type of boat altogether. The old boat we had, known as the *General Warren*, was an abandoned boat that was under the control of the War Department and was loaned to us. We need that licensed fireman in this new boat. That is the boat that hauls our freight. We have not yet a passenger service. It hauls manure and supplies from Washington, and it brings our supplies, wood, stone, and brick, the products that we are making, from the institution to the city.

Senator LEA. I notice you have asked for an increase in the salary of your chief electrician from $900 to $1,500.

Mr. WILSON. Yes; we feel that that is a proper salary. We have had a great deal of trouble getting a good man.

Senator SMITH of Maryland. Does he get his board?

Mr. WILSON. Yes, sir. That is an isolated institution, and men object to going so far from the city.

Senator SMITH of Maryland. Has he a house? Has he a family?

Mr. WILSON. No. If he has a family, they will have to live outside. We can not provide for his family.

Senator SMITH of Maryland: But he gets his board?

Mr. WILSON. Yes, sir. You understand, this institution is isolated and it provides its own heat, light, and water.

Senator SMITH of Maryland. $1,500 for an engineer, who also gets his board, is a large compensation.

Senator LEA. That is a large increase, too.

Mr. WILSON. We have never had the type of man we ought to have that is efficient.

Senator SMITH of Maryland. That may be, but that is a pretty big salary to pay an engineer.

Senator GALLINGER. The only trouble is that if that is allowed here, there is a long list of engineers all through the bill who will come in and want their salaries raised to the same amount.

Mr. WILSON. My information is— although I have not definite information— that the engineer in the District Building would get about as much as that.

Senator SMITH of Maryland. He does not get any board.

Mr. WILSON. No, sir; he does not get board; but this is the largest plant we have and is a very extensive mechanical plant.

Senator SMITH of Maryland. Have you any data to show what revenue is derived from that plant? They make brick there, do they not?

Mr. WILSON. Yes, sir; it would run about $20,000 this past year. We hope it will be much more this year.

Senator SMITH of Maryland. It may be that all of the members of the committee do not know that that is quite a new institution. Does this superintendent of the brick kiln get his board?

Mr. WILSON. Yes, sir.

Senator LEA. I think every employee there gets his board, does he not?

Mr. WILSON. Yes; unless he desires otherwise. Some of them have their homes near and go to them. There are one or two items on the next page that I would like to speak of in detail.

REPAIRS TO BUILDINGS.

On page 74 there is the item "For material for repairs to buildings, roads, and walks."

Senator SMITH of Maryland. How much more have you to speak about?

Mr. WILSON. There is just one page, Mr. Chairman. That item is in lines 4 and 5. We recommended $5,000 and the House has granted $4,000.

Senator SMITH of Maryland. What did you get previously?

Mr. WILSON. We had $4,000, I think, in the current bill.

Senator GALLINGER. That is right; you had $4,000.

Mr. WILSON. The only thing I want to say is that our buildings there are of a temporary character. Instead of building a great big so-called modern prison, a brick and stone structure, they have put up little wooden shacks of one story, and the scheme has proved admirable. They are inexpensive, and it will take quite a little to keep them in repair from year to year. What we have there is a prison farm, which has excited a great deal of interest among people who have visited it.

Senator GALLINGER. Are you now constructing substantial buildings?

Mr. WILSON. Not yet.

Senator GALLINGER. No concrete buildings?

Mr. WILSON. No concrete buildings, except the punishment cells, where we are afraid of fire, and a concrete basement for a very large barn, which is a wooden structure. Almost all of the buildings have been constructed from lumber produced on the place. The trim has been purchased outside.

FARM IMPLEMENTS.

Coming down to line 14, "For farm implements, including wagons, plows, planters, harrows, drills, and so forth," the superintendent tells me, after conference with the auditor, that he would like you to include the word "harness," so as to make it read "wagons, harness, plows, planters," and so on.

Senator SMITH of Maryland. Have you any on hand now?

Mr. WILSON. We have few good farm implements yet.

Senator GALLINGER. If they should buy harnesses from this appropriation, the auditor might not allow it. Is that it?

Mr. WILSON. Yes; that is the point. We would urge that the amount be made $3,000 instead of $1,500. The land there is 1,000 acres in extent at present, and we have very little farming, only 200 or 300 acres. In the course of two or three years it will be three or four times as much as that. We have cut the trees where they are to be cut. Some of the land is reserved in wood. They are taking out the stumps, and we have never had an equipment of farm implements, and of course in the first two or three years, where we are taking out stumps and plowing the ground where there are stumps, it is a little harder on our implements.

Senator GALLINGER. I notice in that item the words "and so forth." Under that there might be purchased almost anything, it seems to me.

Mr. WILSON. That is what we thought, but we went to the auditor and he said: "Those words are so general that we are not disposed to give them any meaning." He said: "We have not any use for 'and so forth.'"

Senator SMITH, of Maryland. That would be unlimited.

Senator GALLINGER. Yes.

Senator LEA. I notice that they have omitted several items, which amount to $14,500, in regard to duplicate electric machinery, etc.; new building for machine shop, and equipment for same; canning factory, including building and machinery, and slaughterhouse and equipment. To my mind the only justification for that would be that you would reduce the cost of maintenance.

DUPLICATE ELECTRIC MACHINERY.

Mr. WILSON. Except in the first item, that is correct. The first item, duplicate electric machinery, there is a great danger of a breakdown. We have no duplicates. The other items are purely for economy in maintenance.

Senator LEA. Have you any estimates on the last three items, which amount to $8,500, of reduction in the cost of maintenance, if these improvements were made?

Mr. WILSON. No. In this institution we do not use the money we earn. It goes to the Treasury. The money for the brick, stone, etc., that we sold, that goes into the Treasury.

Senator LEA. Then put it the other way. Have you any estimates to show the additional profits that would be made, the additional sums that would be covered into the Treasury, if these items were appropriated?

Mr. WILSON. I can not say definitely, but I can say with a good deal of confidence that during this coming year our income will, I think, be double what it was this past year. For instance, we have eight brick kilns operating. Last year we had only two. We have this year two stone crushing plants, one large and one small. Last year we had only one small one.

Senator LEA. As one member of the committee, I think the most important data you could give us would be estimates from some responsible persons showing the increased production as a result of that expenditure.

CANNING FACTORY AND SLAUGHTERHOUSE.

Mr. WILSON. I will endeavor to estimate the saving as closely as possible and put it in the record. I would say with reference to the two last items, the canning factory and the slaughterhouse, that those are not urgent.

Senator SMITH of Maryland. A canning factory?

Mr. WILSON. Yes. We propose to can our surplus vegetables, and use them for the other institutions.

Senator SMITH of Maryland. How many acres have you there?

Mr. WILSON. 1.100.

Senator SMITH of Maryland. But how many are tillable?

Mr. WILSON. The land is all tillable, as much as they reclaim. We expect to till from 600 to 800 acres.

Senator SMITH of Maryland. When?

Mr. WILSON. In the next three years, we think. We have something like 400 acres now, and we have other acres that are cleared.

NEW BUILDING FOR MACHINE SHOP AND EQUIPMENT.

The second item we urge very strongly for economical reasons; that is, the new building for machine shop, and equipment for same. We have no machine shop, and we could do our own work there. For instance, recently a propeller of the boat was broken by a snag. We go up the creek from the Potomac River. To get that repaired it not only cost us something, but we had to send it away to be fixed. The plant is so large that we think a machine shop a decided economy,

Senator SMITH of Maryland. Then, you would have to have machinists.

Mr. WILSON. We do not ask for any additional employees, and we promise not to do it on account of this particular item. We now have some mechanics and we get as prisoners some skilled mechanics.

Senator SMITH of Maryland. I know, but if you go into these repairs——.

Senator LEA. You would have to have some skilled laborers to do the work.

Senator SMITH of Maryland. Could you build a machine shop for $5,000?

Mr. WILSON. Yes, sir.

Senator SMITH of Maryland. How much would your repairs on your machinery cost? That would be only for repairs, as I understand it. You would not make any machinery?

Mr. WILSON. Yes, sir. We would make the smaller articles, like tools.

Senator SMITH of Maryland. There is the interest on that, besides the depreciation, say $250 a year interest, at 5 per cent, besides the depreciation. It seems to me with an arrangement of the kind you have there, it would be cheaper to hire it done, for the present, anyway.

Mr. WILSON. I will be glad, Mr. Chairman, to put in some notes on that. There is not only the cost of the repairs, which I happen to know would be quite large—I happen to know the amount of those, because I see the vouchers as they go through—but we are obliged to ship this machinery out to have it repaired and have it shipped back.

(The following statement was submitted by Mr. Wilson:)

COMMISSIONERS OF THE DISTRICT OF COLUMBIA,
Occoquan, Va., February 12, 1914.

Mr. GEORGE S. WILSON,
    Secretary of the Board of Charities,
      Municipal Building, Washington, D. C.

DEAR SIR: I have hastily taken from our records the amount that has been spent in the last 18 months for repairs that could have been saved for the institution had we had a well-regulated machine shop. In fact, the amount would have been $3,000, but it seems to me that this is sufficient to satisfy the committee that a machine shop would save us money.

    Yours, truly,

          W. H. WHITTAKER, *Superintendent.*

Repairs on tug Louise	$134.00	G. W. Forsberg.
Do	445.55	Do.
26 wood rollers, 10 inches long	13.00	E. M. Freese.
1 idle roller, 10 inches long 5 inches in diameter	.75	Do.
1 set of liners (brick machine)	13.00	Do.
1 eccentric babbitted and riveted	82.35	Do.
1 brake pin hub	16.70	Do.
1 pair wearing plates	7.60	Do.
Repairs to General Warren	21.25	J. & H. Atcheson.
Do	164.00	G. W. Forsberg.
Threading 7-inch pipe	3.00	Thos. Somerville.
Repairs to pump	98.80	Henry Worthing.
Do	10.00	Do.
Do	4.00	Do.
Do	7.00	Do.
Do	14.00	Do.
Repairs to crusher	8.80	Austin Manufacturing Co.
Do	77.15	Do.
Do	2.70	Do.
Threading pipe	8.00	Thos. Somerville.
Do	2.00	Do.
Machine work on bolts	3.35	G. W. Forsberg.
Set of liners for brick die	78.00	E. M. Freese.
Repairs on crusher	31.50	Austin Manufacturing Co.
Do	22.65	Do.
Repairs on pump	12.72	Thos. Somerville.
7 rollers	5.25	Amer. C. Mec. Co.
1 clutch shift collar	6.50	Do.
1 lever	2.50	Do.
6 threaded nuts	3.00	Do.
Repairs on engine	65.70	American Engine Co.
Expansion joints	7.16	Thos. Somerville.
Repairs on dry pan (brickyard)	111.50	Stephenson Co.
Repairs on pump	10.96	Deane Pump Co.
Do	30.52	Henry Worthing.
Repairs on General Warren	500.00	G. W. Forsberg.
Repairs on tug Louise	55.05	J. & H. Atchison.
Do	83.45	Weber & Thomas.
Do	35.60	J. & H. Atchison.
Repairs to stone crusher	27.00	Henry Martin.
	2,225.46	

Above is expenditure for repairs, District of Columbia Workhouse, from July 1, 1912, to February 1, 1914; this amount does not include the reseating of valves and small items that could be saved with an up-to-date machine shop.

    Yours, truly,

          W. H. WHITTAKER, *Superintendent.*

Senator SMITH of Maryland. How far are you from Washington?

Mr. WILSON. We are 25 miles from Washington. And then s' of the machinery we can not have repaired in Washington.

Senator SMITH of Maryland. I know, but it is a matter of or two only, is it not, to get it anywhere you want it? You c it to Baltimore in a day.

Mr. WILSON. Yes.

Senator SMITH of Maryland. E¢

Mr. WILSON. But we do not fin   thing we send them.

Senator SMITH of Maryland. Of course you do not get them done in a day; but so far as the matter of distance is concerned, it takes no longer than that coming and going, and you can get the work done as quickly in one place as another.

Mr. WILSON. The particular thing back of all this is our labor. Among our prisoners we find a good many mechanics.

Senator SMITH of Maryland. Yes; I can see that.

Mr. WILSON. That is what we are trying to do there. We are setting these men at this brick-making work. We have one superintendent, who is a very good man, and we are making very good brick.

Dr. KOBER. I may say that the superintendent, apart from having repairs made, also intends to manufacture tools and small parts of machinery. The machinery used in the manufacture of brick and in the stone-crushing department is liable to much wear and tear. I had very much the same feeling that the Senator has on the subject of economy, but the superintendent convinced me that there were a number of ways in which money would be saved by making a great many of the tools and drills right at that plant, to say nothing of the actual inconvenience incident to delays in making the necessary repairs. Operations will many times be suspended for lack of prompt repairs.

Senator SMITH of Maryland. Most of this stuff you can have duplicates of. Most people who use large machinery have duplicates of parts that are liable to break, and get around it in that way. I am only offering that for consideration.

Dr. KOBER. I believe the superintendent provides as far as practicable for such contingencies. I hope some day the Senators will see the plant. Senator Ransdell went there, evidently at the suggestion of some friend, and he volunteered the statement that it was really a remarkable institution, and was greatly impressed when he saw how those people were put to work; and how the system is likely in a few years to become self-supporting. We are not quite so optimistic, because we know it will take time.

Mr. SMITH of Maryland. How many people have you there?

Mr. WILSON. The number has increased since the passage of the new liquor law. We have nearly 700 now.

Senator LEA. You asked for a total of $197,150 for the workhouse, and the House allowed you $177,010, which is $10,140 increase. That is on line 16, page 74.

Mr. WILSON. Yes; I think that includes all these items we have been speaking about, some of which are not strictly annual maintenance.

Senator GALLINGER. I observe that this bill transfers this institution to the control of the Commissioners of the District of Columbia. I ought to remember, but will you state under what control it is now?

Mr. WILSON. I think I can say that that is the result of a misapprehension. We do not ask that that be changed, because it does not change the existing law. At the time of the hearing in the House committee there seemed to be a little doubt whether the commissioners had control. Now, the fact is that the commissioners have always had control.

Senator GALLINGER. That is why I wondered at this language. I did not understand it.

Mr. WILSON. I was giving their interpretation of its meaning. The Board of Charities believes that in all these municipal institutions of which we have been speaking the control rests entirely in the commissioners, and it always has, and should be so.

The original legislation for the organization of this workhouse specifically provided that it should be under the control of the commissioners and it has hever been changed.

Senator GALLINGER. Yes.

Senator LEA. We have had the hospital for the inebriates and the municipal lodging house discussed very fully.

Dr. KOBER. You have heard arguments involving them?

Senator SMITH of Maryland. Yes; I think we heard those two items very fully. There was a little said about the municipal lodging house.

Dr. KOBER. These institutions are very much needed, and you probably have heard all the arguments that are needed.

Senator LEA. Have you the appropriation for this Board of Charities and Corrections? If so, just let that be put in the record.

Mr. WILSON. Very well. The appropriation for 1914 is $1,234,007.

On this same page, page 74, line 22, in order to avoid a possible tie-up with the accounting officers, beginning with the words "and for the beginning of construction of such buildings," we suggest that these words be used, "including personal services."

The thought in that is to employ mechanics and laborers only.

Senator LEA. Then why is that necessary?

Mr. WILSON. The purpose of that paragraph is the preliminary work for this reformatory. We would need some draftsmen, and we would not have those among the prisoners.

Senator LEA. Yes; I understand that; but if this is for construction work, construction work would certainly include draftsmen. If we put those words in there, "including personal services," does not that open it so that you can use it for purposes other than construction work?

Mr. WILSON. It possibly does, but as I understand the law the fact that the appropriation is for construction work does not give us the right to employ personal services. Indeed, I think that the law requires that if it is over a very small specific amount it must be done by contract.

Senator LEA. Over $500, or something like that, I think.

Mr. WILSON. Yes, sir.

Senator LEA. My object in making the suggestion was to prevent a part of that appropriation being used for the employment of personal services for other than construction work—such as drafting plans.

Mr. WILSON. There is no thought of using it for other purposes. It would undoubtedly open the way to use it for other purposes, for any other purpose that was legitimately connected with the work, but I do not know of any other language that we could use except "personal services." Our own idea is to do the work ourselves and hire men, instead of doing it under contract. Of course, we hope with the aid of prison labor to do many times the amount of work represented by this money, and that is the reason we ask that it be done not under contract.

Senator LEA. Yes. The total estimates for charities and corrections for the year 1915 amount to $1,463,517. For last year the amount was $1,184,457.

Dr. KOBER. I desire, on behalf of the board, to thank the gentlemen of the committee for their courteous consideration and for their patience.

(At 6 o'clock p. m. the subcommittee adjourned until tomorrow, Thursday, February 12, 1914, at 10.30 o'clock a. m.)

SOUTHERN RELIEF SOCIETY.

STATEMENT OF MISS NANNIE RANDOLPH HETH, PRESIDENT SOUTHERN RELIEF SOCIETY.

Miss HETH. Mr. Chairman, we have come to you in behalf of the work we are doing. We have 65 people we are taking care of at a very small sum per month. These people are indigent Confederate veterans and their widows and wives who become stranded here, and there is no other place for them to go but the poorhouse. We have come to ask you, when this money is appropriated for the District charities, if you will include us in this, and help us toward taking care of these people. We have with us our treasurer, Mrs. Rollins, who is bonded for the money we have raised to take care of these people, and we have the chairman of our relief committee, Mrs. Covington, who has been untiring in her work in looking after them. We have given these indigent people $5 a month and $3 a month, and we have built a little home over in Georgetown for them, and the way we support this home is that we literally beg the bread for them. That is all we have. We have 14 of them there now. We have to take care of them when they are sick, and bury them when they die. We have merely the sum of $5 a month for them, and we want to ask if you will do something for us?

Senator GALLINGER. Do you own that building?

Miss HETH. No, sir; we rent it for $40 a month, and there we have 14, and we have an old Confederate soldier and his wife there, and they are very helpless, and we are taking care of 65 of these people, all together, and they are in a very great state of need and destitution here in this city. They would have no place to go to except the poorhouse if we did not do this. The annual proceeds from our ball are divided between the Veterans' Association and the Southern Relief Society, and that is all we have except our annual dues, which are a dollar, from the members of the society. We also have to beg people to help us in this work. We have a bread committee and an ice committee and a potato committee and an incidental committee, who look after them and supply them in that way.

Senator GALLINGER. The title of your organization is the Southern Relief Society?

Miss HETH. The Southern Relief Society.

Senator GALLINGER. Do you confine your work to the relief of Confederates, or the descendents of Confederate soldiers?

Miss HETH. Yes; we do.

Senator GALLINGER. Entirely so?

Miss HETH. Yes, sir. These people are stranded here in the District of Columbia, and they nave no homes to go to. Some of them lived here before the war, and some of them came here after the war, and they find themselves here completely stranded. There is no place for them to go to; there is no State to which they can go to be taken care of. They have been living here, and now they are barred from their States. They have been living here for nearly 50 years, many of them.

Senator GALLINGER. You say you have 14 in this home, but you are caring for how many, altogether?

Miss HETH. Sixty-five, altogether.

Senator GALLINGER. Do you mean that you have 65 now that you are looking after?

Miss HETH. Altogether; yes, sir.

Senator GALLINGER. I suppose it might be more or less to-morrow?

Miss HETH. Yes; we might have more to-morrow, and there might be some deaths.

Senator GALLINGER. But you have 65 now?

Miss HETH. We have 65 now.

Senator SMITH of Maryland. Where do you take care of those other than the 14?

Miss HETH. We take care of them in their little rooms.

Senator SMITH of Maryland. What do you pay for them in those rooms?

Mrs. COVINGTON. I brought my receipts, in case they were needed. I have been the chairman of the relief committee for about eight years, and those that we can not put into the home we just care for them on the outside by paying their room rent; and the churches help in a small way, because we could not begin to give all of them what they need.

Miss HETH. We send physicians to look after them and put them in hospitals, and we give clothing to them at the home, and we bury them when they die. We have not any money at all, and we beg for clothing for them.

Senator GALLINGER. These are either Confederate soldiers or the descendants of Confederate soldiers?

Miss HETH. Yes; Confederate soldiers, their wives and widows.

Mrs. ROLLINS. Every case is investigated.

Senator GALLINGER. You do not extend relief in a general way to southern people who are stranded here?

Miss HETH. No, sir.

Senator GALLINGER. You are taking care of a military class, Confederate soldiers, and also their wives and widows?

Miss HETH. Yes, sir; and we have done it in this way, by what we could beg and the subscriptions we have had.

Mrs. ROLLINS. We do not pay any salaries, of course, to our officers.

Mr. DE LEON. If you will allow me to make a remark, there is a letter here from the chairman of the relief committee of the Confederate Veterans' Association, and likewise a letter from the chairman of the relief committee of the Southern Relief Society, and then there is a letter from Miss Heth, the president of the society, which clearly states what she desires and which puts the whole thing before you. These are all here in form, so that the members of the committee can inform themselves exactly of the status of things. There is likewise a letter from a lady who is in very destitute circumstances, showing the sufferings to which these people are subjected.

Miss HETH. Last week a Confederate soldier was buried at Arlington. He was a major in the army. He had not a dollar—not a penny. That will give you an idea of the destitution and suffering here that nobody else knows anything about, and we do want to do more for them than the $5 a month and the $3 we can give them.

Senator SMITH of Maryland. Did you ask for anything in the House?

Miss HETH. No; we only came here. We only wanted a part of such money as was appropriated for the District for similar purposes.

Senator SMITH of Maryland. I understand; but it has to be agreed to by both sides.

Miss HETH. Yes. we know it has to be agreed to by both sides.

Mr. DE LEON. It is exactly similar to the appropriation for the Florence Crittenton Home, only the amount is larger.

Senator GALLINGER. Do these people that you good ladies are looking after make application to the hospitals of the city for lodging and treatment?

Miss HETH. Yes, sir. We have one there now, and we have some more that we want to go in now; and sometimes they die in the hospitals, because we have not any place for them. They have not any homes. We took one woman out of the eighth floor of the Farragut, who was starving, not long ago. We found that she was starving there, and we took her to a hospital and paid a dollar a day for her, and she died there. We thought we could make her more comfortable in a pay ward; and she died there and we were responsible for her funeral expenses, and somebody came forward and said they would pay the funeral expenses for her.

Senator SMITH of Maryland. You are asking here $16,000. What amount would you think would be necessary to take care of one of these people a year?

Miss HETH. If we could give them from $15 to $20 a month, that is what we would like to do.

Senator SMITH of Maryland. From $15 to $20 a month?

Miss HETH. Yes; that was what we figured on.

Senator GALLINGER. Do you not think that if we appropriate here for your association, as an outside matter—I mean outside of our hospital benefactions—your numbers will rapidly increase?

Miss HETH. I do not think so.

Mrs. ROLLINS. We do not think so, because we are only looking after the old men and their widows, wives, and daughters, and their numbers are decreasing all the time.

Miss HETH. The wives and widows and the old men. Our expenses, of course, are increasing, because they become more infirm all the time.

Senator SMITH of Maryland. You are not looking after the children?

Miss HETH. Only two.

Senator SMITH of Maryland. Putting the amount at $15 a month, if you had 60 of these people it would not amount to anything like the sum named here.

Miss HETH. That amount covers what is asked for the Confederate veterans, too.

Mr. DE LEON. Will you allow me to make a remark, please?

Senator SMITH of Maryland. Go ahead, sir.

Mr. DE LEON. I first consulted Senator Works on this subject, whom I found very sympathetic, and desirous of introducing a bill of this character, but on the advice of friends I afterwards concluded that it was better to appeal to this committee and have put in the District appropriation bill a clause similar to what you have for the Florence Crittenden Mission. I figured that it would cost about $1,000 a year rent for the widows' home, and then $1,200 for the veterans' home and $900 for salary of the chairman of the relief committee, which would be about $3,100, leaving something over $12,000, which would be less than $20 apiece for those people. This letter will explain the whole situation. It tells exactly what the ladies are desirous of accomplishing.

Senator GALLINGER. Just there, let me say that the most we have ever done in the direction of taking care of soldiers and their families has been in a provision that will be found on page 71, where we have this item:

Temporary Home for ex-Union Soldiers and Sailors, Grand Army of the Republic: Superintendent, $1,200; janitor, $360; cook, $360; maintenance, $4,000; in all, $5,920.

It is also provided that veterans of the Spanish-American War shall be admitted. We do not undertake to care for wives or widows of Union soldiers.

Miss HETH. Well, we will take anything you will give us and be mighty glad of it; but you see, the only thing was that while we were about this we were thinking that they were dropping off so; you know I do not think that the ladies know as much about these things as gentlemen. We wanted to get all we could to make them as comfortable as we could, because they were dying so fast. Their wives will be here and their daughters will be here. That is the reason. We have this little home over here, and we will be thankful for anything you will give us; won't we?

Mrs. ROLLINS. Indeed, we will.

Senator SMITH of Maryland. Of course, we can not discriminate, and we have to show a good reason why we appropriate, and how much we appropriate would be taken into consideration. I think the feeling is to help you. I feel that way myself. But this amount of $16,000 I do not think we could give you.

Senator LEA. That is $21.60 a month for these people.

Senator SMITH of Maryland. That is, for the number you have now, and they are decreasing, of course.

Miss HETH. Yes, sir.

Senator SMITH of Maryland. We have heard what you have to say, and we will take up the matter and endeavor to do what we can.

Miss HETH. We thank you.

STATEMENT OF MR. PERRY M. DE LEON.

Mr. DE LEON. Gentlemen, this relief is in connection entirely with veterans, widows of veterans, and their dependents. I will say to you gentlemen that we have 25 men and widows that we are taking care of. The men are differently situated from the ladies, because men will not beg, and we have $1,800 a year to support 25 men, which is thoroughly inadequate.

Senator GALLINGER. Mr. Chairman, I would suggest that the letter I have in my hand, signed by Miss Nannie Randolph Heth, president of the Southern Relief Society, be put in the proceedings.

Senator SMITH of Maryland. Very well.

(The letter referred to is as follows:)

WASHINGTON, D. C., *February 11, 1914.*

Hon. JOHN WALTER SMITH,
Chairman of Committee on District of Columbia,
United States Senate.

DEAR SIR: The Southern Relief Society is endeavoring to care for some 65 to 70 indigent old Confederate veterans and widows, some of whom are bedridden; but the situation has reached a point where we must have help or greatly increased suffering will ensue.

The only means we have is the profit from the annual charity ball and occasional small contriutions, which, of course, are painfully inadequate. There is dire poverty and much suffering among these unfortunate people, who, by reason of non-residence, are debarred from any aid from their States, and have only our society to aid them, which it has done and is doing, even to the extent of soliciting bread from the baker. Their destitution should elicit the profoundest sympathy. The bill is not a pension measure, but simply a bill to care for destitute people who otherwise would be a charge upon the public. Congress aids several charities and homes in the District, so why not this?

It certainly will be favored by the Union veterans, for at Gettysburg last July they expressed a desire, both on the platform and in conversation, to see Confederate veterans properly cared for.

The Southern Relief Society and the veterans are endeavoring to care for the southern cases of indigency, but our means are so meager that in no case can we allow over $5 a month and in many cases only $2 or $3. Fourteen of these unfortunates, however, are fed and sheltered in a small home in Georgetown (in which they are somewhat crowded) by the most constant and ceaseless efforts of the ladies and by the charitable contributions of the butcher, baker, grocer, and others. The aid asked of Congress will diminish year by year, for these poor old people will soon be where the weary are at rest.

The chairman of our relief committee for eight years has, without remuneration, unselfishly worked early and late aiding the sick and destitute, but must now be salaried, having been widowed within the last year and left with scanty means.

Should Congress accede to our request, we shall create a board of control of four ladies and three gentlemen, of such character as to be a guarantee that the funds will be conscientiously and economically disbursed.

Our society is incorporated and our treasurer bonded.

Sincerely hoping our appeal will not be in vain,

Respectfully,

(Signed)   NANNIE RANDOLPH HETH,
President Southern Relief Society.

The following letters were submitted by Mr. De Leon:

WASHINGTON, D. C., *December 19, 1913.*

Capt. PERRY M. DE LEON.
Washington, D. C.

My DEAR COMRADE: In reply to your verbal inquiry as to the number of beneficiaries of the limited charity fund which I disburse, I beg to say that the monthly average is about 25 veterans, and widows of veterans, whose wants are acute and urgent, and other applicants for occasional aid whose calls are met only partially, and then with great difficulty.

I am deeply interested in your plan, as outlined in our conversation of yesterday, and wish with all my heart that the measure of success in its accomplishment may be as abundant as the enthusiasm and sympathy for your suffering comrades, which prompt your efforts in their behalf.

You and I know how pitifully small the individual allowances are, because of the fact that our only source of revenue is one-half the sum realized by the annual charity ball of the Southern Relief Society, and an occasional contribution from some friend and well-wisher whose liberality is greater than his financial ability.

The Confederate Memorial Home, at 1322 Vermont Avenue NW., has a debt upon the building of something over $12,000. To meet the interest on this debt and to pay the running expenses we have been compelled to rent most of our rooms, and are unable to house but two or three veterans.

This property is well adapted for the purpose contemplated, and could easily be made to accommodate all who would likely be eligible for admission or claim its benefits as a home.

Heartily wishing you godspeed in your laudable undertaking to care for our utterly dependent comrades, whose fast-thinning ranks mutely appeal for succor with an eloquence not to be expressed in words, I remain,

Cordially and fraternally, your friend and comrade,

J. T. PETTY,
Chairman Relief Committee.

WASHINGTON, D. C., *December 3, 1913.*

MY DEAR MRS. COVINGTON: I thank you and other members of the Southern Relief Society for the kind remembrance inclosed in your note.

I am truly grateful to you for your kindness in asking for a basket for me, and very grateful to those who so kindly and generously acceded to your request, and also to the kind gentleman who came through the rain to bring a large well-filled basket of choice groceries, vegetables, fruit, and a fine chicken. I was almost afraid to take the gift, fearing that it was intended for some one else, but Mr. Elliott assured me it was for me.

I was without fuel, so I had to prepare my chicken and leave it until Friday afternoon, when your note came with the money which enabled me to buy it.

Dear Mrs. Covington, I can not express the gratitude I feel for all your kindness; we are indeed sadly in need of clothing of every kind. I have been suffering since January with acute rheumatism; this is the first time in 10 months that I have written anything more than my name. I wanted to go to see you months ago, but was not able to do so, nor had nor have I a dress fit to wear in the street; any clothing that you have to spare will be thankfully received. I hope that you and your little boys are well and happy.

Yours, with love and esteem,

G. C. W.

NOTE.—The writer is a lady, an educated woman, and bears a name highly honored in South Carolina, of which State she is a native.

JANET DORSEY COVINGTON.

SOUTHERN RELIEF SOCIETY,
WASHINGTON, D. C., *December 22, 1913.*

Capt. PERRY M. DE LEON,
1016 Massachusetts Avenue, Washington, D. C.

MY DEAR CAPTAIN: In response to your inquiry I would say that the Ladies' Southern Relief Society has now in its rented home at 1518 Thirty-first Street, Georgetown, 12 widows, besides a helpless old veteran and his wife—14 in all—as many as our home can hold. In addition, I had during the last month 26 pensioners, 40 in all, on my list to whom I afforded such relief as I could. Of course you are aware that the means at my command, all voluntary contributions, except half of the proceeds from the Southern Relief Charity Ball, are utterly inadequate to properly provide for these old indigent unfortunate people, who become each year more infirm and helpless. They certainly deserve to be cared for, and the ladies are unremitting in their efforts to listen to their woes, but unfortunately I am only able to give the scantiest relief, and there are many cases which appeal to my sympathies and cause me great distress at my inability to do for them what I would had I the means at my command to do so. I inclose copy of a letter which is a type of many I receive which wring my heart by my being unable to aid them as I desire.

Sincerely trusting the aid you are seeking may be accorded.

Sincerely, yours,

JANET DORSEY COVINGTON,
Chairman Relief Committee, Ladies' Southern Relief Society.

THURSDAY, FEBRUARY 12, 1914.

The subcommittee met at 10.30 a. m.

Present: Senators Smith of Maryland (chairman), Gallinger, and Dillingham.

MUNICIPAL LODGING HOUSE.

A. H. Tyson, Mrs. Archibald Hopkins, Miss Aline Solomons, and Mrs. Philip Henry appeared.

The CHAIRMAN (Senator SMITH of Maryland). Mr. Tyson and ladies, we will hear what you have to say on the subject of the proposed municipal lodging house. We understand that the appropriation was thrown out in the House of Representatives.

Mrs. HOPKINS. Mr. Chairman and gentlemen, I am chairman of the woman's department of the National Civic Federation. I came here simply to make an appeal to you. Senator Gallinger, who is here, knows me, and he knows why I am interested in these things. I have lived here all my life.

After the appropriation for a municipal lodging house was thrown out, as I understand, by the committee of the House of Representatives, the superintendent, Mr. Tyson, wrote me a letter, which I will read. Hearing that the item had been thrown out, I asked him some questions, and this was his reply:

"MUNICIPAL LODGING HOUSE,
"Washington, D. C., January 10, 1914.

"RESPECTED MADAM: As per your request, I am pleased to give herewith reasons why a new municipal lodging house is needed in this city, viz: The house here, at 312 Twelfth Street NW., is a very small building, 23 by 100 feet, three stories, without cellar or basement, with low ceilings, very badly lighted, ventilated, and cramped, and, as stated by the Board of Charities in its report to Congress, to be unsanitary and altogether inadequate.

"There are usually 300 or more stranded men, especially in winter season, in the city of Washington, and the municipal lodging house is provided with 50 beds (two or three times as many as should be, crowded into its little sleeping rooms) to care for these men. The house at present is more than packed to its full capacity, often a dozen or more men being compelled to sleep on the dining-room floor.

"We have plans in this office for a new and suitable loding house for the District with a capacity for 200 persons, with provision where boys of tender years could be segregated; also provision for women is made, there being no proper place centrally located for a respectable stranded woman to find temporary shelter in this city."

There is no provision for a woman here who finds herself stranded. No matter how respectable she may be or how innocent the cause, she must be sent to the almshouse here temporarily.

We thoroughly believe in a work test for the unemployed who appeal for assistance, and this institution should be known as the municipal industrial department rather than simply a place of charity, where free meals and lodgings are doled out to the unemployed, as worthy poor men would rather work than beg for what they receive.

Fortunately, here in Washington, we could furnish all who need it temporary employment in the way of sawing, splitting, and handling wood. The District government uses a thousand cords per annum. The Federal Government uses 350 to 500 cords per annum, and if Congress will provide the city with ample accommodations for the men and a woodyard of sufficient capacity, we could easily do the work, besides supplying some of the wood dealers in the city as we are doing at present.

"The rule now is to allow a man to stay three nights at the lodging house, and then he must move on. The great majority of these men are compelled to leave before they have time to find employment; but if they could be allowed to stay even a week at the lodging house it would often help them to obtain permanent employment, and thus a needy man would be helped, and at the same time the city would be nothing out, for his work would fully equal his keeping, he being required to do about one-quarter of a day's work, thus giving him the major part of the day to look for a job.

"The ' bum' element of the unemployed do not come to an institution of this character because of the work test, but worthy men are glad to render the amount of work required to tide them over a rough spot in their lives.

"Could we be furnished with proper facilities, the institution would be largely self-supporting.

"The present lodging house was donated to the Government by the honest night lodging house association two years ago and was accepted by an act of Congress. (The building is estimated at $20,000, including the lot.) The running of the institution has been maintained by appropriations made by Congress for 20 years; but the present site is many times too small for such a building as is needed, with ample wood-yard accommodations. Moreover. the permanence of such a building south of Pennsylvania Avenue is uncertain, as Congress may acquire these blocks for Federal buildings at any time.

"Such a lot as is needed, well located, will cost not less than $20,000, this cost being practically offset by the donation of the property at 312 Twelfth Street NW. to the Government, as above stated. An ample iron, cement, and brick structure erected on said lot would cost with equipment $110,000, which would finally be a saving to the Government in the manufacture of fire wood, as there is an abundance of timber south of and within easy reach of the District to furnish its institutions with firewood for generations to come.

"The present appropriation for maintenance is $1,820, and for salaries $1,710; total $3,530. A year ago Congress took away the foreman, and left the superintendent to handle from five to eight thousand men per annum alone, except for the aid of the night watch, for six months in the year. It is a big job to stand over these men all day and until 10 o'clock at night, to see that they perform their task, and to see that the wood is correctly measured out to the wood dealers; to check their clothes at night and morning, and to fumigate the same; to say nothing of other things too numerous to mention. Therefore the superintendent is compelled to pay for a helper out of his own funds; and without the constant assistance of his wife, who draws no salary, could not get through with the work of the institution.

"Very respectfully,

"A. H. TYSON, *Superintendent.*"

Senator GALLINGER. I observe that the commissioners recommended that an appropriation of $50,000 be made and that a building should be constructed on the site of the present municipal lodging house.

Mrs. HOPKINS. Yes, and I have since seen the commissioners and Mr. Newman told me he felt he had made a mistake in that point of view, and that he would gladly withdraw that suggestion and say to the Committee on Appropriations that it would be a very unwise expenditure to be made on that site.

Senator GALLINGER. What is the appropriation suggested in Mr. Tyson's letter?

Mrs. HOPKINS. One hundred and thirty thousand dollars. That is to cover everything. For the building and equipment the estimate is $110,000. It is to be a fireproof building of course.

Senator GALLINGER. You said a moment ago that there is no place where a certain class of stranded people can be taken care of in this city. Do not the Associated Charities look out for that class of people?

Mrs. HOPKINS. Yes, but it has no place to send them. In the instance I speak of a very nice women from Maryland about two months ago found herself stranded here with two boys of 14 and 10. The Associated Charities had money to pay for food but no place to send them. In this lodging house with men of all classes there is no place to send boys. Mr. Tyson felt so strongly about not putting them with this class of men in the municipal lodging house that they sent them out at their own expense. What we want particularly to have you observe is the fact that this municipal lodging could be made almost self-supporting by the wood cutting work for the District.

Senator SMITH of Maryland. Where would the wood come from?

Mrs. HOPKINS. The wood that is used in schools for kindling and for fires in furnaces in the engine houses and the District Building and the Federal Building.

Senator SMITH of Maryland. You would get the wood by the cord and manipulate it?

Mrs. HOPKINS. Yes; by wholesale, without any middle man?

Senator GALLINGER. Is that wood used to a very large extent?

Mr. TYSON. From 350 to 500 cords are used here by the Federal Government.

Mrs. HOPKINS. It is wood for kindling for the furnaces, too.

Senator SMITH of Maryland. What do you get for changing it from the large size into kindling?

Mrs. HOPKINS. I may explain that the contractor for the District of Columbia buys that wood for $5.50 a cord and receives nearly $8 a cord for it.

Senator SMITH of Maryland. He receives a profit of about $2.50 a cord for manipulating it?

Mrs. HOPKINS. For manipulating it. Mind you, there is another man between us, the wholesale dealer, who furnishes us with wood and makes his profit.

Senator SMITH of Maryland. What do you mean by wholesale dealer?

Mrs. HOPKINS. They get a supply of wood down the river from persons who produce it. It comes to the schools. They sell to wood

Miss SOLOMONS. I think if by any possibility any member of this committee could go down and see it the place would speak for itself more strongly than any argument we could make.

Senator GALLINGER. How many people do you accommodate there

Mr. TYSON. We have accommodated between 5,000 and 8,000 people a year.

Senator SMITH of Maryland. How many do you average in the winter months?

Mr. TYSON. There are more in the winter, about double the number.

Senator SMITH of Maryland. How many?

Mr. TYSON. About 25 would be the average.   Last year there were 55 and a number of them had to sleep on the floor.   Of course, in the summer time the number falls off to the minimum.

Senator SMITH of Maryland. How many can you accommodate?

Mr. TYSON. We have beds for 50, very closely packed.

Mrs. HOPKINS. Three, one on top of the other.

Senator GALLINGER. How do you manage to do that upon the small maintenance sum that is appropriated?

Mr. TYSON. The superintendent is a pretty lively gentleman.

Senator GALLINGER. For maintenance the sum allowed is only $1,820.

Mr. HOPKINS. Mr. Tyson's wife does the cooking.

Senator SMITH of Maryland. You give them lodging and what else?

Mr. TYSON. We give them a meal in the evening, lodging, and a meal in the morning, and require from them an hour and a half to two hours' work, generally about two hours' work.   It is a measured task. We require them to saw a pile of wood 4 feet wide, 6 feet high, and 8 inches long.   That for a capable man would be work for about an hour and a quarter.   He might do it in less time if a real expert, or if he is not so gifted it might take him two hours or even three hours to get through with it.

Senator SMITH of Maryland. How long have you been superintendent of the lodging house?

Mr. TYSON. I am in my eleventh year.

Miss SOLOMONS. I assure you that every one who has seen it knows that the place is most immaculate; it is a clean place, well cared for.

Senator SMITH of Maryland. You had 55 last year.   I understand that you can accommodate 50.

Mr. TYSON. Fifty.

Senator SMITH of Maryland. In the winter you have more than ordinary?

Mr. TYSON. More than ordinary.

Senator SMITH of Maryland. Do you often have more than 50, the number you can accommodate?

Mr. TYSON. Not so often, but in the wintertime it runs from 40 to 50 right along and the conditions are such that they are crowded in very close quarters.

Senator SMITH of Maryland. Mr. Superintendent, if you took a contract for municipal lodging you would meet a condition that you could not very well govern.   You do not know how much help you are going to require.   Sometimes you might have three times as many persons as at other times.   You could not gauge the work.

Mr. TYSON. I think it could be done in this way.   For a very small wage paid to those who would have to stand at the machine these

Mrs. HOPKINS. We have believed that by using the sawdust furnace we would heat the water and the wood would be disinfected. The equipment would cost about $2,000, but the whole thing practically would be run by that labor. Your idea, Mr. Tyson, would be to have very little paid labor?

Mr. TYSON. Very little.

Mrs. HOPKINS. It would be run almost exclusively by these people and it would obviate having to send them away after only three nights. It would enable them to stay longer on account of the work. We all who are in this sort of philanthropic work feel the very great necessity for such an improved plant. We are far behind other cities in that regard. I will ask Mr. Tyson to give the Senators the figures about the self-supporting condition of the plant.

Senator SMITH of Maryland. Just leave them with us and we will look over them.

Mr. TYSON. I think that will be better than to go over them.

Mrs. HOPKINS. In many things it can be self-supporting.

Senator GALLINGER. Have you statistics from other cities as to lodging houses of this kind?

Mrs. HOPKINS. Yes; we have figures from other cities. There are only two municipal lodging houses in the country, I understand, in Chicago and New York.

Senator GALLINGER. I had the impression that there were not many.

Mr. TYSON. There is still another in Denver, Colo., but it is a small affair. Since we drew the plan for this municipal lodging house Montreal sent an architect down to see what Washington had and to look over the plans, and now they have built a $150,000 lodging house in Montreal, equipping it with disinfecting apparatus. The way I found out the exact cost of the building was because the gentleman was in my office.

Miss SOLOMONS. I will state——

Mrs. HOPKINS. Miss Solomons's father you know, and she takes a very great interest in these matters.

Miss SOLOMONS. The cost is due to the necessity for caring for four classes of people—the men, the women, the colored people, and the boys.

Senator GALLINGER. Is the title of the house you now occupy in the Government or some association?

Mrs. HOPKINS. It is in the District government.

Senator GALLINGER. And it is worth $20,000?

Mr. TYSON. $20,000.

Senator GALLINGER. Exactly where is it located?

Mr. TYSON. West of the city post office directly in front of the Twelfth Street door?

Senator GALLINGER. It is likely to be taken by the Government?

Mr. TYSON. Likely. It is an unwise position.

Mrs. HOPKINS. That is why I spoke to Commissioner Newman and urged that that point was not considered.

Senator GALLINGER. Of course, if put on the present site we would have to dismantle it and do without a lodging house for two or three years.

Mr. TYSON. Partially self-supporting.

Senator SMITH of Maryland. As Senator Gallinger has just remarked, you would come in competition with labor. The country is full of laws now prohibiting penal institutions and other institutions from manufacturing. They are throwing out their machinery, and they are putting the inmates at work on roads instead of working them in the prison.

Mr. TYSON. That would be for convict labor.

Senator SMITH of Maryland. This is not convict labor, it is true, but it would be considered in the same light. It is the Government in competition with labor. I am not saying anything about whether it would be right or wrong. I am only stating the fact as it exists to-day. That is what you would run up against.

Mr. TYSON. That question might be raised if we put in a laundry, but it would not be raised on the wood yard, and that would be a great assistance to us. The profit we could make out of that would be a great assistance to us in running the institution.

Senator SMITH of Maryland, I think it is a worthy charity. There is no question about that.

Mrs. HENRY. It would teach them how to work.

Senator SMITH of Maryland. I understand that many of these are good people, and if they only had help to get started they might get along well.

Mr. TYSON. We have had some very honorable people.

Senator SMITH of Maryland. I am sure of that.

Mr. TYSON. One gentleman came there some years ago, and he afterwards made a success in life. He came back here and took Mrs. Tyson and myself up to the New Willard and he showed us his curios from Europe and said he was clearing $10,000 a year. That was one poor stranded, down-and-out fellow.

Senator SMITH of Maryland. There are a great many people who are unfortunate, and sometimes if they get a little help and you take them by the hand they get a start and go right along successfully.

Senator GALLINGER. Mr. Tyson, what about dissolute people and people suffering from intemperate habits and all that? Do you take them without any special examination on those points? Do you take anybody who comes?

Mr. TYSON. Anybody who comes if they are sober and willing to perform work for their keeping. If they are ill, then of course we take them in. If a man is not sick enough to go to a hospital we keep him two or three days to help him along.

Senator GALLINGER. Mrs. Hopkins, pardon me for asking you a question. I think likely you know, being connected with various charities here, what is the exact function of the Associated Charities? In other words, what do they do? I think that the board of charities acts upon every application for relief which comes to the Associated Charities, does it not?

Mrs. HOPKINS. It has nothing to do with it.

Senator GALLINGER. Are you sure?

Mrs. HOPKINS. I am, sir. The secretary of the Board of Charities, George S. Wilson, is the person who passes on the money used, here in Congress given to the various institutions.

Senator GALLINGER. But we do not give the Associated Charities anything.

Mrs. HOPKINS. You do not give the Associated Charities anything?

Senator GALLINGER. That is the charity I am inquiring about.

Mrs. HOPKINS. The Associated Charities is an organization of philanthropic persons here who investigate and save me the trouble of investigating. If anybody comes to me for anything of any kind I call up the Associated Charities and say, "Please investigate this man or this woman and see if the circumstances are so and so."

They go to them and if the circumstances are what are represented they either give the immediate relief of fuel or food or shelter or they show the organization to which the person has any right to appeal, first, their family, then their church, and then any philanthropic people, or they come to me and ask me to help them.

Senator GALLINGER. Pardon me, Mrs. Hopkins, I was wrong. It is the Associated Charities that make the investigation rather than the Board of Charities, and the Associated Charities reports to these other organizations.

Mrs. HOPKINS. It reports to the other organizations, and they work together with the Board of Charities. For instance, if the Associated Charities feel that they should put a woman into the Home for Incurables of which I am president, they request the Board of Charities to assume the maintenance of that woman, and out of the appropriation which Congress gives the Home for Incurables, $5,000, Mr. Wilson authorizes that she shall be taken into the Home for Incurables and they pay so much for her maintenance.

Senator GALLINGER. Could you approximately state how much money the Associated Charities raises annually?

Mrs. HOPKINS. From outside?

Senator GALLINGER. From outside.

Mrs. HOPKINS. I ought to know absolutely, but it is a very composite body. There is the Associated Charities and the Citizens' Relief, and then the summer camps, and outings, and all its various organizations, I would say about $30,000 a year; but I would not be sure about that. I would rather send you their report.

Senator GALLINGER. There is a citizens' relief association?

Mrs. HOPKINS. That is the side of the Associated Charities that gives actual help, food, and clothing.

Senator GALLINGER. In other words, the Associated Charities is also called the Citizens' Relief Association?

Mrs. HOPKINS. They work together. I will see that you have the data, Senator.

Mr. TYSON. Mr. Chairman, the object of the municipal lodging house is not only to afford free temporary shelter to various classes of persons who are temporarily stranded, such as the old and feeble, boys of tender years, and ofttimes boys who are turned over to Probation Officer Massey by the police court, who are also sent to the lodging house for two or three days, and persons who are affected with some degree of illness, yet not ill enough for hospital treatment, and those recently dismissed from hospitals, cripples, or the blind picked up in the streets, etc., some of these classes being kept in the lodging house pending transportation to their homes out of the city.

But the municipal lodging house is not free for able-bodied men who are temporarily stranded, who should be required to perform work sufficient to fully compensate the institution for their temporary stay therein. This policy should be rigidly enforced. This house is often a boon for a few days to the poor fellows just out of the workhouse or jail, without a cent in the world to his name. But the labor of all these men should be utilized in manufacturing the nearly 1,500 cords of wood into kindling and firewood used by the District and Federal Governments for their various institutions.

In addition to wholesome, very plain food and a decent bed, an abundance of natural ventilation, breathing space, and light is provided for in the design for the new lodging house; also shower baths, and fumigation, which will not only be a safeguard from disease and vermin, but this hot-air fumigator will also dry out their clothing. So, though the men come in, as they often do, wet to the skin by rain or snow, they will receive, possibly, all the clothing they own nice and dry in the morning.

An up-to-date steam laundry is provided, which will not only wash the linens for the house daily, but will also disinfect the same under 10 pounds of steam pressure in the washer. Provision is also made for the men to do their personal washing.

The building is designed for a lot centrally located for the convenient distribution of wood to all the Government institutions. There is an admirable lot on Second Street NW. between B and C Streets. This lot is accessible from all sides, and is desirable not only for the hauling of wood to and from the building, but also would afford perfect light and ventilation. This location is neither desirable as a residential nor as a business section; therefore can be had at reasonable figures.

The main part of the building is to be 66 feet by 101 feet, four stories, viz: Basement and main floor, with second and third floors for sleeping rooms, dormitories, and baths, and is designed to accommodate 200 persons, including the help.

A very important feature of the Municipal Lodging House is the wood yard, joined thereto at the rear, 66 feet by 66 feet, which should be equipped with the most improved appliances for the manufacture and handling of kindling and firewood, so that the greatest amount of profit possible might be realized from the work performed by the men. This wood yard is one story, with heating plant, coal room, laundry, etc., in the basement beneath the same.

Another important feature of the designing throughout the entire building is that it may be run by the fewest possible number of paid employees—men being selected to assist in the management and working of the inmates—therefore there will be but very few additional paid employees needed. Take, for instance, the kitchen, which is so in touch with all who are to be fed, that one cook, without a paid assistant, could easily cook for a full house. And again, the steam fumigator, being equipped with electricity to operate it, a licensed steam engineer night and day will be eliminated; and so on throughout.

The structure should be thoroughly fireproof. No part of the building is constructed over the wood yard.

The men, boys, and women are all three entirely segregated.

Cost of building, including heating and plumbing, estimated by the municipal architect, District of Columbia	$90,000
Cost of lot, about 11,000 feet, at $2 per foot	22,000
Wood-yard equipment	2,000
Disinfecting plant	6,000
Steam laundry	2,650
200 beds and bedding	4,000
Sawdust furnace, heating coil, and hot-water tank	1,000
Tables, chairs, benches, office furniture, gas range, window shades, fire extingushers, shelving, etc	1,350
Lighting	1,000
Total amount asked for in the amendment	130,000

Why the building and equipment should cost $108,000 is that the building should not be a death trap, but should be made fireproof—constructed of steel, cement, and brick.

Also that the inmates are to be cared for in separate groups—white men, colored men, boys, and women. This requires separate rooms, lavatories, and dormitories.

As to the size of the building, the space is needed in the rooms and sleeping apartments, and is barely sufficient to meet the requirements of the law, without forced ventilation, which would be too expensive. Last, but not least, is the necessity of a wood yard of ample proportions, properly equipped.

I also wish to submit to the committee the following letter, which I addressed to Senator Lodge in January.

MUNICIPAL LODGING HOUSE,
312 TWELFTH STREET NW.,
Washington, D. C., January 22, 1914.

Senator HENRY CABOT LODGE,
Washington, D. C.

HONORABLE SIR: As per your request, I have the honor to furnish you herewith figures taken from the annual reports of several institutions similar in kind to the municipal lodging house of this city, where able-bodied, stranded men are required to perform work in return for meals and lodgings furnished, showing to what extent said institutions are self-supporting, viz:

In the third annual report of the board of public welfare of Kansas City, Mo., it is shown, on page 133, that the institution there known as "The Helping Hand" was 52.5 self-supporting, their only industry being that of breaking stone.

The Whosoever Gospel Mission, of Germantown, Pa., in its eighteenth annual report, October, 1913, on pages 7 and 12, shows that the running expenses, which include materials, salaries, insurance, interest, etc., amounted to $47,263.33, while the receipts from sale of goods manufactured and labor of men was $44,698.82, leaving a deficiency of only $2,563.51, therefore being nearly self-supporting.

Prof. Charles Zueblin's book American Municipal Progress (P. 102), states that in Syracuse, where the lodgers do street work to pay for their accommodations, there was earned $151.98 above expenses.

The Friendly Inn Association, in its annual report fiscal year ending October 31, 1913, which conducts a wood business in a very clumsily arranged building for such an enterprise at 309 South Sharp Street, Baltimore, Md., shows that while it was only a little over 21 per cent self-supporting, yet at the same time states that on 691¼ cords of wood sold at $6,810.84, costing $4,755.82, made a profit of $2,375 (including the value of 64½ cords more of wood on hand at the end of the fiscal year than at the beginning of the same); or, in other words, there was a profit of over $3 per cord on the wood sold.

I am informed by Government officials that there are nearly 1,500 cords of wood used in the District of Columbia, between the District and Federal governments. This, in addition to what could be sold otherwise in the city, would give employment in all probability to all able-bodied applicants for help, and thus the Municipal Lodging House could easily supply this wood if proper accommodations for the men and modern equipment for the institution was provided.

Therefore, considering the possibility of profit in the wood business, as shown by the Friendly Inn Association of our near neighbor city of Baltimore (though with modern equipment the men could accomplish several times as much as they now do), and this corroborates our own experience in this institution in years gone by, when we bought the wood directly from the producers, and looks as though the profits on a well-conducted wood business in a suitable municipal lodging house in this city would go a long way toward the self-support of such an institution.

Very respectfully submitted.

A. H. TYSON, *Superintendent.*

Mrs. HOPKINS. We are very much indebted to you, gentlemen of the committee, for listening to us.

Senator GALLINGER. We know the work you are doing, and we appreciate it.

STATEMENT OF S. W. CURRIDEN.

EASTERN HIGH SCHOOL BUILDING.

Mr. CURRIDEN. My labors here, Mr. Chairman and Senators, are practically in continuation of the labors that were embodied in the work referred to in Senate Document 648 of the Sixtieth Congress, second session, in connection with the procurement of a new site for the jail and workhouse. Former Senator Chandler aided in that work, and Senator Gallinger has been of great aid in years past to thus promote the larger interests of the city. Last night, learning that a partial presentation on behalf of the East Washington Citizens' Association was before you, I drafted a brief statement, which I was asked to come up and read to Senator Gallinger. This paper briefly presents matters, as the Scotch would say, for men of "far ken," for men who do not merely look for to-morrow morning's breakfast, but for next Sunday's dinner.

If you will permit me to read what I have written here, this will be the foundation for any questions you may wish to ask.

Senator SMITH of Maryland. Go ahead, sir.

Mr. CURRIDEN. The eastern section of the city for near 10 years has pleaded for enlargement of its high-school facilities. It has long outgrown the buildings used for the purpose. The purchase of a new site for this project has been delayed pending the selection of one that would be of ample size and accessible alike to all parts of the eastern section of the city.

The transfer of the workhouse organization, its inmates as well as those in their charge, to Occoquan, and of the almshouse organization, its inmates as well as those in their charge, to Blue Plains, has taken away the largest proportion of the unfortunates who were here detained for lack of long-needed facilities for their better care. All the buildings used for the care of the workhouse and almshouse inmates are old and antiquated, insanitary, separated one from the other, and expensive to maintain. Two brick structures are to be found here, neither of which has ever been put to use. One of them may have been put to use for one year.

Senator GALLINGER. One was used for one year; yes.

Mr. CURRIDEN. They are parts of a workhouse structure that, when completed, it was estimated would cost close to $700,000. The construction of this costly building was in violation of the express provision of the act of Congress limiting its cost to $150,000.

Senator SMITH of Maryland. Where did they get the money to make the difference between the two figures? How did they exceed the appropriation? Pardon me for interrupting you, but I do not understand how they could spend $700,000 when they estimated for $150,000, and that limitation was made.

Mr. CURRIDEN. When the representatives of the East Washington Citizens' Association, including myself, went to Senator Cockrell, at Senator Allison's suggestion, there had been an appropriation, given by a previous act, of $50,000; then a second appropriation of $50,000 for continuing the erection of this building was found in the District appropriation bill then being considered by the Senate.

When this item giving a second $50,000 for continuing the erection of a workhouse structure attracted the attention of Senator William E. Chandler, of New Hampshire, who had knowledge of many conditions at the workhouse and the almshouse, and did not know of any new construction going on or that any had been appropriated for, Senator Chandler tried to secure an amendment to this clause and, thus having the matter considered in conference, appropriate aid could be given to both these institutions. But on the statement to the Senate by Senator Allison that the amount asked for in the bill was necessary to enable the commissioners of the District to complete existing contracts, no further action was insisted upon by Mr. Chandler. Then, at the next session of Congress, when a third $50,000 for this workhouse construction was under consideration in the Senate, when other representatives of the citizens of East Washington, including myself, called upon Senator Allison, he stated that the desire of the association to limit the expenditures on the proposed workhouse buildings was wise—that he concurred in the plan of making no construction on that reservation beyond what was called for temporary requirements. He then sent us to Senator Francis M. Cockrell, then chairman of the subcommittee of the Committee on Appropriations in charge of the bill making appropriations for the District of Columbia. If I remember correctly Senator Dawes, of Massachusetts, and Senator Isham G. Harris were present. These gent e en heard the statements presented to them and as a result of that conference the clause making appropriation of the third $50,000 for this workhouse structure was amended by the addition of the following provision, drawn up and presented by Senator Cockrell:

Provided, That the total cost of the building shall not exceed $150,000, including the $100,000 heretofore appropriated; and said commissioners are hereby authorized, in their discretion, to expend for temporary frame structures to meet present institutional needs not exceeding $20,000 of the sum heretofore appropriated for this purpose.

Our association, as well as myself, rested in the belief that this clause subsequently enacted into law would settle the business. In the meantime plans for this ambitious structure, to cost between $600,000 and $700,000, were being discussed in the papers, and pictures of it were printed in architectural and other professional papers.

But in spite of the above prohibition the powers in charge of the construction used nearly all of the $150,000 in expensive plans and in the erection of but one wing, a small portion only of the building costing in the end sums vastly in excess of half a million dollars and this for a permanent construction and a permanent occupation of Reservation No. 13 in complete violation of Senator Allison's understanding of the desire of the Senate.

If you will pardon a personal statement, about this time I was compelled to undergo a series of severe surgical operations and gave no further thought to workhouse construction. Other matters pressed upon me. My attention to the construction of only a wing— only a small part of the great building—was called by Mr. William F. Downey, one of the best of men, and at whose funeral services (going on at this hour as you listen to me) I would be present if not here. He took me down there in his private carriage, and both of us were amazed beyond words.

Thereafter a second wing was built and when a clause authorizing a fourth appropriation was pending before the Senate I called upon Senator Gallinger and reminded him of the facts as I have here stated them to you.

Senator SMITH of Maryland. Then there was no estimate made for this building by the Government architects or officials who do that work?

Mr. CURRIDEN. No, sir.

Senator SMITH of Maryland. They just went on from time to time adding to it until they had spent this amount of money?

Mr. CURRIDEN. Certainly. Then we came to Senator Gallinger and he, with the aid of Representative Gardner, of Michigan (who was chairman of the subcommittee of the House Committee on Appropriations in charge of the District of Columbia appropriation bill), instead of the item giving $110,000 for a fourth wing, got subs.ituted a clause by which the President was afterwards enabled to appoint the commission to consider and report upon this jail and workhouse problem. This commission was composed of Hon. Wendell P. Stafford, Mr. William V. La Dow, of the Department of Justice, and Hon. John Joy Edson, representing the citizens and the institutional work of the District. For the expenses of thi: commission $3,000 was appropriated, and as a result of their labors the workhouse and almshouse have each been placed in a new location; all this in line with the earnest labors covering many years of citizens interested in the welfare of the eastern section of the city of Washington.

That is the genesis and the present condition of this great project, much being given in detail in Senate Report No. 648, Sixtieth Congress, now left with you.

Senator GALLINGER. To shorten this a little, Mr. Curriden, your argument to-day is in favor of taking the present site of a jail for a site for an Eastern High School?

Mr. CURRIDEN. Yes, sir.

Senator GALLINGER. And what is your suggestion about those buildings?

Mr. CURRIDEN. Allow me to finish reading this statement.

Senator GALLINGER. Certainly.

Mr. CURRIDEN. The completion of this costly structure for the purposes of confinement of workhouse prisoners was in 1906 deemed unwise, and in lieu thereof Congress authorized the purchase of a tract of land near Occoquan, Va., of about 1,000 acres, where the men, and women also, are all given out-door tasks suitable to their years and to their varying capacities, where they are each and every one compelled to contribute their labor to the support of themselves and the institution. Under the wise management of Col. Whitacre the workhouse institution of Occoquan will, it is believed, soon be self-supporting.

All of the foregoing buildings, including the jail, are located on reservation No. 13 on the original plat of the National Capital. It contains about 40 acres, this area to be increased when the improvement of the Anacostia River, now under way, is completed.

This reservation No. 17, extending between Nineteenth Street east and the Anacostia River, will supply the long-desired site for the long-needed Eastern High School and its correlated educational institutions. Our two brick structures, designed to be parts of the ambitious workhouse structure, can be adapted for laboratory buildings at small expense; and when the jail structure is no longer put to its present antiquated and needlessly expensive uses, that structure can be converted into a gymnasium in connection with the proposed Eastern High School.

Senator GALLINGER. What about a jail?

Mr. CURRIDEN. That I will explain later on. To resume my paper: On this great space can be placed the proposed stadium with a seating capacity of 20,000 to 30,000 people, supplying to this great and growing city an opportunity to witness competitive drills and contests of all the schools of this and near-by cities, as well as other functions to which great multitudes are drawn as in other cities of the world having such structures. The topography of a portion of this reservation will lend itself to the inexpensive construction of this great work. Thither will come vast crowds of the best of our people, and the street railways will gladly extend their lines eastward to get the benefit resulting from this profitable patronage.

The present uses of the jail are limited. It is stated that it is now used (1) as a place of detention of prisoners held for trial and (2) as a place for detention of prisoners after trial, pending their transfer to Atlanta, Ga., or other places of prolonged confinement.

Senator SMITH of Maryland. This is a United States Government jail?

Mr. CURRIDEN. Yes. For many years the erection of a house of detention close to the courthouse building has been strongly urged for the benefit of prisoners pending trial as well as for convenience of the courts. The great distance from the courthouse to the present jail causes needless delays and expense.

It has been urged by some that a building close to the courthouse should be provided that would furnish accommodations for (1) the heads of the police department of the District, whose offices are in the District Building between Thirteen and a half and Fourteenth Streets fronting Pennsylvania Avenue—bringing to that building many undesirable characters, and at times crowds of sight-seers drawn thither to see persons under arrest, or under suspicion; (2) also for the new central police station to take the place of police station No. 1 on Twelfth Street NW., south of the Avenue—an old, unsanitary, and undesirable structure, year after year denounced by every police-department head, and this earnestly confirmed by successive committees of the board of trade and other civic associations of the city. It is just alongside of the lodging house you have heard spoken of in this hearing. Finally (3), in this building, under the same roof, the proposed house of detention can well be placed, the control uni-fied, expense gradually lessened, prisoners pending trial given needed opportunity to confer with counsel, and counsel long-denied oppor-tunity for quick and proper access to their clients.

These are some of our arguments as to some of the temporary uses of that building.

Senator GALLINGER. Just a question or two on this point, Mr. Curriden. Do you think it is desirable to carry the Eastern High School across this plateau and locate it on the Eastern Branch of the Anacostia? It is at one extreme end of the populated district here.

Mr. CURRIDEN. This is a matter of growth, of development. The contention in East Washington has been for years to secure the site for an Eastern High School that was taken for the District stables. There was the Wallach Building; but when Maj. Judson came in he said that was no place for the high school; it needed a 'larger place. If you will study the conditions there you will agree with him. I respect Maj. Judson; he is a man of far ken. That stable, located down here, has not been proved to be a nuisance, and the only site now available for the needed Eastern High School is on this reservation No. 13, lying between Nineteenth Street and the river. When the Eastern Branch is canalized every street-car line in the city will be glad to extend their lines to it. Let me here relpy to the question as to the remoteness of this site for the Eastern High School.

When the Western High School was located some years ago by Commissioner Ross at the then extreme end of Georgetown, I thought it was remote and that the location was unwise, but now the city has grown up to it, and I think it was one of the wisest investments that could have been made.

Senator GALLINGER. The difference is that the city is growing to thn northwest because there is land there, and on the eastern side you rue into the river. That is the point. You are putting the Eastern High School right on the bank of a river.

Mr. CURRIDEN. But you see, gentlemen, we are now living for the future. You and I will all have monuments over us when some of these things are done. Here in the east is Twining City, and the time will come when the eastern section will have the needed bridging over. The canalization of the Eastern Branch is sure to come.

The stadium I am speaking of has been a matter of discussion, and Maj. Judson, who was a man of far-reaching vision, first suggested that on this reservation was the best site for the proposed stadium. Now comes the suggestion that it be put down on Potomac Park, which is all one level stretch of ground, and would be inaccessible to the various street-car lines, whereas here is a place that would be associated with educational institutions.

Senator GALLINGER. Your suggestion involves this, as I look at it: Of course it can not be done this year. First, the building of a new municipal hospital to take care of the inmates of the Washington Asylum; next, the building of a new jail to take care of prisoners and the conversion of that Government reservation into a site for a high school and playground. However worthy it may be it is a great big scheme, is it not?

Mr. CURRIDEN. Well, Senator, the first time I climbed up Mount Kearsarge and saw that stretch of landscape it took my breath away. What we need is to see the great city of Washington as men of far ken.

Senator GALLINGER. Mount Kearsarge is now just as it was when you climbed it. It has not changed.

Mr. CURRIDEN. That is true; but many of us, I hope, are changing, and this for the better. I was treasurer for nearly four years of Garfield Memorial Hospital of this city. I gave much work to that, for my heart was in it. I then antagonized a municipal hospital as originally planned that would cost $3,000,000. In the present plan the municipal hospital might well be given a better name, and the present plans of the Board of Charities would be widely and earnestly approved. On this reservation 13, since the workhouse and almshouse have both been removed, there remain only this rambling lot of little ragged ends of institutions. The removal of these can be made a very easy task if you set about it. Such a plan, humane and inexpensive, is embodied in the report printed by the association a year ago, copies of which I leave with you. That report is as follows:

WASHINGTON, D. C., *December 23, 1912.*

To the East Washington Citizens' Association:

The subject matter of this paper was referred to the undersigned for consideration and report by the following vote adopted at the June meeting:

"*Voted*, That the chairman of the committee on public health, Dr. Charles M. Emmons, be, and is hereby, requested, in company with our president, William M. Potter, to visit the present Washington Asylum Hospital and Jail, and as a result of such visits and inspection to submit a report to the next meeting with such recommendations as they deem proper."

To help consideration of the subject, let us consider the number and present use of all the buildings on Reservation No. 13.

This reservation covers an area of over 50 acres, exclusive of what will be added to it when the Anacostia River improvement now under way is completed.

LIST OF BUILDINGS.

The accompanying plat shows the location on this reservation of buildings which can be designated as follows:

1. United States jail, having an average daily population in 1912 of 175; its capacity, 400.

2. Old workhouse building (not used); in bad condition.

3. Two detached workhouse buildings, each containing steel cages (neither building used).

4. Female workhouse building; not used; in bad condition.

5. Almshouse building, old and in bad condition; now used for care and treatment of alcoholics and insane, in which white and black are mixed, and of both sexes, quartered in separate apartments. In this building, also, are quartered some nurses of both sexes. This building was condemned many years ago for almshouse purposes, being defective in design as well as in construction, also insanitary and not adapted for present uses.

6. Tuberculosis building, brick; not used, but in usable condition; close to above building, No. 5.

7. Smallpox hospital, brick, consisting of one administration and one hospital building; very rarely used; located on the extreme edge of the reservation; dangerous to patients as well as to present caretakers.

8. A detention house, infrequently used; not far from No. 7; practically a quarantine for suspects of smallpox. In this is also a caretaker.

9. A crematory; this within a few hundred feet of No. 8 and the jail, No. 1.

10. Sundry frame buildings, old and dilapidated, known as stables and shops.

11. Sundry frame buildings, all old and dilapidated, except the so-called nurses' home building.

12. Residence of superintendent, of brick; in good condition.

13. Four buildings of brick, near No. 4, used as dwellings of employees; also one old frame building occupied by employees.

14. Two brick sheds of one story, not used. Formerly used as an almshouse for colored people.

USE OF BUILDINGS.

The use of the buildings described in the above 14 classifications can be summarized as follows: The daily average of prisoners in the jail is given at 156 in 1911 and 175 in 1912.

The daily average of chronic sick, including insane and alcoholic cases, acute cases, and maternity cases, in 1911 was 156, of which there were 37 maternity cases. In 1912 there was a daily average of 175 of the above classes of patients, including a total of 56 maternity cases. Most of the foregoing were colored, and they were housed in buildings numbered 11 in the foregoing list.

There have been few, if any, smallpox cases or suspects during the past two years. For this group of buildings another and more suitable location should be secured.

The building No. 9 is the crematory, used for the incineration of unclaimed remains of unknown and paupers.

The control of all these buildings, with but one exception, and the inmates and patients therein, as well as of those in their immediate charge, is now vested in the superintendent of the jail. The one exception above referred to is the smallpox hospital, the control of which is in the hands of the District health office.

In the 13 sets of buildings, exclusive of the jail, there was, as stated, in 1911 a daily average of 156. Of these 83 were colored and 67 white. In the year 1912 the daily average of 175 consisted of a like proportion of colored and white, except the maternity cases. These have been classified in the official reports as acute and chronic, as alcoholics and drug habitués, as syphilitic and other chronic sick, male as well as female.

NO PLACE FOR MATERNITY CASES.

The care in the asylum hospital of 37 maternity cases in 1911 and 56 cases in 1912 excited surprise in the minds of your committee. Such cases should have been sent to the Columbia or other hospitals with which the District authorities have contract relations.

MENTAL CASES SHOULD GO TO GOVERNMENT HOSPITAL FOR INSANE, NOT TO THIS PLACE.

The care in this asylum hospital of the so-called mental cases is notoriously unsatisfactory to patients, as well as to the authorities. Your committee sees no reason why the old system of temporory commitment to the observation ward of the Government Hospital for the Insane, still authorized by law, is not greatly superior to the present practice, where appropriate segregation of white from black and of mild from excitable cases can be had, and all this at an enormous saving of expense to the District. Under this system, and in accordance with existing law, a patient so committed can be discharged at any time within the temporary commitment of 30 days if he be found of sound mind by the superintendent of the Government hospital.

This proposed return to the old and better system of temporary commitment would have lessened the number of patients treated in the Washington Asylum Hospital by 425 in 1911 and 550 in 1912.

OTHER PUBLIC HOSPITALS BETTER FITTED FOR CARE OF THESE CASES.

Of the remaining cases treated in 1911 and 1912, a large proportion might have been sent to other hospitals of the city which receive large appropriations from the Government and are far better prepared to render timely and skillful care.

The Freedmen's Hospital has recently increased its capacity, and this can now be availed of. A slight outlay for a ward for chronics will enable it to take care of all the chronic colored sick.

At Blue Plains there are at this writing accommodations for 30 additional cases. That place has a resident physician, with trained nurses and hospital equipment.

All maternity cases can be cared for at Columbia Hospital, or at either Garfield, Georgetown University, or George Washington University Hospitals, at far less expense and with vastly better accommodations and treatment.

HELP FOR THE HELPLESS AND INCURABLE.

The hospital for Incurables has appealed to Congress for a small appropriation to enable it, with funds already in hand, to build another wing for incurables. If such aid be given, the grant could be made under conditions of care for a large proportion of undesirable chronics, resulting in humanitarian care of them, and greatly lessening the burdens on institutions giving special care to acute cases.

From the financial point of view this is worthy of immediate consideration. From a humanitarian standpoint not a day should be lost in the distribution of these cases, as suggested, and in the closing of the Washington Asylum Hospital.

Your committee can not express too strongly its opinion that from the asylum hospital, without delay, all the above-described cases should be transferred, as suggested. For this, it seems to us, there is needed no additional legislation, only a determination on the part of the District authorities to secure to the very poor and needy better treatment than is now within reach, and this at less cost than at present.

EXISTING CONDITIONS VERY BAD.

Your committee found all the buildings but two of those named unfit for present use and practically beyond repair or reconstruction. We found the common drinking cup used alike by tubercular and other acute and chronic sick. We found that for a period of one month no registered pharmacist was on duty. We found alcoholic and mental cases of both colors, black and white, shut up together, with no opportunity for segregation of quiet patients from noisy. A like mixture was found among the female alcoholics. It seems to be almost impossible to keep the nursing staff up to the required number, due, no doubt, to unsatisfactory surroundings and the amount of work placed upon them. In hot weather the mental and alcoholic cases are closely confined in insanitary, cooped-up quarters, a disgrace to civilization.

JAIL EXPENSIVE AND OUT OF PLACE.

As to the jail, this serves at this time no purpose but that of a place of detention for prisoners waiting to be sent to prison and those under indictment. For many years the relocation of this institution close to the courthouse has been advocated—this, as in other cities, for reasons of economy and the speedy and convenient access to those therein confined. A capacity of 150 would cover all needs, and in this building also could be placed the headquarters of the District police department.

REMOVAL AS URGED HEREIN WILL GIVE NEEDED SITE FOR EASTERN HIGH SCHOOL, STADIUM, AND OTHER PUBLIC INSTITUTIONS.

The removal at an early date of all the patients in the Asylum Hospital, their admission to, and appropriate care in other hospitals now maintaining a high standard of service, and the construction of the proposed House of Detention for the care of prisoners close to the courthouse will remove from the eastern section of this city all the objectionable structures which have long been its bane, which have worked needlessly to its hurt. Thus cleared off, reservation No. 13 can be given to the Eastern High School and to the stadium and a college for agriculture for the boys of the District of Columbia.

CHARLES M. EMMONS, M. D., *Chairman.*
WILLIAM M. POTTER.

Take the present so-called municipal hospital, for which we have purchased sixty-some acres out between Seventh and Fourteenth Streets NW.

Senator GALLINGER. No; a little over 30 acres, to be accurate.

Mr. CURRIDEN. I am sorry it is so little. I thought it was 60.

Senator GALLINGER. No.

Mr. CURRIDEN. They spent $60,000 for it.

Senator GALLINGER. Yes.

Mr. CURRIDEN. Here is one building for tuberculosis patients. As I understand the Board of Charities—and what I am doing is in cooperation with the Board of Charities, Dr. Kober, and Dr. Hickling—if they could get an enlargement of the power capacity of that building out yonder, which is merely a part of a necessary plan for each municipality's caring for its chronic infirm and defectives, and if they could get this additional heating power plant, they would be able to construct an additional building, and thus they would be enabled to take away many of the inmates now held in the old almshouse buildings.

Senator GALLINGER. That is right up to us now.

Senator SMITH of Maryland. I should like to ask a question for information. As I understand, this reservation consists of 40 acres to start with. Is that right?

Mr. CURRIDEN. Forty acres.

Senator SMITH of Maryland. Then I understand further, that there are various propreties on that ground that have cost six or seven hundred thousand dollars?

Senator GALLINGER. No; much more than that. The brick buildings cost that much.

Senator SMITH of Maryland. Yes; the brick buildings cost that much. On that property there is a jail and a workhouse. Am I right about that?

Mr. CURRIDEN. Two segments of a workhouse; yes.

Senator SMITH of Maryland. And an almshouse?

Mr. CURRIDEN. Old buildings.

Senator GALLINGER. And a smallpox hospital and a crematorium.

Senator SMITH of Maryland. And quite a number of buildings. They are being used by the Government?

Mr. CURRIDEN. Yes.

Senator SMITH of Maryland. Do you not believe that property could be utilized to greater advantage for some other purpose than to take it for a high school? Would it not handicap a high-school institution to try to utilize property of that kind? Could it not be used for some better purpose, and more economically for some other purpose, than it could for a high school? Would it not handicap the high school to say: "We are going to utilize this building for such a purpose, and that building for such a purpose"? When you build high schools now, you know, you are building them for children, and you are looking after their health, and all of that. Would it not in a way handicap the erection of a proper institution of that character?

Mr. CURRIDEN. I will answer you frankly and honestly and conscientiously, no. A couple of Sundays ago I went over to Anacostia, and saw the work progressing in the canalization of the Eastern Branch. That will go on up north of the Congressional Cemetery, then continue on to the District line. Then, to this 40 acres will be added about 10 acres of riparian land, by reason of the improvement of the river frontage.

Senator SMITH of Maryland. Have you use for that much land for a high school?

Mr. CURRIDEN. Take our State institutions. There seems to be no end to the possibilities of their growth, and likewise of our Eastern High School.

Senator GALLINGER. Before building a high school on that site we certainly would have to build a new jail and a new hospital.

Senator SMITH of Maryland. And we would have to appropriate for them.

Senator GALLINGER. We would have to appropriate for all those things.

Mr. CURRIDEN. You do not need a new jail. You need a house of detention.

Senator GALLINGER. Well, it is the same thing

Mr. CURRIDEN. Why not put it on Judiciary Square, or east of that place?

Senator GALLINGER. I hope it will never go on Judiciary Square.

Mr. CURRIDEN. Well, I hope not, too.

Senator GALLINGER. We have too many buildings there now.

Mr. CURRIDEN. What I am speaking of, Mr. Chairman, is merely as the result of visitation of the jail several years ago as a member of a committee of the board of trade. With the party were the then commissioners and the heads of the police department of the city, and we spent several days inspecting every police station in the District. In many of them we found the conditions for prisoners as well as for the police force in their charge to be awful—and I use that word guardedly. As to the Twelfth Street station, all agreed that there should be a new station, and this on another site, to give the city what it needs.

Senator SMITH of Maryland. My only object in asking the question was that it struck me that if you are going to build a high school you would need a clean, clear space to build it, according to the modern ideas of a high school, rather than handicap it with a lot of buildings that probably are not suitable for purposes pertaining to a high school.

Mr. CURRIDEN. There are only two buildings there, Mr. Chairman, which could be at all adapted for any institution—the two parts of that large workhouse.

Senator SMITH of Maryland. Well, sir, we shall be very glad to take up this matter.

Senator GALLINGER. The commissioners made an estimate, Mr. Curriden—perhaps you are familiar with it—of $150,000 for the purchase of a site for a new Eastern High School, to be located east of Tenth Street and north of D Street south. That was their estimate. It came to Congress, I suppose, through the board of education.

Mr. CURRIDEN. Yes; and my object is to divert that from purchase of a site, small and inadequate, to the erection of buildings on a plan in which all sections would concur in ultimately.

Senator GALLINGER. Mr. Curriden, I believe you said to me that you wanted to say a word in behalf of the institution at Blue Plains?

Mr. CURRIDEN. I have been down to Blue Plains; I was there at the time of its purchase, and subsequently, and the superintendent recently came into my office much depressed. He said: "See here, the House has turned down this appropriation, and I am in distress." I said: "You mark out what you must have," and so on, and he designated the recommendations in red ink. The point that seemed really the most pressing was increases asked by him to retain his steam-heating force. The comfort of all the many inmates are dependent on securing good help in the care of the lighting and heating plant in his charge.

STATEMENT OF CHARLES C. LANCASTER.

STREET IMPROVEMENTS.

Mr. LANCASTER. I will state that I am president of the Citizens' Northwest Suburban Association, a member of the Brightwood Association, the Columbia Heights Citizens' Association, and the Board of Trade.

Senator SMITH of Maryland. What is the object of your visit, sir?

Mr. LANCASTER. Senators, here is a copy for each of you of our recommendations for our northwest section. As you will observe, those estimates are printed. We do not do anything under cover. They are gone over by our citizens' associations in open meetings, carefully, and we put in the most important and necessary improvements for our section. These are sent to the commissioners before they take up their estimates, for them to go over and see what they can do for us, and then we bring them here to Congress so that you can see what we are doing.

The first point I want to call your attention to is the matter of the improvement of streets. That is on the first page of our recommendations. The first item there, you will observe, is Audobon Terrace, from Albemarle Street to Broad Branch and Rock Creek Park.

Senator GALLINGER. Mr. Shoemaker presented that to the committee.

Mr. LANCASTER. Yes; Mr. Shoemaker is a member of our association, and chairman of the executive committee, and he is interested in that as a tax-payer, with other citizens. I may say that the "$1,500" there is a clerical mistake in printing; it ought to be "$15,000."

As president of that organization, I find that our people are unanimous in advocating the inclusion of that item in the bill. The House neglected to put it in the bill, but the commissioners have recommended it, and we desire the committee to insert it in this bill. We have given the reasons, as you will see in reading along there, why that is necessary. Now, we have made recommendations there for other improvements in our section which have not been recommended by the commissioners.

The next item that is recommended by the commissioners is on page 2 of our estimates. The first item there is Davenport Street. That has been included in the bill. Of course we need not say anything about that. I presume your committee will retain that.

The next one is Harrison Street, from Wisconsin Avenue to Belt Road: To grade and macadamiz , $5,000.

Senator GALLINGER. That is in the bill, is it not?

Mr. LANCASTER. No, sir; that is not in the bill. That is reported by the committee. It is schedule 44. Gentlemen of the committee, we as taxpayers believe that is an important item. It is a small item when you think of the great figures that have been presented to you here to-day and other days during the hearings on this bill, but it is important for the development of this section. As we state in our recommendations there, which you can read at your leisure in going over the bill, Senator—it is item 44 there—this item is important to fix up that street. The land has been given by the property owners, and there are buildings on this street, and they come down the street there with nothing but a dirt road. When the property owners and taxpayers donate the land and start to put buildings on the street, we think Congress ought to go to work and aid the people in developing that street, so that they can improve it and get sanitary facilities. We ask you to put that in the bill.

Right in connection with that is Garrison Street, right below. Now, that was not approved by the commissioners, but it is——

Senator GALLINGER. You had better not waste much time on it, then, Mr. Lancaster?

Mr. LANCASTER. Senator, I want just briefly to explain that that is a very important matter. We people are the originators; we are the taxpayers, and the commissioners are simply our agents. If they do not concur in our recommendations, we appeal to you. This has strong foundations. It is an important street and it ought to be improved. There are sixty or seventy thousand dollars' worth of improvements along in that section, a nice class of houses. Those property owners want that $5,000, which will improve the street and enable them to drive over it and get their coal and wagons over it. As it is, in the wintertime there is mud there and you can not get through the street. It is a small item, but it will be of great advantage to that section.

Now, you will see that we ask for a good many other things there, all of which are important, but we have not got them. The commissioners have not recommended them, and we do not want to burden you with items that you might not feel inclined to put in, in view of the fact that the commissioners have not recommended them. We think they all ought to go in. The whole lump does not amount to a great deal of money. We think they all ought to go in, because we have recommended them and have given you substantial reasons for them, and there is not a man in this town who can deny the necessity of them. There is not a man in our section, or anywhere else in the city of Washington, who can deny the merit of the items that we have asked for. That is just about 25 per cent, say, of what we ought to have out there; but this is done in open meeting by our citizens, knowing, of course, that these things will be shaved down, and opposition will be made by the commissioners, probably before Congress, so we try to put in only what is absolutely necessary at this time, and we have put that in. That is the situation; that is what we ask for, and we hope you gentlemen will include those items in the appropriation bill.

FIRE PROTECTION.

The next item we want to call your attention to is in regard to the fire department. That is in the bill, so I do not know whether we ought to say anything about it or not. There is a fire department station on Wisconsin Avenue and Idaho Avenue. There is some controversy about the location of that fire department station, but, so far as our people are concerned, we are not so much interested in the location as we are in the appropriation. We think there is a public necessity for that additional fire apparatus. We consider it absolutely necessary.

Senator GALLINGER. That is in the bill now?

Mr. LANCASTER. That is in the bill; yes. Then I do not need to press upon it?

Senator SMITH of Maryland. You had better let that alone.

Senator GALLINGER. We might take it out if you discuss it. [Laughter.]

Mr. LANCASTER. I hope not.

PLAYGROUNDS.

The next item I want to call your attention to is the question of playgrounds. According to the bill here, it is on page 27 and goes over to page 28. It is on lines 16 and 17 on page 27, or page 28 it is here. If you will notice, gentlemen, that provides that the playground fund shall be paid wholly out of the revenues of the District of Columbia.

Senator GALLINGER. Mr. Lancaster, if the chairman will pardon me, you know we have fought that out three or four different times, and the House has been absolutely immovable on that subject.

Mr. LANCASTER. Well, Senator, I am familiar with the situation as you have stated it. As far as that is concerned, Mr. Tawney was the man who started that scheme. You held this bill up, as chairman of this committee, for three or four months, fighting that provision in the bill. Mr. Tawney is not there now. We have a new class of men. There is a feeling all over the community here now, and I think all over the country, that the act of 1878 ought to be preserved in its entirety.

Senator GALLINGER. The House does not feel that way.

Mr. LANCASTER. I believe the House will feel that way if the Senate will take the stand that you took here two or three years ago. Mr. Tawney was responsible for that.

Senator GALLINGER. I have taken that stand since Mr. Tawney left the House.

Mr. LANCASTER. I know you have.

Senator GALLINGER. And the House conferees have been immovable on the proposition.

Mr. LANCASTER. We feel that we ought to call your attention to this matter. We feel very deeply in this matter. The Columbia Heights Association, of which I am a member, passed this resolution, which I will read just to show you what the feeling is:

VIOLATION OF ACT OF 1878.

Whereas in the bill (H. R. 10523) making appropriations for the District of Columbia for the fiscal year 1915, which passed the House on January 12, 1914, and is now pending before the Senate Committee on Appropriations, the following provision is contained therein, on page 30, in these words: "In all, for playgrounds, $31,295, which sum shall be paid wholly out of the revenues of the District of Columbia"; and

Whereas this provision is a clear violation of the organic act of 1878, which ordains that, "To the extent to which Congress shall approve of said estimates, Congress shall appropriate the amount of fifty per centum thereof, and the remaining fifty per centum shall be paid out of the taxes of the District of Columbia": Therefore be it

Resolved, By the Columbia Heights Citizens' Association, in public meeting assembled this 3d day of February, 1914, that we solemnly protest against this plain violation of the act of 1878 by the House of Representatives, and we earnestly appeal to the Senate of the United States to oppose the action of the House by insisting upon the payment of the aforesaid fund on the half-and-half plan: Be it further

Resolved, That the president appoint a committee of five members to appear before the Senate Committee on Appropriations and present this resolution and to urge the Senate to stand for the organic act and not to permit its repeal in this particular.

A true copy.

GEORGE C. GERTMAN, *Secretary*.

That is the action of the Columbia Heights Citizens' Association, the citizens' association of which I am president, the citizens' association of the northwest, has passed a resolution, the Brightwood

Citizens' Association has passed resolutions, and the board of trade has passed a resolution, and it is unanimous in this town that that is a violation of the act of 1878.

I want to call your attention to another feature, at page 44 according to the old bill. I have not looked at it here. It is page 44 of the bill. You have the original bill there. Now, Senator Gallinger, will you please look at page 42 there? Now, to show the inconsistency of the House and the conferees on this point, and to show you how they have acted on this point, lines 21, 22, 23, and 24 contain the provision for the identical same purpose as this other one that I showed you, where they want to make it wholly out of the District, and here they make it on the half-and-half plan. Can you see any sense in that? Is there any wisdom in that? There is $3,300 that they propose to put on the half-and-half plan, on the playgrounds—identically the same purpose as this other.

Senator GALLINGER. The only difference, which you do not observe, or do not suggest, is that the second is for school playgrounds, while the first is for general playgrounds.

Mr. LANCASTER. Is there any reason why they should discriminate?

Senator GALLINGER. I am not arguing it.

Mr. LANCASTER. Of course; I notice that; but there is the point. Why should the House go to work and discriminate that way? I believe the Senate ought to stand by that proposition there and maintain the act of 1878 in that particular. I believe that the House will recede from that position when you take it up, and our people feel very strongly on that subject, and we hope that you will insist upon it.

The next point that we want to speak on is in regard to the Borland amendment, an amendment to tax the abutting property owners half of the cost of paving the streets. That is new legislation—never has been in the District before—and our people are unanimously opposed to it, and we appeal to the Senators to oppose that provision of this bill. Probably others have spoken to you on that subject, but we felt that we ought to present this matter to you. It is a matter affecting every property owner in the District of Columbia, and we put it upon this ground. The taxpayers under the law of 1878 now pay one-half of all the expenses of the streets, and the Government pays the other half—abutting owners as well as others who are not on that particular street. Every property in the city is on some street, but whether it is in one square or another square does not make any difference. In addition to that, if you make the abutting property owner pay for that half, you are making him pay double taxation, and we do not see the necessity, or the wisdom, or the philosophy of making the property owner pay double taxation, when the single proposition will carry out the purposes of the improvements of the city; and we oppose the Borland amendment very bitterly, and we think it is a great mistake, and an innovation upon our present law and our present practice.

That, gentlemen, is all I desire, as president of our organization, to call your attention to. Dr. Chappell and Mr. Heider desire to say something as to the improvement of those streets that I spoke of, as they are living in that particular neighborhood and are interested in that; and if you desire to hear them, I would ask that Mr. Heider be heard now.

STATEMENT OF MR. FRED J. HEIDER.

Mr. HEIDER. I reside on Harrison Street. Harrison Street has been dedicated to the District; that is, by us and parties who bought the ground adjoining, and there are, I guess, about $40,000 worth of buildings that have gone up on Harrison Street. Of course we put it on the established grade, and put sidewalks on it, but the street at present is in such a condition that we can not travel it at all, and we have spent money on it as I say, putting new buildings on it, and we have paid for the grading of it and put the sidewalks in.

Senator GALLINGER. Have you sidewalks and water and lights?

Mr. HEIDER. We have water and gas and sewers, of course, and sidewalks. We have paid for that, too, you know.

Senator GALLINGER. Yes.

Mr. HEIDER. I have a house there on the corner of Forty-second and Harrison Streets that has been vacant since September, for the simple reason that the people will not live there in the wintertime. They can not get to the building. It looks to me like after doing all these things we have not derived one cent's worth of benefit, so far as the District is concerned in making any improvements. The sewer and water of course we had to pay for, and it seems to me like the condition of that street is such that we ought to be entitled to some improvement. It has got so now that my tenant who was in this house moved out in September. He stayed there last winter, and he got enough of it.

Senator SMITH of Maryland. How many houses are there on that street?

Mr. HEIDER. There are six houses on Harrison Street between Belt Road and Wisconsin Avenue.

Senator SMITH of Maryland. Six houses?

Mr. HEIDER. Yes.

Mr. LANCASTER. What was the cost of those houses?

Mr. HEIDER. The cost would be about $40,000.

Senator SMITH of Maryland. I thought you just said $30,000?

Mr. HEIDER. No; the house that I built, and the one that is vacant.

Senator SMITH of Maryland. When the square was filled, how many houses would it contain?

Mr. HEIDER. The square, if it was filled?

Senator SMITH of Maryland. Yes.

Mr. HEIDER. I guess each square would be about 350 feet long. There is a part of the ground subdivided.

Senator SMITH of Maryland. In the usual way?

Mr. HEIDER. I guess there would be 20 houses on each side.

Senator SMITH of Maryland. On each side of the street, that many?

Mr. HEIDER. Yes.

Senator SMITH of Maryland. How many houses would there be if the square was filled up; how many would it hold?

Mr. HEIDER. There are two squares, you know.

Senator SMITH of Maryland. I understand.

Senator GALLINGER. The frontage of house lots out there would average 40 or 50 feet, would they not?

Mr. HEIDER. Yes.

Senator GALLINGER. You would not make them 25 feet, would you?

Mr. HEIDER. No, sir. They would average 40 or 50 feet.

Senator GALLINGER. If the square was 350 feet long, that would be only seven houses to a square, with 5 feet left on each side.

Mr. HEIDER. Seven houses?

Senator GALLINGER. Yes.

Senator SMITH of Maryland. That would be 14 houses to each square, taking both sides of the street.

Senator GALLINGER. If the square is only 350 feet long.

Mr. HEIDER. No; it is about 700 feet. There are two blocks there, you know, and there would be that many in each block; that is, you might say between Forty-first and Forty-third Streets on Harrison Street.

Senator SMITH of Maryland. Taking both sides of the street, there would be 28 houses in the two squares, and you have built only six houses on those two blocks.

Mr. HEIDER. Yes; but as I say, people have just got disgusted with the street, and they will not build more.

Senator GALLINGER. The appropriation for this street is submitted by the commissioners, is it not?

Mr. HEIDER. Yes; I think so.

Senator GALLINGER. And was left out by the House?

Mr. HEIDER. Yes. I wish, gentlemen, you would put this back.

In addition, I notice that the taxes have been raised about 90 per cent, but we do not get any benefit from that. We have tried to improve things around there, but so far as the District is concerned, we have not had a cent's worth of benefit.

STATEMENT OF DR. J. W. CHAPPELL.

Dr. CHAPPELL. I do not know that there is anything I could say that would have any effect upon the committee, because I believe the point that I regard as most beneficial has been left out by the District Commissioners. Having been a resident of that section all my life, and my ancestors having lived there for some generations, I think perhaps I am in a condition to know what the opinions of the people of that section are, to some extent. This item asked for, of $100,000 for the widening of Wisconsin Avenue, I think is the most essential thing for our section, essential from every standpoint, and I understand that it has been left out. Personally I believe—and I think I also know the sentiment of the community—that the majority of the members of the community would be in favor of your leaving out every other item, if this one thing could be obtained, and could be gotten at this particular time. In the written discourse there it explains very fairly why we should have that avenue. It is now but 60 feet wide. It is an important highway, the main highway for our entire section, and one-half of it is occupied by the street railroad.

Senator DILLINGHAM. You are speaking about Wisconsin Avenue?

Dr. CHAPPELL. Yes; about Wisconsin Avenue. Personally I believe that the sentiment of the community would be in favor of striking out everything else, at least so far as the streets are concerned, and giving us that one item. If we can not obtain it this year, we should like that little entering wedge to be made this year, so that we will not fail to get it for another year, not only for the benefit of the traveling community, but for the benefit of the lives and safety of those who live upon that road and travel upon that road. We have had repeated instances of accidents there.

Senator GALLINGER. Doctor, this seems to be a new proposition.

Dr. CHAPPELL. I do not know how new it is, but our association has been trying to get it accomplished for 15 or 20 years.

Senator SMITH of Maryland. Have they recommended it?

Dr. CHAPPELL. I believe not. Mr. Lancaster tells me they left it out.

Mr. LANCASTER. It is in our bill. It is our item.

Senator GALLINGER. Was it presented to the House committee?

Mr. LANCASTER. Yes; it was presented to the House committee. If you will turn to our estimates there, you will find that we asked for it.

Senator GALLINGER. From what point to what point is it proposed to widen this avenue?

Dr. CHAPPELL. From Thirty-seventh Street to the District line.

Senator GALLINGER. That would mean pulling down a good many buildings and removing them, would it not?

Dr. CHAPPELL. Not so very many, and not the condemnation of so many houses and lots; a good many along in the village; but they are not very valuable houses. They are frame structures, and it can be done at reasonable expense, and it ought to have been done. We have had a number of accidents, and some people have been killed. The car track is absolutely up against the narrow sidewalk, and you have to be awfully careful—anyone does—and walk in single file, to keep from being run over by those cars. Some years ago this road belonged to a pike company, and the District government bought out the interest of the company, and immediately turned over to the railroad company one-half of the street, without any consideration whatever. If this committee could let us have this or see its way clear to make a beginning this year, it would be a godsend.

Senator GALLINGER. What is the estimated cost?

Dr. CHAPPELL. Of course, it is only a rough estimate, but we have thought that $100,000 would do it.

Senator GALLINGER. Probably it will be much more than that.

Dr. CHAPPELL. I do not know. I think Mr. Lancaster has considered those things very carefully.

There are but two other items, and both of them we are in favor of, and both are extremely essential. Here is Wisconsin Avenue and here is the Conduit Road, and there is absolutely no highway that can be called such, nothing but a dirt road a greater part of the way that is covered with mud and ruts in the winter that make it absolutely impassable in this part of the District of Columbia at this late date. There is not one road there that can be traveled upon with any degree of comfort and satisfaction.

Senator GALLINGER. There is scarcely a house on that road.

Dr. CHAPPELL. That is right; the Little Falls Road. That is on page 8, at the bottom. Right at the juncture of this road and the Conduit Road is the National Training School for Girls, and it is inaccessible so far as our Tennallytown fire engine is concerned, for it could not reach there in bad weather, and I do not know that it could reach it in good weather at all in case of fire. We ought at least to have one road leading from our section, Wisconsin Avenue, west to the District line. People to-day, when the weather makes it at all permissible, in summer go through there; you find automobiles almost continuously going over that road. It is traveled a great deal whenever it is passable and the weather is suitable. That is the second item, and I think next to Wisconsin Avenue—well, I would not say next to Wisconsin Avenue, either, but it is an awfully important thing.

The third thing I should like to call attention to is from a sanitary standpoint, and that is the item we have on page 9 for sweeping and cleaning suburban streets and roads, cleaning out the gutters, $20,000, for which $25,000 is asked. We succeeded a few years ago, I believe, in having an item put in the District bill for that purpose, but for some reason or other it was included in the general appropriation for street cleaning, and the suburbs have been left out. In fact, our suburban villages need to be cleaned just as much as the streets in the city, and I have been advocating the plan and asking for it for a number of years, but we have failed every time. If you could see some of our streets out there, I am sure you would have no doubt as to the necessity for doing something.

I have nothing further to say.

Senator SMITH of Maryland. What are you representing, a board of some kind?

Dr. CHAPPELL. I am representing the Northwest Suburban Citizens' Association. I am one of the committee.

Senator SMITH of Maryland. You are here representing that association?

Dr. CHAPPELL. Yes, sir.

Senator SMITH of Maryland. Are you in any way connected with this property?

Dr. CHAPPELL. No, sir; I do not own a foot of ground on Wisconsin Avenue.

Senator SMITH of Maryland. No; or any of these properties that you speak of? You have a right, of course.

Dr. CHAPPELL. No, sir; I do not own any property on either one of these roads. I live on Grant Road, which would be benefited if we got the street-cleaning proposition through.

Senator SMITH of Maryland. But you are here in the interests of that association.

Dr. CHAPPELL. I have said nothing about anything that concerns me personally, except that one particular item.

Mr. Edelin is here, and I would like you to hear him.

STATEMENT OF MR. D. W. EDELIN.

Senator SMITH of Maryland. Do you represent any association?

Mr. EDELIN. The Columbia Heights Citizens' Association. I am chairman of the committee on streets and alleys.

I will take only a very few minutes of your time. We recommended, after very careful consideration, a certain number of streets to be improved. The commissioners recommended most of these streets. The House has given us only two of them, Fifteenth Street from Euclid Avenue to Columbia Road, and Harvard Street east from Sixteenth Street to the paved street, a matter of only a block. I want to call your attention to Eleventh Street principally. That has a street-car line that is used by a great many people taking the street cars. This is on page 22 of the bill. That was recommended by the commissioners.

Senator SMITH of Maryland. What street is that?

Mr. EDELIN. Eleventh Street from Columbia Road to Park Road. We recommended Columbia Road to Monroe Street. Monroe Street is where the cars stop. All the people north of that have to come to that point to get on these cars, and the road at that point is dirt or macadam. I take the cars there myself, and I have seen there in bad weather people walking in mud considerably over the soles of their shoes, and it covered their shoes; and it is that way all the way down Eleventh Street. Of course, we have had a remarkable winter this winter, but I saw one time when they had to put boards and bricks down to get out to the car tracks on Eleventh Street.

Mr. Chairman, we have three schools on the west side of Eleventh Street, the Normal school, the Ross School, and the Hubbard School. All the people east of that have to cross to Eleventh Street, and in winter weather and wet weather those streets are in very bad condition, and all the people that go downtown use that street, and I think it is one of the most important streets to be paved. I should like to see it paved up to Monroe Street, which is one block farther, and I think that is the most important block of that street, because that is where the cars stop, and all the people who live north of that street have to come down there to take the cars. Park Road is one of the most important streets out there. That connects the Soldiers' Home and Rock Creek Park. It is, of course, principally used by automobiles.

Senator SMITH of Maryland. It is item No. 8, "Park Road, Fourteenth Street to Sherman Avenue."

Mr. EDELIN. Yes, sir. The commissioners recommended that it be graded and improved from Sherman Avenue to Fourteenth Street. The automobiles that come along there in the summer are very numerous, sometimes. I think my wife counted 64 there in 30 minutes going by.

Senator DILLINGHAM. That connects what?

Mr. EDELIN. That connects the Soldiers' Home and Rock Creek Park. It is the only through street in that section to Rock Creek Park at the present time, and it is a very prominent drive. That street is very dusty, and it is impossible for the housekeepers there to keep their houses clean. They have been complaining of it for a long time. The commissioners recommended that to the House, but the House struck it out.

Senator GALLINGER. It is built up very solidly there.

Mr. EDELIN. Yes, practically solid. We have only two or three vacant lots there.

Senator GALLINGER. I happen to know about that.

Mr. EDELIN. Of course, other streets have been recommended, but those are the two most important streets.

I do not want to take up the time of the committee any further. If we get this, it will be a big improvement over what the House has given us. Of course, there are two or three more streets there that we thought were almost necessary, and we should like to have them also, but these two especially, Eleventh Street and Park Road, I think are absolutely necessary.

Mr. LANCASTER. We have another matter up here that the Columbia Heights Citizens' Association are interested in, and that is in regard to that inebriate hospital, for which the commissioners have recommended $75,000. Dr. Gleeson is chairman of the committee of the Columbia Heights Citizens' Association, and is really the author of the proposition, which originated about a year and a half ago. Dr. Gleeson is here, and I should like to have him have an opportunity to present the views of the association.

Senator SMITH of Maryland. That was recommended by the commissioners and left out by the House?

Mr. LANCASTER. Yes; left out by the House.

STATEMENT OF DR. J. K. P. GLEESON, CHAIRMAN OF THE CITIZENS' ASSOCIATION COMMITTEE ON THE ESTABLISHMENT OF A HOME FOR INEBRIATES.

Senator SMITH of Maryland. You are representing what, Doctor?

Dr. GLEESON. I am chairman of the committee of the Columbia Heights Citizens' Association on this subject of an inebriate hospital.

Senator SMITH of Maryland. You are here in what interest?

Dr. GLEESON. I am here in the interests of the public, generally.

Senator SMITH of Maryland. I assume that, but what special interest?

Dr. GLEESON. And especially representing the Columbia Heights Citizens' Association.

Senator SMITH of Maryland. What subject do you want to speak on?

Senator GALLINGER. Dr. Hickling yesterday spoke on the subject of an inebriate hospital.

Dr. GLEESON. Yes; he asked me to come to-day. I will state that through a period of many years in the practice of medicine I have had occasion to come in contact, either freely, of my own will, or by force of circumstances, with the evils growing out of the habit of drinking. I speak especially of the habit when it has reached that point where a man or a woman can be termed an inebriate. I have watched what has been the policy, especially in the District of Columbia, where, as I say, I have lived for forty-odd years, and have watched very carefully the methods of handling these cases of drunkards in this city, and I suppose that it has been one of the worst systems and the least successful in the way of any benefit to the victims of that terrible disease, because I shall treat of this matter simply as a disease—that can be possibly adopted. To make it as brief as possible, I will say that the method has been to treat these cases as criminals—these victims of the drink habit. I have very little sympathy with the man who deliberately, with his eyes wide open, goes, like walking into a furnace, and makes a drunkard of himself; but when he has gone that far that drink has become his master, he is not, in my opinion, responsible after that for what he may do under those conditions, and at that point this becomes a disease.

The custom was here— the custom has been in this city— that when a man was found drunk on the streets he used to be arrested and taken to the station house, thrown into a cell, and left there to sober up until morning. If in the will of the police it was thought fit to turn him loose in the morning after he had gotten straightened up, it was done so with him; if not, he was brought before the court and fined; or, of he could not pay his fine he was sent to jail or to the workhouse— generally to the workhouse. Cases are on record— a number of cases during the past few years— where men have been thrown into those cells in the police stations and left there and found dead in the morning. Mistakes have been made where men have been taken up on the streets, or perhaps found unconscious on the streets, and supposed to be drunk, who were diseased or were suffering from some attack of some kind and thrown into a station house, where they died without help and without a proper examination.

These patients have been sent down to the Washington Asylum, which, by the way, I want to say is an institution the history of which is not creditable to the District of Columbia or to any other part of the country, and I certainly am sustained by the testimony of Dr. Hickling, who has been the superintendent or the medical attendant of that institution for years, and if you refer to his report of last year you will find that he says in that institution the drunk and the sober, the crazy and the sane, the white and the black, are all thrown in together, and there they are kept, all mingling one with the other; and those are conditions that have prevailed down there, and that has been the condition for many years. Although the matter has been brought up by the authorities in the District and bills had been introduced for establishing some kind of an asylum or a place for treating this class of cases, still nothing had been accomplished, and in view of that situation I offered in our association on the 4th of April, 1911, these resolutions:

RESOLUTIONS ADOPTED BY THE COLUMBIA HEIGHTS CITIZENS' ASSOCIATION, APRIL 4, 1911

Whereas there is no place, institution, hospital, or home in the District of Columbia where inebriates or the victims of the drug habit can be sent for treatment and be lawfully committed so that they can be absolutely restrained from access to either intoxicating liquors or injurious drugs other than the District workhouse; and

Whereas the proposition to establish such a hospital has been before Congress in some form for the last 10 years, and has been advocated by past members of the and the present Board of Commissioners, many of our public-spirited citizens, and prominent physicians, also the board of trade, thus far without result: Therefore be it

Resolved, That the Columbia Heights Citizens' Association most heartily approve of the proposition for the early establishment of such a hospital, and the members thereof pledge themselves, individually and collectively, to do all in their power to bring about such a result as early as possible.

Resolved, That the secretary be instructed to send a copy of these resolutions to each of the citizens' associations of the District of Columbia, the chamber of commerce, and the board of trade, with the request that they take favorable and prompt action upon the same, thus securing a concerted action upon the proposition by the several associations, and also a copy to the District Commissioners and to the chairman of the Committee on the District of Columbia of the Senate and House of Representatives, respectively.

These resolutions were adopted or approved by the various citizens' associations throughout the District of Columbia, by the chamber of commerce, the board of trade, the Federation of Citizens' Associations, and other civic organizations.

I will say that, based on these resolutions, the result was that a bill was introduced in both the House and the Senate covering the proposition to establish an asylum of this kind, or a hospital. Those bills, S. 2676 and H. R. 12107, were introduced in the Sixty-second Congress.

Our committee worked in concert with the commissioners on this matter as far as we could, but there were certain points of disagreement. At that time the commissioners were in favor of locating such an institution, if it was established, on the old Washington Asylum grounds, which you have heard discussed here this morning to some extent, and utilizing one or the other of those buildings down there. I personally opposed that, and my committee backed me in opposing that location, because of the fact that the association, in the first place, felt that, it being connected with the jail and the workhouse and all its associations in that line, it would not be very largely conducive to moral reform; and, furthermore, that from a sanitary point of view the location itself was not desirable. Neither was there in that plot or reservation, No. 13, sufficient ground upon which properly to establish an institution of this kind.

This idea contemplates not only, not simply, a hospital. If we are going at the thing in the proper way, if we are going to follow precedents established by other States and other communities, we want not only a hospital building, but we want ground around the building, and we should have ground enough so that those diseased persons who shall be committed there in accordance with the proposed law can be placed at work in the open air as far as possible, many of them, and kept employed in different lines of trade, and manufacturing industries, by which they will not only have their minds and bodies occupied, but they will at the same time contribute largely to making such an institution self-supporting. In support of that phase of the question, I will refer simply to what is probably the largest institution of the kind in the country—so far as I know, the largest by all odds—that is the State institution at Foxboro, Mass. There they have probably the most model institution of the kind that has yet been organized. Now, according to the records—and I have their reports here for several years—they started, and in 1910 they had 20 acres of ground, and they have been adding constantly to that, so that now they have means to employ, in one way or another, these patients, and it is preferable where they can do so to employ them out in the open air and keep them occupied.

Senator SMITH of Maryland. They have about 107 acres, I take it, from this report.

Dr. GLEESON. Yes, sir; so that they are now utilizing that method, and they have been very successful in the matter of treating those cases and reforming many of them. Of course the patients are kept there under legal commitment, and they have to stay there until they are legally discharged.

Senator SMITH of Maryland. Do you know the population of this town of which you speak?

Dr. GLEESON. Foxboro?

Senator SMITH of Maryland. Yes.

Dr. GLEESON. I do not know, but it is a small town.

Mr. LANCASTER. This is a State institution.

Dr. GLEESON. Yes; it is a State institution.

Senator GALLINGER. As an old resident of this city, you are aware of the fact that the acreage of the District is becoming rather small for purposes such as you are arguing for.

Dr. GLEESON. Precisely; and that is why I am arguing we will have to go outside of the District if we want to have an institution of this kind.

Senator GALLINGER. Then, we have got to get action by the State legislatures, unless there is a general statute covering it. We will run into the objection that is constantly raised, that we are dumping our undesirable institutions into Maryland and Virginia. We will have a good deal of trouble on that score.

Dr. GLEESON. That question may be raised, of course.

Senator SMITH of Maryland. Do you believe that these people would stay in long enough to do much work—to benefit themselves? It is not your object to keep them any length of time in this institution, is it?

Dr. GLEESON. The proposition is, I suppose, to have them committed by the courts under a provision of law for a period of two years. It will be provided that in the discretion of the superintendent they can either be let out on parole or discharged; that is the present practice in the other institutions.

Senator GALLINGER. I observe that before the House committee, when this matter was discussed by Dr. Kober, a question was raised by Mr. Sisson which seemed to be rather serious. I read from page 417 of the House hearings, as follows:

Mr. SISSON. Before any appropriation is made, is it not necessary to ascertain whether there is a law authorizing adjudication by any authority of the case of an inebriate? If a judgment or order is found in pursuance of a statute declaring a man to be an inebriate, that finding makes it a crime.

Dr. KOBER. There is no law now. A law has been proposed, and it is urged by a great many people in the community.

Mr. SISSON. Why spend this $75,000 until you have ascertained whether or not you can get the law?

I am not a lawyer, but I suppose the point is that you have got to adjudicate a man an inebriate before you can confine him.

Dr. GLEESON. I do not know what law there is, either in Massachusetts or in other States, bearing on that point. Iowa has a large State institution, and in a recent article I saw that Minnesota has recently appropriated over a quarter of a million dollars for an inebriate asylum, and all those institutions, so far as I know, are provided with this land for the purpose of carrying out these objects of reform.

In the first place, the commissioners this year have apparently practically conceded the point that my committee made—that is, as to removing the location from Reservation 13, the Washington Asylum grounds—and have now proposed to put it out there in connection with the proposed municipal hospital. In my opinion, the objection to that is that there will be no opportunity for grounds about that place. It will be simply a house of detention, and that is all you can make of it; and it is also in conjunction with the Tuberculosis Hospital, which is objectionable in many aspects, and will never be possible to develop it into an institution in accordance with the ideas of men who have had experience in the treatment of this class of cases. So that the real gist of the thing would be to secure an outside location, where we would have the proper facilities for carrying out this work. But I am so much in favor of an institution of this kind, by which means we can remove this class of people, treated as criminals, from that criminal class, and treat them as they should be treated—as diseased persons; and so much in favor of bringing about that much of a change, that I am willing almost to have it located anywhere, although I do not think it is good policy or advisable to begin anything on a scale that we really know does not promise to work out as we would like to have it. But if that is the best we can get, if we can get an institution or a building at that point for that purpose at the present time, we certainly will be glad to accept it.

The amount here is $75,000. If that was properly invested or handled it strikes me that outside of the limits of the District of Columbia a tract of land might be found which could be purchased for a small percentage of that money, and the balance of it could be utilized for putting up buildings, and the thing could be started on a small scale and gradually worked up as the growth of conditions would require, and eventually we would have an institution which would meet the requirements of the case, and provide what is certainly a necessity in this community.

In my opinion, there is no use to talk about doing away with the liquor business. You can restrict it and all that, but men are going to have liquor, they are going to get it some way as long as it is manufactured, and these men who are strictly in the inebriate class are, as you all know, unproductive themselves. They generally become dependent upon the community, and their friends and relatives suffer and are under a certain amount of disgrace from the results of their conduct.

Senator GALLINGER. I was interested in your suggestion that these men are not criminals, but are diseased men; that is, suffering from one form of disease.

Dr. GLEESON. That is the point.

Senator GALLINGER. What is your view as to heredity, and how large a part does that play?

Dr. GLEESON. In my personal opinion, Senator, it does not cut a very large figure. I do not believe that a large proportion of cases are inherited. That is the result of my observation and study of the question, and it is the opinion of many others who have studied the subject.

Senator SMITH of Maryland. You do not think they inherit the weakness of the parents, which allows them to go on to excess?

Dr. GLEESON. No, sir; I do not think so.

Senator SMITH of Maryland. Do they not inherit the disposition of the parents?

Dr. GLEESON. Not altogether. I have seen cases where I thought there was some evidence of that.

Senator SMITH of Maryland. I have known families where it seemed that it went on down from one to another.

Dr. GLEESON. We can all appreciate this. Take a decent, respectable family; the father perhaps may be a drunkard, and you may get a whole family of children, or boys, and the father is drinking off and on, and he goes on sprees, and he himself is discredited, and his family feel that. The very fact of that state of things, in my opinion, tends to keep the sons from getting into it and following in his tracks; it would prejudice them against it, you know; and I have known of cases of that kind where I know it has had that effect; so that I do not take so much stock in that.

I want to say just a few words here on that very subject. I have something in print here which expresses the thing better than I could, perhaps, otherwise. Referring to these bills providing for the establishment of a hospital for inebriates, and so forth, attention is called to the fact that there is no place in the District of Columbia where the unfortunate victims of the drink or drug habit can be lawfully committed and detained for treatment except the District workhouse or Washington Asylum Hospital, which is located on the same reservation as the District jail building and near the same. This is intended to include the liquor and drug habits, as the liquor habit is a drug habit, and the worst form of drug habit, in my opinion.

Under this jurisdiction drunkenness is not a criminal offense, and therefore no person found on the street or any public place simply in an intoxicated condition can be arrested and locked up, except it may be under some extraordinary conditions, when as a precautionary measure and for his own protection from bodily harm he is taken in charge and lodged in a police station for a night, and the police records will show that in several instances the person has later been found dead in the station-house cell. If such cases had been sent to a hospital for treatment, doubtless their lives in most cases would have been saved. The fact stands, then, that no inebriate can be committed to the said workhouse or Washington Asylum Hospital except under a charge of disorderly conduct, profanity, threats, etc., which involves a trial in the police court.

All persons so committed are simply treated from a criminal standpoint, the whole proceeding having a degrading influence upon all concerned.

To remedy this crying evil, the movement has been made by the citizens of the District of Columbia for the permanent establishment of a special hospital where this class of unfortunate and diseased persons can be lawfully committed and detained for a definite period and treated by proper medical methods and upon strictly humanitarian principles, entirely removed from any idea of criminal conditions.

The movement started by the unanimous adoption, after discussion by the Columbia Heights Citizens' Association, of the series of resolutions which I have already read to you.

Senator GALLINGER. I would say, in passing, that I have been importuned for a great many years on this subject. I think I have had correspondence with you on it.

Dr. GLEESON. I know you have had a great deal to do with it.

Senator GALLINGER. I have been very much embarrassed in certain directions. In the first place, it never seemed to me that the reservation where the workhouse is was a proper place for an institution of that kind.

Dr. GLEESON. Not in any sense.

Senator GALLINGER. In the second place, it is a fact that the tract of land where the Tuberculosis Hospital is now located is not large enough to put the institution there. If we relieve the old Washington Asylum of its inmates and give them better quarters, we will have undoubtedly to build a hospital on that tract for that purpose; and then the question came, and it was a broad question, whether we could secure land outside of the District, and if so, where and at what cost; and in that way the matter has drifted and we did not seem to reach the point where we could take action, and hence the matter has gone by default. Bills have been introduced, of course.

Dr. GLEESON. Yes, I understand the difficulties that have followed this whole question all the way through; and yet at the same time, to my mind very clearly the fact remains of the necessity of such a thing.

Senator SMITH of Maryland. Do you not think it would be unwise, speaking about this Tuberculosis Hospital, to put an inebriate hospital where the inmates of the Tuberculosis Hospital and the people who are committed as inebriates would go together? Would not that be rather an unwise proposition?

Dr. GLEESON. Positively objectionable, Senator, I think.

Senator SMITH of Maryland. It so strikes me.

Dr. GLEESON. And while I do not want to appear as opposing the wishes of the commissioners to that effect——

Senator SMITH of Maryland. The tuberculosis patients are allowed to go around, and they have to.

Dr. GLEESON. Yes, certainly; they are kept in the open air as much as possible.

Senator GALLINGER. Yes.

Senator SMITH of Maryland. To mix those two classes of people together it seems to me would be a very unwise proposition, and one that would help to destroy the object for which you had your tuberculosis hospital.

Senator GALLINGER. I notice that you class the liquor habit as a drug habit, and doubtless you are correct about that. I want to propound a question to you which I propounded, I believe, to Dr. Hickling. It is this: We have been very diligent in this District, and I have taken great interest in it, in trying to prohibit the sale of these habit-forming drugs, like cocaine, and we have a very strict law on the statute books on that subject, and yet they seem to get these drugs. Where do they get them? Are those drugs being sold here contrary to law, to any extent, or do they get them from outside?

Dr. GLEESON. They get them often from outside. We have very stringent laws on the question of smuggling, you know, but they smuggle things, just the same.

Senator GALLINGER. Yes.

Dr. GLEESON. Persons addicted to the habit of morphine, which they can get in powder or tablets, can not buy it here; or, even if they could, in the course of my professional experience I have run upon cases like this. For instance, a woman with either a drug habit or the drink habit is the worst possible example of the effect of those two habits. Women are worse than men in every respect. They become more demoralized, I believe, more degraded, really, and they become absolutely untruthful and unreliable; you can not rely upon anything they say, etc. I have known cases where a woman wanted morphine and she did not want people to know that she was getting it; she was laboring under the impression that she was deceiving her friends. She would write to a druggist or a friend or a party in a distant city and have them buy morphine and put it up in little packets and seal it up in newspaper packages and mail the newspapers to her containing it.

All kinds of tricks are used to bring it in. So that to-day there are undoubtedly people bringing in cocaine from outside, in different ways.

They get it in some way, and people will get it. So that those are very difficult matters to control absolutely; but it is very important that they should be controlled. You take the extensive agitation that we have had recently—an epidemic, so to speak—that has arisen out of the first case reported in years of poisoning by bichloride tablets. It is a remarkable thing how that has spread. As soon as one case happened there were 20 cases. We have rules governing the sale of poisons, and yet I saw in the newspapers here some time ago where some woman bought a bottle of bichloride tablets.

Senator GALLINGER. Some years ago a London physician, Dr. Elam, wrote a book entitled "A Physician's Problems."

Dr. GLEESON. Yes; I remember it.

Senator GALLINGER. Dr. Elam argued that there were mental and moral as well as physical epidemics, and inebriation perhaps comes under that head. I suppose you have seen the thing in your experience and practice, often?

Dr. GLEESON. Yes. You have had the experience of striking a certain disease that you have not had a case of perhaps for a year, and within six months you would get six or eight or ten cases of that same thing; not a general epidemic, but somehow it seems to be in the air, and it happens that way.

Senator GALLINGER. Yes.

Dr. GLEESON. Gentlemen of the committee, this is a matter in which I feel a great deal of interest. I do not want to consume more of your time. It is a matter which I think is of interest to every member of the community, and I am anxious to see the time come when this class of unfortunate human beings will be treated from a humanitarian standpoint. That can only be brought about by Government supervision, in my opinion. You take your private sanitariums; I have had experience with those. I do not know one where I could send a drunkard or a victim of any other drug habit, and place them with absolute safety or security that they would not be able to get what they wanted; because they will not exercise the care and supervision over them that ought to be given them, and they have not the authority, oftentime, to do it; and unless a man has the will power to reform himself, he is not going to be saved in that way, because these men lose their will power. There is the trouble. Their will is gone, and they can not control themselves, they can not resist this, and they will go through fire and flood to get a drink.

I knew a man up in Maine some years ago who tried to reform. He made a pledge to his friends that he would not drink for a certain length of time, and he stood it out for three or four days, but on one Thursday night, about the fourth day, this craving for liquor came upon him. It was up in Maine, where there was prohibition, but he knew a place where he could get it. It was a cold, stormy, sleety night, a terrible night in winter, but he finally got up out of his bed— he knew the place some 12 miles distant where he could get a drink of whisky—and he put his clothes on and walked that 12 miles and got his drink of whisky and brought some back with him, and got back the next day. You know, that is a terrible power over a man, a thing like that.

Senator GALLINGER. While treating a man holding a very high official position in New Hampshire, I made an appeal to him. He was my friend, and I had been his friend, politically and otherwise.

I said to him, "Why don't you give it up?" He said, "Doctor, there is a spot in my stomach that beefsteak doesn't touch." He died a drunkard.

Dr. GLEESON. Well do I remember the state of things in New Hampshire when Medford rum was the popular drink. I have seen men walk miles to get a drink, in the coldest of weather.

Now, gentlemen, I have laid before you the principal points, I believe. Here is a copy of our brief on this subject, if you have not seen it. The matter is condensed there, and we would like to have you read it.

Senator GALLINGER. As I understand the matter, you think that if an institution of this kind was established it ought to include an area of 100 acres, or thereabouts?

Dr. GLEESON. It ought to be all the way from 50 acres up to 100 acres, so that you could start it that way, so that you could have the facilities for putting those people to work in some way.

Senator GALLINGER. When we passed the bill establishing the workhouse, as I recall it, it was provided in that bill that it should be an area not less than 1,000 acres, and 1,100 acres were purchased at Occoquan for that purpose. We likewise at that time passed a bill—perhaps it was a provision in the same bill—for an equal area for a reformatory, and an equal amount of land was purchased near Mount Vernon; but there was such a protest against that on the part of those interested in Mount Vernon that that land was sold and never was utilized. I think we would have to go outside of the District, Doctor, to get a site, and we might find it difficult to procure land for an institution of this kind.

Dr. GLEESON. I think so. That is my personal idea of it. I think that is the proper way to go about it. That is what I should like to see done.

Senator SMITH of Maryland. Do you know a State which has an institution of the kind of which you speak?

Dr. GLEESON. Iowa, Minnesota, and Massachusetts are three States that I know of that have model institutions, as I understand. I know more about the Foxboro institution, because I have been in correspondence with the superintendent and have had the reports.

Senator SMITH of Maryland. Those States that have these institutions are the exceptions?

Dr. GLEESON. Yes; so far as I know. I do not think a large number of States have them at the present time, but the question is being agitated, and it is a thing that is growing, and those who have gone into it have gone into it to make an institution that would reach the matter in a proper way.

Senator GALLINGER. Did you ever investigate the Keely institutes with a view to determining what proportion of cures in these institutions are permanent?

Dr. GLEESON. I have never had the opportunity of studying a sufficient number of cases to form any definite opinion. I have known of some individual cases where they apparently were absolutely cured. I know a case of one man that I now recall—he is dead, however, at this time -- who reformed under the Keely cure, and for 18 years he never touched a drink of whisky.

Senator GALLINGER. You have an institution of that kind in your State, Senator Smith?

Senator SMITH of Maryland. A Keely institute, yes. That is at Laurel, Howard County.

Dr. GLEESON. But this matter is a matter of a great deal of interest, and it is a matter that I certainly hope public men will take hold of and see if you can not do something about it. It can not be done in a year, but it is worth the effort on the part of every good citizen to try and establish an institution of this kind in some way.

Senator SMITH of Maryland. And there is no better place to start it than at the seat of the Government of the United States, where it may serve as an example.

Dr. GLEESON. That is the way I look at it. They can afford it. I heard you raise another question in another connection, about the working plan— if you put people to work in these institutions. There is another side to that question. As I said a moment ago, these inebriates, common drunkards, habitual drunkards, and all that, are dependent; they are nonproductive; they have to be supported and taken care of by somebody, and the State has to do it if nobody else does it. If they can be reformed, and if they can be put into an ·institution where they can be made self-supporting, it is a help to the community generally. There can be no reasonable objection raised to it, that I can see.

Senator GALLINGER. With your knowledge of that class of men, is it your opinion that, supposing we had 100 acres, a good deal of work could be gotten out of those people?

Dr. GLEESON. Unquestionably. As a rule, the report of the superintendents of these institutions is that these people are glad to be employed. They enjoy it. They like to be out, and they like the exercise. If a man has a trade, they will let him work at his trade, and do what he can. If not, they put him on the grounds, and he gets interested in improving and embellishing and parking up the place, and getting fruit. They become interested in the institution.

Senator GALLINGER. The grounds at Foxboro are beautifully ornamented.

Dr. GLEESON. Yes.

Senator GALLINGER. They have been improved to a high degree.

Dr. GLEESON. Yes; and they are productive. They state in their report the amount of stuff they raise. I think they raise a great deal there that they supply to other State institutions.

I am very much obliged to you, gentlemen, and I hope you will give this matter careful consideration, as I am quite sure you will.

Mr. LANCASTER. We are very much obliged to you.

STATEMENT OF MR. EVAN H. TUCKER, PRESIDENT OF THE NORTHEAST WASHINGTON CITIZENS' ASSOCIATION.

Senator SMITH of Maryland. What is the special subject you want to speak of?

Mr. TUCKER. We have two or three questions that we want to speak of, briefly. We have the question of the Patterson Park proposition, which the commissioners recommended in their estimates, which the House did not honor, and I should like, after I say a few words on other subjects, to introduce the chairman of our committee on parks, Prof. Hall, to say something to you.

Then we have the Eastern High School, and I might say it is a whole high-school situation at the present time. I suppose the committee has learned from others that there is at the present time a great congestion in the high schools, and that is more perceptible in the Eastern, Business, and McKinley schools. We naturally want to see what is the remedy. What are we going to do? The Business High School occupies a site which covers a square, with no spare ground around it whatever. The McKinley School occupies a site uptown, where the adjacent property is built up by dwellings. If any land was acquired for the enlargement of that school, it would be at a very large cost. From figures furnished me by the superintendent of schools I find that the enrollment in the Business High School of pupils residing in east Washington on December 1, 1913, was 426. Those pupils resided, mind you, up here on Capitol Hill and in east Washington, and they had to be transported to and from that uptown school every day at an expense to those people, and those are the people in our community who are least able to pay car fare. The McKinley School at the same time had an enrollment of 292 pupils residing in east Washington who had to be transported, and the Central High School had at the same time 161 enrolled, making a total of 879 pupils residing in east Washington who attended those uptown schools and either had to walk or pay transportation.

Our Eastern High School is doing a very good work, but it is too small. It is a building that was constructed to accommodate comfortably about 400 pupils. On December 1, or thereabouts, Prof. Small, the principal of the school, tells me they had an enrollment of in the neighborhood of 460. His present enrollment is 471, which requires classes to occupy sometimes the assembly hall, corridors, and so forth; and I am told by him—and he is here to verify it—that in this present stage of the transfers of pupils from the schools to the high schools he had to turn away a number who desired to come there. Those who went to the uptown schools had to put up there with the crowded condition at those schools.

The question of a remedy is one that has been in our minds for a great many years. I have thought for a great many years that we should have an Eastern High School to accommodate the pupils of Washington, of all the various classes, business classes, technical classes, academic classes, and scientific classes, so as to allow our children to be taught there. If that kind of a building was provided at the present time, it would relieve the Business High School of these 426 pupils, so that that school would not need to be enlarged for some time to come; it would relieve the McKinley School of 292 pupils; and it would relieve the Central School of 161 pupils; so that, you see, the solution of the present condition of our schools will be in the immediate providing of an Eastern High School building. That solves the whole problem for the present, and it is a question as to how that shall be done. Senator Lane's proposition, not to build such a large Central High School at this time, but to give immediate relief here in East Washington, seems to me a reasonable one. It would be perfectly reasonable to build a Central High School on the site provided to accommodate 1,500 or 1,600 pupils, which would be about 400 or 500 pupils more than would go there at the present time, if you gave us facilities here to take care of our own; and that building could be built so that it could be enlarged as conditions changed, and if that was done, a part of the appropriation which you would make now for a large building, which looks forward to the future, could be placed for furnishing immediate relief not only for the Eastern High School, but for these other schools whose buildings can not be enlarged, the Business and the McKinley High Schools.

It looks to us, with all due respect to those who are not in favor of that—and I know that my good friend, Senator Gallinger, is not—as though that is the most reasonable way out of the proposition at this time, unless we can get a large enough appropriation to go right ahead and purchase a site and build us a new high school at the present time. But, you see, if we do as the commissioners recommended in their estimates, provide now $150,000 for a site, and purchase the site, it may be three or four years before we have a building, and we need it now, at this very minute, and owing to the rapid increase of population in East Washington—it is the one of the urban sections that is growing faster than any other—-the conditions are going to be terrible in a short time. I read in the paper the other night where 124 houses are going to be built out north of Florida Avenue. You can imagine how that is going to increase attendance in the schools, because the people who occupy those little houses are the kind that have children, and plenty of them.

In case the judgment of the committee is not in favor of the plan to separate appropriations for the Central School, and give us immediate relief, the best that we can ask of the committee is to provide money for the site, and if possible, to provide means to go right ahead with that school, and build us a school.

Senator GALLINGER. All that the proposition to divide the appropriation for the Central High School involves is that we should take out of the appropriation a sufficient amount to buy a site for the Eastern High School.

Mr. TUCKER. If I understood the commissioners' recommendation, they provide that $400,000 shall be separated from the other appropriation for the purchase of a site, and toward the erection of a new Eastern High School. That is the way it reads, according to my recollection.

Senator SMITH of Maryland. Is it not your observation that the schools that have been built in the past have proven in a few years inadequate, and have had to be added to?

Mr. TUCKER. Yes, sir; that is so.

Senator SMITH of Maryland. Then do you not think that in building a school you should build a little for the future, and not just build a house that is large enough to hold those that may go at the present time?

Mr. TUCKER. I do. I agree with you.

Senator SMITH of Maryland. Personally, I think it has been pretty thoroughly demonstrated to this committee—and I think it is due to you, to be frank with you, that the building that it is proposed to build for the Central High School will soon be filled.

Mr. TUCKER. The new Central School?

Senator SMITH of Maryland. Yes.

Senator GALLINGER. I would make this suggestion, Mr. Tucker, in all seriousness: We all feel that you good people in East Washington—and you know you have always had my sympathy——

Mr. TUCKER. I know that, and your support.

Senator GALLINGER (continuing). Should direct your efforts now to procuring an Eastern High School, and not get involved in the controversy concerning the Central High School. I have no doubt you will get that school in the near future, if you will just bend you energies in that direction. Of course we are now confronted with these complications as to the location of that building. Gentlemen come in here and argue that we ought to put it on the reservation on the Eastern Branch, which would mean the tearing down of a lot of buildings and the construction of new buildings, and that seems to be not feasible.

Mr. TUCKER. I am not in favor of that.

Senator GALLINGER. The commissioners have suggested a site, I believe.

Mr. TUCKER. We are not in favor of any particular site, but the general location is what we look at.

Senator GALLINGER. Do you not think it wise for you gentlemen to advocate to-day an appropriation for a site? Of course it follows that we have got to make appropriation for a building, but that comes along naturally in the next year or so, as a rule.

Mr. TUCKER. It would mean a delay.

Senator GALLINGER. Oh, yes. Well, we can not get a new high school without delay. No matter what we do, it is going to take time. It has been a good many years that we have been agitating a new Central High School. We purchased the land several years ago for the Central High School, but the building has not been erected. Necessarily, there will be delay.

Senator SMITH of Maryland. My judgment is that you will get a better high school by going on your own hook and trying to provide a school for yourselves than you will by trying to divide what has been appropriated for another purpose.

Mr. TUCKER. I am willing to leave that to the judgment of the committee.

Senator SMITH of Maryland. I think both sections ought to have schools, myself.

Mr. TUCKER. In answer to the chairman of the committee, the point I was making in regard to the Central High School is this: I understand that the enrollment at the present Central High School is 1,200, and we could take from that school those that live in East Washington, if we had provision for them, and probably that would leave at the Central High School in the neighborhood of a little over 1,000 at the present time, and a building that would accommodate 1,600 would do for them not only now, but for several years to come.

Senator SMITH of Maryland. It would do for the present?

Mr. TUCKER. Yes; and then if you would provide so that that could be enlarged it seems to us that would afford us a chance to get immediate relief, and then you could look after the other afterwards.

Senator SMITH of Maryland. In building these buildings you do not build for the immediate future?

Mr. TUCKER. Yes.

Senator SMITH of Maryland. You want to build for the future?

Mr. TUCKER. Yes.

Senator SMITH of Maryland. Money sufficient to buy that ground and build a school has been appropriated.

Senator GALLINGER. And the plans are all made.

Senator SMITH of Maryland. And the plans are all made; and if you should now attempt to divert part of that fund in the interests of your own section I think you would make a mistake. I think it is perfectly fair to speak and let you know what the sense of the committee is, so that you may not waste time in attempting to argue in favor of something that is not likely to occur.

Mr. TUCKER. I will not argue that point further.

There is a condition in the Business High School that is very congested. That is on a square, as I said, where there is no adjacent ground available and you can not enlarge it. The only reasonable way that I can see would be to keep our East Washington children there, 426 pupils, almost as many as we have in the Eastern High School at present, who attend that school, and it would save them car fare and be a heap better than making larger appropriations uptown for those children.

Senator SMITH of Maryland. The thing to do now is to lay your foundation, and you will get your school. I am for educating the children myself, and I am for giving all the facilities that are necessary in a proper, economical way; and you had better lay the foundation.

Mr. TUCKER. Well, then, in the name of all the citizens of East Washington I am going to ask this committee to include in the bill that you will frame, or in the amendments to the House bill, the appropriation that is in the estimates for a site for this high school, located as the commissioners request. We do not want to put it down there on the jail site where our children will have to keep on forever paying car fare.

Senator GALLINGER. I am very glad you feel that way, because I fear it would be a mistake to put it down on the border of the river at the extreme end of the populous part of that section of the city.

Mr. TUCKER. We want it as near the center of the urban population of the city as possible.

Senator GALLINGER. I want you to excuse me for interrupting your argument, but I think it would be futile to go on with that matter, and it might be against your interests.

Mr. TUCKER. The next proposition I am here to speak about is a site for a graded school in northeast Washington, which is a matter of very great interest.

Senator GALLINGER. Is that estimated for?

Mr. TUCKER. It is estimated for at $45 000, and there is a piece of ground there that is located exactly right for building on. If we let it go and let speculators get it and build on it we will have trouble finding a suitable site. As I said, that northern part of our section is building up very rapidly, and the schools are now congested, and we have got to look out for the future. In this division we have not a school building that has an assembly hall. That project is now going all over the country, of having the school buildings open for public meetings, and among the schools in our section there is not a single school building that has an assembly hall.

Senator SMITH of Maryland. Do you think it is well to allow the school buildings to be used for those purposes?

Mr. TUCKER. I think where they have an assembly hall, that would be all right.

Senator GALLINGER. I will say that so far as I am concerned I do not believe in opening the schools for gatherings of all kinds, as is proposed.

Mr. TUCKER. That is very frank.

Senator GALLINGER. In my State they do not allow it. The buildings are used for school and educational purposes alone.

Senator SMITH of Maryland. In my opinion, it is not the wisest thing.

Senator GALLINGER. When the Government pays one-half of the bills for building schoolhouses here, and maintaining them, I do not propose that they shall be turned into dance halls.

Mr. TUCKER. The assembly hall, anyway, is a very important part of the school work, and where they have these halls, they make very good use of them, as Dr. Small can tell you about the Eastern.

That is not the point. The point is that we need this building for the graded schools. It is very much needed. The population is growing very rapidly, and we have had no school buildings there for several years, so that the school buildings are not keeping pace in any way with the population of that section; and what we ask is that you will restore to the bill that $45,000 for that site. That is all we are asking at this time for that school.

Here is a matter that Senator Gallinger is specially interested in—and I am sure we all are—the Anacostia Flats. That is not new legislation. The last two or three years, through the influence of Senator Gallinger, we have had $100,000 appropriated, half out of the General Government revenues and half out of the District revenues.

Senator GALLINGER. As I understand, the Engineer Commissioner says that he can not use any more money this year, and does not need it.

Mr. TUCKER. That is a question. They have gotten hold of the Bieber property now, and they can go ahead. That is what held them up. Whether that is a fact or not, that statement has been made; but it is my duty to present this. We fought for this for years and years, and we want to see that work go on, and we do not want to see any halt in it on account of lack of funds.

There is a balance available of $245,000 for this work on the Anacostia Flats, so that this work will go along. You need not worry.

Senator GALLINGER. That is going to be one of the best investments that has been made.

Mr. TUCKER. There is no doubt about that, and we appreciate your part in the matter.

The next thing is an appropriation that is in the estimates, for a public convenience station at the intersection of 15th and H Streets NE. That is a point where many important roads meet. There are an avenue and two important streets that cross at that point, and there are two roads that come in there from the State of Maryland.

Senator GALLINGER. That is right at the White House Station, is it not?

Mr. TUCKER. That is right at the White House Station, and a large number of people go to that point, and that necessity has been felt for a long time there. The estimate provides $1,000 for a site, and $10,000 for a building, which makes a very modest sum, $11,000).

Mr. SMITH of Maryland. That $11,000 is for what purpose?

Mr. TUCKER. $1,000 for a site and $10,000 for a building, making $11,000 altogether.

Senator SMITH of Maryland. For what purpose?

Mr. TUCKER. For this public convenience station at the intersection of all these important streets and roads at Fifteenth and H Streets NE., where the White House Station is.

Senator GALLINGER. I will venture to inquire whether or not, if we should undertake that work, we would be able to go through with it without a public meeting being held to denounce the idea of locating a public convenience station at that point. We appropriated for and had partly built one in the northwest section and we had to pull it down, after $8,000 had been expended. We tried to get one at another congested point, and we had such a storm of protests that we did not dare to start in on it. As a result of that, in the last year or two we have not tried to do anything in that line.

Mr. TUCKER. Yes; that is a fact. Those people up there are human, and they have the same failings that humanity has generally, but I do think that the necessity for it is pretty well felt, and I believe that a site could be selected there that would not interfere much with private interests.

Senator GALLINGER. You could not get an underground station for $10,000, could you?

Mr. TUCKER. No, sir.

Senator GALLINGER. That is the most desirable form of convenience station.

Mr. TUCKER. Yes; in my opinion that would be the best. The commissioners have looked into it pretty carefully, and I think they understand where they are to put it. We try to keep away from the question of sites. We do not want anybody to think we have an interest in real estate, and we do not suggest to committees sites; but we would like you to allow us $11,000 for that needed improvement.

I have here the question of the inebriate hospital. I simply want to say that our association has indorsed that as a general proposition. You have listened to arguments on that matter, and I do not want to go into it, but we have seen the necessity for that for years, and we want it. We have some of those people in our section, as they have them in other sections.

Now, I am down to the question of the Borland amendment. I want to say just a few words on that. As a general proposition, we do not believe that it is right to assess abutting property owners for the paving of these streets.

Senator GALLINGER. That has been presented to us by quite a number of gentlemen, and I think the chairman will agree with me that we pretty fully understand it.

Mr. TUCKER. Yes; but now, as to the special proposal, it would not be right to do it at this time, because of the bearing that it would have on us. The streets in the northwestern section have been paved until they are less than 4 per cent unpaved to-day, and we have had to pave them out of the general funds, and have had to repave them over and over again out of the general funds, and it would hardly seem fair now, when it comes our chance to get a little improvement in East Washington, to say, "Gentlemen, put your hands in your own pockets and pay it all."

Senator GALLINGER. No.

Mr. TUCKER. This is an opening of new subdivisions, and especially in these narrow streets, where a man is not able to pay, as against a wide street, to help him out if it is a wide street. Here will be a street, and then there is a 40-foot avenue and a little house going back from that street, and the owner would have to pay for paving that avenue and the street, too.

Senator SMITH of Maryland. I think we understand that.

Mr. TUCKER. I have given you the facts on this as briefly as I could. I should like Prof. Hall to make a little statement to you about the Patterson Park proposition.

STATEMENT OF PERCIVAL HALL.

Mr. HALL. I am chairman of the Committee on Parks and Spaces of the Northeast Washington Citizens' Association. Mr. Chairman and gentlemen of the Committee, Mr Tucker asked you to kindly give me a few minutes here in regard to the Patterson tract for a public park. This Patterson tract park was advocated in the estimates of the District Commissioners, and an estimate was made in that report for $375,000 for the acquisition of the tract. That was cut out of the bill as it was finally reported.

The Northeast Washington Citizens' Association is very anxious to have that public park. I will call your attention to the fact that Northeast Washington has no public parks of any consequence. There is Stanton Square, some 3 acres, which is all cut up by walks and fountains and flower beds, and so forth, and we could say that half of Lincoln Park is also in the northeast. That is also 3 acres. That is 6 acres altogether. Really, we have no public parks at all.

Senator GALLINGER. Did you not think, when we made parks out of the grounds surrounding two forts in the eastern part of the . District that it was a benefit to your section?

Mr. HALL. I should like to call your attention to the fact that this ground you are speaking of, on the other side of the Anacostia River, is inaccessible at present.

Senator GALLINGER. Yes.

Mr. HALL. In regard to the Patterson tract, I should like to say a word in regard to its accessibility. It is on Florida Avenue, and the Capital Traction Co. runs cars by there every six minutes or so. Those cars come from the navy yard and go right by the tract, and it makes it easily available to everybody, including the boys and girls of our high schools, as they are now situated. Any athletic team from any of these high schools can get there in 15 minutes without change of cars.

As to the general situation of the tract, that is enough.

As to its present condition, I should like to say a word. It is already a natural park. The part on Florida Avenue is level and is being used now by boys and various teams, and so forth, to a great extent, through the kindness of the owners, as a park. The northeastern part of it is covered with one of the most beautiful pieces of woods that is now in the District of Columbia so close in to the city, and it lends itself most beautifully to the purposes of a park.

Further than that, I should like to say one word more, that this tract is included in the park scheme. I understand that nowadays the commissioners will not recommend any tract that is not so included, and I think that is correct. We believe in that, too. We feel that that tract should be acquired as one of the links in the park system. It was so arranged in the McMillan park scheme that this should be one of the links; but it is available for building at any time and will soon be taken up, and one of the links in that scheme will be gone forever. I think it is very important, to carry out the McMillan park scheme, that this should be acquired.

There is only one other point, I think. The East Washington Citizens' Association differs from the proposal of the Commissioners of the District of Columbia on one very important thing, and that is with regard to the assessment of benefits. In regard to that it is very much the same as in regard to the paving of the streets. For many years, without any protest, the citizens of the northeast have been assisting in buying these tracts of land in the northwest—Montrose Park, in Georgetown, and so on—and it is now proposed that large tracts shall be bought along Rock Creek. We are glad to have them. All of those will be purchased on the basis of half and half. The proposition, as it appears in the recommendations and estimates of the commissioners, is that one-third of the cost of this tract, of $125,000, shall be assessed as benefits—at least that much shall be assessed as benefits. The location of that tract is between the railroad and New York Avenue on one side. If you will look at this map you will see this in blue is the tract. This is the Columbia Institution for the Deaf, which is held in trust by the Government of the United States [indicating on map], and these are the railroad tracks and the roundhouses here, and so forth. This section is all full of poor people here, and that would mean an assessing of $125,000 down to an area in here [indicating on map]. We feel that we should like to have that one thing changed. We should like to have $1,300,000 for the acquisitions in Rock Creek Valley on the half-and-half principle, and we should like to have Patterson Park on the same basis, $375,000, appropriated on the half-and-half plan.

We want the tract, and we should like very much to have it in the same way that the northwest and the other parts of the city have had their parks, for which we have helped to pay. I thank you, gentlemen.

Senator SMITH of Maryland. Would you rather not have it if you had to pay the one-third?

Mr. HALL. Our citizens have taken that stand, that they feel that it should be on the half-and-half basis. We have never had any parks in that section. As I understand it, some of those little squares were simply acquired by chopping off the ends of streets, and there was no assessment made for them—Stanton Square and Lincoln Park.

Senator GALLINGER. The owners of that land are not inclined to sell at the price named by the commissioners.

Senator SMITH of Maryland. Did not the trustees of that estate appear before us?

Senator GALLINGER. Yes. When it comes to condemnation of that land, what do you suppose it will cost the Government?

Mr. HALL. I do not know. They have condemned a strip, I think, up on New York Avenue. It could be ascertained how much that cost.

Senator GALLINGER. We have not had a very satisfactory experience in condemning land in the District for the Government.

Mr. HALL. The assessment is $3,500 per acre, and figuring on the basis of two-thirds of the value, that would mean $5,000 per acre. There are eighty-one and a fraction acres, so that $400,000 would be, I should think, a fair price for it. Three hundred and seventy-five thousand dollars is put down there. In a personal talk with the commissioners our association suggested $400,000, and exactly why they took that figure, $375,000, I am not aware.

Senator GALLINGER. It is not a matter of what this committee would do or what the Senate would do, if it had its own way. If I had my way, there would not be any suggestion about turning money back into the Treasury this year. I would use the money that the District has raised, and put an equal sum of the money of the Government with that, and do these things; but others do not agree with that. Now, considering the urgency of the various interests in the District, the building of schoolhouses, the building of a new hospital, the building of an inebriate asylum, and the fact that we ought to have a building for the feeble-minded —it is a shame that we have not one——

Mr. HALL. I have heard of that.

Senator GALLINGER (continuing). In view of all those things, do you really think that at the present time it is good policy for the Government to spend much more money for parks?

Mr. HALL. Well, I do, yes, sir; in regard to our section there. There has been a complete change in the last 10 years. Formerly there were whole blocks that were vacant where the boys got out and played ball. Since the building of that car line through there, there have been blocks and blocks of houses, as Mr. Tucker told you, built there; and those people that live there are the kind of people that have families, and they have not big yards and places for the children to play. The building up of that section has resulted in depriving them of the playgrounds that they ought to have. On Sunday that place is full of teams playing, and there are teams there every day, and one of the things is that this has already been laid out in streets and might be subdivided at any time. Already the surveyors have laid out a tentative plan for cutting that up. Patterson Avenue runs through there and several other streets. All of that land is flat and all ready for building, and any time anybody wants to start there, the plan is laid out for cutting the ground up and putting the street through. If we lose that land, we lose the best chance for a convenient park, and that important link in the McMillan park plan is gone forever. I really think it is a very pressing and important thing.

Senator GALLINGER. This matter was pretty thoroughly discussed before the committee.

Mr. HALL. I want to emphasize the fact that we would rather not have the park than to impose upon those poor people the assessment of one-third of the cost. There is no speculative land there. It is simply a matter of those poor people there.

Senator GALLINGER. I think it is an injustice that any such thing should be proposed. That plan was not applied to the parks in any other portion of the city, and there is no reason why it should be applied in the eastern section of the city, where the people are less able to pay than in some other sections.

Mr. TUCKER. I am sorry that Prof. Small, of the Eastern High School, was not able to remain any longer, but he has left a map, with a statement attached. I do not know what is in it, but I will present it to the committee.

STATEMENT OF MARVIN M. McLEAN, PRESIDENT OF THE BROOKLAND CITIZENS' ASSOCIATION.

Mr. McLEAN. We noticed that our items for Brookland were presented to the House committee, but this year they left us out.

Senator GALLINGER. This is for streets?

Mr. McLEAN. Yes, sir; for street improvement. The commissioners estimated for $25,000 worth of improvements, including 10 items. As president of our association, I have gone over that list as carefully as I could, and selected three that we consider most important.

Senator GALLINGER. Address yourself to those three items.

Mr. McLEAN. The first is "Otis Street, Twelfth Street to Fourteenth Street, grade." That amount is $4,200. That item was included by the Senate committee last year, and got into the bill, but was struck out by the House. It has been well considered, and we think it is a very fine item, and we should like for it to go in.

Senator GALLINGER. It was dropped in conference, I believe.

Mr. McLEAN. Yes; it was dropped in conference.

The next item is not a very large one, but is most important. It is "Thirteenth Street, Franklin Street to Irving Street, grade, $2,600." Two blocks have been improved on that street coming from Rhode Island Avenue north, and this is a continuation of the work, and really puts it in very much better condition, and opens the street up to the Episcopal Church of Brookland, which is attended from several directions, and this would be a very important improvement for that church and for that section of the city.

The next item that I marked was "Kearney Street, Fourteenth Street to Eighteenth Street, grade and improve, $5,500." That is to macadamize. Kearney Street has been graded from Fourteenth Street to Eighteenth Street. That street has been about one-half completed, and if you macadamize four blocks, that completes the work that was intended originally, and it extends through the heart of Brookland to Sherwood's Addition, and that is nearer grade than any other street in the center of our city.

There is one little item that was not estimated for, which personally I am extremely anxious to see go in, and that is to grade the two lots adjacent to the Brookland Public School, that were acquired last year. We acquired the lots, and they are now being used as playgrounds, and some apparatus is on them. One corner is about 5 or 6 feet below grade, and it could be graded for a very small amount, and fenced. The amount we have estimated is $500. If you can consider that without a recommendation, we have gone over it very carefully, and it would make the ground just like it should be for use.

Senator GALLINGER. Have you gone over the matter with the Engineer Commissioner as to the probable cost, or is that your own estimate?

Mr. McLEAN. That is our estimate. I live right across the street from it, and I understand the cost of grading, and that is a good, close estimate. That is to fence both sides of the ground and fill it in with dirt. That is all the grading amounts to. That would also fence off an objectionable stable that is there now, that is within 20 feet ot the school building.

Senator GALLINGER. We do not often make appropriations to build fences.

Mr. McLEAN. In grading and improving you have fenced out there. I do not know where you made the appropriation, but it is done. Ours is fenced.

Senator GALLINGER. Last year we appropriated $100,000 for repair and improvement of school buildings and grounds. This year the House ga e $115,000 for those purposes.

Mr. McLEAN. It is possible that we might be able to get it out of that.

Senator GALLINGER. I was just wondering if you might not get this particular thing out of that item. Is this to repair the street?

Mr. McLEAN. No; to grade the ground.

Senator GALLINGER. I think that is where you have got to look for it.

Mr. McLEAN. If we can get it there, it will suit us just the same as that.

Senator GALLINGER. I think you had better get it there.

Mr. McLEAN. Those three we have considered very carefully, and we should like something to go in for our section.

Senator GALLINGER. You are certainly very modest in your demands.

Mr. McLEAN. I am president of our association, and I think I speak the sentiment of the members generally when I say that we are very much opposed to dividing that appropriation for the Central High School. We think that is one of the best things ever done for the District, and we hope it will stand.

STATEMENT OF EDWARD J. NEWCOMB.

Mr. NEWCOMB. I represent the Public Improvement Association of Congress Heights. The commissioners have recommended to Congress the improvement of eight short streets in Congress Heights, and the House has seen fit to cut out every one of them. Cur section, as you know, Senator Gallinger—I have seen you there frequently and in my place of business—is a poor section. It was built up entirely by the working class of people, and the people all own their own homes, and therefore they are people of moderate means, and can not afford to be put to much expense. In the last five or six years we have been very fortunate in getting such improvements as water and sewer and gas, and we are now trying to get sidewalks, and in some section of the town we have sidewalks. In those sections in which we have asked improvements of the streets, the commissioners have informed us that sidewalks would be impossible until these particular streets had been improved, and as the place has grown up and become thickly populated, we feel that these improvements are absolutely necessary. We have not asked for any other thing whatsoever in the way of an appropriation for this section. In some of the streets we have tried to get our automobile fire department to go through, and in their efforts to go through they have gotten stuck and had to send for the wreck wagon to get out. These improvements, as I say, are absolutely essential and necessary, and we would ask that your honorable committee restore them to their proper place.

Senator GALLINGER. Have you a list there?

Mr. NEWCOMB. Yes, sir.

Senator GALLINGER. Could you select four out of those eight streets that you think are the most important?

Mr. NEWCOMB. Mr. McKay is the chairman of the committee, and he will answer that question.

Mr. McKAY. The streets are so short and it is so small an item, that it seems a shame not to have them all in.

Mr. NEWCOMB. We will be glad to omit one particular street. Take No. 11, "Highview Place, Nichols Avenue to Brothers Place, grade and improve, $500." That should have gone through to Raleigh Place, two blocks. That is a street that is 8 to 10 inches deep in sand, where the fire department could positively not go. I had occasion some time ago to take home in my machine a lady who fell and broke her arm, and I was three hours getting out. In fact, I had to shovel my way out.

Senator GALLINGER. That would extend to Raleigh Place?

Mr. NEWCOMB. Yes, a distance of one block further.

Senator GALLINGER. That would make $1,000 instead of $500.

Mr. McKAY. It ought to be $1,500, because it is quite a deep cut.

Senator GALLINGER. Highview Place to Raleigh Place.

Mr. NEWCOMB. Yes.

Senator GALLINGER. We will consider that. Is there any other street that you are interested in?

Mr. McKAY. "Fifth Street, Alabama Avenue to Savannah Street, and Savannah Street, Fourth Street to Randle Place, grade and improve, $1,800."

Senator GALLINGER. That is $1,800?

Mr. McKAY. That is $1,800, and it should be $2,500.

Senator GALLINGER. I am afraid if we go to increasing any of these things——

Mr. McKAY. All right; just make it $1,800. Then we have Waclark Place and Fourth Street, Nichols Avenue to Savannah Street.

Senator GALLINGER. "Waclark Place, Nichols Avenue to Raleigh Place, grade and improve, $800."

Mr. McKAY. That amount is $800.

Senator GALLINGER. Then you have another?

Mr. McKAY. Yes, "Fourth Street, Nichols Avenue to Savannah Street, grade and improve, $1,000."

Then there is also "Sixth Street, Alabama Avenue to Savannah Street, grade and improve, $1,100."

Then there is "Seventh Street, Alabama Avenue to Nichols Avenue, grade and improve, $2,300."

It is very important that that should be improved, because the church is situated there, and it is almost impossible to get there for a funeral.

The commissioners for years have asked for an appropriation for "Trenton Place, west of Nichols Avenue, grade and improve, $4,200." They have asked $5,000, and now they ask $4,200 for making that improvement; but if we could get the others they are more important than this one.

Senator GALLINGER. Then I will just mark that one off.

Mr. McKAY. I might state that 75 per cent of the abutting property on these small streets is improved and is owned by the property owners who live there, and the commissioners made a special trip out there and picked out these streets to improve.

Senator GALLINGER. Can you give any reason why the House did not allow you an appropriation for some of these streets?

Mr. NEWCOMB. I think it was because we did not come down and ask for it.

Mr. McKAY. I think it was because they just made a general cut, and cut everything.

Mr. NEWCOMB. Last year we asked for appropriations and did not get any.

Senator GALLINGER. We will give careful consideration to these items. I know your neighborhood pretty well.

Mr. NEWCOMB. Yes, sir; we see you out there frequently.

STATEMENT OF HERMAN J. SCHULTEIS.

Mr. SCHULTEIS. I only wanted to ask if the amendment which was in last year's bill, which went out in conference, would be restored this year. This is the bill H. R. 28499.

I will say that Mr. Swan, the secretary of the Columbia Polytechnic Institute for the blind, called down at the office of the commissioners, and he was asked to sit aside somewhere, for the last two days before the estimates were completed at the District Commissioners, and he did not get an opportunity to present the matter. On the third day they sent for me, saying that he had been put in a side room there, to sit down, and had not had an opportunity to see the commissioners. I went personally and saw the commissioners, and they said they were in favor of it, but they had sent up the estimates that day; that if they could get them back, they would recommend it, and in case they did not get them back they would make the fact known to the committee in any way that was desirable, either by telephone or by writing a letter stating that they approved of it and that it should have gone into the estimates this year. Unfortunately, the matter was dropped out of the last bill, out of the deficiency bill of the last Congress in conference. It had been agreed upon and was in one of the printed bills—I saw it in print—that they should have part of this money. I think the committee agreed on $3,000, but that $3,000 would not buy even the Merganthaler machine, because I have a list here, sent to me from the secretary of the Coulmbia Polytechnic Institute, in which he gives the items that are necessary, and he asked for $6,000 to be appropriated, to be expended under the direction of the Commissioners of the District of Columbia, that list is as follows:

Item: for the $6,000 appropriation to be expended under the directions of Commissioners of the District of Columbia.

1 Mergenthaler linotype machine	$3, 600
1 12 by 18 Golding jobber press	400
1 Monitor stitching machine	200
16 post-card cuts	300
Instructions and employment for the blind	500
Instruction by linotype and switchboard operator for the blind	1, 000
Total	6, 000

I want to state that this switchboard matter adds another trade to the number that the blind people can follow. It has only been recently discovered that they can do that, just as it has been discovered recently that they can operate a linotype machine, and the Linotype Journal, a paper that is published by the Linotype people, in this month's issue, has given a long and very interesting story about the particular lady who does that work here in the city. This is the first blind person in the world who has been able to operate—who has ever tried to operate—a linotype machine. This is a bulletin of the linotype people.

In their journal or magazine called "Voices from Darkland," on page 22 they give a description of the way it was discovered that blind people could do this work. It will add a new trade for the blind. They have only 18 trades at present. I have here a list of them. These trades are, printing, stitching, binding of books, broom making, chair caning, chair repairing, seine making, crocheting, hammock making, machine sewing, hand sewing, music teaching (pianoforte, organ, and violin), voice culture, massage, and typewriting.

There are just those 18 professions and trades that are open to the blind, and this will add two more. It will add linotype operating and switchboard operating. This would give employment in telephone offices to large numbers of blind people, because in the Baltimore hotels, where they have three of them now operating switchboards, they say that the blind girls give much more satisfactory service than those with sight. They have a keenness of hearing that people with sight do not seem to have. They can operate a telephone switchboard much better than people who can see, and, as there are in these offices a great many positions of this kind, there is great opportunity for their employment.

Senator GALLINGER. You say there are now three girls so employed in Baltimore?

Mr. SCHULTEIS. Yes, sir; and it is presumed that as soon as it is discovered that they can do this work just as well as if not better than those who have their sight, and that they give better satisfaction, it will open a new employment to the blind that has never been opened to them before.

Senator GALLINGER. Let me ask you about this Mergenthaler machine. Notwithstanding that I have a knowledge of printing, I am not very familiar with the operation of the linotype machine. How is a blind woman going to read her copy?

Mr. SCHULTEIS. She has to have a reader. They have to employ a reader, whom they can employ at about $6 a week. Any little girl that knows how to read and write can act for them, and the pay for linotype work is so great—about $29 a week—that they can afford to pay $6 for a reader, and then they will make more than they can at any of the trades or crafts that I have enumerated. They can afford to pay a person to read for them, and that has to be done.

Senator GALLINGER. Can they afford to pay a person to read, and yet do that work at less than a person with sight would be willing to do it?

Mr. SCHULTEIS. Yes, sir; and the printers—the linotype operators—do not object to this invasion by the blind people. They say, "If they can do that work, all right; we are not going to do anything to lay a straw in their way."

Senator GALLINGER. Now, I want to ask you a couple of questions about the Polytechnic Institute. We have made some appropriations for that institution.

Mr. SCHULTEIS. Yes, sir; two appropriations in Congress in the past.

Senator GALLINGER. I thought there were three.

Mr. SCHULTEIS. You may be right about it.

Senator GALLINGER. How many people have they there at the present time?

Mr. SCHULTEIS. I do not know. I have here one of their magazines, which gives a number of cards, and their pictures, and what they do.

Senator GALLINGER. Never mind that. You do not know?

Mr. SCHULTEIS. No, sir; I do not know.

Senator GALLINGER. We made an appropriation for the purchase of a printing press for them to make colored post cards.

Mr. SCHULTEIS. Yes, sir.

Senator GALLINGER. Have they ever done anything with those post cards?

Mr. SCHULTEIS. Yes, sir; they have done remarkably well.

Senator GALLINGER. Somebody made the suggestion to me that the post cards were purchased, and were not made by these people.

Mr. SCHULTEIS. Whoever made that suggestion was in error. I have here samples of the various processes the cards have to go through. Here is one card in one color, and here is another card in another color. They have made a great deal of profit out of those cards. They are able to live on the proceeds.

Senator GALLINGER. Do they not necessarily have the help of people with sight in the making of these cards?

Mr. SCHULTEIS. There is one instructor, Mr. Dineen, who superintends the work and helps them. I do not know what particular part he does. I know that they do stitching. For this magazine, for example, they do everything.

Senator GALLINGER. They could not determine the proper coloring on these cards, could they?

Mr. SCHULTEIS. No, sir. They can put the red through, for instance, and the other colors they can put through.

Senator GALLINGER. If they are told how to do it?

Mr. SCHULTEIS. Yes. Then they can put through another on another plate, and then the third one.

Senator GALLINGER. What does that read on the corner of that card, there? Does it not say "Clinedinst Photograph Company"?

Mr. Schulteis. Yes, sir. Clinedinst made the photograph from which that plate was cut. Clinedinst took a picture of that building, and this plate was cut from that photograph, and Congress appropriated the money to have that cut made. Clinedinst had nothing to do with making that card; never saw it or had it in his office. Nobody but the Polytechnic Institute handled that card. They have been able to do so well with these cards that they can take this entire legacy that was left to them a short time ago and apply it to the payment for the building, every penny. They were left $5,000, and then $10,000. They will have left the interest to pay on the debt that remains. There is still a mortgage on the building. But they are making enough money, on what Congress has enabled them to do, to be able to be self-sustaining; and if they get this linotype machine and the switchboard they can give instruction to all the blind in the city without any cost. They have a letter with the District Commissioners now, offering to educate any blind white person in the District of Columbia.

Mr. Schulteis. I want to add that it is my belief that if Congress gives them the money to get this linotype machine with, other institutions in the different States, when they find that it is possible for blind people to do this work, will also buy machines, and it will enable people who are sightless, all over the world, to add one more trade to their narrow, limited number now, as well as the switchboard matter.

Senator Gallinger. You say that this will add two more trades?

Mr. Schulteis. To the number that they are now able to perform; yes, sir.

Senator Gallinger. How many are there in this lsit?

Mr. Schulteis. There are 18 there. That is all there are anywhere in the world. There is not another thing that they can do that is profitable; and this will be highly profitable, and it will be more in the nature of a profession than anything they are now doing, except possibly printing.

(At 2.10 o'clock p. m., the subcommittee took a recess until 3 o'clock p. m.)

AFTERNOON SESSION.

The subcommittee met, at the expiration of the recess. at 3 o'clock p. m.

EMERGENCY HOSPITAL.

STATEMENTS OF SURG. GEN. C. F. STOKES, CHIEF BUREAU OF MEDICINE AND SURGERY, UNITED STATES ARMY, DR. WILLIAM P. CARR, AND MRS. T. T. GAFF.

Senator Gallinger. Mr. Chairman, these good people are here relative to an amendment which Senator Brandegee offered, appropriating $50,000 toward the construction of a new Emergency Hospital, to take the place of that of which they have been dispossessed by the Government buying the land on Pennsylvania Avenue, between Fourteenth and Fifteenth Streets, or of which they will be dispossessed immediately, and they have purchased a lot and raised a good deal of money, and they will tell us all about it. They want a little government^l ^^l^ ^eyond what they have heretofore received

Senator SMITH of Maryland. I think you formerly got an appropriation for this institution.

Senator GALLINGER. There was an appropriation of $50,000 two years ago.

Senator SMITH of Maryland. I think that some time ago I had some talk in my office about it. You have raised something over $100,000?

Surg. Gen. STOKES. Yes, sir.

Senator SMITH of Maryland. And also I believe you have purchased a lot, as I remember, and have had the design of the buildings, and all that, to cost about $300,000; is that correct?

Surg. Gen. STOKES. That is correct.

Senator SMITH of Maryland. I think that I have heard about it. Some one else was present, I believe, at that time.

Mrs. GAFF. I was with Dr. Stokes.

Senator SMITH of Maryland. If there is anything further you want to say about it, we shall be glad to hear you.

Mrs. GAFF. The only thing I wanted to say was that the reason we felt that we ought to have more help was because the conditions in Washington were very different from those in other cities, and it was increasingly difficult to raise money here for that reason. The people here are not able to contribute large sums as they can and do contribute them in other cities, because there are practically no industries here, and the population consists principally of Government people and retired Army and Navy officers, and people who live on fixed incomes, and of course in that case they can not give any very large amounts; so that in the campaign we got up, while they very gladly contributed, we had but $120,000 contributed when we were trying to raise $300,000.

Senator GALLINGER. How much did you raise?

Mrs. GAFF. We raised only about $120,000. That is all we could really count on. There was a little more raised.

Senator SMITH of Maryland. That is a good deal of money, we think in the country.

Senator GALLINGER. Yes. You raised over $100,000?

Mrs. GAFF. Yes; $120,000, of which we had to spend $10,000 for the expenses of the campaign and one thing and another, and then there is $10,000 which the people who signed are not able to pay up, so that that brought us down to $120,000, so that in reality that is all we have.

Senator GALLINGER. You have $50,000 that has been appropriated previously?

Mrs. GAFF. Yes; two years ago.

Senator SMITH of Maryland. That $50,000 is not included?

Mrs. GAFF. No, sir.

Senator SMITH of Maryland. Now you are asking for $50,000 more?

Mrs. GAFF. $50,000 more, because we feel that here it would take us so long a time to raise that amount of money.

Senator SMITH of Maryland. You have a lot, have you not?

Mrs. GAFF. Oh, yes; we have our lot.

Senator SMITH of Maryland. In whose name is that lot?

Mrs. GAFF. Dr. Carr can answer that.

Dr. CARR. It is in the name of the Central Dispensary or Emergency Hospital. It is an incorporated institution, under the direction of a board of directors of 33 men.

Senator GALLINGER. How much did your lot cost, approximately?

Mrs. GAFF. About $57,000 I think our lot was, all told.

Senator GALLINGER. That is all paid for?

Mrs. GAFF. Yes; and we have two little houses which I think are all right, if we spend a thousand dollars on them, for the nurses' home. Then we have to build a garage.

Senator SMITH of Maryland. What is the estimated cost of the building you want to put up?

Dr. CARR. Mr. Chairman. I have those figures here, and I thought that after Mrs. Gaff got through with her statement I would give you those figures.

Mrs. GAFF. Senator Smith would like to have them now. I have said practically everything that there is to say, except that the feeling is that if the Congress could help us so that we would start well equipped and not have to borrow so much, I think other people will be much more willing to give us the balance of the money we need—about $85,000 or $100,000—if they feel that it is a successful cause they are contributing to.

Senator SMITH of Maryland. As I understand, you have now $170,000, have you not?

Mrs. GAFF. We have now $178,000 that we can really count on absolutely.

Senator SMITH of Maryland. And you have bought your lot?

Mrs. GAFF. We have our lot and our nurses' home, except that it has to be fixed up a little.

Senator SMITH of Maryland. And how much money is the building you propose to build going to cost, according to the estimate which I presume you have?

Mrs. GAFF. The estimates are that it will cost, complete with everything, about $315,000.

Senator SMITH of Maryland. $315,000?

Mrs. GAFF. Yes, sir; but then you see, Senator, we have to have from $10,000 to $15,000 in bank for running expenses. We can not take out every cent we have.

Senator SMITH of Maryland. Where do you get your money for running this institution?

Mrs. GAFF. How do you mean?

Mrs. GAFF. How do you mean? What do we earn? It is from our pay rooms, and I think the X-ray gives something.

Senator GALLINGER. And a small appropriation from Congress each year for indigent patients.

Senator SMITH of Maryland. We appropriate a sum for that, too?

Senator GALLINGER. For the indigent patients, $17,000.

Mrs. GAFF. The money you appropriate for the indigents we have to earn, and the Board of Charities now makes the contract, and they allow us $1.20 a day and so much for ambulance calls, and so much for emergency cases, and of course what they allow does not really cover the cost.

Senator SMITH of Maryland. Oh, no; I can see that. I think you people who do this hard work deserve a great deal of credit and ought to be helped.

Mrs. GAFF. We raised a good deal among ourselves.

Senator GALLINGER. Mrs. Stotesbury gave you $10,000?

Mrs. GAFF. Yes; Mrs. Stotesbury gave us $10,000. That was a kind of a wedding gift. I spent $3,000 for the electric ambulance, and $1,000 for building a little shed and buying some things, and then I had to take $2,500 of it to go into the campaign fund, and now I have $3,500 left.

Surg. Gen. STOKES. The directors asked me, if you cared to hear me, to point out the needs of such a hospital and what it really means in this community.

Senator SMITH of Maryland. We will be very glad to hear you.

Surg. Gen. STOKES. I have just finished my tour of duty as surgeon general, and I am absolutely disinterested. The chances are that I shall leave this community. I am here on a public-spirited errand.

It has always seemed to me, and I always find, that when I go before your committees in the Senate or in the House I never bring any real new facts to the committee, and if I can succeed in refreshing your memories and emphasizing certain points, I shall be very glad.

It seems to me that there is an obligation on the part of Congress to take care of the thousands who come here repeatedly, annually. There is no proper provision to-day.

We have a large number of residents here in the diplomatic service. What is to become of them in case of emergency?

When these big crowds gather here, a stand may give way if it is at an inaugural parade.

We may have, and have had, large fires in theaters, or stampedes there.

I had unusual experiences years ago, in New York City, in three big hospitals, two of which were emergency hospitals; one on Chambers Street, in 1883, when we had a stampede on the Brooklyn Bridge the day that it was opened, and some 50 people were disabled there and 12 or 14 were killed. Suppose that we had an emergency of that sort here. There is no provision whatever for it.

Every day we have street accidents, street car accidents, and motor mishaps.

We are putting up new buildings. Structures fall and injure people, and they need immediate care and attention, and that attention and care can not be given in a makeshift emergency plant and relief station. These people can not be moved. It may be a case of hemorrhage. It may be a question of preventing infection. One of my friends in your distinguished body had an attack of vertigo and was carried from a park to that hospital; and there have been others.

Take cases of sunstroke, where what is done in a few minutes means a question of life or death; or you are in convulsions; or you may take any one of a thousand and one conditions that might be mentioned, and if that hospital is not built, there is no provision. The man who is picked up in the street might be—although it makes no difference who he is—some one from your body, or he might be some millionaire who was temporarily residing here, or he might be a poor man in the District. You can not discriminate. He must be looked after properly. To put up a makeshift structure and not have it properly equipped is, in my opinion, not doing our full duty; and I feel, too, that good is coming to this community through the training that the internes get, and there are many of them located here.

I am on the board of regents of the College of Surgeons of America, that has to do with the passing on the qualifications of surgeons as to their fitness. The surgeons in this community are hampered by reason of the fact that the facilities for qualifying are decidedly restricted. I think that is another feature of it. We want a good representation here, just as every State wants representation, in that college.

Take cases of gas poisoning. They are very common, as well as ordinary suicides or accidental poisonings.

I could go on still further, but I do not want to burden you with that.

In our building program and hospitals in the Navy, we have built more hospital establishments, probably, than any other organization in the world. Within the last two years we have built about 12 hospitals.

In connection with the plans for this new hospital we have had the benefit of the advice of some of our skilled men, so that our plans have been drawn up in an economic way, and every feature has been carefully considered.

Of course, for a building like this the Emergency Hospital is a little more expensive than where you have great space. When you come to consider the cost per cubic foot, it is broken up into small surfaces for purposes of administration. So far as my experience goes on that board of administration it has been excellent. I feel, too, that it is not the board of directors' intention to lie down, if we are fortunate enough to get money, and not seek further help, but I think if Congress will recognize us with an appropriation, and we get something going and have something to show what has been done, others will follow and we will get further help. I think if you saw the building and plans you would be very much pleased with the whole project.

I am about to leave the board of directors, but I think that if you do side with the board of directors it will be in a public-spirited and disinterested work, which deserves some recognition. It is a very interesting work, and will help a lot of people, but all they get out of it is the pleasure of doing that work, and it takes a lot of time. I hope I have not spoken too long.

Senator GALLINGER. Before Dr. Carr addresses the committee, I want to say that two years ago this matter was very acute. There was great danger of this hospital being lost to the city absolutely, and as some of these good people know, I took quite a lively interest in it, and my judgment then was that it a success the appropriation ought to have been $100,000; but there were conditions surrounding it then, and difficulties, that I will not enumerate, and eventually, in conjunction with my associates, we put in the bill $50,000, and that was allowed in conference. I have many times since then regretted that I did not make a more strenuous effort to get $100,000, because I felt then, as I feel now, that that is an amount that the Government can well afford to invest in this institution; so that I feel very warmly in favor of the amendment that is now before the committee to add another $50,000, which undoubtedly will result in the completion of this splendid institution. As I understand it, if this $50,000 is allowed, Mrs. Gaff and others who were instrumental in raising over $100,000 by a campaign in the city, will again take up the work with a view of getting whatever may be needed in addition to this. I think I am right in saying that.

Mrs. GAFF. Absolutely.

Senator SMITH of Maryland. I want to say that in regard to this matter, I am in full cooperation with you. I think these people have shown a spirit, and have secured results, that should be encouraged by the Government. The Government gets the benefit of this, largely, and I do think that private parties, the ladies and those who are giving their time and working for it, should be rewarded and helped out, and so far as I am concerned I feel that I am willing and glad to help you.

Mrs. GAFF. That is very kind of you.

Senator SMITH of Maryland. If you were to get the $100,000, you would have $65,000 yet to raise?

Mr. GAFF. Eighty thousand dollars.

Senator SMITH of Maryland. You are raising more than the Government is giving you. The Government is not giving you one-third of what is required?

Mrs. GAFF. No, sir.

Senator SMITH of Maryland. And then you have to support this hospital by private contributions, I understand?

Mrs. GAFF. Yes, sir.

STATEMENT OF DR. WILLIAM P. CARR.

Dr. CARR. It might seem useless for me to say anything, when you are all so favorable to the proposition. I wanted, though, to give you just exactly the state of affairs, as I have been a sort of custodian of records. We came before the committee just a few years ago with this proposition, which was a resolution passed by the board:

If Congress will appropriate for this purpose $100,000, we agree to add to this sum the money and property now in possession of the hospital, and we agree in addition to build and equip on the lot which we own an emergency hospital, modern and adequate in every way, suitable for its intended purpose in city.

Senator Gallinger has just told you that we did not get that appropriation of $100,000, although this committee did recommend the $100,000, but we did get $50,000. In conference it was cut down $50,000. With that encouragement, the directors made a strenuous campaign and succeeded in getting from the citizens of Washington pledges and money to the amount of $141,000. Ten thousand dollars of that was spent in the expenses of the campaign, however. The net results of the campaign are $86,000 in cash now in bank, and $46,000 in pledges still out, of which, from the way they have been paying up, I think, we can reasonably expect to get $36,000.

An ideal site has been secured and paid for at a cost of $57,000, and this property includes two houses which are well suited for a nurses' home. Plans have been very carefully prepared, after visits to city hospitals in other cities—New York, Baltimore, Pittsburgh, Detroit, Cleveland, Buffalo, Chicago—by members of the building committee and the architect, and we had the advice of the naval architect and Dr. Stokes, in getting up these plans, and they have been very carefully prepared.

Senator SMITH of Maryland. Who is your architect?

Dr. CARR. Mr. Wyeth, and Mr. Southworth, who is naval architect under Dr. Stokes, has been assisting him in considering the plans, and they have been consulting experts in Baltimore and New York hospitals, and we are of opinion that we have an ideal plan for this hospital.

The present financial condition is as follows:

Estimated cost of the proposed Emergency Hospital, complete and ready for patients, is as follows:

Lowest bid for building	$259,750
Fixtures and elevators	36,781
Renovating nurses' home	1,000
Garage	3,000
60 beds and bedding, $24	1,400
Furnishing 30 rooms	3,000
Furnishing operating room	300
New instruments	100
Architects' fees and inspection	10,000
	315,371

To meet this demand our resources are as follows:

Congressional appropriation	$50,000	
Cash raised from citizens	86,000	
Cash in special fund	4,000	
Cash out at interest	2,500	
Cash in treasury	13,000	
Total cash in hand	155,500	
Pledges in course of collection, total, $46,000, of which we can reasonably expect to collect	36,000	
Total building resources	191,500	191,500
We have also 4 lots purchased for building site, at a cost of	57,000	
Making our total assets	248,500	
Cash needed to complete and equip hospital		123,871

A reserve fund should be held for running expenses until we are are fairly started in the new hospital, and for contingencies, of at least $12,000; making the total amount we need $135,871.

We propose to continue our efforts to raise the rest of this money from private sources and individuals, but we can hardly hope to raise that much, and many members of the board feel that it would be a very great handicap to start with such a debt. We are willing to start with a debt of $50,000, but not with a debt of $140,000.

We have made a very careful and conservative estimate of the probable cost of running the proposed hospital and of the income we may expect from private rooms and from other sources, and we have carefully checked these estimates by comparison with other hospitals in this city and in many other cities, and we are of opinion that the new emergency hospital will be practically self-sustaining, even though we keep in the wards every day of the year from 40 to 50 charity cases, cases which will cost us an average of $2 a day, and for which we expect to be paid by the Board of Charities only $1.20 a day.

For the last 10 years the hospital has had no direct appropriation of money from the Government for treating these cases, but we board these cases in the hospital at the rate of $1.20 a day, although the cost has been $2.27 a day.

Senator SMITH of Maryland. Is not that a pretty high price, $2.27 a day?

Dr. CARR. It is just about the average of all hospitals in cities all over the country. I got the figures for 37 hospitals in this city and in New York and other cities, and the average was just about $2 a day.

Senator SMITH of Maryland. That includes overhead charges?

Dr. CARR. Yes; everything; including overhead charges and everything. The overhead charges in the new hospital will be a little less than they are in the old, because every provision has been made to cut down expense by installing labor-saving devices and making it convenient and compact.

Senator SMITH of Maryland. I understand you take anybody in this hospital, it does not matter how poor, but you get $1.20 a day from the Charity Board for poor patients; is that right?

Dr. CARR. Yes, sir.

Senator SMITH of Maryland. And you bear the balance of the expense—$1.10?

Dr. CARR. Yes. We make up that difference by the income from the private rooms.

At the last hearing before this committee the question of the complete separation of the public and private charities consumed most of the time. The Board of Charities wanted to separate entirely public and private institutions, and I take it that that question was settled at that time, and need not be discussed again. I have here a little pamphlet which contains the arguments as given at that time.

Senator LEA. I understand you have a loss on account of our appropriation of $17,000?

Dr. CARR. Yes, we lose; but we are very glad to do it, because we can make it up from the pay patients.

Senator LEA. Really the institution is losing money.

Senator SMITH of Maryland. They are helping us. These ladies are going out and begging for money in order to run this place.

Dr. CARR. The Emergency Hospital has two very distinct functions, I think. One is to take care of charity cases or emergency cases, and the other is to take care of well-to-do individuals, and you can not separate them. When you take a man up on the street there is no time to investigate and see whether he is rich or poor, whether he is a valuable citizen or a tramp. The thing to do is to take him to the hospital immediately and give him the best treatment.

Senator SMITH of Maryland. Take care of him?

Dr. CARR. Yes; no matter what he is.

Senator SMITH of Maryland. What do you charge for pay patients?

Dr. CARR. We charge them from $15 to $25 a week for rooms.

Senator SMITH of Maryland. Does that include a nurse?

Dr. CARR. No; that does not include a private nurse. It includes nursing; but if they want a private nurse, they pay extra.

Senator LEA. I understand you are asking for $50,000, and you state that if you get $50,000 you will still have to go in debt to carry out your plan. Suppose we gave you $75,000 on the condition that the entire amount was raised, so that you could start off even; would that be any incentive?

Dr. CARR. We would, of course, be glad to get it, but we would be glad to get the $50,000.

Senator LEA. You would rather have the $50,000 without conditions than the $75,000 with that condition?

Dr. CARR. We only hope it will not be cut down in conference, as it was last time. We think we can get a little ahead as we go along, and gradually wipe out that debt.

Senator GALLINGER. Perhaps you may have to put a small mortgage on your buildings when you start.

Dr. CARR. We will have to put a right good mortgage on them, I think.

Senator GALLINGER. That depends on how successful you are in your second campaign?

Dr. CARR. We have already started work on the building.

Senator GALLINGER. Yes, I understand.

Dr. CARR. We are taking the chance of getting the rest of the money before it is completed; but I do not believe we can raise all of that money, and we will be pretty badly handicapped.

I should like to ask one thing. Is this going to come up before the Appropriations Committee of the House?

Senator GALLINGER. If this committee agrees to it in the first place, and then the Senate agrees to it, it will go to the House, and either the House will agree to it, or what is more likely, the House will send the entire bill to conference, and this will be before the conferees of the two Houses.

Dr. CARR. Thank you very much.

Senator GALLINGER. I want to say to you, Dr. Carr, and to Dr. Stokes and Mrs. Gaff, that it is very gratifying to me to find my associates so kindly disposed toward this amendment.

Dr. CARR. It is very gratifying to us to find you gentlemen so favorable.

Mrs. GAFF. It is one of those unexpected pleasures.

Senator GALLINGER. As you know, this has been very close to my heart, this new hospital, and we had to fight to save it.

Mrs. GAFF. I think if we get this it is going to be an absolute success, and we are really going to get the rest of that money.

STATEMENT OF HON. DAVID J. LEWIS, A REPRESENTATIVE IN CONGRESS FROM THE STATE OF MARYLAND.

Mr. LEWIS. Mr. Chairman and gentlemen of the committee, I desire to speak of bill H. R. 24126, introduced by Mr. Sterling for Mr. Jackson. It relates to the privilege of attendance at the schools of the District of Columbia by people residing outside of the District line.

Senator SMITH of Maryland. I want to say, Mr. Lewis, for your comfort, probably, that I think we have gone fully into that matter, and I think we have gotten about all there is in regard to it, and the committee feels that it is fully informed. What is this bill?

Senator GALLINGER. This is a bill that seems to have been referred to this committee, Mr. Chairman.

Senator SMITH of Maryland. Go ahead, then, and make your statement.

Mr. LEWIS. Just one fact which probably may not be familiar to the committee.

Senator GALLINGER. This is to change the law in that particular?

Mr. LEWIS. That fact is this, that considerations of reciprocity seem to justify extending to the residents in the neighborhood of the District, over the line in Maryland, the privileges that they have had here for many years, for it developes that the State of Maryland is treating the people of the District in just that way. I have information to the effect that the Maryland Agricultural College, an establishment of the State of Maryland, maintained almost exclusively by the State of Maryland, has been giving free tuition.

Senator SMITH of Maryland. The Government makes an appropriation for that institution.

Mr. LEWIS. It does, as it does to those institutions in all the States.

Senator SMITH of Maryland. Yes.

Mr. LEWIS. The people of Washington have been availing themselves of its facilities to a very great extent.

Senator GALLINGER. It must be to a very limited extent.

Mr. LEWIS. My information is not complete, I must confess. I just have the information that they are availing themselves of this free tuition in the Maryland Agricultural College. Of course, that institution is not confined to the teaching of agriculture.

Senator GALLINGER. No.

Mr. LEWIS. I thank the committee for this hearing.

STATEMENT OF SENATOR BLAIR LEE, OF MARYLAND.

Senator SMITH of Maryland. Senator Lee wants to have a word to say in regard to the same subject.

Senator LEE. Mr. Chairman and gentlemen, there was expected to be a delegation here from Montgomery County this afternoon to say something to you on the school situation. There was a very sudden change in the relationship of the two jurisdictions a few years ago, when a charge was put upon children coming into the National Capital from the surrounding States, and it naturally caused a great deal of disorder in the school system of, I imagine, both Virginia and Maryland. Certainly it did so in the Maryland counties. It called for a sudden increase of school compensation. We want to suggest that not only in respect to schools, but in respect to a great many other things, there is a relationship between the Virginia counties and the Maryland counties and the National Capital that is commercial and natural and ought to be respected in every respect. There ought to be, perhaps, more kindliness of relation between the National Capital and the adjacent portions of the same country than there would be between a commercial center and the adjacent portions of the States around it. Certainly there ought to be in this case, as half the support here comes from the country at large.

In respect to the matter of manual-training schools and centers of that kind, they are a very important phase of education that are very much appreciated by the adjacent population, and very much needed, and if you should make any special conditions that would encourage children to go long distances, even for the purpose of getting this manual-training education, it seems to me that it would be entirely appropriate for the National Capital to make concessions on that proposition, even more markedly than you should on any other phase of education.   We have lately in Maryland had a school of technology founded in connection with Johns Hopkins, and it is a pretty expensive school, as all such schools are, and in connection with that there was a considerable appropriation, both annual and for constructive purposes.   One of the provisions in connection with that school of technology was that there should be a certain number of free scholarships to be assigned to the various counties in Maryland, and the theory of the school was that it would fit on to the high-school system of the city, so that the boy graduating from a high school would be capable of entering this Johns Hopkins School of Technology in the lowest class.   This school has been going for about 18 months or a year, and we have already had some experience in those matters, and we find that there is some little gap between the theory and the facts.

We find that it is very hard to get the boys leaving the high schools with the ordinary high-school equipment to qualify for this school of technology.   I have had some experience in connection with three boys from my own county who had had high-school eductions.   One of them had been to a college in the West, and one or two of them had been to the manual-training school here.   When it came to the question of qualifying for the John Hopkins Technology School, those boys who had had that manual training-school experience were way ahead of the boys who had had, say, the junior year in an ordinary college, and it was an illustration of the importance of these manual-training schools in connection with the development of technical knowledge, which this section of the country is so particularly in need of from the constructive standpoint—the engineering standpoint.   So that if you gentlemen are disposed to extend a more liberal relationship to these adjacent counties I would particularly urge upon you that you make some special consideration of this in connection with these technical schools here in the District.

STATEMENT OF SENATOR LEE S. OVERMAN, OF NORTH CAROLINA.

Senator OVERMAN. Mr. Chairman and gentlemen, I come here on behalf of a matter of charity.   I have here a letter from Miss Margaret Wilson, who is very much interested in this matter.   This provision is as follows:

Then there is a provision for two guards for the swimming beach $480.   It seems that there is a misleading idea that it provides for both, and a letter that I have here from the District Commissioners recommends that they be allowed.

On the Rosedale and Howard playgrounds, the first of which is for white people, and the second for colored people, an amendment is prepared by us in such form that it can be introduced as an amendment as it stands.   The amounts provided are based on estimates which are made by the municipal architect.

Senator GALLINGER. The Commissioners did not include this in their regular estimates?

Senator OVERMAN. It is not estimated for, but they say they have had the architect make the estimate.   I should like to have you put that in.

Miss WETMORE. I should like to say that I am representing not only the National Civic Federation, but I am speaking for many of these ladies.   Miss Lathrop is here, and she is very much in favor of these school nurses.   Miss Elizabeth V. Brown, superintendent of primary instruction, is here, and Mr. Ufford is here, as well as Mr. Baldwin.

Senator GALLINGER. I made the suggestion I did for the reason that it is love's labor lost for this committee and the Senate to put in this bill a provision if the House is hostile to it; and in view of what has already happened, it occurred to me that a very strenuous effort ought to have been made before the House committee to persuade them.

Miss WETMORE. I quite agree with you, and I hope something will be done.

Senator GALLINGER. Nothing can be done without their cooperation.

Miss WETMORE. Oh, Mr. Senator, I fully realize that.   I know a good deal about the difficulties.

STATEMENT OF MISS ELIZABETH V. BROWN, SUPERINTENDENT OF PRIMARY INSTRUCTION.

Miss BROWN. I should like to ask Senator Gallinger whether it is too late now to do anything with the conferees.   We are ready to do anything we can.   We are here in full panoply for war at the present time.

Senator GALLINGER. Of course, you will have to wait and see what the Senate does.

Miss BROWN. You know, this has been a waiting game, so far as the Senate is concerned, for 10 years.

Senator GALLINGER. I would suggest that you might, at the proper time, well try your persuasive powers on the House conferees, provided the Senate amends the bill as you desire.

Miss BROWN. Of course in my work I am going hither and yon into the schools of the city, and this is just the particular time when, if you could find time to go through the schools, you would find that diseases are very prevalent, especially among the younger children, measles, whooping cough and scarlet fever especially.   We have eliminated infection to a certain extent.   The medical system gives part-time service to our schools.   That will have to be broadened in Washington, as it is in other cities, to include supervision, where school physicians will be employed to give all their time to the school work.   The teachers themselves can not see, they do not know, the incipient signs of diseases which spread through the schools.   Just a few days ago I was in a school where there are only about 25 children, and there should have been 35 or 40.   I looked at the small number and I said "Where are your children?"   "Excluded."   "Why?"   "Oh, well, pediculosis, and ringworm, and the itch.   All those diseases fashionable in this particular neighborhood."   These troubles have gone through the schools, and one of these troubles, what they call the itch, is a thing that is communicable through the free textbooks and papers used by the children; and yet those books we do not destroy as we destroy books that have been the property of children who have had scarlet fever or some more malignant disease than this form of skin disease.

These teachers are wholly incompetent to deal with this. They do watch the children and they do send the children home, and report them to the medical inspector; but the difficulties are frequently in the homes. At the time that we did have the services of the school nurses, for that short period I think the most effective work was done by the visits that were paid to the homes of the children. There are many sections of our city where the parents really do not know how to take care of their children.

Yesterday morning I was talking with a teacher who told me about a little girl who, a few minutes after school opened the other day, seemed to be very faint. The teacher said "Sit down a little while and put your head on your desk and rest. Why are you sick so early in the morning? What did you have for breakfast?" "I didn't have any breakfast. I don't have any breakfast when I come to morning school." Our nurse inquired among the little children who came to morning school, and she investigated in this one school and found that there were three children that did not usually have breakfast. In one case she found a child eating a piece of candy, what is popularly known among the children as a "two-day sucker," a lump of candy on the end of a wooden skewer, a little after 9 o'clock in the morning, and she said, "You must not eat candy so early in the morning. Why did you buy that? What did you have for breakfast?" The child said, "I didn't have no breakfast. Mama didn't get up in time. She gave me a penny and told me to get something to eat on the way to school." And I suppose that for her penny the two-day sucker might be considered as a good investment so far as its lasting qualities were concerned, but it was a pretty poor substitute for breakfast for the child.

In another case the teacher went to see the mother of a little girl who fainted one day in school. The mother said, "Yes, she don't never eat no breakfast." The teacher said, "What do you give her?" She said, "She won't eat any." The teacher said, "Did you ever try to give her oatmeal?" "No." She said to the little girl, "Will you eat oatmeal?" "Yes." She said, "Why do you not get that ready for the child?" She said, "Will you eat eggs?" And then she thought that she was perhaps unwise in saying eggs, but it turned out that they had plenty of eggs; they kept chickens. The mother said, "We have plenty of eggs, but if she does eat eggs she won't eat any bread." Then the child said, "I want meat; mama had some meat with horseradish on it, and she wouldn't give me any of it." The teachers do not know what to do.

In other cases the nurse said to the mother, "Will you listen to what I say and help to put this child into a healthy condition?" Some of the nurses have gone to particular homes, so they have cooperated with the teachers.

Of course, I could multiply stories from one end of the city to the other. It is not the general rule, but there are so many, many places where we as school people are in need of the sympathetic and the expert services of a nurse who can do the follow-up work of the medical inspection, and often get the homes in the right condition for giving the children sanitary surroundings, and give them good food and nourishment on which they can count to sustain the work of the school day. It is useless to repeat the things that Miss Wetmore has brought out about the other cities that are doing this work, and that are feeling that it is a great cooperative force in making for strong, healthful conditions of city living in these days.

Senator GALLINGER. Miss Brown, let me ask you, how often do the medical inspectors visit the schools?

Miss BROWN. They try to get around about once a week. We have not very many of them. They give about two hours a day, do they not?

Miss LATHROP. Two or three times a week.

Miss BROWN. In the city, where there are larger groups of schools, they do not come in so frequently. They do work very efficiently, but they need the follow-up help of the nurses.

STATEMENT OF MISS JULIA C. LATHROP, CHIEF CHILDREN'S BUREAU.

Miss LATHROP. I was just saying to Mrs. Beale that I think one great point showing the usefulness of the school nurse is that there are records that show that the ordinary inspection has increased about fourfold where the nurses have been used for this follow-up work. Otherwise your doctors do not go to the homes, and the children do not get the benefit of their work there. By excluding the child from the school you get rid of tuberculosis and these other diseases, and you get those common results that we all know about; but a child may soon become a chronic truant; whereas those New York records show that there was an approximate reduction of 90 per cent, if I remember, or rather over that, I believe, in the amount of absenteeism from these preventable causes, chronic trachoma and the like, just because the nurse followed the case to the dispensary and to the home, and did the work that no doctor could do.

STATEMENT OF MISS FLORA L. HENDLEY, SUPERVISING PRINCIPAL, PUBLIC SCHOOLS.

Miss HENDLEY. I am supervisor of a section of the city in the northeast, and I was the fortunate one who received the services of a nurse from the Instructive Visiting Nurse Association. Through the kindness of the association I had a nurse at the school every school day up to June for one school year, and part of the time in another school year. The contrast is very strong between the cases that were taken care of in that way and the cases that during the next year were not taken up. Of course I need say nothing more about the absence of these preventable diseases, but there is another side to it.

The child who is not in good physical condition does not take the education which the State provides for it, and we find among the children so many cases of some childish trouble which needs more than simply being followed up by a nurse, which needs medical attention, and the nurse in my division was especially successful with such cases, besides keeping these other children in the school. To go back to that subject for a minute, no child was out more than three days for any one of these easily communicable troubles, any of the skin troubles or little troubles that keep the children out. No child was out over three days during the period when I had a nurse, and other times I have had the same children sent out and stay out for a week at a time, three or four times a year. That shows the contrast between the follow-up work that Miss Lathrop speaks of and the unfollowed exclusion by the medical inspector.

During the eight months that I had the school nurse we had a number of important operations, 18 for the removal of adenoids and tonsils, and those would not have been performed if we had not had a nurse. I will have to explain how the ordinary inspection acts. If a teacher has any idea that a child needs medical treatment, she refers that child to the medical inspector. A blank is made up, and if the child noes need medical treatment that is sent back to the parents. The teacher aids as much as she can; but in the section of the city where I am the mother is busy; it is a section of small homes, small salaries, with several children in the family usually, and the mother is too busy to take the child down and have its adenoids taken out; but if the nurse comes and says she will take the child, the mother is very willing to have the child go. That nurse had 18 important operations performed. These cases were taken care of: Fifty-eight cases of defective vision, children needing glasses; 18 cases of defective hearing; 22 cases of adenoids; 59 cases of enlarged tonsils; and 149 cases of miscellaneous troubles, catarrh or things of that sort.

One hundred and fifty-four children were taken to the dispensary, and 81 others were sent to the dispensary to get care. That was the year that I had a nurse. Last year I had no nurse. I have these few cases that I have picked up, and this number does not represent all that should have had treatment and received no medical attention: Two children with both defective sight and hearing; 93 with defective sight; 10 with defective hearing; 1 with ear and throat trouble; 2 with defective eyes and bad throat; 25 cases of pediculosis that could not be followed up; 20 with skin disease; 11 cases of vague throat trouble; 15 with diseased tonsils; 1 child with defective sight, adenoids, and diseased tonsils; 8 with adenoids and diseased tonsils; 2 with nose and throat trouble; and 55 with nasal obstruction. Those children received no medical attention, and that represents quite a number of children for a small section. They really are not receiving the education that is being given them, because they are not in physical condition to take it. When any of these children have had attention, it is shown very plainly by their progress that the treatment was needed.

Senator GALLINGER. If the medical inspectors do their duty, would not at least some of those children get attention? Do the medical inspectors simply go in and diagnose the cases?

Miss HENDLEY. That is it; the medical inspector is not allowed to go to the child's home. He indicates on a slip of paper what attention the child needs, and the teacher usually follows it up by a note to the parents. The average mother, when she gets a note of that sort saying that Tommy's throat needs attention, says "What does the teacher know about Tommy's throat?" Then we send a paper for the parents to sign, which certifies that the child has or has not received medical attention, and if the child has received that attention, the word "not" is to be struck out; and we get those papers back with the word "not" not only not struck out but heavily underscored, which is as much to say "has not, and will not."

Senator GALLINGER. It would seem that the value of the medical inspection is a negligible quantity?

Miss HENDLEY. It is, without the nurse. It really is. But the nurse has a sort of semiofficial position in the family, so that the mother will listen to the nurse when she will not listen to the teacher.

Senator SMITH of Maryland. How many children received the care of the nurse?

Miss HENDLEY. One thousand two hundred and twenty-four. There were about 3,200 children in the division, and the visits to the children amounted to 1,530. There were about, I should say, 800 different children.

Senator SMITH of Maryland. What was the number of the children?

Miss HENDLEY. There are 3,200 children in the division over which I am supervisor.

Senator SMITH of Maryland. And the nurse had those under her care as nurse, as I understand it?

Miss HENDLEY. Yes. Of course when children were sent to her that needed medical attention, she did not do any inspecting.

Senator SMITH of Maryland. Was she able to take care properly of such a large number, according to your judgment?

Miss HENDLEY. She did wonderful work. Yes; I think one nurse to a division can accomplish a great deal. She made 1,530 visits during that time, and accomplished a great deal of good.

Senator SMITH of Maryland. Visits to their homes?

Miss HENDLEY. To their homes; yes, sir. Of course, some of those cases had to be followed up for three or four visits. She took children to the dispensary and saw that they had medical treatment. She really did a wonderful amount of good.

Senator GALLINGER. From your knowledge and experience along that line, what would you suggest as the minimum number of nurses that would be required to adequately do this work?

Miss HENDLEY. Thirteen.

Senator GALLINGER. The commissioners have recommended three.

Miss HENDLEY. Of course three could take care of the most pronounced cases, the cases that we are getting all the time. I have in my possession a file of papers, I suppose a foot or two high, each representing a child needing medical attention. I got one yesterday, "a child having but one eye needs medical attention immediately," and I feel sure, knowing the family, that she will not get attention; but the teacher said she would take the child to the dispensary at 2 o'clock on Wednesday, and the mother said, "I would be glad to have her go."

Mrs. HOPKINS. The second point we would call to your attention is the Board of Children's Guardians, and the general secretary of the Associated Charities, Mr. Ufford, will tell you what is needed on that.

CHARITIES AND CORRECTIONS (AGAIN).

STATEMENT OF MR. WALTER S. UFFORD.

BOARD OF CHILDREN'S GUARDIANS.

Mr. ÙFFORD. The Monday Evening Club is very much interested in -adequate provision for the neglected and defective children of Washington. The Monday Evening Club, furthermore, is on record as favoring school nurses. It is also on record before the Commissioners of the District, at a hearing which was given us during the preparation of the estimates, in favor of more visitors of the board of children's guardians. In Washington the situation is different from what it is in many of our large cities. There is no private organization in the city which does work for the prevention of cruelty and neglect in behalf of abandoned and defective children. That is all consigned in Washington to a public board, known as the board of children's guardians. We often hear private and public charity compared, and we who are engaged in private charity see no reason why our public charities should not be as efficient as our private charities.

As a matter of fact, Mr. Chairman and members of this committee, the best children's agencies in this country—such, for example, as you have in Baltimore, and in Maryland, and the one in Pennsylvania, in Philadelphia, and the one in New York, and the one in Boston—would not begin to think that they could care for the wards committed to them with the number of employees that are given to the board of children's guardians in Washington. In brief, the board here has but six visitors and inspectors, dealing with approximately 1,700 wards of the city. The records of that board, as investigated by the Children's Council, a group of people that are at work with children in Washington, show an average of approximately 300 children committed to the care of each of these visitors, where the best standards in these private organizations to which I have referred is 50 and 60 children to each visitor. The board of charities, which, as I understand it, presents the estimates of the board of children's guardians, has asked for four additional officers.

The associated charities, a private organization, receiving no public money, in its study of the situation and in its annual report, a copy of which I should like to file with you for the purpose of incorporating this portion in the record, has estimated that six would be the minimum that would meet this situation—six additional inspectors—and when we are asking for those, we believe we are asking for what will in the end produce economy in the District. We believe that instead of spending so much money for the care of these children their cases will be more carefully studied, the responsibility will be placed in many cases upon their parents, and other means will be found to care for them, so that by increasing your personal service to these children you are doing preventive work of the highest character. Many of them are feeble-minded, many of them are defective, many of them, like these children in the public schools that have been cited, need medical attention. As a matter of fact the board is so underequipped that, from its own records, the average number of visits to each child placed outside of the District during the year for the year was one. The Boston Children's Aid Society reports that it means to visit its wards six times a year.

That is the comparison between the standards that have been established and recognized by private agencies and the standard in the District of Columbia of this governmental agency, supported by appropriations by Congress; and, Mr. Chairman, the Monday Evening Club, the Children's Council, the Board of Charities, and the Associated Charities, and I am sure the woman's department of the National Federation, are tremendously interested in seeing that these children who can not speak for themselves - the defective, the orphan children of the District, and the neglected children of the District, so many of whom are committed to the care of the board by the juvenile court—shall be properly supervised when they are once given into the guardianship of the District.

The extract from the report of the associated charities, referred to by Mr. Ufford, is as follows:

CHILDREN—WARDS OF THE CITY.

Notwithstanding the efforts made by the Associated Charities, the St. Vincent de Paul Society, the United Hebrew Charities, and other private philanthropies to keep children with their parents, there is a large number who, because of orphanhood, neglect, improper guardianship, incorrigibility, or feeble-mindedness, require the protection of the municipality. This is afforded through the Board of Children's Guardians, which stands at the present time (October 1) in loco parentis to 1,728 children. Of these children, 440 are in institutions, 302 in boarding homes, 418 in free homes, 429 with relatives and friends, and 139 missing. Who should be a model parent if not the State? The responsibility, as well as the opportunity, of this legal guardianship, or oversight, of hundreds of children is enormous. Here is the material, if improperly handled, for the perpetuation of pauperism and crime indefinitely. Yet how is the District of Columbia, backed by the freest, richest nation in the world, meeting this responsibility?

Where the best of our private agencies average not more than 50 children to each visitor—the number which holds good also in juvenile court probation work—the following is the number of children cared for by the agents of the Board of Children's Guardians last year:

Two visiting inspectors averaged 375 each.

Three placing and visiting officers averaged 221 each.

Usual number of visits to children placed outside District during the year, 1.[1]

For six years the Board of Children's Guardians has petitioned for a larger visitorial corps. The present investigating clerk deals, on an average, with 149 children each month, an impossible number for efficient service. The Associated Charities, from its own experience with many of these children, maintains that wise economy, as well as the conservation of childhood, calls for the most painstaking inquiries as to conditions in the family before bringing these cases into court. In many such instances resources would be found within the family group to care for the children. In other instances, such as cases of gross neglect, the children should be more quickly cared for without the present delays.

The moral is plain. The Board of Children's Guardians, charged with the grave responsibility of caring for over 1,700 public wards of the District of Columbia, needs a large increase in its present force in order to meet its responsibilities. To make the work of this board as efficient as that of our private children's aid societies means that instead of 6 visiting, placing, and investigating officers it should have at least 12.

THE FEEBLE-MINDED.

The figures quoted above as to the wards of the Board of Children's Guardians do not include 93 feeble-minded children under the care of the board. In addition to this number, the board has information regarding 84 of the feeble-minded class in the District of Columbia for whom it appears essential that custodial care and special training should be provided. It is believed, however, by students of the local situation that a complete census of the feeble-minded in the District of Columbia would show a much larger number needing custodial care.

---

[1] The plan of the Boston Children's Aid Society is to see each child at least six times a year, and more frequently as the case may demand.

Washington has within its own borders no institution for the care of the feeble-minded. At present such children must be sent beyond the reach of their parents to private institutions elsewhere. The appropriation is a limited one, and many feeble-minded children are left at home or permitted to attend the public schools. Under this system feeble-mindedness is bound to increase. It is most important in dealing with this great problem—this fruitful source of pauperism and crime—that all feeble-minded women of child-bearing age should be placed under custodial care. A similar policy should, in fact, be followed as to all feeble-minded persons. Furthermore, the community should be educated to the acceptance of a policy of compulsory sterilization for its feeble-minded and its congenitally degenerate.

Mrs. HOPKINS. I will ask you next, Mr. Chairman, to hear Mr. William H. Baldwin on the subject of the juvenile court. He has made a study of the subject.

JUVENILE COURT (AGAIN).

STATEMENT OF MR. WILLIAM H. BALDWIN (again).

Mr. BALDWIN. I was requested to come here with these good people from the Monday Evening Club and present this subject in connection with the others, because it is of so much importance to the work in which the club and those associated with it are connected.

I have made a study of it, not only because of my connection for some years now, with different phases of the juvenile court work, but also as chairman of the juvenile court committee, and I ought first to say—and I am glad to have this opportunity of saying it, although I did not expect at the time the hearing was kindly granted us here, some time ago, to come again in this way, to have this opportunity to say that yesterday we made the discovery of a great mistake in the estimates that have been sent up here. We had a meeting of our juvenile court committee, and we asked, gentlemen, for not a cent more than we needed, the very smallest amount we could get along with, and we were told, and it came with a very cruel sound, that of course we would not get what we asked for. I want to say to you, therefore, that the remarkable thing about this estimate is that it does not contain one cent that is not necessary for the proper work of the court for the coming year.

The circumstances are that the estimates were carefully prepared by Judge Latimer in connection with the commissioners for presentation to the Subcommittee on Appropriations in the House. As Judge Latimer was ill, I was asked to represent him in presenting this matter to them, and was much gratified with the interest that the subcommittee showed and the questions that they asked, and the matter was presented to them in a way that the commissioners thought would enlist their support for practically all of the appropriations as the schedule came up. I was glad to have Judge Latimer say that in the sort of general reduction that occurred he thought perhaps the matter had been presented fairly well, because they had left more in the Juvenile Court appropriation than they had in some of the others; and I am sure that so far as that was done, it was done because the committee was convinced that the court certainly ought to have that much, even though they left out the other items, according to the general principle that they applied to the appropriation bill for the District.

Working from that, and feeling the setback—the unfortunate setback, that the judge felt very deeply, in connection with the action of the House—in asking the Senate committee here for what ought to be restored, he made the amount just as small as he could and made some reductions, about $1,800, as you see, in the first group of items, as to the employees, from the amount that had been asked for in the House, not because these items were not needed, but because he did not want to ask for too much, hoping to get from the Senate all that was needed; and I need not speak again of the increase in the item of the deputy clerk, who takes care of, I should say, double or perhaps treble the amount of money that he did, because of the growth of the work of the court, or many times the amount of the money that he did when the salary was fixed. The increase of $300 asked for there is but justice, and it is not in proportion to the additional amount of work done.

As to the chief probation officer, the judge has been obliged to get a new man, a man of experience, who comes here from St. Louis, and who came at the salary that is now being paid, $1,500, with a statement from the judge that he was asking for an increase in that salary, which the man is well worth. Now, I have no idea—although the judge has not made any improper representations to him—but that he expected to get this, leaving it entirely with Congress. If that man does not get more than $1,500, I have no idea that he will stay; and as you already know from the record, the probation officers in other cities of the size of Washington get anywhere from $2,250 to $2,500.

In talking to the committee before, I spoke of the probation officer at Cleveland, Ohio, who is a good man, who greatly assists Judge Adams, and who gets $2,500. This $2,000 ought certainly to be given to this man.

As to the probation officers, the House has allowed one more, making the total number of probation officers four.

I have already explained that the average number of boys—probationers—last year, all of whom are delinquent, was about 450. In the House hearings I read from a statement made by the vice president of the state probation commission of New York, to the effect that the probation officer ought not to be required to take care of more than 50, or at the very most 75, probationers. The work can not be well done with more than that number. Judge Latimer has reduced the number that he asked for here to six, asking for one more probation officer at $2,400, and two more at $1,000. I might say that I think one reason why the House granted this single probation officer that it gave was that one has been provided and piad for by the Daughters of the American Revolution, and they certainly did not want to have volunteers pay for work that the United States ought to pay for. They need that money, and I want to say again that when the judge took office on the 1st of July, or in July, the number of children on probation had dropped to 400, and the judge found that with three probation officers the work was not being well done at all, the probationers were not receiving the proper attention, so that he dismissed 235 boys, not because they were not in further need of probation, but because he had to dismiss them in order to reduce the number to the number that the probation officers thought they could take care of; that is, practically, to 165.

Now, there is another point about that, and that is that these boys that need probation are turned loose on the community, and they are liable to do something that is bad, some of them, and they are liable to be sent out to the National Training School. If they are sent out there, the care of five or six of them would cost the Government as much as the salary of an additional probation officer. If there were 10 boys sent out there that this probation officer could take care of, it would cost the Government twice as much as the salary of the probation officer; so that in the interests of economy it is apparent that this probation officer should be furnished.

The salary of the bailiff we ask to be brought up to the salary received by a number of bailiffs in the police court, and the item for the larger salary is made necessary, it having been put in before, because we have found it necessary to move the juvenile court to other quarters, where it will be necessary to have some one to take care of the rooms.

Senator GALLINGER. There was no estimate for a larger sum submitted to Congress.

Senator LEA. I think they made a supplemental estimate.

Senator GALLINGER. I do not know where it is.

Mr. BALDWIN. I do not know about that, Senator, but the matter has not been entirely overlooked. If you will look on page 94 of the House hearings, you will find that in speaking about the general situation as to the court it was explained that these estimates contained nothing—the requests that were made at that time contained nothing—that related to the necessity to move the court, the expectation being that when that matter came up some different estimates for a new building proposition, for proper provision for the court in views of its being obliged to be moved, would be submitted. This really comes in for that, and that leads to what I am going to speak of in the last item in the group, where you notice that the request for the compensation for jurors has been reduced from $1,300 to $900, and that the item for rent has been largely increased.

There has been a nominal rent of $20 a month, because the building belonged to the Government, simply, I suppose, to preserve its right. There has been a notification from the Treasury Department—I saw the notification from one of the architects in the Treasury Department, yesterday—that they are obliged to move, and the time is fixed about August, so that it will be necessary to provide other quarters, and that is what makes this item of the larger amount necessary. The circumstances will be different.

There has been put down an item of $2,400 for rent, and we discussed that yesterday at our juvenile court meeting, with the judge, and I do not believe that suitable quarters can be furnished for that amount, based on the information that comes from inquiries that have been made since we have been looking around. Judge Latimer in his modesty has fixed the amount too low. This is his first experience with that. I hope you will have some consideration for him on this item. I would be very glad to have you make that $3,000. Now, I am just telling you the circumstances. The responsibility rests with the committee here in view of the circumstances.

The item of furniture, fixtures, equipment, and repairs to the courthouse and grounds, and the contingent expenses, have somewhat overlapped in previous sessions on account of the wording.

Senator GALLINGER. Judge Latimer went over with us the item of rent, and he said that it ought to be $2,400. Now, you have got it up to $3,000.

Mr. BALDWIN. I am telling you of the information that came to the committee. I am only telling you the circumstances.

Senator GALLINGER. We would be very much more likely to be s 'ayed, if at all, by the representations made by the Judge.

wMr. BALDWIN. Well, if you will give the Judge what he asks for here, I will not ask you for more; only, I am telling you why it should be that much; and these items of miscellaneous and contingent expenses grow out of the same circumstances.

The matter of the new building was spoken of yesterday, and the committee passed a resolution that a bill be presented providing for a suitable building for the juvenile court and the detention rooms, which will no doubt come before you and will take care of itself in that way.

HEALTH DEPARTMENT (AGAIN).

Mr. BALDWIN. Mrs. Hopkins has said that I would also say something about the needs of the health department. I represent also the Association for the Prevention of Tuberculosis, and I happen to be chairman of the legislative committee of that association, and the increase in the amount that is asked for for contagious diseases, together with the release of the limitation of the amount, or at least the extension of the limitation of the amount, that can be used for personal services is very important in taking care of these diseases and especially in the matter of attention to the persons that have tuberculosis. There are quite a number in the District now who are not being properly taken care of because the health department has no nurses to use in that way. That is another argument for school nurses, and I heartily indorse all that has been said in regard to that, because if the matter is put in the proper way it might be possible for these nurses on Saturday, if they are put under the general supervision of the health department, to assist in looking after some of this other work that would help out with the work that is now done by the sanitary inspectors.

If you will notice the item in the estimate, it explains that quite a little of the work that has to be done now about contagious diseases is done by the more highly paid sanitary inspectors, and it takes their time, and they can not do their work as well as they ought to. If the Health Department is given a little more latitude in regard to the use of the money that is appropriated, better work can be done in providing for the needs of the District.

There is an assistant bacteriologist asked for, with something more for the traveling expenses which are made necessary for the Federal inspections that they are trying to get of milk, etc., to take care of these diseases. I believe that it would be money saved to grant all of these things, from a health standpoint.

I am glad to have the committee give us such consideration here, and I want to say that, although we come up here unofficially, we do feel that the responsibility of providing for the needs of this city and the government of this District rests equally on the Senate, with the House. I know that the Senators and the Members of the House also have many other things; other local things, and national matters to attend to. We were told by a gentleman who has had some experience that the matters of the District were somewhat incidental; but they are not, because the Constitution of the United States puts this responsibility on the Senators, and that is why we come here.

ADDITIONAL STATEMENT OF MRS. ARCHIBALD HOPKINS.

Mrs. HOPKINS. At this point I wished to bring up the question of a municipal lodging house, but you were kind enough to give us a private hearing this morning on that, and I will not bring that up.

Senator SMITH of Maryland. You were heard on that; yes.

MUNICIPAL HOSPITAL (AGAIN).

Mrs. HOPKINS. A municipal hospital is made absolutely necessary by the fact that the present almshouse consists of dilapidated, antiquated buildings, in close proximity to the jail. The buildings are beyond repair, and any new building erected should be placed on the site already provided by Congress. The present overcrowded condition is shown by the fact that beds have to be placed at times in the basement, as many as 24 at one time. There should be a place to which inebriates could be taken and treated and straightened up on an indeterminate sentence.

HOSPITAL FOR INEBRIATES.

I believe that the secret of the whole thing is in doing away with drink. If you will do away with drink, you will do away with all these other things. Drink is the foundation stone of all our troubles, and incidentally of yours, as it makes it necessary for us to come here and drive you almost crazy, and we feel very strongly that that is the keystone of the situation.

Senator SMITH of Maryland. I feel that you will have to continue to come here, then, because I can not abolish it.

Mrs. HOPKINS. But you can make a place where inebriates can be held, and where they can be given medical treatment to enable them to resist temptation.

Senator GALLINGER. We had a physician before us this morning who eloquently and at great length argued this question. He says we will have to have 100 acres at least upon which to plant this inebriate hospital, and we will be unable to find a tract in the District of that size, and we really do not know where to go for it.

Senator SMITH of Maryland. One of the troubles we have had is that we have different sets of people come here and want us to build an institution, and we have had several appear before us in regard to this inebriate asylum, and there are no two that agree as to how it should be built and where, or how much land it should have around it, or whether it should have any. There is one of the difficulties.

Mrs. HOPKINS. I know.

Senator SMITH of Maryland. We are puzzled to know what is the proper thing to do.

If you will pardon me, I will say there does not seem to be any agreement as to the proper thing to do. I am not quarreling, you understand, but you put us in a position so that we do not know where we are.

Mrs. HOPKINS. We who are here are entirely agreed, and if you will give us the names of the other different people you speak of we will see if we can not get them to come together in an amicable way, and we will make them come to some conclusion and bring them up here.

Now, I want to ask you one other thing, for the care of the feeble-minded. Miss Lathrop and everybody concerned feels that this is one of the greatest questions in the District.

Senator GALLINGER. Right there, you ought to have gone to the House. I have twice introduced a bill, reported it, and advocated it, for building in the District of Columbia an institution for the care of the feeble-minded. The bill passed the Senate, but died in the House. I think you need not argue that before the Senate or before a Senate committee.

Mrs. HOPKINS. Then we will go before the House.

Senator GALLINGER. I have reintroduced that bill in the present Congress. I know Senator Smith will report it, and I feel sure it will pass the Senate again, and then if you will go to the House you can deal with it there.

Senator SMITH of Maryland. There is nothing reasonable you can ask for here, for those who can not take care of themselves or the children, that I will not try to do, but the difficulty is that you can not get these bills through without the approbation of the House. There is the difficulty. I have no doubt they look at it from their standpoint, and I have no doubt they are doing just what they think is right.

Senator GALLINGER. Certainly.

Senator SMITH of Maryland. And you ladies must try to convince them that they are not.

Mrs. HOPKINS. We always apply to the Senate, because they are always with us and really try to do what we want, and therefore we come to you.

We are infinitely indebted for your courtesy and patience, and if one of you will kindly tell us when is the psychological moment to go to the House, we will do so.

Senator SMITH of Maryland. Whatever we may do here with regard to matters, that has not been done by the House, when they fix the conference committee you had better let after them.

Mrs. HOPKINS. We thank you very much indeed.

Mr. BALDWIN. In view of the remarks that have been made about the arrangement with the House——

Senator SMITH of Maryland. I do not want to curtail your statement, Mr. Baldwin, but have you not covered everything?

Mr. BALDWIN. I want to say that in the House hearings you will find discussed the question of the building for the juvenile court, and the expense of moving, and it was there stated that that matter would be brought up. The increase in these items ought to have been put down, as a matter of fact, as a part of that, and a bill will come in for the building later. If you will give us a good juvenile court building we will let you locate it where you want to. We are quite satisfied with that.

(At 5 o'clock p. m. the subcommittee adjourned until to-morrow, Friday, February 13, 1914, at 10.30 o'clock a. m.)

FRIDAY, FEBRUARY 13, 1914.

The subcommittee met at 10.30 a. m.

DISTRICT REVENUES.

George Truesdell, Henry B. F. Macfarland, Aldis B. Browne, and Ralph P. Barnard appeared.

The ACTING CHAIRMAN (Senator Gallinger). The chairman of the subcommittee, Senator Smith, is unavoidably detained this morning. He may be in later. As our time is very valuable just now, if agreeable to the gentlemen present the hearing will proceed.

OPENING STATEMENT OF GEORGE TRUESDELL.

Mr. TRUESDELL. Mr. Chairman, the board of trade is very deeply concerned about section 8 of the appropriation bill as it came from the House, and requested its committee on municipal finance to ask for a hearing before this committee, which you very generously and courteously granted. As chairman of the committee I have requested Mr. Macfarland, who is chairman of the subcommittee to whom the matter has been specially referred, to occupy the larger part of the time which you feel you can grant us at this hearing.

Senator GALLINGER. Mr. Macfarland, you will proceed.

STATEMENT OF HENRY B. F. MACFARLAND.

Mr. MACFARLAND. Mr. Chairman, I believe this is my first appearance before your subcommittee since 1910, when I completed my 10 years of service as one of the Commissioners of the District of Columbia. I would not be here this morning if I did not feel that the National Capital is facing a crisis affecting its entire future. I am here under the introduction of the chairman of the committee on municipal finance and under the direction of the Washington Board of Trade, but I should like to speak as a citizen of the United States, just as if I had come here this morning from Philadelphia, my birthplace.

In international law the word "national" is not only used as an adjective but as a noun, and we of the District of Columbia can certainly claim to be "nationals," as well as residents of the National Capital. It is as a "national," as a citizen of the United States, that I should like to present the outlines of an argument which is very familiar to you, sir, but which may not be so familiar to all the members of the present Committee on Appropriations. I shall proceed briefly but comprehensively to review the history of the National Capital, so as to show the roots of the tree the trunk of which at the present time certainly has come to be the arrangement which is now menaced by section 8 of the District of Columbia appropriation bill as it has come to the Senate from the House. We can understand the present only by knowing the past.

The half-and-half principle, as it is commonly called, of the act of June 11, 1878, under which the greater part of the progress of the National Capital has been made, is menaced by the action of the

House, even though that action was taken without discussion, without division, without considering a point of order which would probably have lain against section 8 as new legislation, and with a very small attendance of the Members of the House. But it is here as the action of the House, and it is accompanied by another provision, commonly called the Borland amendment, which in itself involves a serious departure from the same half-and-half principle. It contemplates a fatal blow at the wise policy of general, harmonious, continuous highway improvement out of general funds for the common use and advantage of all the people, and therefore properly to be paid for by all.

I shall not dwell upon the Borland amendment, because your committee has dealt with that in former years, and we have no doubt that it is perfectly understood by your committee. The injustice of it to the small property owner, of whom we have over 50,000, who has heretofore contributed to the common improvement of the highways through his taxes, and who might be called upon for the whole expense of improvement of the highway in front of his property, and its inconsistency with the systematic and orderly development of the entire National Capital will be so apparent to your committee that you need no prolonged argument against the Borland amendment, which repeals the "half-and-half" provision as to street improvements.

Besides these two important measures now pending before this committee, the Senate District Committee is considering two other measures sent by the House which ought to be defeated because they, too, strike at the life of the National Capital. One exempts from distribution under the half-and-half agreement a half million of the District's revenues from licenses, simply one form of taxation; and the other the so-called Johnson-Prouty bill would compel the District revenues to bear the whole of two years' instalments of interest payment on the 3.65 bonds, directly contrary to the legislation of Congress in 1874 and in 1878, and for 35 years continuously since, and contrary to the interpretation of the Treasury Department ever since 1878. These bills, like the measures before this committee, were passed when only a small minority of the House was present and, it must be believed, without due consideration of the facts. It is proper to say that if there is to be any reopening of the careful final settlement of accounts made by Congress in 1874–1878, the arrears of the United States in its dealings with the National Capital will have to be considered and, according to the reports to Congress by its own committees, those arrears would amount to many millions of dollars.

In appearing before you, sir, I feel very much as Paul felt when he appeared before Agrippa, not that I am any more like Paul than you are like Agrippa, but he was thankful to appear before one who was familiar with the history and customs of the Jews, and whom he regarded as sympathetic with their aspirations and purposes, yet I shall have to ask you to pardon me for speaking of things which are very familiar to you. It is necessary to speak of them for the orderly presentation of this argument, not only for your consideration, sir, and that of the subcommittee, but for the consideration of the entire committee, and possibly for the consideration of the Senate, if it should be used by your committee.

Speaking, then, as I said, as a national, as a citizen of the United States who might have come here this morning from Philadelphia to present the national view, let me say that the Nation has a greater interest in the National Capital than any of the people who live in the District of Columbia, that the Nation deliberately chose to have a capital under its exclusive control and for which it should be exclusively responsible. It deliberately left the large city of Philadelphia and chose to come to this particular place. It had had full experience of the disadvantages of a capital in large commercial cities—New York as well as Philadelphia. George Washington, of course, had suggested it, after the Congress had been obliged to leave Philadelphia and go to New Jersey because of the onset of the unpaid Revolutionary soldiers in 1783, and the clause in the Constitution so familiar to you which gives to the Congress "exclusive legislation in all cases whatsoever"— to use the peculiar phrase not found anywhere else—over such tract, not exceeding 10 miles square, as might be ceded by the particular States to the United States for the purposes of a National Capital, was without doubt inserted in the Constitution largely upon his recommendation.

When the National Government came here from Philadelphia in 1800 there were of course few people in the Federal City. The old town of Georgetown, 50 years old, was over on the western hill, but that was not considered a part of the Federal City. There was, in 1790, no one here except the 19 proprietors of the farms that are now the city of Washington, the 6,111 acres, and their families and slaves. And the Government brought only 126 Government officials and employees from Philadelphia to Washington. So we may say there were few people here at that time, and the National Government, representing the Nation, undertook to found a National Capital without population and without regard to the few people who were here, except as to what they might give to the National Government.

I shall ask you to listen to a brief extract from a unanimous report made by Mr. Poland, of Vermont, for the Committee on the Judiciary of the House of Representatives on the 1st of June, 1874, in connection with the investigations made at that time as to the relation of the National Capital to the National Government and to the people resident here by that committee and by the joint select committees of the two Houses and by the District Committees of that time. The leading lawyers and statesmen of both Houses took part in those investigations and reports including Allison, Thurman, Bayard, Morton, Whyte, Poland, Morrill, Rockwood Hoar, Blackburn, Abram S. Hewitt, Eugene Hale, Hunton. I find it in a comprehensive and admirable document prepared by Col. George Truesdell, chairman of the special committee on municipal finance of the board of trade, in 1912, a copy of which I shall be glad to leave with the committee, because it contains the fruit of considerable and thorough researches.

Every student of American history—

says Mr. Poland—

knows that few questions aroused greater attention in the Continental Congress at the close of the Revolution, than the question as to the seat of government. The archives of the Government are full of debates on that subject. Not only the future tranquillity and well being of the United States was thought to depend upon it, but that every principle of pride and honor, and even of patriotism, were involved in it. The act to establish a permanent seat of government was approved July 16, 1790.

He alludes then to the location of the Capital, which as you know was the work of George Washington himself. He was left free to choose 100 miles along the Potomac and he chose this particular spot. The report then speaks of the Nation's purpose and of the transfer by the 19 original proprietors of the soil of the Federal city of Washington, and it is that to which I now particularly invite your attention: It says:

The language of the act declares distinctly the object of the Government to be to mark out, within the 10 miles square mentioned in the Constitution, a tract "for the use of the United States," the purpose of Congress being to provide a Federal Capital, and not to make provision for any other interest whatever.

Then Mr. Poland says:

This is clearly evidenced by the deed of conveyance made by the original proprietors of the soil, on the 29th day of June, 1791.

He refers to the deed in trust, to Gantt and Beall, who were trustees for this purpose, and says:

The conveyance was made upon certain special trusts, some of which it is important to notice in this connection.

Then he quotes from the deed:

That all the said lands are hereby bargained and sold, or such part thereof as may be thought necessary or proper, to be laid out, together with other lands within the same limits, for a Federal city, with such streets, squares, and parcels and lots as the President of the United States for the time being shall approve.

Then Judge Poland continues:

The proprietors parted with all the soil for the purpose of building here a Federal city, leaving it exclusively with the President to select from the whole whatever he might deem necessary or desirable for that purpose. No reservation was made in the deed for the benefit of the proprietors other than that after the President had indicated all the streets, squares, parcels, and lots that he should deem proper for the use of the United States there should be "a fair and equal division of the remaining lots," and the United States should pay for its reservations and lots at the rate of £25 sterling per acre.

Which amounted then to $66.66 per acre, and aggregated about $36,000 to the proprietors, obtained, however, from the sale of some of the lots, only one-half of which they retained, as is shown by other official documents quoted in this Truesdell report.

The deed—

Continued Mr. Poland—

does not provide for the dedication of any public squares, streets, or avenues to the public use; but the absolute fee simple vested in the United States, so that the Government could at any time close a street or occupy a public square for such purposes as it deemed proper.

As is shown by the deed itself and by the transactions under it, which are mentioned in this report, the Government took what it wanted for its reservations and for public buildings; it took the streets absolutely, and it took one-half of the lots remaining, leaving only the one-half of the lots to the original proprietors.

Senator GALLINGER. Mr. Macfarland, did the Government take lots alternately or en bloc?

Mr. MACFARLAND. Alternately, in many cases. The trust deed provided that the commissioners for the time being should decide exactly how the lots should be apportioned fairly and equally, and that they should be alternate lots unless otherwise agreed. Over one-half of the 6,111 acres of the city site, or about 3,600 acres were devoted to streets, the largest proportion of street area in the world at that time or at any time.

The question—

Continues the Poland report—

as to the scope of the deed in this regard came up early in a dispute between the commissioners and proprietors. The latter thought that the United States had the right only to use the streets as public highways, and not to alienate them or divert them to other uses. Attorneys General Breckenridge, Wirt, and Cushing, advised that the fee-simple title to the streets, avenues, and reservations was in the United States, and it was so held by the Supreme Court in the case of Van Ness et ux v. The City of Washington (4 Peters, 213).

Six-sevenths of the soil of the Federal city, in brief, was given by the original proprietors to the Government, and the only exception to the word "given" lies in the fact that $36,000 was paid the proprietors under the provision for the payment of $66.66 per acre for the land actually taken for the reservations and lots, and that money was paid out of the sale of lots. The whole transaction is given in detail in the Southard report of 1835 to the Senate, of which I shall speak later, and which I shall leave with the committee.

This is a comment of the Polard report.[1]

It is perfectly manifest from a moment's examination of this plan——

the great plan which George Washington had prepared with the advice of Jefferson and Madison and with the assistance of L'Enfant and Ellicott as engineers—

that a city was laid off here for the use of the United States upon a scale hitherto unknown in this or any other country, upon a plan to carry out which would inevitably lead to an expenditure entirely beyond the requirements of a city for business purposes. It was a plan having reference peculiarly to the wants of the Government and not to those of its inhabitants; its streets and avenues, in number, length, and width, are upon a scale that was appropriate for a national capital, but was entirely inappropriate to the demands of a sparse population not engaged in manufacturing or commerce and when manufactures and commerce were not encouraged to come.

And have never been encouraged to come from that day to this.

Not only are the streets unusually wide and numerous, but throughout the city are large reservations, so that it may be estimated that the whole area thus set apart embraces much more than one-half of the whole city, the streets and avenues alone, of which there are 260 miles, varying in width from 90 to 160 feet, amounting to one-half of the entire area of the city.

The mileage of the streets has largely increased since. In the last annual report of the Commissioners of the District of Columbia (p. 38) the total mileage is given as 470 miles, of which 310 are improved.

The Poland report next gives the ratio of street areas of certain cities: Paris, 25.08 per cent; Vienna, 35.08 per cent; Philadelphia, 29.08 per cent; Berlin, 26.04 per cent; Boston, 26.02 per cent; New York, 35.03 per cent; and Washington, 54.08 per cent.

The report contains extracts from the famous unanimous report of the Senate Committee on the District of Columbia in 1835, through its chairman, Senator Southard, of New Jersey, which you, sir, had reprinted by the Senate in recent years, and a copy of which I have here and shall file with the committee.

Of course, 35 years from the founding of the city many men who had taken part in it or were cognizant of all the facts were still living; some of them were then in Congress; all the facts were familiar to public men. The Southard report was the result of a very careful consideration of the history and the circumstances on the petition of the bankrupt corporation of the city of Washington, bankrupted by the patriotic endeavor to develop the Capital, together with the cities of Georgetown and Alexandria (then in the District), which were affected by the financial conditions, and it was also practically the work of the House committee as well, for, although the two committees did not sit together, they considered the measures of relief together.

That report reviewed, of course, as the Poland report reviewed and as the reports of the joint select committees of 1874–78 reviewed, the history which I have so briefly outlined.

It then comes to the question of the duty of the Government in this respect, and we can adopt the language of the Southard report as conservative under all the circumstances. He had said in the report before this that the people who lived here had brought about this really terrible condition for them, there being only 20,000 people here at that time, including slaves and free negroes, that they brought it about in their efforts to develop the George Washington plan as far as their small resources would permit, and also in connection with the George Washington desire to connect the Capital with the West by means of the Chesapeake & Ohio Canal, in which they had made unfortunate investments, with the express authority and approval of the National Government and, following its example. They brought the city to that condition by their attempts at National Capital making. Senator Southard's report approved what they had done, although he thought they had been misled into doing more than they ought to have done. His report says:

The committee are of the opinion that the Government was bound by every principle of equal right and justice to pay a proportion of the expenses incurred upon this subject equal to the amount of property which it held.

Then the report says again:

If the streets are its property, and to be regarded as altogether under its control, it is not easy to perceive why it should call upon or permit others to keep that property in order; and if the streets are to be regarded as for the joint convenience of the Government and the inhabitants, the expenses of maintaining them should be joint and in proportion to their respective interests.

In the investigation of the subject committed to them, and of the relief to be proposed, the committee have been unable to separate the interests of the District from the interests of the United States. They regard it as the child of the Union.

They regard it as the child of the Union—

as a national I should like to emphasize that and also the next clause, namely—

as the creation of the Union for its own purposes.

The report continues:

The design of the founders was to create a residence for the Government, where they should have absolute and unlimited control, which should be regulated and governed by them without the interference of partial interests in the States, which should be built up and sustained by their authority and resources, not dependent upon the will or resources of any State or local interest.

If this had not been the design a temporary or permanent seat of government would have been selected in some populous city, or some territory subject to State jurisdiction; and if this was the design it is not easy to comprehend either the principle which would prevent the Government from a liberal appropriation of the national resources to accomplish the object, or the policy which would confine the city to the means possessed by the inhabitants for its improvement.

Every word should be emphasized.

In the Southard report itself there is a sentence not quoted by the Poland report, which I should like to quote in this relation:

It—

That is, the plan for the National Capital—

It is a plan calculated for the magnificent capital of a great nation, but oppressive, from its very dimensions and arrangements, to the inhabitants, if its execution to any considerable extent is to be thrown upon them. No people who anticipated the execution and subsequent support of it out of their own funds would ever have dreamed of forming such a plan.

Now, note this language:

It would have been the most consummate folly.

That, without doubt, was the judgment of the men of 1835 and of the men of the time of the founding of the National Capital, as the correspondence of Washington and Jefferson and Madison and the commissioners who laid out the Capital between 1790 and 1800 and many official and public utterances of that time will distinctly show.

There is an interesting passage from the address of President Adams in 1800 to the first Congress which assembled here, the Fifth Congress, which suggests what was the common thought of that time as to the National Capital:

You will consider it—

he says—

as the capital of a great nation, advancing with inexhaustible rapidity in arts, in commerce, in wealth, and in population, and possessing within itself those energies and resources which, if not thrown away or lamentably misdirected, will secure to it a long course of prosperity and self-government.

Again I quote from the report of the joint select committee of 1874. In its report after months of investigation the committee said:

The streets, avenues, squares, and general plan of the capital city bear the impress of paramount and exclusive nationality.

As a national I like that phrase.

Spacious and grand in design, dedicated to the sacred uses of a capital, onerous and intolerable as a charge upon private property, the provision for supervision of all suitable improvements and decorations obviously, properly, and imperatively devolves upon Congress, and it will, as it respects the character of its jurisdiction and the dignity of its trust, exercise a jealous care over it.

May this be always done.

The Judiciary Committee in the Poland report, from which I have already quoted, made a quotation from the opinion of the Supreme Court in Van Ness v. The City of Washington, in which the court held that the Government had absolute control over the streets; that they were its absolute property in fee simple; that it could close them if it desired; that it could sell them or could do anything it pleased with them. As a matter of fact, the Southard report says it actually exercised this power. At the bottom of page 3 it says:

It has even closed one of the streets and sold the ground which formed a part of it.

In that Van Ness opinion the Supreme Court said:

The grants were made—

(by the original proprietors)—

for the foundation of a Federal city, and the public faith was necessarily pledged when the grants were accepted to found such a city.

Again, in the same opinion:

The city was designed to last in perpetuity—capitoli immobile saxum.

Then the Poland report continues:

The Federal city was to be a temple erected to liberty, toward which the wishes and expectations of all true friends of the country would necessarily be directed, and, considered under such important points of view as evidently controlled the minds of the founders, it could not be calculated on a small scale. Everything about it was to correspond with the magnitude of the object for which it was intended. It foresaw a far distant future when it was to be the center of a continent under one form of government looking to it for its laws and for its protection. It was to be a city where all improvements made and expenses incurred were to be for the benefit of the whole people.

Viewing the Capital City in this national aspect, we may well understand the motives which governed its founders in imposing upon all who were to come after them such duties and responsibilities toward it as would be peculiar to the Capital City alone and which would fully justify a liberal if not a munificent policy in expenditures.

In December, 1874, a joint select committee reported (S. Rept. No. 479), after many weeks' consideration, very fully on this subject. As submitted by Senator Lot M. Morrill to the Senate, that report says in part:

From the unqualified authority conferred upon Congress, and that the object to be effected thereby is the capital of the Nation, all legislation for the District must be held to be national in its character, and primarily in the interests of the American people at large, and that will be so whether the legislation be direct by Congress or by delegated authority. If this proposition needs to be enforced, it is believed to be necessary only to refer to the objects and circumstances of the acquisition of the territory exclusively for the seat of Government of the United States. That the National Capital might be exempt from the contingency of conflicting local and general authority, the particular States were to concede all jurisdictional rights over the territory to be acquired, and Congress was to "exercise exclusive legislation in all cases whatsoever over said District." The seat of the supreme executive, legislative, and judicial departments of the Government, serene in its isolation alike from conflict of factions and the necessities of commerce, was to symbolize the national unity of a people in their purpose "to form a more perfect union, establish justice, insure domestic tranquillity, provide for the general defense, promote the general welfare, and secure the blessings of liberty." Congress, by the terms of the Constitution, becomes the trustee of the nation, administers its trust in its interest, and may not share its trusteeship with another to the prejudice of the cestui que trust—the body of the American people. Committed to its exclusive care, for a special and sacred purpose, to Congress will be imputed the results of its execution, however deputed. It is believed that the purpose for which this District was acquired will be best accomplished and the interests of all connected with its growth, prosperity, and destiny best subserved by the direct exercise by Congress of the authority devolved upon it. While the primary and paramount obligation and duty is and will be to the National Capital, it may not be overlooked or forgotten that the Capital is the residence of many tens of thousands of American citizens, to be supplemented, in the progress and development of the country, by other tens and hundreds of thousands, and that, independent of any question of conflicting interests or authority, it is plain that as regards expenditures for the improvement and adornment of the capital of a great nation, having at the same time a proper respect to the convenience, privileges, and immunities of a resident population and of those connected with the administration of the Government, a unity of interest must be assumed, and it is believed, may be accredited to exist, in that the general welfare would necessarily seem to be included in the proper development of the design of the city. The demand for expenditures, as indicated in the disposition of its avenues and streets and numerous squares, will necessarily be upon a scale beyond what might reasonably be imposed upon or drawn from the resources of a business and resident population. These may properly be required to make that just contribution to the current annual expenses the interest of the public debt and its ultimate payment which a people so situated as compared with other communities may be required to pay for like protection, privileges, and immunities.

The question is, of course, raised by Senator Southard in the report of 1835 as to why the National Government, in view of the purpose of the founders, had not built up its Capital as it should have done. Of course, there are several answers. Many of the lots given the Government were improvidently sold, though those sold brought altogether about $2,000,000. It was evidently the intention that those lots which were given to the National Government should be used by it, as Thomas Jefferson says in a letter which is appended to the Southard report, for the interest of the National Capital, not only for National Government purposes, but as a residuary interest for the improvement of the city. But that was imperfectly done. When the National Government came here it was penniless and was obliged to sell lots early in order to provide its public buildings and even to borrow money from Maryland and Virginia for that purpose. Then, the talk of the removal of the capital began very early. In 1814, after the visit of the British troops, the House of Representatives, adopted a resolution that it was no longer expedient for the capital to remain in Washington. That was defeated subsequently. The local residents furnished a building for the purposes of the burned-out Congress.

Then the winning of the West began when Jefferson acquired the Louisiana territory, and the people who poured over the Alleghenies began to talk of removing the Capital to the West. Following this report of 1835, when Senator Southard suggested that the Government should pay one-half of what had already been expended by the people here in the vain attempt to make a national capital and to do the Government's task, and also suggested the half-and-half principle of expenditure for the future, came the panic of 1837. Then came the panic of 1857, and then the Civil War. The national neglect of the National Capital continued. The Civil War, however, brought to Washington thousands of men from all over the United States who had never seen the Capital before, who found it, of course, a neglected village in the mud, but who became interested in it, one of whom became Lieutenant General of the Army and President of the United States. Ulysses S. Grant had never seen the Capital until he came here then, and his interest, with that of patriotic men in Congress and patriotic men in the city, brought about the first attempt to improve the city and to carry out the George Washington plan.

After the contending armies had fought for the possession of Washington, after the best blood of the country had been poured out over it as the symbol of the sovereignty of the Nation, it had a new meaning to the country as the expression of its nationality, its patriotism, its wealth, and its power in the eyes of all the world. The Civil War endeared it to the country.

When they came to 1870, the municipal authorities here, on account of the city's efforts to do the Nation's work, were $5,000,000 in debt, and the period of improvement of streets and sewers under the direction of Congress, but at the expense of the District, from 1870 to 1874, started with that debt, and during that period $17,000,000 more of debt was added.   That improvement, which lifted Washington out of the mire, was done legally and entirely by agents of the United States, led by that remarkable man, Alexander R. Shepherd, appointed by President Grant first as member of the board of public works and afterwards as governor, except that the people here by a popular vote did indorse one loan of $4,000,000.   But the work was done by agents of the National Government, and the whole debt was recognized, of course, in the settlement that followed as a legal debt of the United States for which it was primarily responsible.   Congress created and the President appointed the board of public works for the purpose of beginning the new Washington on the old plan of George Washington, and once more the District people, then 109,000, one-third colored, were plunged into bankruptcy by capital making.

From 1874 to 1875, under the temporary commissioners, we were practically in the state of those in the hands of receivers in bankruptcy.   They were ascertaining the assets and liabilities, they were ascertaining the situation of affairs, and they were making a settlement and preparing a new arrangement for the future.   Of course that arrangement is found in the act of June 11, 1878.

Joint select committees of both Houses, the Judiciary Committee and the District committees, made investigations and reports, and from the congressional records and debates we know the entire history of the act.   It was recognized that this was the National Capital.

Speaking now as a national, I may say that after three-fourths of a century of neglect the obligation of the Nation to its capital was for the first time definitely recognized and acted upon.   The reproach was removed, the "half-and-half principle" was adopted and incorporated into that act, and local suffrage abolished.   The act was entitled one to establish "a permanent form of government for the District of Columbia," and while, of course, it can be repealed at any time, it is significant that Congress did all it could to show the design to have it a permanent form of government, even to the extent of voting down the customary provision reserving to Congress the right to repeal that particular act.   Congress can repeal it, but it did all it could to make it a permanent provision for the government of the National Capital, regarding permanency as essential.   The Supreme Court of the United States in Eckloff v. District of Columbia (135 U. S., 240), spoke of the act as being in effect the "constitution of the District of Columbia" and the final decision of Congress as to the government of the District of Columbia.

Mr. Justice Brewer, in delivering the unanimous opinion of the court, referring to the act of 1878, said:

"The court below placed its decision on what we conceive to be the true significance of the act of 1878.   As said by that court, it is to be regarded as an organic act, intended to dispose of the whole question of a government for this District.   It is, as it were, a constitution for the District.   It is declared by its title to be an act to provide 'a permanent form of government for the District.'   The word 'permanent' is suggestive. It implies that prior systems have been temporary and provisional.   As permanent it is complete in itself.   It is the system of government.   The powers which are conferred are organic powers.   We look to the act itself for their extent and limitations. It is not one act in a series of legislation, and to be made to fit into the provisions of the prior legislation, but it is a single complete act, the outcome of previous experiments, and the final judgment of Congress as to the system of government which should obtain. It is the constitution of the District, and its grants of power are to be taken as new and independent grants and expressing in themselves both their extent and limitations. Such was the view taken by the court below, and such we believe is the true view to be taken of the statute."

The fundamental financial principle is the equal division between the Nation and the District of all the expense of developing and maintaining the common Capital, including payment of its debts. That division is a purely arbitrary one adopted for convenience. Various proportions were suggested, from 25 to 60 per cent. The 50 per cent proportion was adopted, without doubt, with the great object of having some definite and fixed amount, so that there might be an orderly, systematic, and continuous development, and that the Capital's progress should not be left, as Mr. Blackburn, of Kentucky, who reported the bill from the House District Committee said, using his language, to "the whim and caprice" of any particular session of Congress.

In the debate in the House, Mr. Blackburn, of Kentucky, in charge of the bill, said:

This is what I desire to say: The people of this District have a right to demand that we shall fix permanently their relations to the Federal Government. It is the Federal Government on the one side treating with the Federal City on the other side. The people of this District have a right to protest against being left subject to the whim and caprice of Congress with each recurring session. They have and can have no tangible value to their real-estate property. Should you go out, any one of you, to purchase a piece of real-estate in the city of Washington, naturally you would ask in the first instance to what taxation it was subject. If the owner is an honest man he can simply reply to you that he does not know.

The repeal clause amendment was offered, as follows:

But Congress reserves the right at any time to repeal, alter, and amend any and all provisions of this act.

In supporting this amendment Mr. Keifer of Ohio said:

"But under this bill, which undertakes to establish a permanent form of government for the District of Columbia, there may be acquired rights which it may be claimed ought not to be vitiated by a repealing act. Very recently arguments have been made in the other end of the Capitol to the effect that it would be unjust to repeal any act having even the semblance of a contract. The object of this amendment, as I understand, is to give notice to all persons who may be interested that Congress claims, and will in its discretion exercise, the right to repeal or alter this legislation. People may come here and, assuming that this is an established law for the government of the District, may invest in property here, or otherwise become interested in this District. To all such Congress, by an amendment in this form, ought to give notice that the power to repeal, alter, or amend the act is reserved."

The amendment was not agreed to.

It was suggested by Mr. Morrill and others that it might be well to have the United States pay the greater part of the expenses, and that the people here pay only the average taxation of cities in the United States. That suggestion was renewed long afterwards in a Senate resolution by Senator Hoar, but the objection then and the objection now to that suggestion is that it would be a floating and uncertain arrangement which would make continuous progress practically impossible. We should not be able then to know what could be done to carry out systematic plans such as have been contemplated by Congress and in some cases authorized by Congress, and that insure the continuous and orderly development of the District of Columbia. One year the Government might give 60 per cent and the next 10 per cent.

Progress would stop. Therefore a definite permanent arrangement was made.

Of course before 1878 there was no possibility of continuous or systematic progress. The whole development of the District was limited to the efforts and resources of the few people who were living here. The Government did not even give the District, as you are very well aware, sir, the grants for public education which were given to the States, and to this day it has not had the benefit of the Morrill Acts, which even Hawaii and Porto Rico enjoy, although you did all you could to bring that about.

The 3.65 bonds which covered the indebtedness of the period between 1870 and 1874 and the $5,000,000 that had been inherited from the former capital-making efforts of the municipality were also guarded by the arrangements of 1874 and 1878. The faith of the United States was pledged in 1874 to the payment of the principal and the interest and to proportionate contribution, and its contribution of one-half for that purpose was pledged in the act of 1878, and until 1924, when those bonds mature, that faith is certainly pledged to that extent to the maintenance of the act of 1878.

Therefore we have a right, I think, to say that there is a moral pledge of the United States that that arrangement should continue, and that it is the intent of the Nation, through its Capital, that it should continue.

May I say, speaking as a national, that the desire of the country is clearly, as expressed in all its organs, that this should be as nearly as possible and in all respects not only physically but otherwise the most perfect capital on earth. Moreover, the people who live outside of the District of Columbia pay such a very small per capita proportion that it is not a feather's weight upon any one of them. Of course only those who contribute to the internal-revenue taxes or the customs duties pay. Those who do not consume any of the things taxed by the internal revenue or any of the things taxed by the tariff do not pay at all; but at most the per capita is very small, 6 or 7 cents at the present time per annum. No one could imagine that they would begrudge that amount. They know also that the Government pays no taxes, although it owns over half the area of the city proper and about 3,000 acres in the adjoining country district. They also know that it has by purchases withdrawn a large part of the land from the tax basis, $7,000,000 worth at least in the last four years, and thus reduced the opportunity for local taxation.

As a National I am struck by the contrasts between my National Capital in the old days of neglect by the Nation and the present days of the Nation's care for it.

Prior to 1871 as official reports show it was an undeveloped, ugly town, without suitable streets, parks, bridges, buildings, lights, schools, or municipal services.

The report of the board of health for 1876 gives a graphic description of the sanitary conditions in 1871:

"It found hundreds of lots below grade, covered with stagnant water, endangering the lives and health of the residents of the neighborhood; hundreds of alleys, receptacles of house offal, giving rise to dangerous effluvia that found its way into the windows of inhabited dwellings; hundreds of hovels, the abode of the poor, with leaky roofs, damp walls, no privy or water supply, and unfit for human habitation; hills of ashes and filth in open lots, the accumulation of many years; 30,000 privy-boxes, many in bad condition or overflowing, and subject to an occasional emptying by a most barbarous and crude system, the operation of which awoke our citizens from their peaceful slumbers to shut out the stench from their sleeping rooms."

"The scavenger, coming in the dead of night like a thief, afraid to be observed; house offal and garbage accumulated in large quantities in yards, subject to a vicious system of removal that cost the city $25,000 per annum; slaughterhouses strewn among our populated districts that claimed as a raison d'être the time they had been allowed to remain and carry on their filthy work in our midst; no quarantine laws or regulations to prevent the incursion and spread of infectious and contagious diseases; no bureau of vital statistics to record births, deaths, and marriages, and to prevent crime; no control over cemetery superintendents or undertakers, so that persons were buried with or without a physician's certificate, whether death had occurred from poison or violence, smallpox, yellow fever, or cholera—the dead were put away under the sod and no questions asked unless glaring and unmistakable evidence of foul play existed; no inspection of food, so that meats, from fly-blown to decomposed, were sold in open market unobserved; no inspection of marine products, so that thousands of bushels of oysters, clams, and other fish unfit for human food found their way from the shambles of the vender to the consumer's table; domestic animals running at large, imperiling life and destroying ornamentation; thousands of hog and cow pens, the inhabitants of which found comfort and food in our alleys, streets, and parks; and innumerable other nuisances were discovered here, tolerated by the apathy of the citizens or their insanitary authorities."

The Washington of 1878 was better but far below the standard of a capital city.

A former president of the Board of Trade, Mr. T. W. Noyes, who resided here in 1878, as now, wrote recently:

Only those who lived here 36 years ago appreciate how infinitely better it is now as a place of residence, how much cleaner, safer, more cultured, more comfortable, and more convenient. The Washington of 1878, was a shabby, ill-paved, ill-lighted, inadequately policed, insufficiently schooled, almost uncleaned city, with surface rent and ridged as by an earthquake, with streets of dust or mud. It had few sanitary safeguards. Its sewers were insufficient. Its water supply was questionable in quality. Crime was frequent, and in certain stretches of the city it was unsafe to walk alone. Deadly railroad grade crossings took heavy toll annually in human lives. There were only poor excuses for street transportation; fire-fighting facilities were insufficient. Washington was a straggling country village, sprawled out over a large area and offering proportionately few benefits to its dwellers in comparison even with those enjoyed by the residents of other cities of that day. To-day Washington is a city of clean, smooth streets, good sidewalks, effective sewerage, pure water, numerous well-equipped and exceptionally well-administered schools, admirable street lighting, one of the best fire-fighting forces in the world, perhaps the best police force for its size in the United States, the finest system of rapid transit anywhere to be found, a complete freedom from disfiguring and dangerous aerial wires, emancipation from the evil of grade-crossing death traps—in short, a city of comfort and cleanliness, of health and education, of protection and progressiveness, a city so close to being a model that it needs now only continued work along the lines laid down since 1878 and pursued until very recently by wise congressional enactments and cooperation with the citizens to become the fairest, most prosperous, and best-equipped city in the world. All this change has occurred, not merely coincidently with the working out of the organic act, but in direct and unquestionable result of it.

Thus, these improvements have made the city more healthful, giving it better protection for life and property, a better water supply, better police and fire protection, better sewerage, better and cheaper transportation facilities, better and cheaper heat and lighting, better and cleaner pavements and sidewalks, cooler and healthier streets, shaded by thousands of additional trees; better schools and libraries, more extensive park areas—the lungs of the city, the people's breathing places—and hospitals, playgrounds, etc., in the old times entirely lacking. Space does not suffice even to recite the infinite ways in which under a system which secures from the Nation equitable participation in the cost of capital maintenance and upbuilding, the city has developed for the physical, mental, and moral betterment of all Washingtonians as individuals, whether poor or well-to-do, however small their tax contributions, whatever their occupation, and in whatever part of the capital they may reside.

The contrast with the conditions in 1878 can be observed by anyone in the city of Washington in 1914, and the results justify the act of Congress of June 11, 1878, without which they would have been impossible.

If you desire its monument, look around you.

As a "national" I must note the fact, whatever the cause, that for three-quarters of a century the National Government did not develop and maintain the National Capital according to the original plan and according to the desire of the country. It left that work chiefly to the District residents. That is obvious from official reports by committees of Congress, beginning with that of the Senate District Committee in 1835 which clearly states the purpose of the founders and the duty of the country respecting the common capital, and is also plainly stated in the reports of the congressional committees making investigation of the whole subject between 1874 and 1878.

As to the relative expenditures by the National Government and the people of the District of Columbia, interesting statements are found in the official reports and speeches of the period 1874–1878, as, for example, the Poland report said:

From a statement of expenditures by the Government by the Treasury Department up to 1871, we find the total expenditures up to 1871 for improvements of avenues and streets by the Government but little over $1,000,000; during which period the local government for the District has expended over nine times that amount.

Representative Hendee, speaking in the House of Representatives, said:

Since the seat of Government was permanently established in this District, the entire expenditures of the United States for improvements in the District have been about $9,000,000, while the amount paid by citizens of the District for the same purpose exceeds the sum of $34,000,000. In other words, the amount taken from the pockets of citizens of the District and put into these improvements is about four times the amount which has been appropriated by the Federal Government. I make these statements upon data furnished from the Treasury Department and other Departments of the Government, which give accurately the items, with dates of appropriations, etc.

These appropriations on the part of the United States have been more frequent or perhaps more liberal within the last six or eight years than ever before. I think that within the first 70 or 71 years of the existence of this Government less than $2,000,000 were appropriated by the United States Government toward improvements in this city; the other six or seven millions have been appropriated since 1871.

Senator Southard's comment, in the historic report of 1835, upon the local objects of the National Government's appropriations up to that period are pertinent to the objects mentioned in the list given by the District Commissioners in their report for 1878 of national appropriations. These objects, like those mentioned by Senator Southard, are chiefly not strictly local but important to the National Government; as, for example, the Washington Aqueduct which was primarily for National Government purposes, and was then, as now, kept under the military control of the National Government, while the whole system of the distribution of the water within the District of Columbia has been constructed chiefly and maintained wholly by the people of the District, the Government paying nothing for the large quantity of water it uses.

That report of the Commissioners of the District for 1878 gives the figures of "the exhibit which has been prepared under the direction of the Treasury Department showing all the expenditures made from the National Treasury for National and District purposes within the District of Columbia from 1790 to 1876." After deducting from the total expenditure of the people of the District $22,106,650 of bonded debt (one-half of which the United States has been paying since 1878), the commissioners report that there still remains an absolutely paid-up expenditure by the people of the District greater than that of the United States by $16,150,770.74. In respect to this amount the commissioners report:

"If an equal division of the expenditures for the local government between the United States and the District of Columbia is a just one, as is now admitted, then the United States is in equity a debtor to the District of Columbia as above shown."

Now, what about the people resident here. If I, a national, had come, as I said, from Philadelphia, and was looking at the residents here I would find about 345,000 people, about 98,000 negroes, the largest negro population in any place in the world, and there are 40,000 civil servants of the Government, many of them, of course, on small salaries, salaries that have not been raised since ante bellum days, and are now inadequate. There are something over 50,000 taxpayers. There is no commerce and no manufactures to speak of; there is no great private industrial plant of any kind, and there are no local multimillionaires. Our winter visitors who are multimillionaires are taxpayers elsewhere.

The people who live here, the residents, are theoretically, of course, free to go if they desire, but they ought not to be forced away; many of them having invested their all here, could not go. The same is true of many of the civil servants. A large number of the present population came here on the faith of the act of June 11, 1878, which they thought would safeguard their property rights. The population has increased from 170,000 in 1878. They have acquired real estate and other property, just as the holders of the 3.65 bonds bought them, in large part on the faith of the United States on the contract, as they considered it, and as it really is, in the act of June 11, 1878. A greater part of those who have come here since that time have, of course, given up, for the sake of coming here, a residence in other places, with political rights, including a direct participation in the National Government and also in State and municipal government so far as taxation and the control of expenditures by voting is concerned. They find that the commercial and industrial conditions here are such that their sons must go elsewhere largely for employment. The District quota being more than full they are ineligible to the civil service of the Government.

Of course the advantages on the other side are great and counterbalance these things or the people would not be here. They have a clean and beautiful city, physically and morally. They have safety, peace and good order, freedom from strikes and riots. They have intellectual opportunities which are unequaled in the country. They have good government, which ought to reduce their tax contributions. They have Congress as their local as well as their national legislature. They contribute through national taxation to the expenses of Congress. Their interests are absolutely in the hands of Congress. It can be trusted to use this great power with justice and generosity.

Now, as a national coming from outside, how do I regard the people of the District with respect to their national obligations? Have the people been good national citizens or are they simply selfish local residents? They have made their full national contribution in every way. In the Civil War they furnished the first defenders of the Capital and sent more than their quota of troops, and more than any except one State in proportion. In the Spanish War they sent more than their quota. In time of peace they pay their full quota of the tariff and internal revenue and income taxes, and in time of war they have paid whatever extra war taxes were imposed, and they have given their moral support in all national undertakings.

The only national taxes that fall directly in ascertainable amounts upon Americans are the internal-revenue taxes. The States and Territories which contributed in the fiscal year ended June 30, 1909, less in internal-revenue collections of the National Treasury than the District of Columbia are Alabama, Arkansas, Delaware, Georgia, Idaho, Kansas, Maine, Mississippi, Nevada, North Dakota, Oklahoma, South Dakota, South Carolina, Utah, Vermont, and Wyoming (16 States), and Alaska, Arizona, New Mexico, and Hawaii (four Territories).

The per capita contribution of the District of Columbia for that year is greater than that of Alabama, Arkansas, Connecticut, Delaware, Georgia, Idaho, Iowa, Kansas, Maine, Montana, Minnesota, Mississippi, New Hampshire, North Dakota, Oklahoma, South Dakota, South Carolina, Tennessee, Texas, Utah, Vermont, and Wyoming (22 States), and Alaska, Arizona, New Mexico, and Oklahoma (four Territories).

The District of Columbia contributed in the fiscal year ended June 30, 1909, in internal-revenue taxation for the support of the National Government more than the combined contributions of Maine, Vermont, Mississippi, North Dakota, Nevada, Oklahoma, and Wyoming.

The per capita contribution of the Washingtonian to this national fund was 17 times as great as that of the resident of Alabama, 18 times that of the resident of Arkansas, 10 times that of the resident of Maine, 16 times that of the resident of South Carolina, 20 times that of the resident of Vermont, and 86 times that of the resident of Mississippi.

As to tariff revenue Washington is one of the large seacoast cities, always the largest consumers of imported goo s.

What is their local contribution as residents of the District? Of course, they perform their jury and their militia duty and their other civic duties. They show as much public spirit as any other Americans.

How about their taxation for local purposes? Is it adequate? The answer to that is in the last bulletin of the United States Bureau of the Census, Bulletin 118, on "Financial statistics of cities having a population of over 30,000 in 1912."

As it is an all important question in our examination of this subject, let us carefully study the comparative table of taxation of these cities, 193 in number, all the principal cities of our country.

What is this Bulletin 118? It is an official document, made after careful investigation by the Bureau of the Census in the long series of municipal investigations which it has made year after year for the purposes of the census. The Census Office now is nearly perfect in its methods of getting this information and of tabulating it properly. Among other things it shows both the taxable basis, what we call the general assessment per capita, and the still more significant tax levy; that is, the amount levied per capita. Both per capita items are greater in the city of Washington, as the bulletin calls the District of Columbia, than in the great majority of the other cities of the country having over 30,000 population. The bulletin shows (P. 18, et seq.) that the Washington per capita assessment is greater than that of 155 out of the 193 cities and its per capita tax levy greater than that of 149 of them. It is a very striking statement of facts— facts unknown even here, for the most part, except by the readers of the fine articles of Mr. Theodore W. Noyes in the Washington Evening Star, which, of course, have brought out all the facts of the whole subject so completely and convincingly.

Since that disproportionate taxation of Washington does not seem to be generally known, I invite special attention to the exact figures as I have drawn them from Bulletin 118. They are of the first importance.

The statistics of valuation and taxation begin on page 18.   The significant figures are those, first, of the per capita assessed valuation of all property taxed, and, second, the per capita levy of property taxes.   The figures for Washington, D. C., are given on page 21, as follows:

Per capita assessed valuation of all property taxed, $1,050.05.

Per capita levy of property taxes, $15.75.

These figures, as in the case of all the other cities, represent exactly the taxable basis of the tax revenues, and afford the only accurate method of comparison between cities.

Now, as an examination of the table referred to will show, the cities which have a lower per capita assessed valuation of all property taxed than Washington, D. C., are as follows (the figures given in the tables being stated in each instance):

Chicago	$409.83	Utica	$715.35
Philadelphia	969.01	Elizabeth	770.59
St. Louis	916.06	Waterbury	886.55
Detroit	898.32	Troy	816.17
Buffalo	845.15	Manchester, N. H	892.19
Los Angeles	857.31	Hoboken	954.96
Newark	1,039.39	Wilkes-Barre	715.50
New Orleans	671.71	Erie	374.50
Minneapolis	779.31	Evansville	553.28
Jersey City	915.27	Peoria	322.15
Seattle	767.53	Fort Wayne	518.79
Kansas City, Mo	672.32	Harrisburg	710.42
Indianapolis	883.04	Savannah	779.79
Rochester	896.00	East St. Louis	207.03
Denver	581.93	Jacksonville	869.08
Louisville	839.00	South Bend	461.54
St. Paul	739.83	Terre Haute	553.71
Oakland, Cal	698.21	Passaic	616.95
Atlanta	926.88	Johnstown	316.54
Worcester	1,011.39	Bayonne	805.09
Birmingham	566.52	Brockton	824.28
New Haven	1,003.26	Holyoke	952.14
Memphis	803.96	Charleston, S. C.	331.76
Scranton	600.14	Allentown	635.86
Omaha	254.05	Springfield, Ill	316.17
Fall River	799.34	Covington	509.63
Spokane	742.18	Altoona	459.26
Grand Rapids	754.87	Pawtucket	959.69
Asheville	684.39	Mobile	600.54
Bridgeport	896.19	Saginaw	520.61
Lowell	779.57	Sioux City	187.60
Cambridge	1,035.71	Binghamton	691.85
San Antonio	834.23	Rockford	398.05
New Bedford	975.48	Little Rock	644.10
Dallas	870.88	Augusta, Ga	665.02
Trenton	705.89	Springfield, Ohio	1,031.66
Albany	1,020.32	Lancaster, Pa	532.85
Salt Lake City	615.46	Pueblo	349.52
Reading	550.16	New Britain	855.84
Camden	575.28	Chattanooga	604.12
Tacoma	779.22	York	527.51
Lynn	867.42	Malden	867.80
Des Moines	247.15	Berkeley	833.63
Lawrence	828.61	Bay City, Mich	392.60
Wilmington	638.74	Haverhill	811.37
Kansas City, Kans	1,015.27	Salem, Mass	820.95
Yonkers	1,000.83	Lincoln, Nebr	211.67
Houston, Tex	895.48	Davenport, Iowa	542.45
Fort Worth	739.71	El Paso	722.38
Duluth	564.43	Tampa	577.20
Norfolk	765.31	McKeesport	547.20
Schenectady	692.16	Flint, Mich	531.45
Somerville, Mass	862.61	Kalamazoo	524.24
St. Joseph	489.04	Racine	623.52

Superior, Wis	$559.08	Perth Amboy	$542.26
Macon	603.06	Taunton	686.80
Butte	596.56	Quincy, Mass	1,022.54
Woonsocket	635.35	Lansing	477.20
Montgomery, Ala	587.43	Pittsfield	987.80
Chester, Pa	468.39	Cedar Rapids	822.73
Pittsburgh	844.98	Oshkosh	665.28
Dubuque	664.69	San Jose	701.36
Galveston	699.91	Amsterdam, N. Y	475.66
West Hoboken	637.61	Jamestown, N. Y	507.34
New Castle, Pa	526.11	Jackson, Mich	610.58
Roanoke	933.90	Williamsport, Pa	465.53
Elmira	658.96	Joplin	309.20
Huntington, W. Va	786.87	Lima	957.72
Knoxville	612.85	Chelsea, Mass	877.10
Lexington, Ky	645.11	Aurora, Ill	228.78
Springfield, Mo	436.90	Austin	705.18
Quincy, Ill	287.42	Newport, Ky	512.67
Charlotte	504.91	Orange, N. J	695.19
Joliet	209.71	La Crosse	665.73
Auburn	632.53	Shreveport	540.91
Everett, Mass	835.14	Colorado Springs	409.02
Decatur, Ill	203.65	Council Bluffs	152.43
Portsmouth, Va	348.06		

Therefore it appears that 155 cities among those having a total population of 30,000 and upward have a lower, and many of them a much lower, per capita assessed valuation of all property taxed than Washington, and that only 37 cities of that description have a higher per capita assessed valuation of all property taxed.

Many of the cities having a lower per capita assessed valuation than Washington are not only larger in population, as in the case of Chicago, Philadelphia, St. Louis, Detroit, Buffalo, Los Angeles, Newark, New Orleans; or about the same population like Minneapolis, but are known to be, as commercial and manufacturing centers, of vastly greater wealth than the National Capital. This comparison certainly shows that the people of the District of Columbia are not underassessed in the valuation of their property for tax purposes.

But more important as a measure of taxation is the per capita levy of property taxes which shows exactly the levy and, in connection with the assessors returns, gives the facts as to tax revenues of any city. On page 21 of Bulletin 118, we found that the per capita levy of property taxes under the head of Washington, D. C., is $15.75. Upon examining the statistics for the rest of the cities we find the following cities show a lower per capita levy of property taxes than Washington (the figures being given in each case):

Philadelphia	$14.30	San Antonio	$12.35
Baltimore	15.53	Dallas	15.85
New Orleans	14.78	Trenton	10.09
Jersey City	12.69	Albany	15.85
Seattle	15.53	Salt Lake City	13.97
Kansas City, Mo	15.47	Reading	7.70
Indianapolis	14.04	Camden	7.18
Louisville	15.02	Tacoma	13.78
St. Paul	12.17	Lynn	14.44
Columbus	13.83	Lawrence	12.47
Toledo	14.07	Wilmington	9.68
Atlanta	11.59	Kansas City, Kans	12.64
Worcester	14.98	Youngstown	11.91
Birmingham	5.67	Houston	15.22
Memphis	12.70	Fort Worth	14.28
Scranton	9.25	Duluth	15.20
Paterson	8.78	Norfolk	12.11
Fall River	13.21	Oklahoma City	15.42
Spokane	13.03	Schenectady	13.51
Dayton	13.02	Somerville	14.19
Grand Rapids	11.36	St. Joseph	11.81
Nashville	10.10	Utica	13.64
Bridgeport	13.17	Elizabeth	8.51
Lowell	12.81	Waterbury	13.26

Akron	$12.91	Racine	$10.72
Manchester, N. H	10.79	Superior, Wis	11.70
Hoboken	11.62	Wheeling, W. Va	9.40
Wilkes-Barre	9.12	Macon	7.66
Erie	8.61	Butte	13.24
Evansville	10.90	Woonsocket	9.88
Ft. Wayne	9.70	Montgomery, Ala	6.61
Harrisburg	11.90	Chester	7.49
Savannah	10.84	Pittsburgh	14.51
East St. Louis	9.98	Dubuque	12.79
Jacksonville	9.84	Galveston	13.09
South Bend	10.34	West Hoboken	5.97
Terre Haute	10.58	Newcastle, Pa	10.52
Passaic	5.86	Roanoke	11.67
Johnstown	7.29	Elmira	13.66
Bayonne	11.89	Huntington, W. Va	7.57
Brockton	14.02	Knoxville	9.81
Holyoke	13.13	Hamilton	9.37
Charleston, S. C	9.21	Lexington, Ky	10.45
Allentown	7.25	Springfield, Mo	7.95
Springfield, Ill	11.30	Quincy, Ill	11.32
Covington, Ky	8.92	Charleston, S. C	6.06
Altoona	9.19	Joliet	11.05
Pawtucket	14.38	Auburn	11.23
Canton	10.44	Everett	14.56
Mobile	6.61	Decatur	9.27
Saginaw	12.81	Portsmouth, Va	5.47
Sioux City	11.95	Perth Amboy	6.70
Binghamton	11.18	Taunton	11.41
Rockford	14.25	Lansing	11.50
Little Rock	7.85	Pittsfield	14.31
Augusta, Ga	8.31	Cedar Rapids	15.53
Springfield, Ohio	10.87	Oshkosh	11.11
Lancaster, Pa	6.93	San Jose	10.89
Pueblo, Col	11.83	Amsterdam	9.08
New Britain	11.58	Jamestown	11.77
Chattanooga	9.97	Jackson, Mich	11.38
York	7.91	Williamsport	9.31
Malden	14.30	Joplin	8.69
Berkeley	11.17	Lima	8.67
Bay City	9.60	Muskogee	12.59
Haverhill	13.40	Aurora, Ill	10.36
Topeka	15.04	Lorain	9.32
Salem	12.40	Austin	11.72
Lincoln, Nebr	14.14	Newport, Ky	8.11
Davenport	15.54	Orange	10.82
El Paso	14.02	La Crosse	9.99
Tampa	9.36	Shreveport	8.36
McKeesport	10.26	Colorado Springs	15.01
Flint, Mich	7.92	Council Bluffs	12.08
Kalamazoo	9.21		

From this it appears that the per capita levy of property taxed in Washington, D. C., is higher than in 149 cities out of the whole number having over 30,000 population: and that only 43 cities have a higher per capita levy of property taxed than Washington.

These official figures, procured, compiled, and published by the National Government, ought to end all charges of inadequate taxation in the National Capital, and ought to convince every intelligent person that the people of Washington are paying more in proportion than the people of the great majority of other cities, including most of the great business cities of the country, and many others which have greater private wealth than the city of Washington. Washington taxpayers are not asking a reduction of taxation, being willing to pay even more than their share toward the maintenance and development of the National Capital; but their fellow countrymen who know the facts will agree that their taxes ought not to be increased, either by increasing the assessment or the rate.

The proposition to compel the assessors to increase the valuation of real property from two-thirds, as now, to 100 per cent of the actual value would, of course, greatly increase the disproportion. There are only a very few cities in the United States, in all, where there is even a nominal assessment of real property at 100 per cent of its actual value. One of these is our nearest neighbor, and one of our best friends, the city of Baltimore, with a population in 1912, according to Census Bulletin 118, of 569,560 (estimated), as against the population of Washington ascertained in the same manner, of 342,776. The comparative table of valuation and taxation in Bulletin 118 from which my statistics have been drawn, gives the total assessed value of the real pro erty in Baltimore in 1912 at $372,651,502, while the same table gives the assessed two-thirds value of the real property in Washington, D. C., in 1912 at $330,322,487. This certainly shows that there is no underassessment of the real property of the District of Columbia. Baltimore with almost twice the population, and very much more than twice the wealth of Washington, is a commercial financial railroad center, commanding much of the trade of the South and West. Since 1912, $40;000,000 has been added to the assessment of real property here subject to appeal.

A similar comparison with the estimates in other places having nominal 100 per cent valuation of real property would yield similar results. Unless all other taxes are to be abolished and a tax on land substituted there can be no reason given for increasing the assessment or the rate on real property. An increased tax on land would of course have the most serious results to the very many small property holders in the city of Washington, where an unusually large proportion of the people own small homes, or rather equities in them, which au increase of taxation would tend to gradually wipe out. An interesting table has been published by Mr. Theodore W. Noyes showing the comparative results of a 100 per cent valuation, according to the statistics of Bulletin 118 for 1912, a group of cities, some of which are larger and others smaller in population than Washington. It is as follows:

Actual assessed valuations (1912) and assessments at 100 per cent.

	Population.	Actual assessment.	Basis.	100 per cent basis.
Detroit	503,445	$316,630,290	75	$422,173,720
Buffalo	439,666	318,552,250	75	424,736,333
Milwaukee	400,279	368,664,865	90	409,627,627
Cincinnati	387,543	375,065,680	100	375,065,680
Newark	369,317	301,209,664	100	301,209,664
New Orleans	350,695	167,177,355	75	222,903,140
Washington	342,776	330,322,487	66⅔	495,483,730
Minneapolis	323,476	163,843,995	50	327,687,990
Jersey City	281,497	190,857,512	100	190,857,512
Seattle	277,420	176,975,528	45	393,278,951
Kansas City	265,977	113,513,040	50	227,026,080
Indianapolis	246,928	163,341,010	60	272,235,016
Providence	235,222	199,193,440	100	199,193,440
Louisville	229,323	123,883,099	70	176,975,855
Rochester	230,414	180,687,350	80	225,859,187
St. Paul	226,300	104,180,969	60	173,634,948
Baltimore	569,560	372,651,502	100	372,651,502
Cleveland	596,970	518,552,210	100	518,552,210

Now, just a word as to the particular kind of local taxation here. The burden of it is on real property, although, of course, there is a large revenue from business licenses and public utility corporations pay a large amount, and there is a considerable amount, larger than in many cities, of what is called personal property taxation. Last year the personal taxes yielded $1,130,840.52 as against $5,101,804.80 from realty taxes.

But it makes no difference, sir, for revenue purposes whether the greater amount of taxation falls upon real property or upon personal property. It is customary here, has been for many years, and since 1878 by act of Congress, to have it fall upon real property. The people are used to it. But it matters not, if it is equitably adjusted, how it falls. The present revenue is necessary. An increase of taxation is not necessary. And of course taxation for the sake of taxation is unthinkable of Congress. It would be like taxation for the destruction of the people who live here, which is beyond our imagination as the action of Congress. The District people are amply taxed in convenient and familiar ways and pay as cheerfully as taxpayers anywhere.

Neither is there any reason why new forms of taxation should be tried here, if a sufficient revenue is obtained from those which are now imposed. And if the revenue were not needed, taxation should be reduced.

In my judgment, speaking now as a national, as a citizen of the United States in the interest of the National Capital itself, the few people who live here should not be subjected to vivisection by experiments in taxation or in any other form of legislation, but should be given the same treatment which is given to the other cities of the United States by the people who control them, since the people of those cities also control this city which has their higher allegiance. This should not be made an experiment station for municipal theorists.

It must always be remembered that the area of the District of Columbia can not be increased (unless Virginia should give back what was retroceded in 1846, because Alexandria was so dissatisfied with the treatment of the Capital by the Nation), and that, therefore, contrary to the experience of other cities which are continually increasing their taxable area, the amount of real property subject to assessment and taxation is constantly decreasing as the Government takes additional portions for its own use.

It must also be remembered that every expenditure here for public improvements increases the tax revenues. Harmonious and continuous development means continual increase of revenues.

There is no point in the argument sometimes made that Washington does not pay State or county taxes. First, it has no State privileges and, second, it does pay county taxes by contributing to the objects covered by county taxes elsewhere, although it has no county privileges. Moreover, its unusually large contribution to national taxation more than offsets the comparatively small State taxation of other cities. The statistics of taxation in other cities in Census Bulletin 118, covers by far the greater pa t of their county taxation payments, as, for example, for school districts. The District is not even a Territory, much less a State, and can not be without an amendment of the Constitution, which might well be made at sometime in the future in order to give a large American population its direct representation in the Senate, the House, and the Electoral College. The Supreme Court has held that the District is not a State for the purpose of allowing its citizens to sue the citizens of the States in the Federal courts, although it is a State for the purpose of a treaty with France respecting real estate; and that it is a State for the purpose of apportionment of direct taxes, although it is not a State for the purpose of the apportionment of Representatives in Congress, both mentioned in the same clause in the Constitution.

Is the money needed? The House, as you are aware, sir, cut the estimates of the Commissioners of the District of Columbia $3,000,000. The Commissioners presented estmates there, as they have doubtless done here, which call for all that additional amount which is available if the half-and-half principle is obeyed, and they justified them no doubt by good reasons. If those particular estimates are not acceptable in any item to Congress, Congress can choose from those which have heretofore been recommended, or from those which occur to it as desirable purposes of expenditure, a sufficient number to utilize all the money, because, as you are well aware, the plans for the District of Columbia are still incomplete, and much remains to be done not only for the physical development but for the development of all the municipal services so as to make it what the people of this country desire.

When in 1900 the Nation joined with the District of Columbia in celebrating the centenary of the founding of the Federal district, the country's interest was centered upon the National Capital as at no other time. In the official celebration on the 12th of December, 1900, fully reported in the commemorative volume published by Congress, and especially in the addresses at the White House and the Capitol, the history of the National Capital was fully set forth, including the George Washington plan, long neglected by the Nation, and the progress which had been made in carrying it out since the Act of June 11, 1878. The first outgrowth of that celebration was the so-called Senate Park Commission of 1900, which reported in 1902 to the Senate a comprehensive project for expanding the George Washington plan outside of the old city limits, and for the location of parks, bridges, and public buildings. At the same time the Commissioners of the District of Columbia, approving the project of the Senate Park Commission, also outlined to Congress plans for the development of the Capital along all other lines, including the development of its municipal services and the amendment of municipal laws so as to make it as nearly perfect as possible. Much has been accomplished under these recommendations but much yet remains to be done, so that there is ample need for the present revenues without reduction. Indeed, it was pointed out by the commissioners to Congress in 1902 that they were counting upon the natural increase in the revenues due to the increase of population and of taxable values to provide for the orderly, systematic upbuilding of the National Capital without detriment to its current maintenance.

During the decade from 1900 to 1910 about twenty-three millions of dollars were expended in extraordinary municipal improvements, besides twenty-two millions more expended by the railroads in abolishing grade crossings and erecting the Union Station, besides relieving the Mall from the servitude of railroad tracks and station. Moreover, all the departments of the District government were modernized and a large number of schools and other buildings of a modern type constructed out of the ordinary municipal appropriations, and many new laws in the interest of social justice and better administration were enacted under the plans suggested, but, as has been said, much remains yet to be done.

The comparatively few people who come here will personally enjoy, of course, the beautiful objects here, but they, with all our countrymen, desire also that the municipal services shall be worthy of the country and not be the subject of reproach. The whole country would rise up in protest if the health department here were so insufficient that the death rate should rise high or if the public education of this community, instead of being as good as it is, was condemned by all educational experts in this country and abroad.

Not more than one-tenth of 1 per cent of our fellow countrymen visit their Capital in a year except at the inauguration of a President and Vice President. But all intelligent Americans take intense pride in their Capital and want it as nearly perfect as possible in all respects. Therefore the idea that it should be considered as divisible into national and local objects of expenditure— the former being those that visitors can see—is fallacious; like any other city, it must be treated as an integral whole, a complete well-rounded city, to be symmetrically developed from a common fund in all its departments and services. Even though the vast majority of Americans can know it only by pictures and descriptions, they all alike want it to be worthy of this great Nation and of its founder, whose name it bears.

It is unfortunate that through the action of the House in a former year the commissioners were restricted in their estimates to the total amount of the District revenue plus the equal contribution of the United States in sight for the next fiscal year, because that prevents their laying all the needs of the Capital before Congress. The estimates of the commissioners can not be called a budget because they have no power of taxation or of appropriation. The only real budget is like the budget of the British Government, where the power of estimating, the power of taxation, and the power of appropriation are in the same hands.

It is only a bill of fare that the commissioners submit to Congress in the estimates, from which it may take what it pleases. Congress, of course, can go outside of the restricted estimates of the commissioners and take up any one of the many objects that have heretofore been recommended or any one which any of its Members thinks should be provided for.

I shall only add that the great thing is to maintain a fixed definite proportion between national and District contribution—the half-and-half division, as experience for 35 years has shown, is convenient. Any proportion must be arbitrary. It is necessary to continue this fixed definite proportion, in order to provide for the orderly continuous development of the National Capitol.

It may seem to some that the National Capital idea is a mere sentiment. Certainly on the day after the birthday of Abraham Lincoln, and a week before the birthday of George Washington, the founder of this city, any American, whether he be a resident of the District of Columbia or a national from some other city, may well dwell upon the great sentiment of the whole people that this capital shall worthily represent the progress and the power and the wealth, physical and spiritual, of the people of the United States.

You have doubtless read the last address which the recent ambassador of Great Britain, Mr. Bryce, made here before leaving for home. It sets forth from a great friend of the United States and of the National Capital what might be called the view of the outside world—which does concern us and for which we do have respect—as to the present beauty of this city through its natural situation and its development under the act of 1878, and as to its possiblities in the future. It reinforces all I have said.

I feel sure that this committee, regarding the history, regarding the facts, regarding the opinion of the Nation and the opinion of the world, will see to it that this attempt in section 8 to destroy the purpose of Congress in the act of 1878 shall not succeed.

If the time should ever come when the merits of the present arrangement under the act of June 11, 1878, are to be seriously reconsidered and reviewed it should be done as was done in 1874; that is, by prolonged, deliberate, impartial investigation, with full opportunity for hearing to all concerned.   It may not take four years, as in 1874–1878, with study by joint select committees, and study by the Judiciary Committee, and study by the District committees, but it should certainly not be hastily done.   Another joint select committee should be created, or an impartial commission.   The House has not passed, it has not even considered seriously, a bill to repeal the half-and-half principle of the act of 1878.   It has not faced the question, but it has sent over here, in section 8 of the pending bill, adopted in a manner with which you are familiar, that which in effect does repeal it and which directly converts money raised by Congress by local taxation for local purposes into a miscellaneous receipt of the United States Treasury that so disappears forever from the account of the District of Columbia.   This was done without such an investigation as that which led to the enactment of the act of 1878—without a hearing to the National Capital; without any consideration worthy of the subject.

The official motto of the District of Columbia is "Justitia omnibus." May not the National Capital confidently expect that Congress will do "justice to all" in this critical situation?   I believe it will do justice to all— justice to the Nation at large in its aspirations for its Capital and justice to the Americans who live in that Capital as well as to the Americans who live outside of it.   All alike are interested in the Capital—proud of it, and zealous for its continued progress toward the ideal city.   Congress has never done injustice to the National Capital in modern times whenever it has given thorough investigation to any question.

I believe that now it will not destroy the half-and-half plan under which the great advance of the past 35 years has been made.   Certainly it will never do so without prolonged investigation and deliberation.   Certainly it will never do so without the general participation of the great majority of Senators and Representatives in that deliberation.   Certainly it will never do so without substituting some plan equally promising for the future of the Capital.

I can not believe that Congress will double the tax burden upon the few people who live here and require them to carry alone the task which is that of the whole people, any more than that it will cut out the Government's contribution and leave the Capital with only half its present appropriation.   Of course, for the vast majority of small property owners, owners chiefly of equities in their homes, doubling the taxation would mean confiscation, and in the end would so reduce the taxable values as to defeat its own purpose.   It would literally kill the goose that laid the golden egg.   As Census Bulletin 118 shows, the people here pay more taxes than the people in the great majority of the cities having over 30,000 population in the United States. Additional taxation would be unjust.   As is shown by the commissioners' estimates and the long list of other things that ought to be done to properly develop and maintain the National Capital, the annual appropriations ought to be more, rather than less.   Believing the money to be needed, the people of the District ask no reduction of the taxation; they ask no change in taxation, but only that their taxes shall be used for the purpose for which Congress has levied them; that no surplus of them be accumulated by failure to make needed appropriations, and that, if a surplus remains, it shall be carried over for appropriation later or applied to indebtedness. Certainly it should not be confiscated into a "miscellaneous receipt" of the United States Treasury, as though it had been raised by national taxation for national purposes, and later spent in Alaska or the Philippines.

STATEMENT OF GEORGE TRUESDELL.

Mr. TRUESDELL. Mr. Chairman, Mr. MacFarland has made such a thorough presentation of the history of the organic act that it will be unnecessary for me to say more than a very little upon this subject. I shall address myself more particularly to the purpose of the eighth section of the appropriation act in covering the surplus revenues of the District of Columbia into the Public Treasury to the credit of "Miscellaneous receipts."

The act of 1878, as you are very well aware, did not contemplate any surplus. The act really did exactly what was proposed in the Morrill Act, except that it made definite the portion which the District was to contribute. It provided, in the first place, for estimates, and that, to the extent to which those estimates were approved by Congress, Congress should appropriate 50 per centum thereof, and the other 50 per cent should be levied as a tax upon the taxable property and privileges of the District of Columbia. The same act provided, however, that not more than $1.50 per $100 should be levied upon property in the District of Columbia in any one year. While it is popularly known as the half-and-half plan, it contemplated that the Government might desire to expend much more than the taxpayers of the District would be able to bear one-half of; so it made the further limitation that the second half should be levied upon the taxable property and privileges in the District of Columbia, provided the total tax in any one year should not exceed the aggregate sum that would be derived from an assessment at the rate of $1.50 per $100.

The revenues of the District of Columbia, therefore, are derived directly by taxation which theoretically and practically is measured by one-half the amount of the appropriations. The revenues of the District are, therefore, practically appropriated in advance for certain specific purposes. Since the passage of that act Congress has placed some very great burdens upon the District—in violation of the requirements of the act, it is true, but nevertheless they are there. A case in point is the highway act, under which all that portion of the District lying outside of the city of Washington is to be laid off in parks, streets, and avenues in strict conformity with the plan of the city, and the cost of laying off the streets is required to be paid exclusively from the revenues of the District. Then, in the act of 1874, Congress pledged the payment by taxation of 50 per cent of the great debt that is evidenced by the 3.65 bonds, some $8,000,000 of which are still outstanding.

From our point of view, one of the most vicious features of this section is, with these great obligations which Congress has placed upon us, that by refusing to appropriate the money raised here by taxation a surplus is created, and that surplus is immediately covered into the Treasury to the credit of "miscellaneous receipts."

That.really appears to be intolerable taxation. The organic act certainly did not contemplate anything of the sort. To tax the people for these specific purposes, and then fail to appropriate the money, and then cover the surplus thus created into the Public Treasury, is certainly a grievous hardship upon the people, and comes very close to being a violation of the plighted faith of the Nation.

In order to economize your time, I have written a few words here of the most general character, which, with your permission, I will read. It will not take me more than five minutes. They sum up in a most general way what has been accomplished under the organic act, and make some remarks thereon.

President Wilson characterized the new currency law as "the constitution of peace." May we not aptly apply this term to our organic act, which the Supreme Court calls a constitution, and call it "a constitution of peace" for the District of Columbia? How aptly the Washingtonians of 35 years ago might have said of their "constitution of peace," as the President so forcefully said of the currency bill as he attached his signature to that important measure, from which so much was expected, and which had been so long coming—

We have slowly been coming to this time, which has now happily arrived, when there is a common recognition of the things that it is undesirable should be done in business and the things that it is desirable should be done. What we are to do now is to organize our peace, is to make our prosperity not only stable but free to have an unimpeded momentum.

How truly we may now say of our "constitution of peace," in the light of 35 years' experience, that it has fulfilled all that was expected or predicted of it; it has "organized our peace and made our prosperity not only stable but free to have an unimpeded momentum." Under its benign influence thousands and tens of thousands of American citizens from every part of our country have been attracted to the Nation's Capital. Its population has increased from 150,000 in 1878 to 350,000 at present, in round numbers. A great system of sewage disposal has been established. A filtration plant has been erected which is giving us pure and potable water. Means of education have increased by the multiplication of public and private schools, and by the establishment of three great universities. Public and private hospitals have increased their accommodations to meet the needs of the growing population. The Potomac marshes, from which formerly emanated disease and disease-bearing mosquitoes, have been converted into a beautiful, health-giving recreation ground for all the people. The death rate has decreased from 25.1 in 1878 to 16.9; a saving of 2,800 lives per annum on the basis of our present population. That, Mr. Chairman, is certainly a great achievement. That alone would seem to justify all of the great expenditure of money that has been made here by the United States and the taxpayers of the District of Columbia together if there were nothing else. A burdensome debt of $22,000,000 has been reduced to $8,000,000, and a large floating debt extinguished. The city has been made practically coextensive with the District, increasing its area from 6,000 acres to 44,000 acres. By wise provisions of Congress, through the act of August 27, 1888, and the act of March 2, 1893, the highway act, many miles of broad avenues and streets have been extended over that vast region in conformity with the beautiful plan of the city, and all future streets and avenues are required to conform to that plan to the end that future growth and development may be in harmony with it.

By our "constitution of peace" a bankrupt city and its over-taxed and overburdened inhabitants, struggling in vain against conditions which they were powerless to overcome, and for which the long delay of Congress in recognizing its primary responsibility under the Constitution for the upkeep of the National Capital was alone responsible, were lifted from their helpless financial condition, permitted to organize their peace, to create prosperity, "to make it stable and free to have an unimpeded momentum." It brought peace and encouragement to a discouraged, hopeless, and tax-ridden people. It has enabled the people of the District to contribute since 1878 toward the extinguishment of the debt of the District of Columbia, and toward capital building, including current expenses, about $125,000,000, the revenues having increased from $1,650,539 in 1878 to over $7,000,000 in 1914.

The United States has contributed to those objects during the same period not far from $100,000,000. Thus, the United States will receive from the taxpayers of the District during the present fiscal year, toward the upkeep of the District, more than 7 per cent of the entire contribution by the United States toward the same since 1878.

Who can justly say, in the light of this result, that the present division of expenses of the Government of the District has not been a wise and prudent one, or that it has not been mutually profitable and beneficial to the Federal and local Governments? Who can say that the expenditures have been excessive, or beyond the needs of the National Capital? What complaints have come from the country that expenditures in the District have been too great, or on an unnecessary or extravagant scale? What protest has come from the legislature of any State or Territory, or from the public press, against the expenditures by the United States toward the expense of the District?

The people of the District are satisfied with the present partner-ship arrangement, and there is little indication that the people of the country at large are not thoroughly pleased with it. There appears to be little or no demand anywhere for a change in our organic act. Yet it is proposed by the House of Representatives, without any assigned reasons, without a hearing, without a report from the Commissioners of the District, and without due deliberation or investigation, by means of a rider on an appropriation bill, to destroy that "constitution of peace" without substituting anything in place of it.

Mr. Chairman, as Mr. Macfarland has remarked, we do not believe section 8 voices the general views of the House of Representatives. There are in this age a good many men who believe that they are born to reform, and that the first step essential toward reformation is to destroy the existing order of things, to destroy something that has proved useful, and afterwards to substitute something else in its place. If Congress had the power to change the form of government in Philadelphia or San Francisco or New Orleans, and it were proposed to be done in the manner in which it is proposed here practically to wipe out the organic act, there would be, of course, a great deal of excitement in those communities.   When you come to legislate as to the form of government in a large city it is a very serious thing to those people, and they naturally feel a great interest in it.

Here in the District of Columbia the people of course have no political power whatever, and they look to Congress.   This is Federal territory, where exclusive jurisdiction resides in Congress.   The people here take it for granted, as they have a right to, that Congress in its wisdom will exercise a just supervision over them.   The President of the United States resides here, and his Cabinet, the Vice President, the Congress, the judges of the courts, all the people who have official relations with the Government, and the people who come here to make Washington their residence.   It is a population of exceptional intelligence; and the people here have a right to expect that they are not only to have the best government that the wisdom of Congress can provide, but that that form of government is to be more or less permanent.

Upon the point of permanency Mr. Macfarland quoted from the speech made by Mr. Blackburn, who was chairman of the District Committee in the House when the organic act was passed, in which he pleaded for permanency.   Whatever might be done, he asked that it should be fixed permanently.   Let me say here that the history of the organic act shows conclusively that the great thing, the important thing, which was held in view, was to create a form of government here which would be permanent, and which would permanently pledge the United States and the District each to bear a certain and definite portion of the expense.   Mr. Macfarland has quoted from the instructions given by the House of Representatives to the Judiciary Committee.   Let me read the resolution to you.   It is very important, as indicating just what the House had in view.

At this time, you will bear in mind, it had been brought home to Congress by numerous petitions and by delegations of citizens that there was a tremendous debt here, and that the city was practically bankrupt; so it became very important for Congress to know just exactly what were the legal relations between the District and the United States.

The House passed by a large vote, 152 to 71, this resolution:

Resolved, That the Committee on the Judiciary be instructed to inquire and report to the House the legal relations between the Federal Government and the local government of the District of Columbia, and the extent and character of the mutual obligations in regard to municipal expenses, and further to inquire and report whether some accurately defined basis of expenditure can not be prescribed and maintained by law.

At the time that committee was appointed there was a joint select committee appointed to look into the affairs of the District.   That committee, after five months of investigation, brought in a report, and along with it a bill which became the act of 1874, which had in one of its sections the requirement that a joint select committee should be appointed to determine what proportion of the expenses should be borne by the United States and by the District of Columbia, respectively.

During the four years that intervened from that time until the final passage of the act of 1878 the matter was continually under discussion in Congress, and it was the one subject that was above every other—what proportion of the expenses was it just and expedient to put upon the people of the District?

It had been demonstrated that it was actually impossible for the people of this community to bear any longer the whole expenses of the District, unaided except by spasmodic appropriations from Congress; so the whole effort of those four years of work, during which three joint select committees and one standing committee, the Judiciary Committee, devoted several months of time to the matter, was for the purpose of determining what should be the basis of division of these expenses.

When finally Mr. Blackburn, who was chairman of the committee, brought the organic act into the House, there were various propositions before the House. The bill provided for an equal division of the expenses. Various amendments were proposed—25 per cent, 35 per cent, 60 per cent, and various other percentages—and they were all voted down. Finally the chairman of the committee, Mr. Blackburn, said:

> There is one point more to which I desire to call the attention of the House, and then I have done. It is the necessity of having some basis of expenditure fixed between the Federal Treasury and the District treasury. How can a property-holder in the District of Columbia determine or gauge the value of his property to-day? Can he tell what tax it will be subjected to as long as he is left the victim of the whim and caprice of Congress? The property holder does not know whether the appropriations made by Congress will be 10 per cent or 90 per cent of the expenditures of the District. No value can be attached to a foot of real estate owned by a property holder within the limits of the District, because the purchaser can not tell what taxation he will be subjected to. The people of the District have a right to demand that you shall fix this question permanently and finally. If you do not intend to bear more than 10 per cent of the burden of taxation, say so. If you will bear 50 per cent of it, then say so; but whatever per cent the Federal Government is to bear should be determined and fixed permanently, so that legitimate and permanent values may be established in this District.
>
> I beg Congress to establish some permanent form of Government.

Mr. Chairman, the title of that act was, "To establish a permanent form of government for the District of Columbia." To my mind no reason can arise for changing that act unless it should be demonstrated in the course of time that the people of the District are not contributing a fair share toward the expenses of the District. That time has not yet been reached. The appropriations never have been equal to those actually needed here in the District. No great surplus has been accumulated at any time. No surplus has been created that could not be used and that has not been used in wiping out the floating debt that has existed here from time to time.

There is no emergency existing to-day requiring a change in the local form of government. There is no reason, so far as I can discover, why the departure from the organic act that is proposed in the eighth section of this bill should be made. No reasons have been assigned. It is in many respects a more harmful act, an act that has in it greater injustice, than what is known as the Crisp bill to repeal the organic act outright, because it practically destroys the act; but, on the other hand, it does more than that. The power that made the organic act can repeal it. No one questions that. When we look back, however, and consider the great deliberation with which that act was framed, it can not be supposed that in the future three joint select committees are going to give months of time, and that the Judiciary Committee of either of the Houses will give months of time, to the consideration of this subject again. That certainly was a most exhaustive study, and in the organic act we have the fruits of that long, laborious, and deliberate investigation.

Why must we throw that into the wastebasket? If it should become necessary, in the judgment of Congress, to change this act and set up some other form of government here surely it ought to be done only after the greatest deliberation and the most careful study by a joint select committee and not on an appropriation bill.

We can not believe that Congress will depart from the practice heretofore. The people of the District of Columbia have the greatest confidence in Congress. They have a right to have. Congress, whenever it legislates deliberately, legislates in the interest of the people. We only ask, if you should reach the conclusion that some change is necessary here, that instead of doing it in the manner proposed it shall be done only in the regular way, by the proper committee having charge of District matters, and after most thorough and comprehensive investigation.

I thank you, sir, for your attention.

INDUSTRIAL HOME SCHOOL.

STATEMENTS OF WALTER C. CLEPHANE AND F. W. M'REYNOLDS, MEMBERS OF THE BOARD OF TRUSTEES OF THE INDUSTRIAL HOME SCHOOL, WASHINGTON, D. C.

Mr. CLEPHANE. We are appearing, Senator, in behalf of the Industrial Home School.

Mr. McREYNOLDS. We are up against a hard proposition there, Senator. Up to 10 years ago we had an appropriation for a supervisor there. We have 100 boys, and we had a superintendent, the only man there, in charge. We had, up to that time, a supervisor and another man who looked after the boys and got them up in the morning, and saw that they were dressed properly and gotten off to school, and saw that they had their baths and went to bed at night properly. We have a public school on the grounds, and a man came there as superintendent of the school, and he was willing to live there at the home for his board and washing and do this work as supervisor. He has been there for 11 years, but he has now been promoted and made one of the supervisors and principals of the public schools of the District, and they have sent a young lady there as head of the school. They said they would send a man if they could find one. We could not find a man who was self-sacrificing enough to do that kind of work. There is such a situation now that there is no one to look after those older boys—that is, no man. A woman can not look after from 12 to 16 boys very well and get them dressed and bathed, etc. We have got to have a man there to do that.

Senator SMITH. When did this situation first arise?

Mr. McREYNOLDS. It just came up this week.

Mr. CLEPHANE. When Mr. Hunter came there as superintendent of this school the salary which we had previously had was stricken out, because he was willing to perform those duties for nothing.

Senator SMITH of Maryland. What are the duties of the superintendent?

Mr. McREYNOLDS. He has supervision of the entire plant. There are 150 children there. We have our gardening and our mechanical work and the greenhouses. There is the buying of supplies, both clothing and food, and the entire superintendence of the plant devolves upon him, and of course he can not, in addition to that, do this other work. It would be a physical impossibility.

Senator SMITH of Maryland. What is it you call him?

Mr. McREYNOLDS. Supervisor of the boys—that was his title before.

Senator SMITH of Maryland. You have once had such a supervisor?

Mr. McREYNOLDS. Yes, sir; over 10 years ago.

Mr. CLEPHANE. Mr. Hunter has been there for 10 years.

Mr. McREYNOLDS. We waived the salary for 10 years, and we have not had it since.

Senator SMITH of Maryland. How many pupils did you have 10 years ago?

Mr. McREYNOLDS. We had practically the same number that we have now. The size of the plant has not been increased.

Senator SMITH of Maryland. How have you gotten along without him for 10 years?

Mr. McREYNOLDS. Mr. Hunter has done all that work.

Senator SMITH of Maryland. Why can he not continue to do it?

Mr. McREYNOLDS. He has been promoted. He has moved away, and they have sent a young lady as principal of this school.

Mr. CLEPHANE. Mr. Hunter, who has been in charge of the public school and of the grounds, because of his duties as a public school teacher, can not live on the grounds. He was willing, in return for his board and lodging and that of his boy, to be there at the school all the time, day and night, and supervise these boys on the grounds outside of school hours, without any compensation. That is the reason the salary which had been previously paid for a boys' supervisor was abolished some ten or eleven years ago. Since that time Mr. Hunter has been doing that work without any compensation, merely getting his board and lodging. Now he has been made supervisor and principal of one of the public-school divisions, and has left the school. We are left entirely without any boys' supervisor. We have been trying to make some arrangements with some other men.

Senator SMITH of Maryland. Then you have really been without a supervisor for 10 years? You have had this man's services and now you have lost him, and you feel that you must have somebody in his place?

Mr. McREYNOLDS. It is an absolute necessity.

Senator SMITH of Maryland. What do you propose to pay a man for that position?

Mr. CLEPHANE. We do not think it would be possible to get a man who is competent to do that work for a less salary than $75 a month. We do not want to ask for any more than we can possibly get a man for. You can see that it requires a man with some strength of character. The last appropriation was $600 a year, $50 a month. But, as you know, the price of everything has gone up, and I doubt very much whether we could get a good man for $50 a month.

Senator SMITH of Maryland. Would you give him his board?

Mr. McREYNOLDS. Oh, yes. He gets up at half past 5 in the morning and sees that the boys are fit for breakfast.

Senator SMITH of Maryland. Is his attention required all the time?

Mr. McREYNOLDS. Except during school hours. He is on duty from half past 5 in the morning until 9, and from half past 2 until 10 o'clock at night.

Senator SMITH of Maryland. He has nothing to do from 9 until half past 2 o'clock?

Mr. McREYNOLDS. And except the lunch hour.

Senator SMITH of Maryland. From half past 5 to 9 is $3\frac{1}{2}$ hours, and from 2 to 10 is 8 hours——

Mr. McREYNOLDS. It is $11\frac{1}{2}$ hours, and a half hour at noon makes it about 12 hours duty in the day.

Senator SMITH of Maryland. About 11 hours, taking out the half hour at luncheon. Did you go before the House with this matter?

Mr. McREYNOLDS. No, sir; it just happened this last week.

Mr. CLEPHANE. There has been no occasion for it heretofore.

Mr. McREYNOLDS. We went down to the commissioners, and they sent us up here.

Senator SMITH of Maryland. It has occurred since this bill has been brought over here?

Mr. McREYNOLDS. Yes, sir; within the last week.

Senator SMITH of Maryland. As what do you propose to designate this man?

Mr. McREYNOLDS. A supervisor of boys.

Senator SMITH of Maryland. You have no supervisor of boys here in the bill.

Mr. McREYNOLDS. We have had no appropriation for one for 11 years.

Mr. SMITH of Maryland. You have three matrons. What do they do?

Mr. McREYNOLDS. They look after the girls and the smaller boys. We take children from 6 years on.

Senator SMITH of Maryland. And two assistant matrons.

Mr. McREYNOLDS. They have the same duties.

Mr. CLEPHANE. They have supervision of the clothing, repairing of clothing, and all that sort of thing.

Senator SMITH of Maryland. I think I know about what you want. Are there more boys than girls?

Mr. CLEPHANE. About 100 boys and 50 girls. We have got to have a man for the boys that are from 12 to 16 years old.

Senator SMITH of Maryland. Very well, gentlemen, I think I understand the situation, and the matter will be given due consideration.

(Whereupon at 2.25 o'clock p. m. the subcommittee adjourned.)

INDEX.

O

Lightning Source UK Ltd.
Milton Keynes UK
UKHW021204180219
337529UK00010B/543/P